# ART DECO

# THE OFFICIAL® IDENTIFICATION AND PRICE GUIDE TO
# ART DECO

By Tony Fusco

*With photography by Robert Four*

FIRST EDITION

HOUSE OF COLLECTIBLES
NEW YORK, NEW YORK 10022

*Important Notice.* All of the information, including valuations, in this book has been compiled from the most reliable sources, and every effort has been made to eliminate errors and questionable data. Nevertheless the possibility of error, in a work of such immense scope, always exists. The publisher will not be held responsible for losses which may occur in the purchase, sale, or other transaction of items because of information contained herein. Readers who feel they have discovered errors are invited to *write* and inform us, so they may be corrected in subsequent editions. Those seeking further information on the topics covered in this book are advised to refer to the complete line of *Official Price Guides* published by the House of Collectibles.

*Appearing in cover photo:* (1) Mahogany marquetry library cabinet by Eugene Printz. French 1920s with hammered iron base and hardware. Valued at $35,000. (2) Ebony and black lacquer side table by Leleu. French 1920s with center bronze medallion and brass edging. Valued at $4,000. (3) Wrought-iron, twofold screen attributed to Edgar Brandt. French 1920s. Valued at $15,000. (4) Sculpture by Hagenauer. Austrian 1930s hammered brass with nickel finish. Valued at $9,000. *All items courtesy of Joia Interiors, New York, NY.*

*Frontispiece:* Poster for the 1925 Paris Exposition by Charles Loupot. *From the collection of Pat Kery.*

© 1988 by Tony Fusco

All rights reserved under International and
Pan-American Copyright Conventions.

Published by: The House of Collectibles
 201 East 50th Street
 New York, New York 10022

Distributed by Ballantine Books, a division of Random House, Inc., New York and simultaneously in Canada by Random House of Canada Limited, Toronto.

Manufactured in the United States of America

ISBN: 0-876-37362-7

10 9 8 7 6 5 4 3 2 1

# TABLE OF CONTENTS

*Acknowledgments*   ix

**Introduction to Art Deco**   1

What Is Art Deco?   3

Today's Market   6

How to Use This Book   13
    Notes on the Price Listings • About the Resource Guide
    • Why Some Dealers Don't Like Price Guides

How to Start a Collection   18

Fakes, Forgeries, and Reproductions   22
    Deco Isn't the Fifties • Furnishings • Statues • Glass
    • Ceramics • Silver, Fashion, and Jewelry • Posters and
    Graphics • 1980s Deco and Postmodernism • A Final
    Note of Caution

An Overview of Art Deco   29

Materials and Techniques   37
    Furniture Materials • Lacquer and Enamel • Fashion
    • Metal • New Materials

# ART DECO

Motifs — 41
    Animals

Decorative Influences — 44
    Art Nouveau • The Opposition Movements: The Arts and Crafts Movement; American Arts and Crafts Movement; Frank Lloyd Wright and the American Prairie School; The Viennese Secession; Bauhaus

Artistic Influences — 57
    Fauvism • The Ballets Russes • Futurism • Cubism • Mondrian and the De Stijl Group • Dadaism and Surrealism

Other Global Influences — 62
    Orientalism • Egyptian Influences • Ancient Architecture • Jazz • Science Fiction • The Machine

The Paris Exposition of 1925 — 67
    Pavillon de l'Esprit Nouveau

Art Deco and America — 73

The Art Deco Revival — 80
    Finch College Museum of Art • The Rediscovery of American 20th-Century Decorative Arts • The Rediscovery of Kitsch

**Objets d'Art Deco** — 85

Architecture — 87
    The Art Deco Preservation Movement • *Special Focus:* Architectural and Interior Design Components • Price Listings

Furnishings — 105
    *Special Focus:* Clocks • Mass-Produced Furniture • Price Listings

Sculpture and Statues — 168
    *Special Focus:* Chryselephantine Statues • Frankart • Price Listings

Glass — 201
    Perfume Bottles • Mass-Produced Glass • *Special Focus:* René Lalique • Price Listings

*Table of Contents*     *vii*

Ceramics     241
    European Ceramics • *Special Focus:* Boch Frères and Longwy/Primavera • Other European Figural Ceramics • English Ceramics • *Special Focus:* Clarice Cliff • American Ceramics • *Special Focus:* Cowan Pottery • Other Art Deco American Ceramics • Price Listings

Silver, Jewelry, and Fashion     289
    Silver • Jewelry • *Special Focus:* Bakelite Jewelry • Fashion and Accessories • Price Listings

Posters and Graphics     335
    Poster Printing Techniques • Typography • Posters • *Special Focus:* Dutch Posters • A Note on the Poster Listings • Pochoir Illustrations • Magazines—Covers and Graphics • *Special Focus:* Louis Icart • *Special Focus:* Romain de Tirtoff (Erté) • Price Listings

Modern Living     385
    Ocean Liner Collectibles • World's Fair Souvenirs • Chrome and Other Metals • Bakelite • Industrial Design • Price Listings

**Resources**     421

Resource Guide     423
    Auction Houses • Dealers • Show Management • Societies and Associations • Preservation Organizations • Tour Services • Entertainment and Production Company • Museums and Collections

*Bibliography*     434

*Index*     439

# ACKNOWLEDGMENTS

As far as we are aware, this is the first price guide ever published devoted to Art Deco, a field in which we are bound to see continued interest and increasing prices. Our research has taken us through scores of scholarly volumes, a huge stack of coffee-table books, and hosts of catalogs from museums, auction houses, and dealers. We have also enjoyed the opportunity of coming into contact with the country's leading authorities and collectors in the field.

In Art Deco today, eyes are on record-breaking prices, new discoveries, enormous shows and sales, and specialized dealerships. New retrospective exhibits continue to offer us great insight into the diversity of styles currently presented and sold under the name of Art Deco.

A guide such as this is just not possible without enormous help, and we want to acknowledge many of those who provided that help.

From the standpoint of scholarship we are indebted to the many talented writers in the Art Deco field, both current and past: Victor Arwas, Martin Battersby, Yvonne Brunhammer, Alastair Duncan, David Hanks, Bevis Hillier, Katherine Morrison McClinton, and others whose painstaking research and insight has continued to illuminate the field for art lovers and historians as well as for collectors. They and many dealers and auction house personnel have set a high standard in the Art Deco literature.

At the auction houses we are extremely grateful to Kathleen Guzman, specialist, Art Nouveau and Art Deco, Christie's East, for providing photographs, mountains of information, and sharp insight into the Art Deco market; Art Nouveau/Art Deco administrative assistant Jane Holcombe, Christie's East; Michael Meek, specialist, 19th century, Art Nouveau and Art Deco, William Doyle Galleries, for numerous photographs and insight, as well as for his candid comments on the market; Maryalice Adams, director of public relations, William Doyle Galleries; and Nancy McClelland, vice-president, specialist, 20th-century decorative arts, Christie's New York, for providing photographs and information.

The information provided by these and other auction houses in the United States and Canada has been used throughout this guide and has allowed us to compare the ranges and geographic differences in prices realized for Art Deco at auction.

We also wish to acknowledge the contributions of many individuals who gave generously of their time and energy to bring together the vast amount of information and photographs contained here:

*Architecture:* Michael Fitzsimmons of Struve Gallery, Chicago; Barbara Baer Capitman and Miguel Seco of the Miami Design Preservation League, Miami, Florida; Arthur S. Lindo of the Cooper-Hewitt Museum, New York; Jim Elkind of Lost City Arts, New York; Eleanor Noel of Radio City Music Hall Productions, New York; and Michael Wallis of "TourLink," Wallis Gideon Wallis, Tulsa, Oklahoma.

*Furnishings:* Leslie Rutz of Gallery Vienna, Chicago; Arnold Kaufman of Fleur de Lis Antiques, New York; Henry Zimmet and Emily Bouchard of French & Company, New York; Gerardus A. Widdershoven of Maison Gerard, New York; Bill Strauss and Nicholas Brown of Helburn & Hoyt, New York; Alan Moss, New York; Bruce Newman of Newel Art Galleries, New York; Audrey Friedman of Primavera Gallery, New York; Arthur and Bronnie Hindin of Retro-Modern Studio, New York; Carolle Thibaut-Pomerantz, New York; Kim Hostler of Arts & Interiors, Philadelphia; Gary and Janet Calderwood of Calderwood Gallery, Philadelphia; Bob Aibel of Moderne, Philadelphia; and Paul Fuhrman of The Warehouse, Allentown, Pennsylvania.

*Sculpture:* Florence Rubinstein and Harry Bradford of Madison Galleries, New York.

*Glass:* Frank Cooper of the Los Angeles Art Deco Society, Los Angeles; Dorothy-Lee Jones, founder, and Nancy S. Eaton, associate curator of The Jones Museum of Glass and Ceramics, Sebago, Maine; John Kaschak and Valerie Kepler of Thunder Road, Provincetown, Massachusetts; and Clare M. Bavis of the Corning Museum of Glass, Corning, New York.

*Ceramics:* Morton Abromson of Brookline, Massachusetts; Louis and Susan Meisel of Meisel-Primavera, New York; Peter Boehm of Dualities Antiques, Larchmont, New York; Everson Hall of Hall China Company, Ohio; and Victoria Peltz of the Cowan Pottery Museum, Rocky River Public Library, Rocky River, Ohio.

*Silver:* Ed Forcum of Rosebud Gallery, Berkeley, California; and Perrisue Silver, Princeton, New Jersey.

## Acknowledgments

*Jewelry:* Barbara Pollack, Highland Park, Illinois; Ian Harris of N. Bloom & Son Antiques, London; and Honore Jewelry, Cambridge, Massachusetts.

*Fashion:* Irena Urdang de Tour of Detour, Deep River, Connecticut; Karen Haas, assistant curator, Isabella Stewart Gardner Museum, Boston; and Katy Kane, New Hope, Pennsylvania.

*Posters and Graphics:* Bernice Jackson, Concord, Massachusetts; Sondra Eddings, Dyansen Gallery, Boston, Massachusetts; Pat Kery, Pat Kery Fine Arts, New York; Jack Banning of Poster America, New York; and George Theofiles of Miscellaneous Man, New Freedom, Pennsylvania.

*Modern Living:* World's Fair and ocean liner memorabilia: Ken Schultz of Hoboken, New Jersey; industrial design: Jacques Caussin of First Half, New York.

We are also grateful to Greg Wittkopp, associate curator of the Cranbrook Academy of Art Museum, Bloomfield Hills, Michigan; William T. Webber and Frances M. Gay of the Art Deco Society of New York, New York; Christopher Wilk of the Brooklyn Museum, Brooklyn, New York; Sanford Smith of Sanford L. Smith & Associates, New York; Irene Stella, Stella Show Management, Paramus, New Jersey; and Peter Rakelbusch of 21st Century Antiques, Hatfield, Massachusetts; for providing us with photographs, information, and numerous additional contacts around the country. We recognize the contribution of many other dealers, auction houses, societies, museums, and individuals in the Resource Guide at the end of this book.

*A special note:* We are grateful to the dealers and others who did not want to be quoted in the book for providing us with the most candid information about Art Deco collecting. We suspect that if we had not been writing a book on the subject but merely inquiring about the field, they would have been just as frank and just as eager to help.

Last, but proverbially not least, we thank Deborah Gilburg, our research assistant. As many of those who worked with us know, she was instrumental in assembling the information recorded here. This book would simply not have been possible without her assistance, patience, and good humor.

# INTRODUCTION TO ART DECO

# WHAT IS ART DECO?

We want to tell you right off that we are not going to attempt a definitive answer to the question "What is Art Deco?" We hope, rather, that by reading this book you will find the answer to the better question, "What is Art Deco for me?"

"Art Deco" as a term really came into regular usage only during the revival of interest in the style in the 1960s, when Bevis Hillier popularized it with the publication of his book *Art Deco* in 1968. Hillier's work was the first attempt to explore the style of the 1920s and 1930s as a whole through its architecture, furniture, jewelry, and decorative objects.

Art historians and critics often express their feeling that the name Art Deco is wrongly applied to the functional, geometric Art Moderne or Modern style of Le Corbusier and American designers, and even less applicable to the "Streamline" style of kitschy chrome, kitchen appliances, and jazzy ceramics of America in the 1930s. They will tell you that Art Deco is truly the opulent, exotic, and colorful style of the Ballets Russes, which came to Paris in 1909, of fashion designers like Paul Poiret and furniture makers such as Emile-Jacques Ruhlmann and Maurice Dufrène. To them, Art Deco is the style that reached its peak at the Exposition Internationale des Arts Décoratifs et Industriels Modernes in Paris in 1925.

Art Moderne, as it was called in France—or International Modern or simply Modern, as it came to be known in America—is the term these scholars apply to the geometric, angular, and tubular work of later French, German, and American designers such as Rene Joubert,

Paul Frankl, Donald Deskey, and Walter von Nessen. And they'll tell you that the term "Streamline" best describes the aerodynamic look of 1930s industrial design, cars, and ceramics.

Dozens of other names have been coined by writers and others trying to come up with something better or more specific to describe a particular style within the movement: Twenties Decorative, Jazz Modern, Style Moderne, International Style, and Streamline Moderne (in architecture), Zigzag Moderne, and others have all been used. In addition, new designations have been added to imply a regional style: Tropical Deco and Pueblo Deco, for example; and specific styles-within-the-style, such as Depression Modern and Hollywood or Screen Deco.

It is true that there was real animosity between the earlier French Art Deco artists and those who fought for modernity and progress via the machine. As the style spread in the late 1920s and early 1930s, it was influenced by other styles. It was also changed dramatically by national tastes and the impact of social and economic forces. Whatever the case, you'll hear the entire gamut of antiques and collectibles from 1909 until about 1939 and the early 1940s referred to as Art Deco, or simply Deco.

Like it or not, Art Deco is the title that seems destined to refer to the "stylish" production of the entire era, from the end of Art Nouveau early in the century to just prior to World War II. While it does not cover specific movements—such as the Viennese Secession, the Bauhaus, De Stijl, or the Prairie School and Frank Lloyd Wright—these movements had such an impact on Deco from all different directions that today's collector is likely to find them, if not on the same table, then at least at the same show.

Because of this, we felt it would be instructive and useful to you, the interested reader, to include some examples of a wide variety of styles from a broad range of schools, artists, and countries. Our hope is that the comparisons will help you better understand both Art Deco and the market for 20th-century decorative arts.

Most academic authors have devoted little time to the inexpensive and more abundant machine-made, mass-produced products that were common in the declining years of the styles we have mentioned. These were dubbed "kitsch," a German word meaning "trash." Today, kitsch is often spelled with a capital *K*—you'll pay more today for a Chase Chrome ashtray than your grandmother did for a Lalique vase.

Because of its tremendous appeal and growing value on the collecting market, we've included kitsch along with the more refined antiques and collectibles. We are sure this will horrify some, but we hope it will be instructive to all.

The key word here is *stylish*. High Art Deco was above all else stylish, rather than pretty. The word applies to much Art Deco kitsch; even though it was cheap, it had style. A hard word to define, but we hope this book will help.

## What is Art Deco?

In America, and in this as well as other collecting fields, there has also been a strong bias for French objects, with only recent interest in American production. Where possible, we have tried to include objects from other countries that have a special place in the market today, such as Dutch poster art from 1920 to 1940.

We have also tried to include furniture and other objects that people buy, not to collect but simply to furnish their homes, such as American and English machine-made furniture. We feel that those who love to collect Art Deco ceramics, chrome, glass, and other "smalls" cannot necessarily afford to purchase a molded glass dining table by René Lalique, but they might find an overstuffed, streamlined mohair chair not only attractive and comfortable but within their price range as well.

That's how we define Art Deco—but it's always open to discussion.

# TODAY'S MARKET

In general, Art Deco was an artistic, highly urban style that appealed first to those who looked for something "tasteful and simplified," then to those who considered themselves "chic," and later to those who considered themselves "progressive" and "modern." It was the chic stage that did the most to expand the popularity of the style. As a fashion trend, Art Deco was endorsed by the women who wore the new sleek dresses and sportswear styles—symbols of their liberation from stereotypic roles after World War I.

Out of fashion for almost thirty years, Art Deco experienced its initial revival in the late 1960s and early 1970s. The American exhibitions and auctions of that time, coupled with new publications in the field, validated Art Deco, making it officially important to collectors.

Today Art Deco is enjoying more popularity than it ever did—in either its own time or the first revival period. Recent years have seen a wealth of exhibitions and catalogs, books and magazine articles. Exhibitions and publicity generated by dealers and auction houses have merely added fuel to the fire, expanding both the market for Art Deco and the range of objects that are considered collectible.

Now a growing number of collectors, stores, and dealers are specializing in objects of the Art Deco era. Even noncollectors are buying Art Deco furniture, posters, lamps, glassware, radios, kitchen items, bookends, and other decorative and household objects because they are easy to integrate into modern apartments.

## Today's Market

The Art Deco market, especially what is called the "high-end" market, is mature and competitive, involving many specialized collectors and dealers. Ten or more American cities have Art Deco societies, and all of the major New York auction houses have Art Deco experts on staff.

The decorative arts have always been considered the "poor cousin" of the fine arts, and have not yet reached heights attained by Van Gogh, Pollock, or O'Keeffe. In fact, universities that offer art history degrees rarely put an emphasis on decorative arts. However, Art Deco and related styles in the decorative arts have seen higher prices in recent years than ever before.

Art Deco has taken its place with the most valued 20th-century decorative arts. In 1986 a new kind of antiques and collecting exhibition was launched by Sanford Smith in New York. Called "Modernism—A Century of Style and Design," this annual exhibition has gone two rounds as of this writing, bringing together the entire gamut of 20th-century design from various movements that occurred internationally and sometimes simultaneously: Art Nouveau, Bauhaus, Arts and Crafts, Art Deco, Vienna Secession, Bentwood, WPA, Revival, Art Moderne, Aesthetic, Surrealism, and even the Fifties.

The broadening interest in the diversity of 20th-century decorative arts has benefited Art Deco collecting immensely.

"You have to look at the trends over a twenty-year period," states Michael Meek, specialist in 19th-century decorative arts, Art Nouveau, and Art Deco for William Doyle Galleries. "Art Deco, like anything else, has gone up and down, but overall the market is up."

Reflecting on what appears to be a turning point in the evolution of Art Deco collecting, Bruce Newman, president of Newel Art Galleries in New York City, says, "The trend now is for people to upgrade their collections. Buyers are looking for better quality and are becoming more sophisticated. They've read the books, been to the auctions, and are familiar with the dealers."

"The better the quality, the better the investment value," he explains. Newel Art Galleries has been in its current location since 1979 and houses six floors of magnificent antiques from the Renaissance to the 20th century.

Newman proudly shows almost an entire floor of the finest Art Deco and Art Nouveau, with exquisite furniture from early French masters: Süe et Mare, Ruhlmann, Jules Leleu, Maurice Dufrène, and others.

In 1984 Newel discovered thirty-two large panels that once formed a wall in the Grand Salon of the French luxury liner *Normandie*, the work of sculptor Jean Dupas and master lacquer artist Jean Dunand. The panels had been removed from the ocean liner before it was transformed into a troop ship for World War II, and they had been installed in another great French ocean liner, *Ile de France*. After being removed from this second liner, they were sold at auction in 1960 to a French family who preserved them for over twenty years. The panels form a wall 18 feet high by 26 feet long and reportedly sold for $2 million only one month after their arrival in New York. As with other discoveries in the Art Deco field, this extraordinary sale had an immediate impact on the prices at auction for the work of Dupas and Dunand; the prices exploded and have been setting records ever since.

Kathleen Guzman, specialist in Art Nouveau and Art Deco for Christie's East in New York City, remarks, "Overall, the Art Deco market is stronger right now than it has been in a long time. Until 1981 I think Art Nouveau held sway, but trends and tastes are changing. Deco is more fashionable now."

As one example, Miss Guzman cites Lalique, which is being collected by more people today than ever before. "Lalique is at an all-time high, although basic and mid-range Lalique is not skyrocketing. However, the best and rarest pieces are up, up, up. A 'Cluny' model vase by René Lalique just recently sold in Christie's Monaco sale for $170,000."

Can the upward trend in Lalique market prices continue?

"I think the market for Lalique will continue to be strong," comments Audrey Friedman, owner of Primavera Gallery in New York City. "Eight years ago you might have said that the market was manipulated by a few dealers who bought up Lalique. When they sold, the market crashed. But the Lalique market has a very broad base today. There are many more serious collectors, and there is a lot of interest in Japan."

"It takes a real financial commitment to collect Lalique today," she adds. "After all, when glass reaches the price of good sculpture and paintings it's hard even for seasoned dealers to keep up with it. People are more willing to pay top dollar for quality than ever before. The stock market crash of October 1987 seems to have had very little effect on the collecting market."

Other dealers note that the most palpable effect of America's economic uncertainty is that Europeans are now in a position to buy back some of the antiques that came to this country from Europe, and the Japanese, with their strong yen, are furiously buying up French Art Deco on the American market.

But some of the skyrocketing prices in the Art Deco collecting field today are due to well-developed and well-implemented marketing strategies followed by dealers and others.

Kathleen Guzman seems to feel that Americans are easily swayed by this kind of marketing. She comments, "Erté connotes Deco to most collectors, but most of his items on the market were made only since 1978. Statues that were made in editions of 350 only a few years ago are now selling for $25,000. The makers pushed the investment potential and many bought into it. The galleries launched an extraordinary campaign with their first Erté collection. They created their own market. People were supposed to buy all twelve—something like a $30,000 investment on which they could later trade."

She adds, "On the other hand, Erté's early gouaches are small, but they are one of a kind, and one immediately recognizes their value."

Carolle Thibaut-Pomerantz, a private dealer who divides her time between New York and Paris, notes, "Too many people are being influenced by whatever is the latest trend." With real flair, she and her associate, Rodolphe Perpitch, one of the pioneer dealers and rediscoverers of Art Deco in France, select original, unusual pieces for their clients.

"You have to follow your nose and your eye," she said, smiling as she showed us around her booth at the 1987 Modernism exhibition and sale. "Within the mass of Art Deco furniture a lot was then, and still is, considered bourgeois and ordinary. Just because it is Art Deco doesn't make it terrific. Fortunately, there are still a few nice things to discover."

The Art Deco field, though widely cataloged and written about, still does hold some rare finds and unusual surprises. For example, the fall of 1987 in New York seemed to be a rediscovery season of André Sornay, a French furniture designer who Miss Thibaut-Pomerantz says was known for having introduced "kit-type" furniture. Her find was one of Sornay's few outstanding special commissions—an eight-foot-long dining room table in Rio palissandre. (See the photo in our color section, "An Art Deco Portfolio.")

A major catalog and exhibition on Sornay's work is in preparation. During his lifetime Sornay was so well known in his region that Art Deco in the area was referred to as "Style Sornay."

"We've handled Sornay for years," states Gary Calderwood of Philadelphia's Calderwood Gallery. "He was a major designer, but because he worked in Lyon and not Paris, he was largely ignored. His work is finally being included in books on Art Deco furniture. In terms of conceptual strength, he is certainly on a par with René Herbst or Pierre Chareau."

"We are always looking for designers such as Sornay or André Arbus—who worked in France in the late 1930s—who are 'undiscovered' and whose work falls into a more reasonable price range," he says.

Commenting on the fact that their gallery is not in New York, Janet Calderwood states, "People thought we were crazy to open in Philadelphia. They thought we wouldn't find a market for Art Deco." Her husband, Gary, adds, "Instead, what we find is that we are dealing with a world market. In addition to our gallery, we also have a two-thousand-square-foot warehouse, and people come from all over. We're not far from both the New York and Washington markets."

Apart from a broadening of the market for Art Deco geographically and the rediscovery of lesser-known European designers, American Art Deco is reaching new heights in general.

One area that Michael Meek sees as gaining in the market is American 1930s furniture. "At the time, there was not really a market for great cabinetmaking in America, and great American stuff from this period is almost nonexistent. People are starting to see 1930s American furnishings as part of the continuum of American design, and it will gain in value."

Kathleen Guzman adds, "There will be a turnaround in all American design. Prices today are mediocre. Someday Paul Frankl, Donald Deskey, and Gilbert Rohde will bring fantastic prices. However, documentation of these pieces is very difficult. How many, where they were made—this information was not handed down to us, and Americans like a paper trail. Today people rely on documentation and don't trust their eye as much."

The whole field of American design is on the rise, especially because of exhibitions such as "The Machine Age" at the Brooklyn Museum, "High Styles" at the Whitney, "American Art Deco" at the Renwick Gallery in Washington, and the Metropolitan's wing on American design.

That's why many collectors rely on reputable dealers to research and document the pieces they offer.

Bronnie Hindin of Retro-Modern Studio states: "I think that most people find it is more economical in the long run to pay the price and get the expertise that a dealer can offer. Fifteen to twenty years ago maybe you would have come across a find in the field, but today it's much more difficult. Dealers go to great lengths to find the best for their clients, and to the client it's worth it."

Many individuals are turning to auction houses as a source for their collections as well.

Reporting on a trend that has also been observed in other auction houses, Kathleen Guzman comments, "It used to be almost exclusively dealers who attended auctions, but no more. It's almost fifty percent individuals now. Going to an auction house is the best education you can get. It's not like a museum—here you can smell, touch, taste, caress. And you'll never find a display and array of objects like this at a museum. Best of all, no one is going to tell you, 'You're not rich enough to look at this,' which is sometimes the feeling you get in certain dealerships."

Miss Guzman continues: "People are also much more savvy about what they have. However, many still don't understand that the market can fluctuate broadly. They see what something they own sold for many years ago and think it must only be higher today, and that's not always the case."

## Today's Market

It is Michael Meek's job to help assess the auction value of decorative art to be sold at William Doyle Galleries. He comments: "People have to remember that the prices we give are for goods in very good condition and are *always* subject to firsthand inspection. It is most important to see the property to determine what it can be sold for."

The property that William Doyle auctions comes for the most part from the purchase of estates, and the auction house has a much higher percentage of purchased property than consignment property for sale. This means that their estimates tend to be conservative, and their auctions have a low unsold rate—that is, relatively few pieces are subject to reserves or minimum bids.

In addition to individual collectors being better educated and attending more auctions, many museums have entered the market in recent years as they try to put together "definitive" collections of 20th-century design. Museums are just beginning to build collections of 20th-century decorative arts and are active in both selling and buying at auctions and elsewhere.

*Real* collectors—those who collect for the pleasure of collecting and not just for the resale value of the merchandise—are often the source of museum holdings. One curator we spoke to feels that people should be encouraged to collect because private collections often end up in public institutions. For example, many of the great collectors of Art Deco give or lend their collections to museums and special exhibitions—people like John Axelrod, who recently lent the Museum of Fine Arts in Boston a full room of Art Deco; Sidney and Frances Lewis, who gave the Virginia Museum of Fine Arts one of the single most important private collections of 19th- and 20th-century decorative arts ever assembled; and Mitchell Wolfson, Jr., whose Wolfsonian Foundation in Miami is in the process of computerizing his massive Mitchell Wolfson, Jr., Collection of Decorative and Propaganda Arts in order to make it available for public access.

Yet, uncannily, in a market so well developed one can still find plenty of dealers displaying a rag-tag collection of objects from the 1930s, 1940s, and even the 1950s and claiming they are selling Art Deco. Generally, what they are selling is the misperception of the style. We hope this book will serve to clarify the field for you.

What force has hurt the Art Deco collecting market the most in recent years? "Reproductions," Miss Guzman answers. "It really hurt Frankart prices because it's almost impossible to tell the difference between an original and a reproduction. A trained eye can still differentiate real Gallé and Lalique from the repros coming from Buenos Aires, but they're getting better. Also, Lesieutre's bronze and ivory reproductions really hurt the market. The original statues were getting phenomenal prices up to 1983."

To make matters worse, "Some second-tier dealers practice to deceive. They may not know a piece is a reproduction, or they may sell it as an original anyway. It is up to the buyer to develop a trained eye."

Many collectors are becoming more eclectic, with chrome, Bakelite, ceramics, Depression glass, and other subspecialties entering the active Art Deco field. Collectors are more interested, learn more about the field through books and publications, and have formed into affinity groups all over the country.

It is only in certain parts of the country (notably rural areas where this urban style of design never really caught hold) that good examples of Art Deco design can still be cheaply found at flea markets, country auctions, and yard sales.

What about the future of the market? Does Kathleen Guzman have any predictions for the future of Art Deco? She laughs. "Oh, if only I had a crystal ball..." But then she adds more seriously, "The auction of Andy Warhol's Art Deco collection of Eileen Gray, Andre Groult, and other designers [April 1988 at Sotheby's] will rewrite collecting history in the Art Deco furniture field. He collected everything and everything he collected was great.

"At one point we were getting very high prices on Clarice Cliff, but they came down quite a bit. I think Louis Meisel's book on her life and work will help create a wider market for her ceramics."

Miss Guzman adds some others to her list: "Industrial Design from the 1920s and 1930s is an up-and-coming field, and the Fragrance Foundation's collaboration with the Smithsonian for a September 1988 exhibition will expand the market for perfume bottles."

No matter what the area—from fine Ruhlmann desks to Lalique glass to European and American ceramics, from lithographic posters and magazine covers to World's Fair memorabilia and Industrial Design cameras, irons, juicers, and toasters—Art Deco is today one of the most popular collecting fields.

# HOW TO USE THIS BOOK

*Please note:* This book is a guide, not a bible. We set out to to report on what we've observed in today's Art Deco collecting market and to provide the reader with an overview of Deco as a whole. We hope that you may discover here objects you would like to collect and also get a general sense of what variety of objects best suits your pocketbook. Rather than an end in itself, this guide is intended to be a starting point for delving more deeply into any of the collecting areas covered here.

The first part of the book will acquaint the unfamiliar reader with the design trends that preceded, influenced, or were affected by the Art Deco and Art Moderne Movements. It also describes some of the general attributes of the Art Deco style.

The relationships and influences between schools of thought and design are rarely clear, so many of the details of the development of Art Deco have not been included here. Yet we hope that our narrative will clarify the connections and differences between Art Nouveau, Arts and Crafts, Bauhaus, Vienna Secession, Art Deco, Art Moderne, and Streamline.

We've introduced each chapter with a narrative to help you understand the scope of each area within the Art Deco field. Unfortunately, we could not mention all of the talented artists, craftsmen, designers, architects, and others whose contributions enhanced the development of Deco. In other words, if a particular name you are looking for is not included here, that does not necessarily mean that category or designer is not worth collecting. However, dates are given for many artists as a reference point so that you can better understand the time frame of Art Deco and get some sense of comparable value.

## NOTES ON THE PRICE LISTINGS

As is often true of any collectible object, the value of an Art Deco piece frequently depends on what the buyer is willing to pay. We interviewed more than one avid Art Deco collector who will pay high-art prices for low-end items he or she needs for a collection.

Also, many of the prices given in the following pages should be taken with a grain of salt by beginning collectors. Art Deco continues to fetch record prices at auction, and more people seem willing to pay higher prices than ever. However, many original Art Deco objects are still within your reach no matter what your income.

We have offered a sample of prices in each category we have covered—again, this is not necessarily an exhaustive list. If you do not find exactly the object you are looking for here, the prices given can still be used for comparison. Also, many reputable dealers and auction houses will always be willing to quote what a particular object is currently worth on the market.

The bulk of the price listings and price ranges in this book were observed by us or reported by dealers and auction houses during the last six months of 1987. We also gathered information about pricing anonymously at exhibitions, flea markets, and antiques fairs. All prices are given for objects in very good to excellent condition unless otherwise specified. Where damage or refinishing is known, it has been indicated in the description.

*Price ranges* given here are based on highs and lows reported to us by collectors, on observations at flea markets, antiques shows, and dealers' showrooms, and on estimated values reported to us from all over the country.

*Geographic variations* exist, with the East Coast (Boston, New York, Washington, DC, and the Miami area specifically) leading the market. Cities like Baltimore, Philadelphia, and Chicago seem in general to be following close behind. The West Coast, notably California, is a strong market for certain popular Deco fields, such as posters, ceramics, chrome, Erté, and other areas, but it seems to be less strong overall in European furnishings and art. Not only is the demand higher in these areas than in other parts of the country, but dealer overhead tends to be higher in major cities as well. Where differences were notable, we tried to take them into account in establishing our price ranges.

*Exact prices* represent prices realized at auction. These are reported only for 1986 and 1987, but the text sometimes refers to previous auction prices. Exact prices are indicated with the year of the auction in parentheses next to them. These prices represent the purchase price, not the final bid. That is, they include the "buyer's premium" charged by most auction houses, which is generally 10 percent. Where there have been notable differences between realized prices for the same object, we have noted more than one price.

## ABOUT THE RESOURCE GUIDE

The Resource Guide in this book gives you the names, addresses, and phone numbers of dealers, auction houses, museums, Art Deco societies, and individuals whom we've consulted in putting this book together. There is also a bibliography that will help you find other books and periodicals of interest to you.

One great advantage for Art Deco collectors is that the era in which they are interested is so thoroughly chronicled. It is not difficult to find information about the artists, designers, personalities, ateliers (workshops), publishing houses, and other key players.

This was not always the case. Because much of what Art Deco produced was "popular" in nature—posters, fashion, ceramics, and advertising design—much of it lapsed into relative obscurity until its revival in the 1960s. Dozens of excellent scholarly books deal with early French Art Deco and Art Moderne, and now numerous popular books, newsletters, and magazine articles are being written about American Art Deco and kitsch. A great number of high-quality books on various Art Deco subjects have appeared in the last five years. In addition, contemporary exhibits have enhanced our knowledge of Art Deco. If you'd like to find out more about any of the areas in this book, the Resource Guide can help.

## WHY SOME DEALERS DON'T LIKE PRICE GUIDES

Some of the dealers we contacted when gathering the materials and prices in this book declined to help. They felt that price guides did little to help, or actually had a negative effect on the collecting field.

You may think that these dealers are opposed to price guides because they don't want you to know the market price of their holdings. Generally, that's not the case. Dealers know that a well-informed client is usually the better client. Rather, they feel that the public does not understand how to use a guide, and that guides have some intrinsic problems.

In all fairness, we felt that we should explain some of their reasoning. It merits some attention.

- "Prices can change so rapidly."

It's true. The antiques and collectibles market, just like the stock market, is subject to rapid upturns and downturns and cyclical changes.

When you go out with the idea of investing in the antiques market, of course you hope that the objects you acquire will always increase in value. But this is just not the case. The market in antiques is governed by supply and demand. Things come into and go out of fashion. Discoveries can push prices up or down rapidly.

There is a great word that they use on Wall Street. When a rapidly rising stock takes a dive, it is referred to as a "correction." Corrections can happen in the antiques and collectibles market as well.

We want you to use the price listings in this book to understand better the general market range of the area in which you are interested—but remember: specific prices can and do change.

- "Someone will come into my store and expect that I can sell or buy an object for exactly what is listed in the price guide."

The prices in this guide do not necessarily represent the price at which a particular dealer will either buy or sell an object.

The scenario that most dealers who oppose price guides envisage goes something like this: A customer comes into the store with an object from the attic that he or she has seen listed in a price guide for $200. The customer offers the object to the dealer for the listed price. Of course the dealer can't pay such a price because he or she is in the business of "brokering" antiques and needs to mark up merchandise to make a profit.

The same scenario with a different twist: A customer comes into the store, spots an object priced at $400, looks it up in a price guide, and sees a price of $300. Ignoring the fact that the market may have changed, the guide may be old, or any number of other factors, the customer wants the dealer to sell the object for the listed price. Another impossible situation for the dealer, whose price is based on the price at which he or she acquired the object. Dealers are in the business of inventory and turnover. On the average, an antique stays on the shelf from six to eight *years*. When dealers acquire something for a very good price, they can offer it for a very good price. When an object costs them more, they have to charge more.

In addition, other costs add to the price tag at a dealership—overhead, the cost of travel and shipping, the time dealers must spend at auctions and elsewhere to find their inventory, and more, as with any service. Part of the price you pay reflects the work that the dealer put into finding, identifying, and possibly even restoring the piece.

- **"People don't understand auction prices."**
  More individuals are attending auctions, but many still do not understand the auction process. First, each auction is a unique event that will never be recreated.
  The price realized at auction depends largely on who is bidding. Remember, if there is just one person in the room who wants an object, he or she might get it at a price much lower than retail. But if there are two individuals in the room who desperately want that object for their collections, you can bet the price will soar.
  Prices realized can also depend on how the auction is promoted. For example, at a recent auction in New England, which had been advertised as a Victoriana auction, the few Art Deco pieces available went for very low prices, simply because Art Deco collectors and dealers had not been attracted to the sale.
  In addition, when the bid runs very high at an auction, it is more likely to be a collector, not a dealer, who is willing to go the distance. Dealers often can't compete at auctions with determined collectors. If a dealer places a retail-level bid or higher, chances are that he or she has gotten the go-ahead from a specific collector who will purchase the piece.
  Auction prices in a guide such as this are generally lower than retail prices because dealers acquire inventory at auctions for resale. In some instances, though, a price realized at auction exceeds the price at which the object is available on the market. So don't expect to purchase an object from a dealer at the auction price listed here. Remember, too, that the auction prices included here do not necessarily always reflect the value of the best or most important work of any given artist, designer, or school.

# HOW TO START A COLLECTION

The finest decorative arts of the Art Deco period in Europe and America are now esteemed on a par with antiques and are collected by serious collectors. Others, such as chrome, Depression glass, some ceramics, and other objects, fall into the realm of "collectibles." While their value is rising on the market, to many their real value is in the fun of collecting them, learning about them, and understanding the era that produced them.

The most important ingredient for starting a collection is a love of Art Deco styles. Flip through the pages of this book, and if you don't see anything that makes your heart leap, then you really should not collect Art Deco.

Art Deco collectors are a highly passionate group, one committed to helping the field, preserving the design style, and preserving architecture all over the world. The best dealers are inevitably collectors, while individuals have acquired collossal collections of the era's decorative arts for both personal pleasure and public benefit.

So where does a new collector begin?

"Know thyself," the philosophers say. We say, "What kind of collector are you? To concentrate or not to concentrate, that is the question."

Most experts will tell you that in any area of collecting you should decide on a theme, an item, a manufacturer, or a specific designer or school and concentrate your collecting efforts. If you are interested in one of the areas covered here, they tell you, you must devote the time to studying it and understanding it. Study the market performance of what you are interested in and read everything you can get your hands on.

However, while concentrating may be the way that most collectors increase their own knowledge and the value of their collection, Art Deco is also a field that appeals to the eclectic collector. You can acquire Art Deco collectibles "just for the fun of it" or purchase museum-quality furnishings for any room in your home, and not necessarily be an Art Deco collector. Many younger collectors are fascinated by a wide range of Art Deco production and collect what they like and what they can find at the right price. Serious collectors will pooh-pooh this type of collecting—but then, they are very serious about their collections.

Whichever way you go, you should set standards and try to collect only the best examples of Art Deco you can find. Even when your collection falls into a kitsch or mass-produced category, why collect chipped ceramics or chrome that is losing its plating when so many pieces in excellent condition are still available on the market?

If you want to start a quality collection of Art Deco, don't spend your hard-earned dollars until you've taken the time to know and understand what quality means in terms of the field you've chosen—both in product and in price. Go window shopping.

One of the best places to start a collection is right in this book. As you read through it, we hope you will become familiar enough with the Art Deco field to begin to know your "collecting self."

We suggest also that you carefully read the chapters "Today's Market," "How to Use This Book," and "Fakes, Forgeries, and Reproductions" to get a better understanding of the market, answers to other questions you may have, and some understanding of what to look out for.

Here are some other tips:

- Michael Meek, specialist in 19th-century decorative arts, Art Nouveau, and Art Deco for William Doyle Galleries, has some general advice for collectors. He says, "In many ways you have to forget about the 'investment' and buy what you love and what you can afford. It's best to look for those things that were innovative and high quality when they were produced. But ask yourself if the price is just trading on the name of the artist. For example, many of Lalique's pieces were not luxury items to begin with. One piece that brought a very high price recently originally sold for $18 at Saks."

- Remember, yesterday's attics hid Colonial and Victorian treasures, and today's attics and garages might hide Art Deco treasures. It may not be as true as fifteen or twenty years ago, when Art Deco collecting began in earnest; however, Aunt Ethel may still have Art Deco treasures packed away in the basement, and Grandma may still be using her Georg Jensen silver. First step: check around the house.

- Many people feel that they can get much better prices by shopping all of the flea markets and garage sales, and/or by attending auctions. In some cases this is true; however, you have to ask yourself, "Am I willing to spend hours, days, or even weeks looking for that special object or take the chance of finding it and bidding on it at auction, or do I want a dealer to do the work for me? How much is that worth to me?"

"It's true that more individuals are going to auctions than ever before," says Michael Meek. "That is one of the biggest changes in the market today."

- The price of an object may depend on geography. We've already noted that we've tried to take regional price differences into account as they were reported to us. However, you should remember also that some objects may have a higher regional value because of their regional importance, such as Teco pottery in Chicago.

- Being able to document an object increases its value. In other words, documentation costs money. Say you have an old desk and you would like to determine its value. Of course, there must be some intrinsic value to the desk—the materials, workmanship, design, etc. However, if you research the desk and find that it was designed by Gilbert Rohde in 1933, then the value immediately goes up. Research and documentation take time, and "time is money." We know of a few dealers who actually have two different prices—one if you do the research, another if they do it.

Good dealers are very well informed and do substantial research. They are also constantly in touch with the market. Because the decorative arts have not been emphasized in the study of art history in universities, many dealers have had to devote a lot of time to original research. Much of what is known today has come about through the efforts of art consultants, dealers, and auction house personnel: Brian Catley, Alain Lesieutre, Pat Kery, Louis Meisel, Alastair Duncan, Nancy McClelland, David Hanks, and others.

You should try to document your collection as you go along, noting where you purchase each piece and at what price, and recording any other information you may have about it. Not only will your collection grow in value if it is well documented, but the pleasure you get from collecting will also be enhanced as you learn more about these objects.

- People always try to buy low and sell high. It's the law of the collecting jungle. You may want to focus on areas that are not so popular today, with the hope that they will become so tomorrow. Try to avoid buying an object that seems to be peaking in the market.

- The market base for collecting in a certain field will help determine the going prices. If many people are attracted to collecting a certain type of object or artist—for instance, Lalique—that is recognized and sought after, the prices will be higher. When an important book comes out or an exhibition takes place, many more people learn about a new field of collecting, and the market base widens. Generally speaking, this means that prices go up. We have seen this happen in a general way with all American Art Deco in the past few years because of the extraordinary number of fine books and exhibitions focusing on it. Find out when the last major book on the subject you are interested in was published, and compare the market prices before and after its publication. Don't be surprised if values underwent a dramatic transformation.

- No matter what a price guide says, *you* have to decide what an object is worth to you. Simply put, don't buy anything you can't afford. On the other hand, if you love the piece you are looking at and can afford the price, then buy it.

# FAKES, FORGERIES, AND REPRODUCTIONS

Unfortunately, the revitalization of interest in Art Deco in the last twenty years has also seen a flood of both expensive and cheaply produced reproductions on the retail market. Some of the well-produced fakes and forgeries have wound up on the collecting market. Today's collector has to be very wary and very well educated when purchasing Art Deco objects from other than reputable dealers.

Of course, many people knowingly purchase reproductions of furniture, lamps, statues, posters, and other objects because of their highly decorative appeal. However . . .

## DECO ISN'T THE FIFTIES

One of the first problems to overcome in collecting Art Deco is to be clear what is meant by the term, how broadly it is used, and what decorative production actually deserves the title. Uninitiated collectors who are beginning an Art Deco collection should be aware that some items sold in flea markets and antiques fairs as Art Deco are really from the 1940s and 1950s. This is partly because the influence of Art Deco lasted much longer in the United States than elsewhere and partly because many dealers don't know what they have.

At a recent auction we saw a typical 1950s cocktail table sold as Art Deco for $65. While cocktail tables are themselves an inspiration of the low-slung furniture of the Art Deco era, this design had nothing to do with Art Deco and was really part of the flamboyant 1950s. Another example is McCoy pottery, which continued using certain Deco-like geometric patterns in their pottery vases well into the 1950s. Train your eye, and you'll soon see these as "Rural Post-Deco," lacking the sophistication of design—the *style*—that was Deco's hallmark.

## FURNISHINGS

There are companies today that create elegant reproductions using the same materials as early French designers. One company reproduces a noted Ruhlmann desk for about $10,000. The original now brings in six figures. Even 1930s American furniture in chrome and aluminum is being reproduced. Other companies are recreating chairs and couches based on the numerous American and English living room designs that were popular at the time. One company in California takes lesser-quality Deco-style bar cabinets of the 1930s and lacquers them in 1980s decorator colors.

In addition, because the Art Deco era was not that long ago, many companies are still issuing the same high-quality designs they were making over fifty years ago: Thonet's bentwood chairs and Knoll's chairs designed by Mies van der Rohe are just two examples. Other manufacturers have reissued their own original designs from the 1920s and 1930s.

If your love of Art Deco is really just for decorating your home, then purchase a 1986 wall sconce rather than the 1926 variety. It may serve your needs better. And who knows?—in fifty years these well-made reproductions may have developed some value on the secondary market.

The kind of product we are talking about here is well made. The only deception comes when someone tries to sell it as the original item. Unfortunately, it is almost impossible to tell the difference in the best-made pieces without the wisdom of an expert.

Furniture of individual designers is often signed and may even be dated. Because this work was often considered "museum quality" when it was produced, it can be very well documented. In addition, quality dealers know the "provenance" of their pieces—that is, they have a record of where the piece comes from. If you are willing to spend the kind of money it takes to acquire pieces of this nature, then ask for documentation.

Good dealers pay scrupulous attention to detail when identifying and cataloging items, as is true of any established auction house. The overall best advice is to buy from dealers and auction houses with established reputations. While even the best can make a mistake, dealers who serve the same clientele year after year would not survive on misrepresentation.

## STATUES

The market for Art Deco statues in bronze, bronze and ivory, and cast metal has been the hardest hit by reproductions and forgeries. (See "Today's Market" for more comments.) Such reproductions are extremely good in many cases, and even experts have problems detecting fakes.

However, educating yourself about the production of the field you are interested in will help you spot fakes and reproductions more immediately. For example, it is good to know that since the early 1980s Saspirilla Deco Designs of New Jersey have reissued numerous 1930s Frankart designs for statues and lamps.

Likewise, you may have seen advertisements for French bronzes and "chryselephantine" bronze-and-ivory statues cast from the original molds. Because original chryselephantine bronzes using ivory bring minimum prices of about $2,000, a good reproduction may look like a steal at $250 or $300.

Again, if you are aware that a statue is a reproduction and are buying it only for decorative value, it may be the better buy.

## GLASS

Today Art Deco glass is being imitated with a wide range of cheap reproductions. Forging a designer's name on glass is a common practice, even though many kinds of glass, curiously enough, were not signed originally. The absence of a name generally means a lower price on the market, so sometimes an unscrupulous individual will simply add a name. A well-done fake signature is hard to detect, and if you are collecting signed glass, your best bet is to arm yourself with a text in which signatures of glassmakers are reproduced. The best of these is *Glass: Art Nouveau to Art Deco* by Victor Arwas.

Such artists as René Lalique were imitated in their own day as well as today. Etling, Sabino, and other manufacturers produced Lalique-like frosted glass, and some of it is superb. American imitators included Consolidated Glass and Lamp Company and Phoenix Glass Company in the 1930s. These imitations are generally of poorer quality and color, but many collectors are still fooled by the better imitations. Etling, Sabino, and even Phoenix are today collected on their own merits, but they do not often command the price of a Lalique.

## Fakes, Forgeries, and Reproductions

Lalique? No. It's a "Fairy Martélé" bowl by Phoenix Glass. *(Photo by L. Ward; courtesy of the Jones Museum of Glass and Ceramics)*

Educate yourself. Go out into the market and learn to compare different designers. You will then begin to see why Lalique had imitators even in his day, and why they don't hold a candle to him in terms of the quality of the design.

Another word of caution about collecting glass. Repairs and damage are generally hard to hide in glass, but sometimes a chip on a rim will be repaired by the entire rim being cut down.

Also, while damaged glass by important artists may be worth the asking price, mass-produced glass that is damaged is not worth keeping. Remember to inspect any object carefully, especially glass, before buying.

## CERAMICS

Recently, a department store advertisement declared, "Art Deco is Back!" and announced a sale of new Hall china cast from original molds, offering pitchers at $11.98 and serving bowls at $9.98. Although Hall did make some designs that can be called Art Deco or Art Moderne, most of its production was not Deco. What is being reproduced and sold today as Art Deco includes the common Ball Jug introduced in 1938. Today's Hall, with its pastel shades of pink, blue, and white is also quite different in color from its original production in Chinese red, delphinium blue, lettuce green, and other colors.

The Hall self-reproduction is particularly disturbing in a market where 1940s and 1950s ceramics are just beginning to take off, including such items as the Homer Laughlin Company's Fiesta Ware. The reproductions of this china are just as nice as the originals, and while a new trend in collecting would like to place Fiesta Ware and other ceramics of the 1940s and 1950s in the world of Art Deco, it just isn't true. Fiesta Ware was somewhat influenced by certain Art Deco motifs, but that's where the similarities end.

In both ceramics and statuary, reproductions and imitations of Art Deco abound: picture frames, lamps, vases, teapots, statues, ashtrays, bookends, frosted glass, clocks, and salt and pepper shakers. These sell anywhere from $5 to $200 and more. Some of the companies involved in reproduction include Silvestri, FF (Japan), Saspirilla, Five & Dime, Mann (Japan), and Keramik (Italy). In all fairness, it should be noted that *most* of the reproductions we have seen are plainly marked with the name of the manufacturer. However, that does not stop them from being sold as originals. In some cases all it takes is peeling off a label. *You* are the one who has to know the difference.

## SILVER, FASHION, AND JEWELRY

Fashion and jewelry from the Art Deco era have been imitated ever since they first appeared. Open any fashion magazine today and you are sure to see the influence of Art Deco design. Some pieces of jewelry reproduced today are exact duplicates of the originals, using the same quality of precious stones and metals.

In fashion, generally speaking, the prices for "vintage" clothing are roughly equivalent to those of modern designs. Because most people who collect in this category collect it to wear, they concern themselves more with the fit and the price than with collecting value per se. A few years ago, men's skinny silk ties with geometric designs were in vogue, but the new ones had the advantage of not coming with old gravy stains.

Generally speaking, forgers in this field choose items that are "hot" on today's fashion market, like Vuitton bags and Gucci designs.

Sterling silver is difficult to fake, but again it is best to buy from a reputable dealer. Some of the silver designs of the day have been remanufactured, such as the coffee set from the *Normandie*, but these are often sold registered and numbered, and from what we've seen, they are worth the prices asked.

Jewelry, especially fine jewelry, is another area where you should trust a reputable jeweler or estate jewelry dealer. The prices you pay for lower-end or mid-range collectible jewelry is about the same you would pay for similar modern designs.

The best advice we can give on jewelry: Don't pay more than you can afford, and don't buy a Cartier watch from a man on the corner of a busy intersection.

## POSTERS AND GRAPHICS

We have not yet heard of any cases of lithographic posters being forged, as it is a very difficult process indeed to create a well-registered lithograph. However, with some posters costing as much as houses, it is probably only a matter of time before the poster world has its share of "Mona Lisas."

The lithographic process, which is described in the chapter on posters and graphics, laid down layers of color on stones and applied them to the paper. Today's photographic printing processes use film negatives, which create a series of very straight lines of tiny dots. If you really have a question about whether a poster is a true lithograph, look for the photographic dots under a magnifying glass. It is easy to tell modern reproductions of popular Art Deco posters in this manner.

As with glass, the most common forgery in graphics is the forging of a signature on etchings, gouaches, and other kinds of designs. Again, you should become very familiar with the signature of the artist or artists you are interested in collecting.

## 1980s DECO AND POSTMODERNISM

In much the same way that the production market in the 1930s became flooded with mass-produced works in the Art Deco style, the 1980s collecting marketing is being inundated with "Deco-inspired" originals. There are numerous stores that on first glance look as though they have windows full of Art Deco. Original sculptures are being produced in Art Deco style once again for those who consider themselves chic, and they are sold through boutiques and department stores. Pottery, lighting fixtures, and other items are available in sleek, Deco-like designs. The quality of this original work varies; some of it is even quite beautiful—but none of it is Art Deco.

In addition to these there is Postmodernism, a design style that has emerged in both architecture and decorative arts over the last few years and that tends to incorporate both classical and modern elements. The Postmodern Movement's leading exponents are architects such as Michael Graves and Robert Venturi. Today both of these men—and others equally as talented, such as Richard Meier, Trix Haussmann, and Ettore Sottsass—have designed dinnerware, tea sets, and silver for companies such as Swid Powell in New York. The influence of Art Deco and Art Moderne can be seen in Postmodern style, and these high-quality pieces may very well become part of the high-end collecting market of the future.

## A FINAL NOTE OF CAUTION

The best rule of thumb to follow is this: If you are browsing in an antiques show and find what you think is an "unbelievable buy" in Art Deco, then don't believe it. Remember that dealers come into many shows before the public does, and in scanning the wares one of them probably would have noticed an original piece selling so far below market value.

In garage sales and flea markets, where the seller may not be aware of the value of an item, take the risk of purchasing what you believe to be an original (a) only if the price is what you would pay for a reproduction and (b) only if you truly like the piece. You may have made a find, or you may find that you have to live with what you have purchased for a very long time.

# AN OVERVIEW OF ART DECO

Before World War I people with "taste" in the United States and France were reading by the light of their Tiffany lamps—the epitome of the Art Nouveau style—and modeling their ideals of feminine beauty on Alphonse Mucha's curvaceous females with tendril-like hair.

Art Nouveau was dominant for a relatively short period of time and was not as widespread a style as one might believe given the enormous market and popularity it has today. Most urban Americans, for example, were still living in modest Victorian or Colonial settings, immune to the lures of the advertising poster and easily shocked by the seductive goddesses of Art Nouveau.

In England and America, the Arts and Crafts Movement, with its moral fervor, looked down on the extravagance of Art Nouveau. In addition, in several Continental countries emerging Modernist design movements were rising against the flowery decoration and asymmetrical design of Art Nouveau and were winning new converts.

Just after the turn of the century, early pioneers of new Modern styles included Viennese architects Joseph Maria Olbrich and Josef Hoffmann (the latter also creating angular silver tea sets and restrained bentwood furniture); the Scottish architect and designer Charles Rennie Mackintosh; German architects Otto Wagner and Adolf Loos, both of whom influenced the De Stijl group of Holland and later the German Bauhaus; and designer Carlo Bugatti in Italy.

These designers initially did not have as much impact in France as did the arrival in Paris in 1909 of Diaghilev's Ballets Russes. Many talented young fashion designers and artists were delighted by the colorful costumes and Oriental influence of its set and costume designs. Among those who were most influenced by the Ballets Russes were such notable fashion designers, interior designers, and illustrators as Paul Poiret, Paul Iribe, Paul Follot, Erté, Georges Lepape, and André Marty.

With a view toward a unified aesthetic, many fashion designers moved into the field of interior design. Poiret's firm, Martine, and Jeanne Lanvin's commissions of talented cabinetmakers such as Armand-Albert Rateau set new tastes in household furnishings. Lanvin's rival designer, Madeleine Vionnet, had a huge collection of lacquer by Jean Dunand. In fact, Martine sought to integrate the "look" of a room by creating its own textiles, pottery, porcelain, wallpaper, and furniture. A room became the vision of one designer, rather than a collection of works by many.

Jacques Doucet, an important fashion designer, was very influential and avant-garde. He collected Cubist paintings, early Surrealist works, and exotic African and Chinese art. He commissioned and bought from such talented artists as Pierre Legrain, Clément Rousseau, Eileen Gray, Gustav Miklos, and René Lalique to furnish his own home. It is said that André Breton, the fiery father of Surrealism, helped Doucet select his contemporary art.

Doucet exerted great influence on the younger generation of fashion designers as well. Paul Poiret was a former employee of Doucet's when his career was at its highest. Poiret, in turn, hired such notable designers as Paul Iribe and Georges Barbier to execute or render illustrations of his own designs. Poiret also traveled to Vienna and Moscow, where he met the young Romain de Tirtoff, who would later become known as Erté.

In France many of the best decorative artists worked to combine exotic or new materials, traditional methods, and simpler design. These *ébénistes*, or cabinetmakers, often worked for wealthy, knowledgeable and status-conscious clients.

After World War I, architect Louis Süe and painter-decorator André Mare founded the Compagnie des Artistes Français. Among the first to bring together artists from many disciplines in their search for "total design," their company designed and commissioned ceramics, glassware, bookbindings, textiles, and furniture, as well as architecture.

Süe et Mare—along with others in this period—considered themselves "tastefully modern." Among their talented contemporaries was Emile-Jacques Ruhlmann, who had his first major exhibition at the Salon D'Automne in 1913. Other designers of this period include Maurice Dufrène, Jean Dunand, Leon Jallot, Edgar Brandt, Raoul Dufy, Jules Leleu, and Paul Vera. These designers dominated French decorative arts until 1925. In fact, it was their overwhelming strength and influence in the right circles that kept more modernist designs from appearing in the 1925 exposition.

Many people believe that Art Deco was a revolt against Art Nouveau, starting in about 1909 and culminating in the 1925 exposition. However, until about 1930, while these artists sought to find new, simple forms, they were really part of a continuum of French traditional design and often looked to French 18th-century furniture for their inspiration. Even when Modernism became more prevalent, the grand style of the early Art Deco artists would prevail in official commissions for ocean liners and public buildings well into the 1930s.

It should be noted, too, that French Art Deco was not a "movement"—it had no name at the time, no books to establish the "rules" of the new style, and no angry theorists arguing for the adoption of Art Deco over Art Nouveau. If a starting point for the new design is to be identified, it would perhaps be 1900, when French decorative artists founded the Société des Artistes Décorateurs, to which belonged many of the designers named above.

Their ideas were articulated in two magazines, *Art et Décoration* and *L'Art Décoratif,* both of which had started in 1897.

Nevertheless, Art Nouveau *was* challenged and finally overwhelmed by this new design style. It also faced pressure from the Modern design movements in other countries. The advent of World War I and the social changes that led to the expansion of the city and the middle class also contributed to its downfall.

Early Modernist designers subscribed to an ethic of handcraftsmanship, but they were less resistant to the use of machines, new techniques, and modern, less expensive materials. One notable event that affected early French Modern designers was the 1910 exhibition of the Deutscher Werkbund in Paris. German workshop and industrial design inspired such French designers as Francis Jourdain, René Herbst, René Joubert, Robert Mallet-Stevens, and Le Corbusier.

Décoration Intérieur Moderne, or D.I.M., founded in 1919 under the direction of René Joubert, was the first French firm to create tubular steel furniture a few years later. The ideals and designs of these modern artists would not gain wide acceptance until after 1925, by which time Art Deco was no longer deluxe in economic and social terms, and influences from other countries were clamoring too loudly to be ignored.

After 1925 the Modern Movement gained strongholds across Europe. The centers of the movement were to be found in the Parisian Union des Artistes Modernes and the German Bauhaus school.

By 1928 the Thonet company was producing tubular bent-steel furniture designed by Le Corbusier. In 1931 Practical Equipment Limited, or PEL, was creating modern furniture for a wealthy clientele in England. And by the mid-1930s, even Süe et Mare were making furniture in aluminum with a Modern style that reflected the busier, faster pace of life. The Machine Age had come to maturity with the wireless," the passenger train, steamships, and of course, airplanes.

Art Deco in its early phase had sustained traditional values and the use of traditional materials, whereas the exponents of the Modern movement clearly broke with the past, dedicating themselves to the use of new materials, and adopting a socialistic vision of their role in society. Modernism did have its doctrines and manifestos, which overtly proclaimed it to be an attempt to bring together art and industry. Its primary goal was to create larger, less expensive, yet still finely designed furnishings and other objects with new materials. Its political goal—a rather optimistic one—was to put the machine to the service of the masses.

In America early modernists were also at work. Frank Lloyd Wright, influenced by Louis Sullivan and by the Arts and Crafts Movement, had been creating modern architectural designs since the turn of the century. Joseph Urban, a member of the Viennese Secession, emigrated to America and founded the Wiener Werkstätte (Vienna Workshops) gallery in New York in 1922. Paul Theodore Frankl was building his "skyscraper" bookcases as early as 1925.

Although Art Deco and Modern were opposed ideologically, both emphasized quality styling. One way of looking at the transition that took place is to note that simplified Art Deco design first reflected handcrafted French luxury and later German and American economically influenced functionalism. The early couturier, or dressmaker, who became an *ensemblier,* or interior designer, saw his prominence in the field slowly fall, first to the architect and then to the industrial designer. Handcrafting was slowly giving way to mass production.

A number of social and political developments, such as the rapid urbanization of Europe and America and the Great Depression of 1929, helped to hasten this transformation.

In the 1920s, as people began to lead more active social lives, the fashion rage was Coco Chanel. Here was a woman who created bold designs for the woman of the time: a woman who had a new role in society and who was confident enough to take hold and run with it.

Perhaps as the after-effect of "wearing the pants" for so long while their men were away in the trenches, women adopted new sporty clothes with masculine tailoring, broad shoulders, and angular styles. They golfed, played tennis, and went horseback riding, and they needed clothes that were comfortable and durable yet well styled.

The new clothing style affected art. Noted German sculptor Fritz Preiss designed bronze and ivory statues of women in swimsuits intead of slinky cabaret outfits. Even the great Diaghilev had Coco Chanel design sporting clothes for his 1924 ballet, *Le Train Bleu.*

## An Overview of Art Deco

The 1920s were nicknamed "Les Années Folles," the "wild" or "crazy" years. Discontented with the affairs of the world and horrified at the atrocities of a war no one could have reasonably imagined, many people threw out the rulebooks and adopted "daring" attitudes. For the first time women smoked in public and made a show of it by using long, jeweled cigarette holders. They wore shorter and shorter skirts and danced in nightclubs without their escorts. Life was better, people had money, and the weekends were full of champagne bubbles, sunbathing, and F. Scott Fitzgerald–style parties.

The Art Deco style was popularized by both French and American department stores and by the major manufacturers of high-quality household and decorative objects, such as Baccarat and Lalique. Each major French department store had its own atelier, or workshop, to create exclusive designs. These were headed by some of the best designers of the day, and commissions were given to still others. The department stores would play a leading role in the 1925 Paris Exposition.

In the United States, French Art Deco was slow to take hold at first. In fact, a number of American manufacturers visited the 1925 Paris Exposition and came away unimpressed.

In subsequent years important exhibitions (which often play a role in the public acceptance of design styles) were held at the Metropolitan Museum of Art and at Macy's and Lord & Taylor's department stores. However, Art Deco continued to be seen as an essentially "foreign" style, one that appealed to those who considered themselves "Continental" in taste.

What is now considered Art Deco in America has less to do with the early French production than with the other Modern styles that were being developed at the same time.

Immigrants from Finland, Austria, Germany, and other countries brought their design talents and ideals here early in the century. Finnish architect/designer Eliel Saarinen became the first director of the Cranbrook Academy of Art near Detroit in 1922. American ceramicists from Ohio exchanged visits with artists from Vienna. Later, such architects as Walter Gropius and Marcel Breuer would establish themselves in this country as they escaped from Fascist Germany.

What French Art Deco did was to awaken interest in and focus attention on the Modern Movement in America. It was a style that fit America's rapid industrialization, and it quickly captured the entire market. It created a staggering variety of both functional and decorative high- and low-cost objects during the 1920s and 1930s, which are sought after by Art Deco collectors today.

While Modern design captured the American imagination, the often extravagant early French Art Deco style influenced Hollywood greatly. For example, Erté, who came to America in 1925, began designing sets and costumes for the screen almost immediately, establishing a sense of glamour and style that would hold sway in film well into the 1930s.

As industrial production increased, manufacturers began to understand the value of advertising. They often turned to advertising illustrators to help them render their cars, trains, ocean liners, and the like on paper. These formative designers—such as Norman Bel Geddes, who worked for one of America's first major advertising agencies, J. Walter Thompson in New York—were highly influential. Walter Dorwin Teague and Raymond Loewy influenced product design as well as graphics. Modern and new Streamline design ideals were applied to furniture, appliances, and personal items.

Part of industry's courtship of the consumer was the instigation of an economic revolution that haunts many of us to this day—personal credit. The advent of credit had the advantage of opening up huge new markets for manufacturers. A new animal—the annual model change—came into being. Wide varieties of shapes and colors were also introduced into the marketplace, inspiring broader lines of consumer items.

It was clear that the new Modernism was the major design style of the day as early as the 1929 Exhibition of American Industrial Art at the Metropolitan Museum. This exhibition highlighted rooms of furnishings that had been designed by architects.

In the following years American architects and designers such as Donald Deskey, Kem Weber, Gilbert Rohde, Walter von Nessen, and Russel Wright would undertake the design of objects both large and small. Many were commissioned to design furniture and other articles for mass production: glass, chrome, appliances, radios, lamps, and office equipment.

For example, Walter Dorwin Teague designed glassware for Steuben Glass, tabletop and floor-model radios, the Kodak Bantam Special and other cameras, as well as a desk lamp for Polaroid Corporation. He also conceived Consolidated Edison's "City of Light" and the giant National Cash Register at the 1939 New York World's Fair.

Mass-produced items in which cheaper materials underscored poor design have left a bad impression of what this aspect of Art Deco really means. Poor chromium plating, base metals painted to appear as bronze, dime-store ceramic statues, and the like are evidence that the style was declining. Kitsch is not a recent term coined by current collectors. This kind of production was dismissed as kitsch in its own day, the moment it hit the stores. However, today all categories of kitsch are hot collectibles and are bringing higher prices.

Earlier in the Art Deco Movement, even when the object was quantity, it was still a controlled production. At that time the word *series* meant "signed and numbered." Today the French term *article de série* is used derisively and perhaps rightly so, for even French manufacturers have succumbed to the need to produce cheaply manufactured household items for the millions of people who now inhabit urban centers.

Much of this kitsch was the result of the demand for "stylish" goods from a swelling population. It was high style adapted to industrial production so that the masses could enjoy at least an illusion of the grandeur that had been the standard of Art Deco since the beginning of the century. The trend toward poorly manufactured goods increased during the Depression. Hollywood movies were the only escape from troubled times, and "having style" was a way of pretending that times weren't so bad.

In many ways the Hollywood films themselves led to the widespread creation of kitsch. After Erté, Hollywood engaged the talents of such designers as Kem Weber, Joseph Urban, Coco Chanel, and Hermes to create the styles on the screen that the masses yearned for.

The Radio City Rockettes, the human geometric designs created by dancers in Busby Berkeley "Goldigger" films, and Cecil B. DeMille's 1934 *Cleopatra* for Paramount, starring Claudette Colbert, are grand examples of how the entertainment world borrowed from, glamorized, and in the process "standardized" the Art Deco style for mass consumption.

One of the secrets of having style and taste, however, is that it belongs to an "in" crowd. When a design becomes truly popular with the masses, it seems to lose favor with the tastemakers. Art Deco disappeared because of new social realities—the Depression and World War II—but even without these it probably would not have endured mass popularization. Artists, always looking for new ground, had begun to turn away from the style years earlier.

Unfortunately, many people think of the cheapest kind of kitsch when they hear the words *Art Deco*. Perhaps that is because kitsch was so omnipresent. In addition, the underlying influence of Art Deco survived World War II in the design of everyday objects through the 1940s and 1950s, especially in ceramics such as Fiesta Ware.

"Dime Store Deco," as it is sometimes called, was vulgarized more and more as the market for it dwindled. The later the production, the smaller the trace of elegance that marked the high Art Deco period.

In the 1960s eclectic collectors revived many different design styles, and Deco was among them. Its regained popularity with collectors is no doubt due to the fact that so many fine examples of the style exist. In addition, it is the last major style to which collectors can look for handcrafted design, smaller production, and quality materials and workmanship.

The enormous size of the market for Art Deco today is due to the fact that the Modern style, which evolved from Art Deco, was truly the last of the great "total styles." It was a complete and international style. This means that there is practically no design area that it did not touch: hotels and ocean liners, cigarette cases and perfume bottles, carpets and vanity tables, tea sets and cocktail shakers, radios and toasters, handbags and hats, sugar bowls and silverware, advertising and typography, homes and cars, bookbinding and magazines—wherever one looks, Art Deco has left its mark. Today, no matter what your collecting interest, you can find it in the world of Art Deco.

# MATERIALS AND TECHNIQUES

Early Art Deco artists worked in traditional woods and other materials, but like the Art Nouveau artists before them, they displayed a love of exotic materials from faraway places. Mother-of-pearl, semiprecious stones, lacquer and enamel, unusual woods, silvered bronze, crystal, and marble came into usage.

Deco and Nouveau were influenced by a growing fascination with the cultures of Africa, the Orient, and the Americas, and craftsmen imported quantities of rare woods such as Macassar ebony, ivory tusks, and onyx from Brazil. The mere rarity of these materials today greatly increases the price of objects produced from them, but many were available in abundance at the time. In fact, the Belgian government at one time held contests to encourage artists to use the tons of ivory being brought back from the Congo. This helped to increase the popularity of chryselephantine, or bronze-and-ivory sculptures.

## FURNITURE MATERIALS

In furniture production, use of the native sycamore came into vogue in France, along with more exotic burled woods such as zebrawood, amboyna, amaranthe, olivewood, Cuban mahogany, Rio palissandre, and palmwood. These gave artists a wide choice of color, texture, and grain for furniture.

The graining on some of these, like palissandre, is so bold that it can be seen from across the room, and it seems to change the lines of the piece.

Another favorite, if bizarre, material was *galuchat*, actually the skin of a dogfish, which was treated and used like leather. Today you'll hear people call it sharkskin, which sometimes substituted for it, or shagreen. Bleached to pale green, gray, or beige, it became a favorite for desk tops. It had its own repetitive design of scales and could also be tooled with geometric, sunburst, or other Deco designs.

As time went on, modern utilitarian materials were used more frequently in furniture: steel tubing for chairs and tables, thick glass surfaces, stainless steel, and plywood of varying thicknesses. Furniture from such materials was at first met with outrage and anger. However, today we recognize that these materials were used with great genius by the designers of the Modern phase of Art Deco. Their work was art suited to industrial production.

For designers like Le Corbusier and Robert Mallet-Stevens, these easily mass-produced materials supported their philosophy and politics as well as their design goals.

## LACQUER AND ENAMEL

The use of lacquer began in earnest with the arrival in Paris of the Japanese artist Sugawara. Paris had a rage for things Oriental, and Sugawara's influence on two noted designers, Eileen Gray and Jean Dunand, to whom he taught the ancient craft, made lacquer an overwhelmingly popular technique. While both artists went down in history for their lacquer work, Dunand is more often recognized as the master.

White was the only color that could not be produced by lacquer, but Dunand discovered that he could use crushed egg shells to create his white geometric design patterns. Lacquered pieces often were rendered in geometric red, black, and silver designs—a favorite Deco color combination. Many other artists began applying lacquer to everything: boxes big and little, panels, furniture, and glasswares.

Fast-drying industrial lacquer would later replace the painstaking ancient finishing process, meaning that more items could be produced in "lacquer" finishes. The use of real lacquer slowly disappeared.

At this time, industrial enamel was also developed. The passion for enamel, which started in the Art Nouveau period, was expressed primarily in jewelry. The new Modern designs, especially those of Raymond Templier and George and Jean Fouquet, created new markets for bold-colored enameled jewelry. Enameling also became a popular technique for enriching pottery vases and other decorative objects.

## FASHION

At the beginning of the Art Deco period, the lamés, interwoven with real gold and silver thread, were extremely popular for evening dresses. Little fabric was man-made, except for artificial silk. Embroidery often enriched the look of a piece, and pure silk crêpe de chine was a favorite for women's lingerie. By the 1930s synthetic textile production and ready-to-wear styles had proliferated.

As more women began to wear jewelry, more semiprecious stones and materials came into use. Often these materials were selected for the color value they gave to the new geometric design, such as turquoise, malachite, coral, and jade. Later, rhinestones and marcasites would make it possible for every woman to afford jewelry that sparkled like diamonds.

## METAL

Traditional metals, especially bronze and wrought iron, continued to be the basic materials for decorative and architectural purposes. As before, wrought iron was used extensively in architectural detail, while bronze served as a medium for sculpture.

However, wrought iron began to be used more frequently in a decorative way, and eventually even wrought-iron tables were available, often topped with glass and marble. This use later extended to lamps and other furnishings. Artists in glass and metal teamed up to create stunning lighting fixtures, highlighting each other's talents to greater advantage.

Precious metals—copper, silver, and gold—maintained their value but were used in different ways. Edgar Brandt is the undisputed master of metalwork in Art Deco; he was commissioned by many designers to execute wrought-iron designs. Dunand also excelled in working in pewter and hammered copper.

New metalcrafting techniques also came into play. Autogenous welding—which allowed two different metals, such as bronze and silver, to be welded together—created new combinations of metals in decorative pieces.

## NEW MATERIALS

Although the Art Deco Movement may have begun with French artists learning and adopting the traditional method of Japanese lacquer application, it evolved into an era in which kitchenware was made from highly polished, machine-produced chrome. For many, chromium-plated objects typify the Art Deco Movement in America.

Ceramics could be fired and glazed in one step, cheap wood veneers were used to hide metal structures in furniture, aluminum became popular for furnishings, and whole walls of houses could be constructed with glass block.

In the 1930s, as Deco style permeated every level of society, cheaply produced radios, ceramics, kitchen utensils, ashtrays, statues, and costume jewelry were made in the style of the day, using a host of materials, including stainless steel and nickel plating, painted low-quality metal, Bakelite and Catalin plastic, soft white metals, frosted or blue mirrored glass, and opaque glass intended to imitate marble or onyx. Such materials were often decorated, by a variety of methods, in bright, jazzy colors or Floridian pastels.

Given the wide variety of materials and techniques used in the Art Deco period—and their relative abundance and scarcity—these alone can greatly affect the price of a piece. It is also important for the collector to know and recognize the materials used in order to avoid deception. For example, onyx bases on clocks are often passed off on the unwary as marble. Industrial lacquering should not command the price of hand lacquering. Early decorative statues used bronze and ivory, while later ones and imitations used "ivorene," a composition plastic.

Today, when numerous reproductions of Deco and Modern designs are being manufactured and sold again, knowing the range of materials can help you avoid well-made reproductions and poorly made imitations when you are looking for the real thing.

# MOTIFS

The motifs of Art Deco distinguish it from other styles. Art Nouveau is characterized by curving, swaying lines, and it uses plant imagery such as tendrils, ferns, flowers, and leaves. Figures, usually women with flowing hair, were more full-bodied and voluptuous than their sleek Art Deco counterparts. Other popular Art Nouveau motifs include morning glory vines, peacock tails, and calla lilies.

The first phase of Art Deco was still somewhat romantic, though it included stylized motifs of bubbles, rainbows, fountains, and flowing water. Lithe women without the flowing robes and hairstyles of the Nouveau period began to appear, often nude. Influenced by Orientalism, Art Deco displayed simplicity of line and use of bright color combinations.

The Modern phase saw motifs become more rectilinear, symmetrical, and geometric in design. Motifs suggesting movement, speed, or progress were popular, especially after the horror of World War I, as the world raced ahead to better times. The flowers and ferns of early Deco gave way to more geometric and abstract plant forms. The fountain motif, with its cascades of water, became simple repetitive line patterning.

Jazzy, offbeat, and angular motifs appeared in both European Modern and American Art Deco, in the shapes of objects and in painted decoration.

The ziggurat, or stepped tower, was influential in skyscraper architecture and skyscraper-motif furnishings. This form was drawn from ancient Mayan and Aztec temples, as well as from the ruins of Mesopotamia, Assyria, and Egypt. By the end of the era, the skyscraper style had been played out ad nauseam.

The stepped look could also be curved into repeating arcs. The Deco "arc ziggurat" looks like scoops of ice cream topping one another or a stylized cloud formation. Half-circles radiating out from a source could represent sound, telegraph or radio signals, and other invisible forces of the age. Sunburst patterns also became popular.

The zigzag, lightning bolt, or chevron became one of the widely used Art Deco motifs in America, in everything from neon signs to designs on the faces of countertop radios and handles of hairbrushes. A lightning bolt turned on its side could represent electricity, and often appeared on kitchen appliances as well.

Modern motifs were used incessantly as the Deco movement took hold in America. Recognizing motifs in everyday decorative objects becomes easier if one studies their use in architecture of the period.

With the advent of the Streamline style, Modernism lost some of its right angles to curved corners and teardrop shapes. Geometric design became aerodynamic, greatly influenced by the shape of airplanes and cars. Three parallel horizontal or diagonal "speed lines" are often seen on Streamline-design objects. The Streamline style is best seen in industrial objects and household appliances such as irons.

## ANIMALS

Art Deco brought a new bestiary to the world of design, replacing the popular animals of Art Nouveau with the exotic, fast, streamlined, even the mythical: antelopes, gazelles, griffins, greyhounds, borzois, deer, horses, and eagles. In Tropical or Floridian Deco, flamingos, herons, and pelicans, either standing or in flight, became part of the popular design menagerie.

Animals also played a leading role in painting and sculpture, appearing more urbane and sophisticated than ever. One favorite family of animals included the big cats: lions, tigers, jaguars, and leopards, which were more exotic than endangered at the time.

Perhaps the best designer and illustrator of the *animalier* movement was Paul Jouve. Many of his sculpted jaguars and other cats were transformed into bronze statues and decorative ceramics that lurked behind low-slung couches and under cocktail tables for decades.

Birds and insects such as grasshoppers found their way onto Lalique glass and set the standard for many of the Art Deco motifs. (See the photo in our color section, "An Art Deco Portfolio.") Parakeets, parrots, doves, and other birds were favorites for decorating vases and clocks. Antelopes and gazelles were everywhere—leaping across metalwork by Edgar Brandt, grazing around a bowl of Steuben crystal, and animating French department store pottery.

In American architecture and design the eagle was a natural, its already angular beak and flat head lending itself easily to the Modern angular style. Its wings and feathers were set straight back, once again in a stepped pattern.

The popularity of some Art Deco symbols and motifs and of bold lines and graphics waned rapidly when they appeared in Nazi propaganda art. To some eyes the Modern style was a Germanic style and therefore associated with the Third Reich. In fact, American Modern design had been influenced by the Bauhaus, the Wiener Werkstätte, and dozens of German immigrants who had come to this country before the war. Just as cans of sauerkraut were taken down from the shelves and replaced with "Liberty Cabbage" during World War I, the German influence in American design was essentially denied well into the 1950s.

In the 1940s in America, a whole new variety of animal would steal the scene. One of the favorite motifs would become Pegasus, the winged horse—a symbol of hope and freedom—made famous as the logo of Mobil Oil Company.

# DECORATIVE INFLUENCES

## ART NOUVEAU

Art Nouveau was the predominant European design style for only about twenty years, roughly 1890 to 1910. The style really reached its peak about 1900 and slowly ebbed in the following decade, flourishing more in Europe than in America. It was a sculptural style that tried to diminish the importance of the Industrial Revolution and totally ignored machine-produced materials. Some critics say it was "denial," that Nouveau could do little more than postpone the emergence of a more modern style.

The term *Art Nouveau* is said to have originated with a shop owned by Siegfried Bing. He sold furnishings and objets d'art in Paris in 1895 in a shop called Maison de l'Art Nouveau. Bing, an art dealer, critic, and collector of Japanese work, exhibited some of the most outstanding artists of the day in his gallery, including Bonnard, Vuillard, and Aubrey Beardsley.

When he visited the United States, Bing was deeply impressed by American architectural achievements and the work of glassmaker Tiffany, heir to the fortune of the famous Fifth Avenue jewelry store, who had established himself as an interior designer in New York in 1879. Tiffany was a master artist in glass, achieving magnificent colors, breathtaking iridescence, intricacy in staining, and extraordinary textures.

René Lalique worked with Bing designing jewelry that was contrary to the traditional forms. He created abstract designs of plants and insects incorporating semiprecious stones and glass paste, and by the beginning of World War I he was considered the outstanding jeweler of Europe. He soon took up glassmaking in earnest. Lalique was a truly original designer, able not only to survive the transition in decorative arts from Nouveau to Deco but able to lead it as well.

Although Art Nouveau was mainly a decorative style used in furnishings, statues, and the like, it coincided with other design movements in Europe that were more architecturally based. It reflected somewhat the fine arts of its day in France by its use of natural motifs and colors, and in some ways it echoed the vision of an Impressionist painter such as Claude Monet.

Art Nouveau was the first French design movement to stress the equality of the decorative and fine arts, and it helped to foster the emergence and recognition of individual decorative artists. In other countries, such as England, the Arts and Crafts Movement had attempted the same reconciliation of roles, but for philosophical rather than aesthetic reasons. Bing encouraged the synthesis of the fine and decorative arts by commissioning such painters as Bonnard and Toulouse-Lautrec to make designs for stained glass windows that Tiffany would later execute.

Most European nations produced some variation of the Art Nouveau style, and by the 1900 Paris Exposition, it was obvious that Nouveau was dominating the design field. Only the Scandinavian countries, under the influence of Arts and Crafts, were still involved in a more sober style.

In Germany the Art Nouveau style was called Jugendstil because it was highly promoted through the journal *Jugend*. However, Germany's economic realities were different, and in the end her artists revolted against the style. In Italy, Art Nouveau was called Stile Liberty because of the popularity of goods from the London shop of A. L. Liberty.

Art Nouveau became so involved in excesses of ornamentation that it seemed the basis of the style was the ornamentation itself, thereby failing to integrate art and life. It reached its final, most elaborate phase in the Turin Exposition of 1902.

Several Italian artists represented at Turin were precursors of what would become the Modern Movement, among them Carlo Bugatti. Father of the engineer Ettore, who gave the family name to an automobile that became synonymous with luxury and speed, he showed a pair of chairs at the Turin exhibition. Created in 1902, they are egg-shaped, connected by one continuous curved support to circular seats, with highly stylized, geometric carvings.

Other significantly modern designs in the exhibition came from Scotland's Glasgow School and its leading artist, Charles Rennie Mackintosh. He had developed his own style, combining the Arts and Crafts Movement in England with Art Nouveau. Mackintosh was attracted to functional furniture, geometric forms, and clean lines. He and his colleagues, Margaret Macdonald and Herbert and Francis McNair, had already exhibited in the Vienna Secession exhibition of 1900 and had a profound influence on the Wiener Werkstätte artists. In fact, Josef Hoffmann eventually married Mackintosh's sister.

The Wiener Werkstätte was represented at Turin as well. It was evident that the works of the Viennese Secessionists were even more modern than those that had inspired them. The Secession was a proclaimed and highly promoted clean break from the overly flowery Art Nouveau style.

Art Nouveau's largely organic ornamentation never lent itself to architecture, except perhaps that of Spaniard Antoni Gaudi and Frenchman Hector Guimard as exemplified in Guimard's Parisian townhouses and his famous Metro entrances of 1900.

Few architects could achieve the fusion of natural forms with architectural forms as Guimard did, and he became Art Nouveau's leading architect as well as a furniture designer. Gaudi's work—especially for the well-known Church of the Sagrada Familia in Barcelona—was clearly a new vision in architecture, but it was costly and would not endure.

In decorative arts, many talented craftsmen gathered around the city of Nancy in France's Alsace-Lorraine region. Foremost among these were the glassmakers, and in particular, Emile Gallé. Gallé had been a botanist before entering the design trade, and his accurate and beautiful renderings of plants and flowers reflects his academic training. Along with glass, he also produced furniture and other decorative and functional items in Art Nouveau design.

Two other noteworthy designers, primarily of furniture, who also worked in the Nancy area were Louis Majorelle and Victor Prouvé. Other glassmakers, such as Auguste Daum and his brother Antoine, worked in Nancy as well. The Daum Nancy factory would survive the transition from Art Nouveau to Art Deco by modernizing both its products and its processes. Gallé was not so lucky, and his fame faded with the demise of cameo glass.

Although there were many fine talents in graphics and posters, the name that stands out in the Art Nouveau era is Alphonse Mucha, who had achieved a reputation as a jewelry designer. Mucha was one of the first to recognize the power of poster advertising, and he helped to set the tastes of his era through his graphic work. Mucha and other artists skillfully used the newest process for fine color lithography.

## THE OPPOSITION MOVEMENTS

The opposition to Art Nouveau was strong in England, coming mostly from the morally zealous Arts and Crafts Movement led by Charles A. Voysey.
 Vienna was more forward-looking. There architect Otto Wagner insisted on a return to straight lines and geometric forms. Although Arts and Crafts shared a similar sense of form, Wagner used modern materials such as concrete, plate glass, and aluminum in his buildings. In 1908 Adolf Loos attacked what he called the "ornamental delirium" of Art Nouveau. He provided a Modern role model two years later with his Steiner house, a concrete cube that would inspire the De Stijl group, the Bauhaus, and L'Esprit Nouveau of Le Corbusier.
 Viennese designer Josef Hoffmann is now recognized as the major individual precursor of the Modern phase in decorative arts. He was known especially for his furniture and silver designs, many of which were produced by the Wiener Werkstätte, which he founded in 1903.
 In Germany, the architect Muthesius proclaimed that art could no longer disassociate itself from the machine, leading to the creation in 1907 of the Deutscher Werkbund, a society of industrialists and artists who were the antecedents of the Bauhaus. The Werkbund exhibition of 1910 hit the world of Parisian decorative arts like a bombshell, but World War I would delay the development of the Modern style in France.
 In France and in America it was architects again who broke with the Art Nouveau style. The Chicago School, led by Louis Sullivan, made use of metal frameworks for buildings that were first and foremost functional. In 1910 Europe discovered and was impressed by the work of Frank Lloyd Wright and his Prairie House. Art Nouveau came to be seen as out of date. In the modern, faster world its fluid, subtle, and often languorous aspect was too slow, and its asymmetrical lines were just no good for mass production.
 In France there was no real equivalent to the Werkbund of Germany, but in 1900 French decorative artists founded the Société des Artistes Décorateurs, and many other organized groups soon followed suit.
 The evolution in style in France was more gradual than in countries with strong opposition movements. Cabinetmakers, potters, glassmakers, and ironworkers set aside the fantastic elaborations of Art Nouveau and agreed to look to more simplified and subtle forms. Yet they continued to work in rare and precious materials for the very rich.
 Meanwhile, as early as 1907 there were calls for an exposition of contemporary arts in Paris. Between 1909 and the outbreak of World War I, the Cubists, Stravinsky, the Ballets Russes, and many other artistic influences were adding to the excitement of what was actually the

golden age of Art Deco. However, because of the war, the Exposition des Arts Décoratifs et Industriels Modernes, originally scheduled for 1916, would not happen until 1925.

The opposition to early Art Deco in France came from Le Corbusier, designer René Herbst, and other artists who would establish the Union des Artistes Modernes in 1930.

Le Corbusier, a Swiss-born Frenchman whose real name was Charles-Edouard Jeanneret, was the theoretical and design leader of the movement in France; his influence had been gradually building for many years. His Pavillon de L'Esprit Nouveau at the 1925 Paris Exhibition was sneered at by the more established Art Deco artists, but it was really the only French pavilion that consciously promoted the Modern style.

We note that of all of the above, only Art Deco was not a movement—it had no founder, no theory, no leaders, no army to disperse its ideas. French Art Deco was a style that evolved in the continuum of French design. It would be given a name only many decades later.

### The Arts and Crafts Movement

William Morris helped set the tone for the Arts and Crafts Movement in England. Rejecting both past styles and traditional ornamentation, as well as the extravagances of Art Nouveau, he looked to the simplicity of a cottage-industry life-style and to nature for inspiration. The movement was encouraged and nurtured by theorists like John Ruskin, who emphasized the moralistic tone of the design movement. Such theorists were as concerned with social reform as with art, and they championed a craft-based—as opposed to a machine-based—ethic.

Arts and Crafts contributed to a renaissance of British practical arts at the end of the 19th century. And in it, one can see some traces of the Art Nouveau Movement that was still flourishing on the Continent.

However, while they celebrated the individual, the majority of British designers condemned the Art Nouveau style as decadent. One of the leaders of the movement, C. F. A. Voysey, an architect who derived his inspiration from Gothic medieval architecture, claimed that the Art Nouveau style was "out of harmony" with the British national character and climate.

Although the style found some favor with people like Siegfried Bing, it never had an impact on the Art Nouveau style. In fact, one can see more of an affinity with Art Deco in the Arts and Crafts economic use of line and color.

William Morris gave numerous public lectures from 1877 until the 1890s, with such titles as "The Art of the People," "The Aims of Art," "How We Live and How We Might Live," and more. For Morris, the renewal of the arts was part and parcel with his belief in socialism. Although refined, his work expressed itself in strong, pure colors in paint or dye, red brick, and solid work in native woods.

Several "guilds" were created for the production of crafts for discerning clients. The first of these, the Century Guild, was founded in 1884. It was the first time artists had banded together to produce decorative arts. The British art establishment rejected the work of the guilds and denied them access to official shows. As would happen in other countries, these craftsmen organized their own exhibitions, creating the Arts and Crafts Exhibition Society in 1888. They held their first show and sale the same year in London and sponsored numerous other events in the years that followed.

The most popular publication chronicling the design was *The Studio*, started in 1893 and later financed by Charles Holme, a wealthy manufacturer who lived in a house designed by Morris. While *The Studio* did much to publicize the work of designers who would become known as the beacons of the Arts and Crafts Movement, it was also the first place to publish the drawings of Aubrey Beardsley, who was, ironically, at the wild fringe of the "decadent" Art Nouveau. Only after many years would it publish the work of Modern designers in England. However, Art Nouveau (and Art Deco, for that matter) never really caught on in England.

The strength and appeal of the Arts and Crafts Movement declined in the face of the many pressures. It could not recapture a past idyllic age as the world went spinning onward, and it failed to recognize the strength and potential of the machine age. Although its influence is felt to this day, it was, like Art Nouveau, a style that could not stand against the economic, social, and political complexity of life in the modern age.

## American Arts and Crafts Movement

American architect Will Price coined the expression "the art that is life" in 1903 as the subtitle of his periodical *The Artsman*. In early 1987, over eighty years later, the Boston Museum of Fine Arts hosted "The Art That Is Life," an important exhibition that has led to renewed interest in the group of design reformers who led the movement against an increasingly industrialized and urban society in America.

The American Arts and Crafts artists, like their English counterparts, condemned routine industrial labor as unfulfilling and dismissed the whole range of ornate styles popular here, such as Louis XIV and the Rococo Revival. They searched for appropriate historical styles from which to borrow, and during the years 1875 to 1920 the movement had a major impact on American art and life. The evangelistic energy of Ruskin and Morris reached across the ocean and had a profound impact on any artists here who considered themselves part of the English tradition, especially in New England.

Again, somewhat like the Modern style, American Arts and Crafts used rectilinear forms instead of ornate curves. Solid native woods took the place of imported veneers. Unnecessary ornamentation was abandoned.

The movement was also affected by Oriental art, with its uncluttered design and emphasis on nature, by Art Nouveau, and later by Art Deco, with its use of simple geometric forms. Adding to these were influences from Native American culture, such as the geometric patterns of Native American pottery, baskets, and blankets.

Hundreds of Arts and Crafts societies sprang up around the country, and the very first, Boston's Society of Arts and Crafts, is still alive today. From their offices and store in Boston, the society now promotes contemporary artists and craftspeople and educates the public about contemporary decorative arts.

Such periodicals as *Ladies' Home Journal* and *House Beautiful* were founded as part of this movement. Women found a new role and were active in teaching skills and handcrafting. They actively applied the ethical principles of the movement to social reform, creating and selling crafts for philanthropic purposes.

The ideal was to teach people to be self-supporting through crafts rather than having to work in a factory. For example, Paul Revere Pottery in Boston, which produced breakfast sets, lamps, vases, and other utilitarian objects from 1907 to 1942, grew out of a Girls Club in Boston's North End where young Italian immigrant women were taught the potter's skills.

The emphasis on the individual craftsmanship of the artist led to the creation of thousands of small studios, shops, and printing presses and even affected factory production at the time. Gustav Stickley's bookcases and chairs, with their clean, straight lines, were produced by the thousands for the middle-class market in the first two decades of this century.

This furniture production, along with anything in the noted Mission style, is currently coming back into vogue with collectors, particularly on the West Coast, after having been relegated to summer home porches for over fifty years.

Mission-style decorative arts were derived in the 1890s from a type of architecture used in the missions built by the Franciscans in the late 18th and early 19th centuries, and they swept California.

Irving Gill, an architect who arrived in San Diego, California, from Chicago in 1893, took up this Mission style in earnest. In 1914 and 1915, as his style evolved, he designed buildings that ten years later might have been taken for examples of what is generally called the International Style, a term sometimes used to describe the Modern Art Deco era in architecture.

The Arts and Crafts Movement, Art Nouveau, and later Art Deco would all espouse the unity of all of the arts, breaking down the distinctions between fine arts and applied or practical arts and creating a total environment.

The wealthy achieved this through commissioning an architect to design not only the house but all of the furnishings, rugs, stained glass, and lighting fixtures. The architect became the unifying element in the design field, employing hundreds of other artists and craftsmen to execute his vision of unified design. Frank Lloyd Wright, whose dining rooms can barely be separated from his windows and lighting fixtures, was the preeminent American example of this trend.

As the early French Art Deco design waned in the 1920s for a variety of reasons, designers in step with modern life turned to other sources for inspiration, such as the Wiener Werkstätte and the Bauhaus. In the same way, the Arts and Crafts Movement offered some inspiration for the Modernists in America, who found little homegrown design on which to draw except for recycled traditional styles.

The style and substance of Arts and Crafts remains today in much contemporary production, appealing to many who find that tubular steel and modular furniture does not suit either their temperaments or their homes.

## Frank Lloyd Wright and the American Prairie School

In 1900 Frank Lloyd Wright was a young man of thirty living in Chicago, a city that was very much alive to the influence of the British Arts and Crafts Movement. A sometime student of Louis Sullivan, Wright believed the machine was the "normal tool of our civilization" and that it could be manipulated to fulfill a humanistic vision. His lecture that year was significantly entitled "The Art and Craft of the Machine."

Many design movements lay claim to Frank Lloyd Wright. Modernists point to his design for the Guggenheim Museum. Art Deco enthusiasts will pay top dollar for his furnishings from the Imperial Hotel in Japan. Dutch Expressionists were influenced by him. The fact is that Frank Lloyd Wright was a towering genius and belonged to none of the above.

Frank Lloyd Wright himself initially saw his work—and that of talented designers working with him, such as Burley Griffen, Marion Mahoney, William Drummond, and Barry Byrne—as a "New School of the Middle West," which later became known as the Prairie School.

Wright's renderings of houses can now cost almost as much as a house itself, and New York's Metropolitan Museum has established a permanent Frank Lloyd Wright room. Even his 1950s designs for mass-produced furniture rarely showed up in flea markets or antiques fairs.

The buildings of the Prairie School of architecture, exemplified by the Ward W. Willits home in Highland Park, Illinois, built in 1902–1903, are characterized by horizontal lines that hug the flat plains of the prairie—hence the name. However, Wright would design homes in Illinois, New York, California, and elsewhere as well. Everything he created for the interiors of his architecture—furnishings, stained glass windows, statuary, even the textiles—is highly prized today.

In December 1986 a Frank Lloyd Wright high-back spindle chair designed for the Ward W. Willits house sold for $198,000 at auction—triple the price ever paid for a Wright chair. In June 1987 a nine-drawer chest from the Francis W. Little house sold for $264,000, breaking the record for a single piece of Wright furniture. A Wright dining room with an almost square table and eight chairs, originally created for the Joseph W. Husser house in Chicago, brought $1.6 million in November 1987, setting a record for 20th-century American decorative art and tripling the highest previous record for a Wright dining set.

Thomas S. Monagan, founder of Domino's Pizza, was the purchaser of all three of the above. He has amassed the world's largest and most important collection of Frank Lloyd Wright designs, valued at more than $13 million. In the spring of 1988 Monagan's collection, which is housed in the National Center for the Study of Frank Lloyd Wright at Domino Farms in Ann Arbor, Michigan, went on view, featuring many works never seen before by the public.

In this book we offer some listings and photos of Frank Lloyd Wright designs, not in an effort to "claim" him for the Art Deco Movement but rather to show the design and market relationships between Wright and modern Art Deco. He was most certainly the greatest design influence in America during the first half of the century.

Wright's Chicago would also become the home of the Bauhaus in America when its leader, Walter Gropius, left the German Third Reich for this country. In much the same way as the Wiener Werkstätte's new home in New York would affect the Modern Movement, the Bauhaus began to affect the architecture of such major Midwestern cities as Chicago, Detroit, and Cleveland, areas where Frank Lloyd Wright had broken ground with his new design style.

## The Viennese Secession

In Austria, Josef Hoffmann established the Wiener Werkstätte in 1903, producing geometrically inspired work that is generally considered a precursor of the Modern Movement and is often found on the Art Deco market. Ultimately, this movement would have tremendous impact on Modern design in America. For example, American ceramicists, particularly those from Ohio, traveled to study design in Vienna shortly after the turn of the century.

Hoffmann himself was influenced by his teacher, Otto Wagner, who was appointed a professor at the Vienna Academy and whose book, *Moderne Architektur*, is generally considered the starting point of the Viennese Secession.

Hoffmann and some fellow students, including some radical painters of the time, created the Wiener Sezession in 1897 and produced work that in many ways highly praised and imitated the work of Charles Rennie Mackintosh of Scotland's Glasgow School. Mackintosh's stark geometric designs had been largely ignored in France. The Secessionists promoted their ideas through a journal called *Ver Sacrum* (Sacred Spring), which was started in 1898.

Highly reflective of Cubism and German Expressionism, and committed to functionality, the Wiener Werkstätte's production was Modern long before World War I.

In recent years the Viennese Secessionist Movement has regained the renown it once enjoyed in Europe, especially since the 1986 Museum of Modern Art exhibition, "Vienna 1900." Secessionist furniture and decorative arts are reaching new highs in the marketplace, while Secessionist graphics and posters, which are generally rare, have roared through the collecting market. Designs by such artists as Gustav Klimt, Berthold Löffler, Marcus Behmer, Koloman Moser, Leopold Stolba, and others are fetching record prices in America.

The Wiener Werkstätte produced works based on geometry, often using black and white as dominant colors. Creations of coffee sets, tableware, and other household furnishings were later inspiration to Le Corbusier and designers in America. Many objects were produced half-finished and sent to subcontractors for finishing. Almost every branch of the crafts industry was involved in carrying out the Wiener Werkstätte designs.

The variety of articles produced was considerable, ranging from ice cream molds, lorgnettes, stuffed toy animals, and enamel matchboxes to furniture of all kinds, cactus pots, pearl bags, and hat and coat racks.

Under the trade law of the time, the early production of the Wiener Werkstätte was classified as handicrafts, but in 1914 the handicrafts trades were reclassified as factories. There is evidence of industrial production along with crafts production right from the start. In 1913 "Wiener Werkstätte" was registered as a trademark for the first time.

The motifs used became the outstanding symbols of the Modern Movement: the zigzag and lightning bolts. Art Deco stylists also copied the geometric forms, "gazelle" fabric patterns, and other motifs.

Perhaps the best known of the Wiener Werkstätte production today are pieces by the undisputed master, Josef Hoffmann, in particular his furniture, clocks, coffee and tea services, flatware, and ice cream molds in silver or alpaka, a nickel-silver alloy.

Other outstanding designers and artists included Dagobert Peche, Karl Breuer, Otto Lendecke, Susi Singer, Vally Wieselthier, and a host of gold- and silversmiths, joiners, painters, and varnishers, metalworkers, ceramicists and glassmakers, bookbinders and leather workers. Their production was large, and much of it is finding new popularity on the high-end collecting market as the taste for things French broadens to include German objects in mainstream collecting.

Joseph Urban was an architect who was perhaps best known for the Ziegfeld Theater of 1927. He was also a stage designer for the Metropolitan Opera. He opened the Wiener Werkstätte gallery in New York in 1922. This gallery was instrumental in familiarizing Americans with the products of the Viennese Secessionist tradition and preparing the way in America for Art Deco. In addition, when the Wiener Werkstätte was forced to declare bankruptcy in 1932, many of its artists came to America.

We have included Wiener Werkstätte furnishings and decorative objects in this book to familiarize the Art Deco/Art Moderne enthusiast with the Viennese style. As the reader will note, many of these designs are now out of reach for the average collector.

## Bauhaus

In Germany numerous *werkstätte*, or workshops, were experimenting with serial production of furniture and other objects as early as 1904. Germany was determined to establish its reputation for design and architecture based on practical as well as aesthetic principles. The economic impulse for such manufacturing was stronger there than in other countries.

International cultural exchange aided the Germans in their efforts. Hermann Muthesius, often noted as the father of the German Modern Movement, spent several years in England before World War I studying architecture and design. He and Henri van de Velde were members of the Deutscher Werkbund, and in 1906 Van de Velde founded the school that would later become the Bauhaus.

The creation of the Werkbund marked the end of the Art Nouveau movement known as Jugendstil in Germany, and its followers launched a campaign of reform directed toward the improvement of

*Decorative Influences* 55

**The Ziegfeld Theater by Joseph Urban.** *(Photo courtesy of the Cooper-Hewitt Museum)*

industrial rather than handcrafted design. They held an important exhibition in Paris in 1910 that would have a long-term effect on French Art Deco as it changed from the early to the Modern style.

Later the Bauhaus became one of the great gathering places for the development of a particular design philosophy. The integration of the arts with industrial culture was the philosophy of the school. The Bauhaus had a mission—one evident in all aspects of design.

The Bauhaus was founded as an art institute in Weimar in 1919. Much more concerned with practice than with theory, it was from the start fairly antiacademic. Its leading figures included Walter Gropius, Mies van der Rohe, Wassily Kandinsky, Marianne Brandt, Marcel Breuer, Lazlo and Lucia Moholy-Nagy, Paul Klee, and Josef and Anni Albers, all of whom were intimately associated with the Bauhaus workshops as they transformed architecture, art, furniture, metalwork, typography, and even color theory. It changed homes several times, moving around Germany to Dessau in 1925 and to Berlin in 1932 before coming to Chicago in 1937.

Marcel Breuer, who pioneered the use of tubular steel, spent some time in England before emigrating to the United States. There he designed furniture for Isokon Furniture Company and influenced English architectural design of the 1930s by such architects as Wells Coates.

Rather than trying to hide from the machine age as the Arts and Crafts Movement had, the Bauhaus tried to create a world of industrially produced high-quality crafts without sacrificing human qualities. The influence of the Bauhaus would be particularly strong in America.

# ARTISTIC INFLUENCES

In Paris numerous artistic influences affected Art Deco, as they would later affect the development of the Modern style. Although Art Deco turned away from much that was traditional or Nouveau in the world of design, it openly accepted all that was "exotic" and much that was "modern"—a strange combination.

The world after World War I had become a much smaller place, and an international exchange brought European culture into contact with many other cultures around the world. In fact, a closer examination of what is called Art Deco reveals complex influences, not only from the performing arts and from numerous schools of fine art, interacting with and borrowing from one another in the applied arts, but from the Far East, South America, and Africa as well.

Generally speaking, the worlds of fine and applied arts had traditionally remained far apart, each drawing on its own traditions, materials, and philosophies. Many of the modern decorative and architectural movements, such as Art Nouveau, Arts and Crafts, the Viennese Secession, and Art Deco, would make conscious attempts to realign the fine with the applied arts. In essence their goal was to gain the title of "artist" for the craftsman.

## FAUVISM

The work of Matisse and artists such as Dérain, Vlaminck, Marquet, Dufy, and Braque would greatly affect design in the years ahead. In addition to developing reputations for their fine arts, several of them were commissioned to execute designs for decorative arts.

These artists were called *fauves,* or "wild beasts," by critics and the more conservative art community after their Salon D'Automne exhibition in 1905. They produced paintings that used pure color and two-dimensional representation. In 1905, though, they did not so much shake up the design world as make a name for themselves; their influence would be seen later.

By the beginning of World War I, the influence of Fauvism was apparent in many of the applied arts and even in architecture. One look at a "Pandorra" poster by Jan Toroop of Holland shows how far their influence had spread. (See the photo in the color section, "An Art Deco Portfolio.")

## THE BALLETS RUSSES

The colorful, opulent sets and costumes by Léon Bakst for Diaghilev's Ballets Russes were immediately popular when they first appeared in Paris in 1909. They greatly influenced fashion, design, and the illustration of such artists as Erté, André Marty, and Paul Poiret, and they had a tremendous effect on such decorators as Paul Iribe.

Through a total of about forty productions in all over the years, the Ballets Russes presented a new kind of spectacle, integrating dancing, music, art, and design. The painter or illustrator was no longer confined to the two-dimensional canvas but actually created decors, accessories, and costumes. The Ballets Russes and its most famous principal dancer, Nijinski, were the rage of Paris until the outbreak of World War I and for years afterward.

The great Russian musicians who composed for the ballets in the early days, such as Stravinsky and Prokofiev, were joined by the likes of Satie, Poulenc, Milhaud, and others among the avant-garde. Painters such as Picasso, Matisse, Braque, Max Ernst, Miró, Utrillo, and sculptors Laurens, Gabo, and Pevsner were commissioned to design sets. The public discovered Fauvism, Cubism, and the other avant-garde movements through ballet designs.

Soon every French stage was employing contemporary artists to take part in theatrical productions. In the years to come, famous writers such as Jean Cocteau and Blaise Cendrars would set their talents to writing for the stage.

## Artistic Influences

Jean Cocteau, a flippant yet introspective poet/artist/filmmaker, became the model for the stylish Deco renaissance artist of the 20th century. In Paris, when you were decidedly modern in your tastes, someone was bound to call you a Jean Cocteau.

One of the most noted Ballets Russes extravaganzas was the 1910 production of *Shéhérezade*, which featured Ida Rubenstein as the sultana, Nijinski as her slave, decor and costumes by Léon Bakst, choreography by Michel Fokine, and music by Rimsky-Korsakov. It was presented by the great impresario Sergé Diaghilev.

With talent like that, it is no surprise that the production's colorful splendor, its extravagant costumes and stage settings, would immediately be seized upon by the designers for their very discerning (and ballet-going) clientele.

A year later Poiret opened his own decorating firm, Martine, and began to do for the world of interior design what he had done for fashion. In his new profession his influence widened, not only through the Orientalism of his own creations but through those of his early protégé, Paul Iribe.

Furniture was redesigned to fit the slinky dresses. Chaise longues, or "long chairs," appeared frequently as salon furniture, and the now-popular cocktail or coffee table emerged as an accessory to the low-slung design.

**Costume for Anna Pavlova by Léon Bakst.** *(Photo courtesy of the Isabella Stewart Gardner Museum)*

## FUTURISM

Chronologically, Futurism was happening in Italy about the same time as Cubism was happening in France. The same year that the Ballets Russes arrived in Paris, a Futurist poem published in a Parisian newspaper proclaimed, "Speed is our god, the new canon of beauty."

One year later, in 1910, the Futurists published *Manifesto of Futurist Painters* to help disseminate their work. Parisians, who had rioted at the premiere of Stravinsky's *Rite of Spring*, were shocked by the violent nature of these paintings, and acceptance was slow in coming.

Among the leading Futurist painters and sculptors were Umberto Boccioni, Giacomo Balla, Gine Severini, and Martinetti. They succeeded at depicting speed and movement in their work through the use of multiple imaging, oblique angles, and shading.

Besides speed the favorite overall themes were power and energy—both industrial and natural. Paintings depicted cars and railroad trains at full throttle, and industrial motifs were juxtaposed with natural ones. Nature itself made the canvas quiver in the form of storms, lightning bolts, volcanoes, tidal waves, and rearing horses.

## CUBISM

The geometric Cubism of Modigliani, Picasso, and other artists was a much stronger influence on the field of French design than was Futurism. Cubism itself had been influenced by the introduction of African folk art and masks to Europe, and the elongated outlined faces of primitive masks were soon evident in modern sculpture by Gustave Miklos and Alexandre Archipenko. Their sculptures were among the first objects to transform into three dimensions what the Cubist painters had been expressing in two.

Even when portraying everyday scenes drawn from traditional genre painting, such as portraiture and still life, it was the nature of Cubism to reveal new dimensions in the volume of seemingly everyday objects and new psychological dimensions in people. Overall form was achieved through a layering and juxtaposing of geometric forms.

Cubism also revealed new dimensions in art, and in the process it gave the decorative artist new freedom in the form and decoration of objects. Coffee- and teapots need not be round; they need only hold and pour hot liquids. Form and function did not necessarily have to match, and whimsy was allowed. Painted design could be purposely abstract and not even pretend to hang onto "stylized" natural forms. Tables and cabinets and doors need not be squared—they could be oddly angled. Carpets could imitate the bold abstract designs of the African Berbers. In addition, like the new design movement that was to emerge, the Cubists rejected decoration for its own sake.

It was the 1907 exhibition of Picasso's famous painting *Demoiselles d'Avignon* that effectively began the Cubist revolt. Picasso and Braque broke with the Fauves and tried to represent volume on flat planes without perspective or light.

Unlike the world of decorative arts, which came to a screeching halt for social and economic reasons during World War I, the Cubists as individual artists and as a school of thought continued to pursue their geometric vision of the world. Their effect would be felt even more strongly much later, in the Modern Movement in applied arts.

## MONDRIAN AND THE DE STIJL GROUP

Dutch painter Piet Mondrian had been influenced by Cubism when he visited Paris in 1911. He struggled to achieve a pure plastic art through the exclusive use of right angles in horizontal-vertical positions and the use of three primary colors with white, black, and gray.

In the creation of its sparse household products, the De Stijl group defended and imitated what some have termed Mondrian's neoplasticism.

Again, this was an artistic movement that would have profound consequences for the future, when Art Deco gave way to the Modern style. It was an early and long-ignored but important influence on design.

The De Stijl group was founded in Holland during World War I. In 1917 one of its most noted artists, Rietveld, designed his now well-known angular chair, an early example of the Modern style.

The De Stijl group also was a tremendous influence on Dutch graphic expression in poster art. For many reasons this poster art has remained relatively unknown until recently. With a new traveling exhibition touring the United States through 1989, Dutch poster art of the 1920s to the 1940s will surely come into its own, in the eyes of both art historians and collectors. (See "Posters and Graphics.")

## DADAISM AND SURREALISM

Dadaism and Surrealism had some effect on the decorative arts, but many would say that the influence of these styles would not be felt until much later. Only a few Parisians knew of the Dada Movement, born in Switzerland in World War I. The work of such artists as Arp, Picabia, Marcel Duchamp, Max Ernst, and later Salvadore Dali would affect later design styles, such as Biomorphism, beginning in the late 1930s.

# OTHER GLOBAL INFLUENCES

We have already seen how the rise of the fashion industry and the changing role of women influenced the development of the Art Deco style. A host of other influences in many fields is also sometimes mentioned in literature on Art Deco, and they deserve some description here to help the reader round out his or her understanding of the style in its historical context.

## ORIENTALISM

As previously mentioned, Orientalism found expression in the work of Bakst for the Ballets Russes and had a profound effect on early French Art Deco fashion and interiors. However, the rage for things Oriental did not stop there. Parisians had toyed with Oriental style in the arts since the turn of the century.

In the Art Deco period both Japan and China influenced design, perhaps Japan slightly more. The Chinese monochromatic ceramic glazes enjoyed some popularity, but ancient Japanese lacquering techniques were overwhelmingly the choice in decorative arts. For twenty years after the end of World War I, lacquer reigned supreme, and its finest artist, Jean Dunand, was treated as something of a national treasure.

In addition, the angles and patterns of Japanese *ukiyo-e*, or "floating world," etchings greatly influenced the advertising and fashion illustration art of the Deco period. These Japanese prints, which are also highly collectible today, were very accomplished in their use of oblique and odd angles, subtle color combinations, plain or screened backgrounds that allowed the figures to be more prominent, and simplicity of line. Place one of these hand-colored etchings next to a fashion illustration for Poiret by Georges Barbier or Paul Iribe and the affinity is readily apparent.

## EGYPTIAN INFLUENCES

The masks and tribal artifacts that so affected the Cubists are not the only African influences to leave their mark on design in this period.

The uncovering of the tomb of King Tutankhamen by Howard Carter and Lord Carnarvon in 1922 brought Egyptian symbols such as sphinxes, hieroglyphics, bright colors, and famous faces such as Nefertiti's to the consciousness of Europeans. The influence was most strongly felt in fashion and in jewelry. Necklaces, chokers, and bracelets were fashioned on Egyptian symbols or were directly copied from Egyptian jewelry. Lapis lazuli and other gemstones came into popularity. English potter Clarice Cliff's "Archaic" vases are direct steals from the capitals of Egyptian columns. (See the photo in our color section, "An Art Deco Portfolio.")

## ANCIENT ARCHITECTURE

The ziggurat, or stepped temple, as mentioned in the "Motifs" chapter, had a strong influence on architecture. Its lines were also abstracted to create many of the patterning motifs commonly associated with Art Deco.

The ziggurat had parallels in the New World: Native American Indian, Mayan, and Aztec pueblo and temple designs and architecture can be said to have influenced the stepped-back look of everything from skyscrapers and other buildings to mantel clocks, radios, and American Paul Frankl's famous bookcases.

In addition, this native American architecture greatly influenced the architecture of the Southwest, in both the line and color of its decoration, friezes, and moldings, to such a degree that some have called this style "Pueblo Deco." (See the photo of Tulsa's Boston Avenue Methodist Church by Bruce Goff in our color section, "An Art Deco Portfolio.")

Aztec ruins, Teolehuacan I. *(Photo courtesy of the Mexican Consulate in Boston)*

## JAZZ

The Jazz Age, like the world around it, was full of new syncopated rhythms and dynamism. Popular dances made their way to Paris: the black bottom, the fox trot, the shimmy, and the Charleston. The style of dancing and of dresses was slyly innocent or coyly seductive. You could miss the ballet and the opera and still find style in a nightclub.

Parisian popular audiences in 1925 thrilled to the *Revue Nègre* of the famed Josephine Baker. In the same year a visitor to Paris might view the Ballets Russes or the Pavillon de L'Esprit Nouveau, where Le Corbusier exploded the Modern style.

Josephine Baker was worshipped in Paris, as were many things "Negro" at the time. Black Americans were exotic talents and became the French nightclub set's prized rare possessions. The poster for *Revue Nègre* by Paul Colin was in a whole new idiom for advertising art and is today's prized artifact recalling the era. Baker, with her feather fans, was as often depicted in chryselephantine and bronze statues as was the dramatic Sarah Bernhardt.

## Other Global Influences

In America, George Gershwin's *Rhapsody in Blue* sent jazz on a dizzying climb of popularity. Jazz designs proliferated in the decorative arts, and today no single Jazz Age piece is better known than Viktor Schreckengost's "Jazz Bowl," created for Cowan Pottery. (See the photo in our color section, "An Art Deco Portfolio.")

## SCIENCE FICTION

Science fiction also played an important "modernistic" and "mechanistic" role. H. G. Wells's books were tremendously popular in the early 1930s. In popular culture and graphics, no influence was greater than that of Buck Rogers or Flash Gordon.

Urban utopian worlds were envisioned where the machine was put to the service of man. Frank Lloyd Wright's 1934 proposals for "Broadacre City" were utopian in concept. Le Corbusier's projects for the "Radiant City," 1930–1936, and the earlier 1925 "Plan Voisin" for Paris were idealistic and socialistic. His idea was to level certain *arrondissements*, or districts, of Paris and create a model city of high-rise structures that would house 3 million inhabitants.

The 1926 German movie *Metropolis* by Fritz Lang showed a utopian city that was mechanistic and populated by human robots. In Germany Lang's film had a profound effect on graphic design and advertising art.

## THE MACHINE

The machine itself was the the greatest influence of all and the one most internationally felt.

The industrial age had shown people that objects could be mass-produced, distributed, and sold at great profit. The style that would eventually emerge could be manufactured on an assembly line and was far removed from the production of the Art Deco Salon des Artistes Décorateurs.

The airplane, the ocean liner, and the automobile came to symbolize a new generation for whom speed reigned. But speed could reign only if designs were aerodynamically sleek. Designs of these new modes of transportation affected advertising art as well.

All other designs would follow in the Streamline style: posters, fashion, tableware, salt and pepper shakers, fur coats, compact cases, earrings, dressing tables—the list is endless. Even public monuments became simpler and more streamlined.

The task of the industrial designer in the 1930s was to create manufactured goods that were stylish. This was especially true after the Depression, when American industry sought to whet the appetite of wary consumers.

Industrial design readily accepted the streamline conventions already established in the applied arts, and design was further broken down into interchangeable parts. While individual artists would continue to create handcrafted expressions in all media, the production of everyday household goods would be increasingly mechanized.

# THE PARIS EXPOSITION OF 1925

The 1925 Parisian Exposition Internationale des Arts Décoratifs et Industriels Modernes was underwritten by the French government. In fact, it was the Ministry of Finance that called for the exposition. The French government controlled important industries for the manufacture of household goods and furnishings—for example, the National Manufacture at Sèvres, which produced porcelain and pottery. The goals of the exposition were blatantly to promote French production and to establish the French as the masters of the decorative arts and the arbiters of "good taste" for the entire civilized world.

Well, it worked to a certain degree!

This grand exposition was not the launching of Art Deco, though many people think so because the name *Art Deco* was drawn from the name of the exhibit. As we have already noted, Deco was really the culmination of many years of innovative French design.

It had been a long time since the last major international exhibition had been held in Paris in 1900. At that time Art Nouveau still dominated the avant-garde. The average Frenchman of the day, however, probably had a home decorated in First Empire or Henry IV, and Madame's bedroom probably had ornate cupids in the Rococo plasterwork.

The 1925 exposition had been planned as early as 1909. At that time a concern about the quality of decorative arts had prompted the department stores to organize competitions. The government agreed that an exposition was needed and started developing plans for it, but it was postponed because of World War I.

The exhibition pavilions were hosted by the large French department stores—Les Grands Magasins du Louvre, Bon Marché, Les Galleries Lafayette, and Le Printemps—and featured objects (furniture, lamps, mantel clocks, glassware, and jewelry) that reflected the new style. It was the exaltation of everyday objects into the realm of art. In fact, the rules for the exhibition explicitly forbade artists from displaying any object that relied on historic European designs or patterns.

This exhibition was by no means comprehensive, although it included work by some of the most notable architects and designers of the time: architects Robert Mallet-Stevens and Konstantin Melnikoff; painters Fernand Leger, Marie Laurencin, and Robert and Sonia Delaunay; and interior decorators Pierre Chareau, Pierre Legrain, Jean Dunand, Paul Iribe, and Jean Puiforcat.

However, Le Corbusier's and Ozenfant's Pavillon de l'Esprit Nouveau, named after a review they founded in 1920 to disseminate their pure Modernist views, was only grudgingly included. The artists who had influenced Le Corbusier—the Bauhaus, Deutscher Werkbund, and Dutch De Stijl Movements—were completely excluded. Josef Hoffmann and some of his contemporaries worked on the Austrian Pavilion. But the French pavilions had little to do with the Modern style.

Economically, the world was not yet "pushed" to Modernism and new materials. Socially, the early deluxe style still held sway. The new style was considered less "tasteful," and the French were not eager to part with bombé-front cabinets, carved tassels on Süe et Mare furniture, and the flowery textiles of Paul Follot. Furniture made of metal tubing was considered crass.

The exposition was really a showcase for the art of the *ensemblier*, or interior designer. It had become the role of the designer both to design and commission fine works and to create an "ensemble" for a room with a single vision, or "look." This was in spite of the fact that most people could not afford the services of the better *ensembliers* and had to make do with what they bought in department stores.

The site chosen was the heart of Paris and embraced a huge area including the banks and bridges of the River Seine and the Esplanade des Invalides where Napoleon is entombed. The pavilions of other countries were spread along the river and included those of Turkey, Denmark, Switzerland, Italy, Japan, Austria, Sweden, Poland, Belgium, The Netherlands, Great Britain, and many other nations. The French sections were the most numerous, with almost one hundred pavilions, and were spread on the South Bank, centering on the pavilion called Ambassade Française, or French Embassy.

## The Paris Exposition of 1925

Whereas the Eiffel Tower had been seen as scandalous and vulgar in 1900, it had now become a symbol of the new modern world. It was illuminated with changing patterns of lights created as a promotional effort by Citroën. The Eiffel Tower was once again a beacon to light international artists to France.

The Ambassade Française held the most prominent position in the exposition and was assembled to showcase the true geniuses of French design. Every room was completely furnished, carpeted, curtained, and fitted with glass and silver, ivory and jade ornaments, sculptures and paintings. The reception rooms contained textiles by Raoul Dufy, metalwork by Edgar Brandt, and glass by Lalique. The series of rooms ended with a winter garden designed by Robert Mallet-Stevens, who also designed the Pavillon de Tourisme, overlooking the court and adjoining music room.

Another of the most talked about buildings at the exposition was the Hotel d'un Riche Collectioneur, designed by Emile-Jacques Ruhlmann and filled with his luxurious furniture, as the "home of a rich collector" should be.

Ruhlmann is a major figure of the Art Deco era, a master cabinetmaker and an extremely talented *ensemblier*. Ruhlmann went to great lengths to obtain rare and precious materials for his clients, and his work was expensive even for the time. He furnished the homes of many of the wealthy manufacturers of the era and had pieces purchased by the French government for the Elysées Palace, the French equivalent of the White House. He collaborated with the leading artists to execute his designs—among them Jean Dunand and Pierre Legrain.

Of almost equal importance to his pavilion was the Lalique pavilion. Lalique, of course, would exploit the use of glass to its fullest and even created a public fountain in the shape of an obelisk that was illuminated at night.

The interior displays of the pavilion of the Galleries Lafayette were designed in their own studio, known as La Maîtrise, under the direction of noted designer Maurice Dufrène. Dufrène's style included curved forms, discreet and indirect lighting, and subtle colors such as rose. Black marble tabletops contrasted with the lemonwood or maple furniture.

The Magasins du Printemps and the work of their studio, Primavera, were housed in a building designed with a hyperbolic concrete dome encrusted with small circular pieces of glass.

By contrast, the Bon Marché pavilion was more rectangular and monumental and was furnished to perfection by Paul Follot, the director of Pomone, Bon Marché's studio.

The work of Studium Louvre of the Grands Magasins du Louvre was housed in a building with a balcony full of flowers and windows where mannequins with bobbed hair and cloche hats modeled dresses from *Vogue*. The door to this pavilion was pure Deco, with multiple moldings stepped back in a frame-within-a-frame pattern.

It is difficult for us to feel as people did in 1920. "The war to end all wars" was over. An entire generation had seen misery on a greater scale than ever before and had turned to color and luxury with a voracious appetite, bearing an optimism about the future that no generation has so completely shared since.

It was a style that appealed to an emerging wealthy population that was reaping the benefits of industrialization and evolving from "tasteful" to "progressive" in their tastes and habits. There was still no sign of the forthcoming Depression, and many felt no need even to look at the mass-produced works of the Germanic nations.

Even more than the movements that had preceded it, Art Deco conceived of a room as a harmonious whole in which each object, functional or artistic, contributed to the overall work of art. Style was seen as the spirit of the era, and the role of the interior decorator was to provide the clientele with a full complement of their own personal brand of style. There was much individuality in the production of this era.

The right of the decorator to equal status with the painter, sculptor, and architect rested on his being able to re-create the effect of art through decoration; that is, to affect viewers emotionally and intellectually and make them feel as if they had glimpsed something for the very first time.

Perhaps the greatest in achieving this effect was Paul Poiret, who displayed his work on three barges anchored in the Seine River. Poiret's real genius lay in fashion design, but his barges were among the most popular features of the exposition although not as financially successful as he had hoped. Poiret succeeded in what had become a highly intellectual and sophisticated art form, achieving a quality described best by that overused word *chic*.

## PAVILLON DE L'ESPRIT NOUVEAU

It was this building and its contents that foreshadowed the new movement in decorative arts, one that would quickly supersede early Art Deco as Modern style, only later to be transformed into what we now call Streamline.

Le Corbusier was not the originator of the Modern Movement. He had been influenced by Walter Gropius and Mies van der Rohe of the Bauhaus, as well as by Josef Hoffmann and the Wiener Werkstätte. He

## The Paris Exposition of 1925

was, however, an intelligent, articulate writer and the leading French proponent of the new style. He was the architect who would replace the interior designer as the trend-setter.

The design of his pavilion faced bitter opposition from the director of the exposition. It was only in the last minutes before opening, because of the direct intervention of the Minister of Fine Arts, that a thirty-foot fence constructed to hide the pavilion was dismantled.

The purpose of the building, bluntly, was to deny the need for decorative art. Furniture, in Le Corbusier's estimation, was "household equipment that a building needed."

He also successfully exploited the new possibilities of steel and concrete architectural construction. According to one chronicle of the period, after the Ambassade Française this pavilion was "like a cold plunge after a Turkish bath."

The first half of the building was designed and furnished as a living space. The second part was an exhibition gallery where he set up his model for his *Plan Voisin de Paris* ("Neighborhood Plan for Paris"). His model showed what was then the ideal city: a series of evenly placed tall buildings that could provide housing for 3 million people, as well as shops, offices, stores, and theaters.

Today we may look at this design and feel lucky that it never came to pass. We already have enough "canyons" of tall buildings in our cities. However, the *Plan Voisin* was not a developer's get-rich scheme but rather a thoughtful interpretation of a utopian future, where the machine served people, and all people were equally served.

In his 1926 book, *L'Art décoratif d'aujourd'hui*, Le Corbusier puts forward his thinking on modern decorative arts and their place in the machine age. While others may have feared that the machine would enslave people by taking away individuality and craftsmanship, Le Corbusier saw the machine as the means for developing a better society. The following composite paragraph is excerpted from various parts of the original text to provide a summary of his thinking.

> The past is not infallible. It had some things that were beautiful and some that were ugly. There are today, and more will emerge, consequences of the crisis that separates the pre-mechanistic society from the new mechanistic society.... Decorative art is an imprecise and inexact term. The decorative arts are simply equipment, beautiful equipment. The machine, that modern phenomenon, is bringing about a transformation of the spirit in the world. Architecture is a spiritual system which fixes in a material way the sentiment of an era ... and everything is integrated into an architectural system. We are no longer in an era of dillentantism, but rather a difficult and epic era, serious and violent, hasty and productive, fertile and economic. Decorative arts were basically anti-technical. They were going in the opposite way as the general direction of the epoch.

In practice, Modernism was not as sterile or as undecorative as it may have sounded in theory. Le Corbusier's now famous tubular steel chair with stretched pony-skin seat and built-in footrest seems elegant and refined.

The extremes of Modernism, however, would not hold sway except perhaps in the field of industrial design. As the movement gained momentum in the United States, it acquired the American taste for color and boldness and was transformed into something that was chic but decidedly American.

# ART DECO AND AMERICA

In 1925, the year of the Paris Exposition, fashion designer Erté set sail for Hollywood, where he would influence the film industry through the elaborate designs for sets and costumes he executed for Metro-Goldwyn-Mayer. Consequently, he set new standards of taste for the American public. Already well known to American fashion-followers, he had been under exclusive contract to illustrate for *Harper's Bazaar* for ten years, and his influence had spread to the hills of Southern California.

But the first real foothold of Art Deco in America had actually been the work of committed museum curators and others who had recognized the importance of the style long before the public did. A fund created in 1922 for the Department of Decorative Arts in the Metropolitan Museum of Art, New York, enabled it to purchase and commission examples of modern decorative art in Europe and America.

Joseph Beck, curator, built a fine collection of Art Deco works during 1922 and 1923. Then, in 1926 the Metropolitan Museum presented the R. H. Macy–sponsored International Exhibition of Art in Industry, featuring some of the best of the 1925 Paris Exposition. Many say that this was the point at which Art Deco arrived in America. Commerce followed art, and Macy's hosted an exhibition and sale of contemporary decorative arts under the name "Art in Trade" in 1927.

The French style of Art Deco could not be accepted in America, however, until it had undergone the kind of transformation that turns the immigrant into an American. Art Deco had to pass through the American life-style and be mutated by American industrialization, by jazz, and by modernist designers already at work here.

The role of the woman in society had changed in America, as it had in Europe, after World War I. Urbanization meant smaller living quarters, and the new industrial age brought with it a host of household goods and equipment that were previously unknown. Modular units that could be easily rearranged became popular. In 1927, for the first time in history, hemlines rose above women's knees—fashion was keeping pace with the popularization of a new image for women as jazz-loving, cigarette-smoking, short-haired, independent, and slim.

As if to bring America and Europe symbolically together, Charles Lindbergh made the first solo flight to Paris that same year. Meanwhile, in other things American, the Babe hit sixty home runs, Jack Dempsey and Gene Tunney met in one of the greatest prizefights ever, and Al Jolson and *The Jazz Singer* brought talking pictures to Hollywood.

Prohibition had been in effect for seven years, encouraging people to flout both the law and convention by going to speakeasies. Flappers drank champagne from high heels. The execution of Sacco and Vanzetti in Charlestown, Massachusetts, provoked unrest among the working class in this country and rioting in London and Paris. Nineteen twenty-seven was the year the Model A Ford was introduced. Radio sales were booming, and George Gershwin's *American in Paris* premiered.

The great Stock Market Crash of 1929 was just two years away.

Until then America had been quietly but persistently moving toward a Modern style in architectural and household design, influenced by a host of talented immigrants from many countries.

Major design talents such as Bruno Paul, Walter von Nessen, and Lucian Bernhard from Germany; Josef Urban, who headed the Wiener Werkstätte in America Gallery; Paul Frankl from Austria; Alexandre Archipenko from Denmark; and Eliel Saarinen from Finland had been working in America before French Art Deco arrived on the scene.

Saarinen, an architect and designer, had emigrated from Finland in 1922 and became the first director of the Cranbrook Academy of Art near Detroit, which provided a nurturing ground for American Art Deco design and would later be the site of one of the major revival exhibitions in the early 1970s. Major artists of the Cranbrook Academy included Saarinen's wife, Loja, who used geometric natural forms in her textiles; ceramist Maija Grotell; and sculptor Carl Milles.

Their work betrays some influence from American design movements such as the Prairie School and from native American style, as in the stylized horses of Maja Andersson Wirde's carpets.

Carpet by Maja Andersson Wirde, designed at the Loja Saarinen Studio. *(Photo courtesy of the Cranbrook Academy of Art Museum)*

Other early Modern influences came from Frank Lloyd Wright's architecture. He was the first to incorporate Mayan architectural motifs in his work. Also in the Midwest, R. Guy Cowan's pottery studio in Cleveland, Ohio, made a direct connection with Vienna through such artists as Russell Aitkin and Victor Schreckengost. These early movements in America were ripe for the encounter with French Art Deco when more than four hundred works from the 1925 Paris Exposition made a countrywide tour in the next two years.

As was the case in Europe, Modern design in America had met with resistance, and artists banded together to promote their new vision in such groups as the American Designers' Gallery and Contempora. Unlike European design, American design received no official or governmental patronage and it was the American Designers' Gallery that hosted the first exhibition of all-American designers in 1928.

Traditional Art Deco had become so mainstream that designers such as Ruhlmann and Dunand survived on official commissions from the government, banks, hotels, and other institutions.

For example, when the luxury French ocean liner *Normandie* was outfitted in 1935, it was a like a commissioned floating museum of the highest in French Art Deco design of its day. Jean Dupas sculpted wall murals that were lacquered by Jean Dunand, and there were textiles by Rodier and furniture by Jules Leleu. Many other ocean liners, such as the *Ile de France* and the *Atlantique,* were also designed with Art Deco interiors.

By that time international travel had become more affordable and more tempting, and the grand ocean liners became everyman's floating dream of Hollywood stardom. Travel posters recapture the grandeur of ocean travel. Today many collectors focus their attention on the Art Deco furnishings, souvenirs, and ephemera from the great ocean liners. However, the lavish early Art Deco was soon to be abandoned entirely by a world faced with grim economic and political realities.

The United States soon rivaled France for preeminence in the Art Deco design field, although the style of design was modified by the strong forces of Modernism in this country. Architects such as William Van Alen, who designed the Chrysler Building in 1930, and Raymond Hood, one of the designers for John D. Rockefeller, led the way. The skyscraper was the dominant motif, and Paul Frankl created his ingenious "Skyscraper" line of furniture from 1925 to about 1930.

Other architects and designers—Donald Deskey, Norman Bel Geddes, Kem Weber, Walter Dorwin Teague, and Raymond Loewy—came to prominence with their Modern furniture and decorative business and industrial designs.

Loewy also designed for the English firm Practical Equipment Limited, or PEL, one of the leading manufacturers of Modern furniture in England. It should be noted that England never really accepted the early Art Deco style but moved forward quickly with 1930s Modern design. This was especially true in the area of porcelain and ceramics, where the English successfully bridged the gap between studio and mass-produced work. For example, the works of Keith Murray for Wedgwood, Susie Cooper for Crown Works, and Clarice Cliff for the Arthur J. Wilkinson Company were industrially produced but hand-painted.

Between 1927 and 1932, when the famous Radio City Music Hall and the Empire State Building were built, the new design style raged through American fashion and life.

In 1929 the Metropolitan hosted its own exhibition to show the best of what was being done in America and to encourage the creation of a new decorative style adapted to the needs of urban modern life. Entitled "The Architect and the Industrial Arts," it displayed a series of interiors by architect-designers.

In 1931 the American Union of Decorative Artists and Craftsmen, or AUDAC, held an exhibition at the Brooklyn Museum, and the range of design shown was broader than any museum exhibition up to that time—fabrics, radio cabinets, architectural models, furniture, and decorative and graphic arts. The show reflected a turn toward a machine aesthetic, promoted by such designers as Russel Wright.

## Art Deco and America

By 1931 the annual exhibition at the Metropolitan was including industrially produced objects. By 1934, perhaps because of the Depression, it was giving emphasis to objects that could be produced easily and cheaply, like Chase Chrome designs by Walter von Nessen.

American Art Deco had survived the Wall Street crash of 1929 in a functional and plainer style due to lowered prices and mass production. The Depression brought with it the new profession of industrial designer, someone whose know-how in technology as well as in design was needed to create products that the food-line-weary public would be tempted to buy.

With the end of Prohibition, an array of bars, bar stools, cocktail shakers, ashtrays, and glasses were produced for "stylish entertaining." Over the next few years handcrafting declined, and mass-produced industrial items flooded the market in the Streamline style and jazzy tilted angles. Jazz affected everything from Erik Magnussen's silver tea sets to designs for women's hand mirrors and decorative ceramics.

Streamlining was an essentially American development. It changed the emphasis of Art Deco from vertical to horizontal lines. Smooth, rounded curves replaced most of the Cubist, geometric influence in Modern design. Streamlined cars and streamlined appliances were well suited to industrial manufacture.

In the 1930s and early 1940s the Art Deco style in America was transformed in yet another way, particularly in Florida and California. Tropical Deco—or Floridian Deco, as it is sometimes called—worked with a softer palette and a different vision from the Industrial Deco of New York and Chicago, with its constant theme of man's progress through the machine. Hollywood or Screen Deco used Deco styling in films—it still figures in many modern productions. Pueblo Deco combined Modern design with native American influences to create elaborately beautiful structures.

The Chicago Century of Progress Exposition in 1933 marked the highest point of art in industrial design in the United States, and souvenirs of this exposition with their Deco styling are very collectible today. Many feel that the last great expression of the Modern style in America came with the New York World's Fair of 1939. Some say it was the more than twenty-five thousand different souvenirs of the 1939 World's Fair, sold to millions, that signaled the end of Art Deco as a predominant design style.

By 1940 Art Deco was almost *too* stylish for a world faced with war and rationing and lost its appeal to unadorned concrete, steel, and glass. Also, the adoption by the German Nazi and Italian Fascist regimes of extremely stylized geometric patterns and designs for their propaganda posters and graphics did little to enhance the style's popularity.

The Art Deco patterns and color combinations were repeated so often they lost their appeal, but there were only drab wartime colors to replace them. Photographic effects began to replace the bold strong graphics of Deco advertising art and illustration. The kitsch quality of Deco designs and novelties increased and was vaguely and superficially perpetuated in cheap ceramics and other dime store items.

Many apartment buildings had Deco-style sconces and fake square columns with Deco-motif cornices, but painted plaster moldings replaced those made from wood or metal. A cheaper aluminum was substituted for chrome and stainless steel.

So broad and universal was the kitsch application of Deco motifs that many people are still conditioned against liking Deco, and many more remain unaware of the mastery and high quality of the style in either its initial or Modern phases.

It was thus more than the onset of World War II that finally ended the Art Deco fever: people's attitudes toward the style of the times changed as its products were marketed in abundance. Designers and artists stopped working in the style and sought new frontiers. The Art Deco era had come to an end . . . or so it seemed.

After World War II it was as if Art Deco had never existed. For example, when he died in 1950, the French artist Louis Icart ws practically unknown. His etchings, which had been produced in extremely large quantities by the Louis Icart Society in New York, could be bought for pennies. In the post–World War II years Art Deco seemed dated, perhaps a bit too elitist, and was largely ignored or forgotten. Art Moderne seemed too cold, too mechanistic for a world that now realized that the machine did not necessarily lead to peace and prosperity—it could also lead to war. Modern materials were used, but Biomorphism, a style that had begun to emerge in the 1930s, was gaining popularity. Biomorphism abstracted naturalistic forms, and soon chair seats were shaped like amebas or, as someone once described it, potato chips.

In the postwar 1950s America went on a binge. The whimsy of the period is best seen in coffee tables that looked like enormous bohemian artists' palettes, outrageous plastic sunglasses, clear-plastic high heels, plastic handbags, and plastic everything.

The flying saucer became a popular myth and symbol and was quickly turned into bedroom lamps, space heaters, and other everyday objects. The molecular structure entered the general consciousness and found its way into design, especially in items such as kitchen wall clocks. Television and rock culture replaced America's wonderment with the radio, smoky urban nightclubs, and sleek cigarette lighters. None of the high styling and tasteful decoration that were the hallmarks of Art Deco and Art Moderne was left. In fact, the 1950s were marked by a renewed interest in the more ornamental Art Nouveau style, fostered by a series of exhibitions in Europe and in 1960 at the Museum of Modern Art in New York.

# THE ART DECO REVIVAL

In the late 1960s and early 1970s Art Deco entered a renaissance among collectors, dealers, and connoisseurs that continues to this day. At the time, some people felt that its resurgence was tied to a sort of historicism, tempered with a touch of nostalgia. Few expected the repopularization of Deco to last or to be so strong.

Like the early popularization of Art Deco, the revival owes much to museum shows. As opposed to its promotion by manufacturers in the 1920s and 1930s, Art Deco's popularity today is due in large measure to the research and promotion done by dealers and auction houses, as well as a host of books on the subject.

The Musée des Arts Decoratifs launched a retrospective exhibition entitled "Les Années 25" in 1966, sending Art Deco shock waves through the design world once again. In 1970 Finch College Museum hosted the first revival exhibition of Art Deco in the United States. This was followed in 1971 by an expanded version of the exhibition at the Minneapolis Institute of Arts, which awakened contemporary collectors to the importance of Art Deco.

Still, Art Deco was far from popular when these museums began to pay it serious attention. Many art and antiques dealers were skeptical of the resurgence of interest and felt that perhaps it was only a passing fad. It was individual vanguard collectors and museums that were most attracted to collecting Art Deco during the revival period—an attraction that was to pay off handsomely.

## FINCH COLLEGE MUSEUM OF ART

The Art Deco exhibition that took place at the Finch College Museum of Art in New York City from October to November 1970 was the first major revival exhibition in this country. The exhibit presented over 550 objects, from furniture to costume jewelry, and helped America rediscover the great European and American designers. In all, the Finch College Museum exhibition opened the doors of nostalgia for Art Deco and embraced the broadest interpretation of the term for collectors.

Among the wide variety of works that were included were the following: bronze and ivory chryselephantine statuettes of dancing and Egyptian figures by D. H. Chiparus, with marble bases; sculpture by Edouard Marcel Sandoz; gouaches from the flamboyant Erté; London subway posters by E. McKnight Kauffer; rare bookbindings; jewelry by René Lalique, Georges Fouquet, Van Cleef and Arpels, and Cartier, including a rare lapel brooch watch in jade, chimera, gold, platinum, rubies, diamonds, onyx, and black enamel.

The furniture displayed was by a broad range of designers and reflected the great divergence of style grouped under the name Art Deco: lacquered screens by Jean Dunand; a chair and dressing table by Paul Frankl; pieces by Léon Jallot, Armand-Albert Rateau, and Emile-Jacques Ruhlmann—such as his sideboard in burled walnut with black marble top and bronze medallions that had been exhibited in 1925 in Paris.

Many additional well-known designers were represented, including metalwork craftsman Edgar Brandt, glass artist Antoine Daum, and English potter Clarice Cliff.

Of course, no exhibition of Art Deco glass would have been complete without the work of Gaston Louis Vuitton and that of René Lalique, whose 1932 "Carthage" vase of clear glass with matte-finish exterior and carved bird motif on each of eight buttresses still made viewers gasp.

Nonparochial in its definition of Art Deco, the Finch exhibition also included a chrome, tubular, steel chair with cane back and seat by Mies van der Rohe; a side chair with octagonal seat and hexagonal back designed for the Imperial Hotel in Tokyo by Frank Lloyd Wright; and from the Wiener Werkstätte, a 1930s bowl with ceramic openwork and a blue-gray water pitcher in the typical circular style with one quarter of the circle indented to form the handle.

Silver on display included pieces from the Orfeverie Christofle and from the master silversmith Jean Puiforcat. Textiles included the exuberant flower designs of Raoul Dufy and a wide variety of wallpapers, draperies, and bedcovers.

Albert Cheuret's 1930 Egyptian-inspired mantel clock was also there, along with a Cartier clock in crystal, mounted with enameled gold and rose diamonds, from the collection of Broadway's *Funny Girl* star, Barbra Streisand. Streisand lent other objects to the collection, including a Czechoslovakian atomizer with etched ruby panels, a gouache by John Vassos, and a glass lamp with colored flowers by G. Argy-Rousseau.

The Finch College exhibition marked the rediscovery in America of both the lavish production of French artists, the early Modern production of German, Austrian, and French designers, and the American Art Deco inspirations of the New World.

This exhibition defined the range of the Art Deco collecting field until very recently. However, the first revival exhibitions paid less attention to American designers who have since come into their own on the collecting market. It also did little to promote the kitsch production of American manufacturers and the Streamline design of industrial collectibles.

Today, almost twenty years after the Finch exhibition, the collecting field for Art Deco has expanded far beyond the well-known names of French Art Deco. It now actively includes a variety of production of other nationalities such as the Dutch, Italian, and Eastern European countries, broadening it even more as a collecting field, and adding new areas of interest.

## THE REDISCOVERY OF AMERICAN 20TH-CENTURY DECORATIVE ARTS

A series of exhibitions that started shortly after the Finch College Museum exhibition has increased knowledge of American Art Deco and other 20th-century American decorative styles. In general, we can also say that the Bicentennial of 1976 refocused attention on things American and rekindled an interest in our own heritage that has also been reflected in the collecting market.

In 1972 "The Arts and Crafts Movement in America 1876–1916" was co-organized by the Princeton University Art Museum and the Art Institute of Chicago. Vanguard collectors in this field were also brilliant publicists, pushing for its recognition in the collecting market. The major auction houses soon joined in, with Skinner's in Bolton, Massachusetts, holding the first theme auction in 1982, followed by Christie's in New York the same year. In 1987 a monumental exhibition, "The Art That Is Life," was sponsored by the Museum of Fine Arts in Boston, and Arts and Crafts collecting went through the roof.

Frank Lloyd Wright, whose work more often than not has set the pace for records in American decorative arts, had his first major retrospective exhibition at the Renwick Gallery of the Smithsonian in 1979.

After the Finch and Minneapolis exhibitions little attention was given to American Art Deco until recently, even though numerous vanguard collectors and dealers, notably in New York City, were busy documenting the best of the field. In 1983 Yale University hosted "At Home in Manhattan: Modern Decorative Arts, 1925 to the Depression." The same year another exhibition, "Design in America: The Cranbrook Vision 1925–1950," organized by the Metropolitan Museum of Art and the Detroit Institute of Art in conjunction with Cranbrook Academy of Art, made a somewhat bigger splash.

Yet it has been only in 1986 and 1987 that exhibitions and shows have had a major impact on the Art Deco market.

In 1986 the Whitney Museum hosted "High Styles," the first in-depth exhibition of American 20th-century decorative arts. While including Tiffany and Art Nouveau, the show emphasized major Modern designers—among them, Joseph Urban, Donald Deskey, Raymond Hood, and Kem Weber. The same year, the Brooklyn Museum hosted "The Machine Age in America 1918–1941" and reintroduced the industrial design and mass-produced furnishings of Walter Dorwin Teague, Walter von Nessen, Raymond Loewy, Russell Wright, and many others.

In 1987 the Renwick Gallery in Washington hosted another exhibition, which has had—up to the time of writing—a major impact in the collecting field: "American Art Deco." The book for the exhibition (same title, by Alastair Duncan) is a major resource for anyone interested in American Art Deco collecting. Already dealers are pointing out photos in it to customers, indicating the merits of a particular artist or style as highlighted in the show.

## THE REDISCOVERY OF KITSCH

Welcome to the long-spurned world of collecting kitsch!

In the 1930s, as the Art Deco style in kitsch permeated every level of society, cheaply produced radios, ceramics, kitchen utensils, ashtrays, statues, costume jewelry, and more were made in Art Deco style, using materials such as Bakelite, other plastics, chrome, tubular steel, and glass, often decorated in bright, jazzy colors. Kitsch is the name given to the entire range of both functional and decorative low-cost objects that are sought after by collectors today.

Kitsch, as one author put it, may not "live up to the original ideals of the movement," but New York City's Frankart Company statues and lamps, which originally sold for only a few dollars, now bring prices of hundreds of dollars or more depending on condition. Cocktail shakers and ashtrays from Chase Chrome, widely distributed in department stores where many Chase items originally sold for less than a dollar, are now bringing $25 to $500 or more. The now famous pink flamingos of the Floridian Art Deco period, bought by tourists for a dollar or two, are very collectible and are commanding $25, $50, and higher prices.

In addition, movie memorabilia of the Hollywood Art Deco years is gaining in price. (Although it is a Deco style, we do not cover Hollywood memorabilia in this book, as it would need an entire volume to itself.)

Today's collectors of kitsch may be less concerned about "high art" and more interested in the fun of collecting these objects, but they can be as passionate as collectors of Lalique and pursue their hobby with the relentlessness of major art collectors.

Republications of manufacturers' catalogs in the early 1980s did much to promote the collecting of some categories of Art Deco kitsch. The Chase Chrome catalog for 1936–1937 was reprinted by an antiques dealer in 1983 and widely distributed. The major Frankart catalog used by collectors was reprinted in 1981.

Numerous books have also appeared on Roseville pottery, radios, plastic jewelry, and other subjects, adding to both dealers' and collectors' knowledge of kitsch. While much of this production can still be found at general antiques shows and flea markets, it is less and less likely that the seller won't know what he or she is selling—and the going price.

The revival of interest that started in the late 1960s and early 1970s has resulted today in an active, mature market for the vast array of museum-quality, high-end, mid-range, and low-end objects in the Art Deco style. We are sure that there are still some discoveries to be made and that the market will redefine itself further, but now, no matter what your collecting interest or financial resources, you can find something in Art Deco that fits your personality and your pocketbook.

# OBJETS D'ART DECO

# ARCHITECTURE

The value of studying Art Deco architecture for a collector is seeing and recognizing distinctive patterns and styles. As we've noted, where French Art Deco took its cue from fashion, the American style of Art Deco evolved in furnishings, decorative objects, and even fashion from an architectural point of view. Today many people feel that the Art Deco style in America and elsewhere is really seen at its best in architecture.

The predominance of architecture in Art Deco is due to a line of great architect/designers starting with Charles Rennie Mackintosh of the Glasgow School. He, in turn, was one of the strongest influences on the Viennese Secessionists. His use of clear, geometric form in architecture extended to the design of furniture, mantel clocks, and graphic designs for wall coverings.

Otto Wagner (1841–1918) and Adolf Loos were architects who influenced Austrian designers, the De Stijl group of Holland, and the German Bauhaus. Loos, a younger compatriot of Wagner, wrote a book called *Ornamentation and Crime*, in which he argued against the use of ornament in 20th-century architecture and attacked false embellishments and facades that did not represent the true building behind them.

Viennese and German architects followed in their wake. Joseph Maria Olbrich (1867–1908) was a leading Viennese architect who began following Modern principles. Josef Hoffmann (1870–1956), one of the leaders of the Viennese Secession and an admirer of Mackintosh, designed the Austrian pavilion for the 1925 Paris Exposition. Peter

Behrens, the teacher of Walter Gropius (1883–1969) at the Bauhaus, designed an Expressionist greenhouse attached to Hoffmann's pavilion.

Today, when one thinks of the architecture of the era, one almost automatically thinks of Le Corbusier or of Walter Gropius, Mies van der Rohe, Marcel Breuer, and the Bauhaus School. However, in actuality, Gropius and his followers were banned from the 1925 Paris Exposition and had to set up their own pavilion to show their wares. One faction among the French was so embarrassed by Le Corbusier's pavilion that they tried to hide it behind a thirty-foot fence. Called Pavillon de l'Esprit Nouveau, it was a model housing unit named for the magazine that promoted his doctrine. (See "Paris Exposition of 1925.") Robert Mallet-Stevens (1886–1945) and Andre Lurçat were two other French architects who had taken up the Modern style.

It was not until the 1930s that the Bauhaus School of design and architecture gained popularity. Many of these talented European architects had emigrated to America, where their ideas, if not immediately accepted, were at least reinforced by the growing popularity of Frank Lloyd Wright (1867–1959), his sometime teacher Louis Sullivan, and the straight lines and flat roofs of the Prairie School. In England, where Breuer lived and worked before joining Gropius in America, he influenced an entire generation of 1930s architects including Wells Coates (1895–1958). German architect Erich Mendelsohn (1887–1953) also worked in England before coming to America, where his work helped to popularize the Streamline style of Modern design. Frank Lloyd Wright's design for the Guggenheim Museum, although not executed until the 1950s, owes a great deal to the Modern movement in architecture.

Gropius eventually taught architecture at Harvard University, and Le Corbusier designed the Carpenter Center for the Visual Arts there. In 1987 America rediscovered the work of this great master and marked the occasion of his hundredth birthday with numerous exhibitions and commemorations.

The Carpenter Center incorporated most of Corbusier's ideas into a somewhat unsettling whole: a building raised on columns, with roof gardens, ramps, and concrete softened with bright primary colors. But Corbusier's greatest contribution to the architecture of the period was the freeing of walls from their supports and the opening up of spaces. In that sense his impact is still very much in evidence.

Another architectural pioneer in America was Austrian-born Joseph Urban, who played a crucial advocacy role for Modern design in America. It was his career as a set designer that first brought him to live in America, where he worked with the Boston Opera Company before moving to New York about 1917 and becoming associated with the Metropolitan Opera Company.

## Architecture

Returning to architecture in 1925, he had six or seven very prolific years, which included the design of Palm Beach residences, restaurants, cabarets, retail stores, and the Ziegfeld Theater in New York. (See the photo in "Decorative Influences.") By 1930 he was in the vanguard of American architecture along with Raymond Hood (1881–1934), Ely Jacques Kahn, and others, many of whom were creating in the skyscraper style.

The Art Deco skyscraper style in the 1920s and 1930s was itself greatly influenced by ancient styles of architecture, including Egyptian, Mayan, and Aztec stepped temples. Another influence was the ziggurat, or temple tower, of the ancient Assyrian and Babylonian cultures, where each step was smaller than the one below it.

This period—the heyday of Art Deco architecture in America—produced some of the most revolutionary and exciting architecture ever known. The skyscraper was a truly American phenomenon and the American answer to urban development. There were no skyscrapers in Europe, while America had a history of multistory metal frame buildings dating back to the turn of the century.

The ever-increasing height of the skyscraper was leading to ever-increasing congestion in American cities, and in 1916 New York passed the first zoning act, which in fact may have helped create the skyscraper style.

This act provided that a building had to be set back from the street and only on one quarter of its lot could it rise to any height. Some say it was this law that forced architects to adopt the new style; others say the new style came along just in time. Whatever the case, the Art Deco design fit perfectly, and the skyline of urban centers came to reflect the era. In spite of this practical beginning, American designers began to use the stepped-back motif in everything from vases, coffeepots, cigarette cases, and earrings to mantel clocks, furniture, and even textile designs.

The speed and movement of the Art Deco style was best expressed in architecture through windows and moldings. The windows in a building were positioned to make the viewer's eye move along at a rapid speed, vertically or horizontally, as did the moldings. These and other designs actually made the architectural volume of skyscrapers seem less ominous.

Every major city acquired outstanding examples of Art Deco architecture during this period. The San Francisco Telephone Building was the first skyscraper to be built outside New York but was soon followed by the Guardian Building in Detroit, the Northern Life Tower in Seattle, and the Richfield Building in Los Angeles. However, it was New York City that was to become the Art Deco skyscraper capital of the world.

# ART DECO

The New York City Landmarks Preservation Commission was established in 1965 to protect the city's most important architectural sites from demolition and alteration. In 1974 the first Art Deco building to be named a landmark was the American Radiator Building at 40 West 40th Street, designed by Raymond Hood. Today numerous Art Deco buildings have landmark designation.

Radio City Music Hall, which celebrated its fiftieth anniversary in 1982, was the first part of Rockefeller Center to be completed. It represents an extraordinary concentration of talents: John D. Rockefeller was the developer of the entire center, with three major architectural firms involved in its creation; René Chambellan (1893–1955) was the architectural sculptor for the Music Hall, and Donald Deskey was the interior designer. The well-known precision dance team, the Rockettes, have been an integral part of Radio City Music Hall since its opening night in December 1932.

The interior was named a landmark in 1978, meaning that all public areas of the theater as well as carpets, drapes, wall coverings, and furnishings had to be maintained in their original design, fabric, color, and style, setting off a nationwide search for original components. The original plates for the silver- and gold-tone wallpaper were located in Germany, and more than ten thousand yards of floor coverings were rewoven. Remarkably, the whirlwind restoration was completed in about one month's time in 1979.

The whole of Rockefeller Center is resplendent with Art Deco sculpture, murals, figural terra-cotta, and glass by dozens of talented designers of the day. It is also perhaps the all-time favorite "Art Deco Walking Tour." Whether you are a Rockefeller or not, you can enjoy

Grand Foyer, Radio City Music Hall. *(Photo courtesy of Radio City Music Hall Productions)*

## Architecture

a tour past monolithic sculptures, such as Paul Manship's "Prometheus" in the Lower Plaza and "Atlas," a seven-ton bronze by Lee Lawrie; magnificent glass relief sculpture and limestone incision designs by Attilio Piccirilli; fountainheads by sculptor René Chambellan; huge wall murals by Jose Maria Sert and Dean Cornwell; and the streamlined stainless steel sculpture by Isamu Noguchi (b. 1904) over the door of the Associated Press building.

Lee Lawrie (1877–1963) created several important works of art for Rockefeller Center, including one sometimes called "Wisdom," carved in limestone and cast in glass. Above the doorway to the RCA Building an imposing God sends his message to mankind: "Wisdom and knowledge shall be the stability of thy times." The real title of the work is "Genius, Which Interprets to the Human Race the Laws and Cycles of the Cosmic Forces of the Universe Making Cycles of Light and Sound." The "Wisdom" inscription was added at a later date. Another work by Lawrie, "Progress," is a limestone carving over the door at 14 West 49th Street, symbolizing the advances of civilization.

The New York City building that many feel epitomizes the American Art Deco architectural style, however, is the Chrysler Building. Both the building and the interior have gained landmark status. Designed by William van Alen (1883–1954), its remarkable nickel-chrome-steel cladding, dome, and spire and its striking Modern design make it an attraction for tourists from all over the world, even though

"Wisdom" by Lee Lawrie for the RCA Building. *(Photo by R. Four)*

"Progress" by Lee Lawrie for Rockefeller Center. *(Photo by R. Four)*

it was quickly eclipsed as "the tallest building in the world." Its direct connection with the automobile is emphasized by the enormous ornamental Chrysler radiator caps at the corners of the thirty-first floor.

The Waldorf Astoria Hotel, the finest piece of Art Deco hotel architecture in New York, is a noble skyscraper that was built when the "old" Waldorf came down to make way for the Empire State Building. Its Grand Ballroom, Park Avenue lobby, and famed Starlight Roof were renovated in the early 1980s to their original 1930s decor. The restoration cost $2 million to uncover the Art Deco details that had been "lost" in the early 1960s when the Grand Ballroom was redecorated in Edwardian style. A new color scheme and advanced lighting techniques have been added. The lobby, which was also renovated, brought back some incredible interior ornamentation, including thirteen murals by French artist Louis Rigal.

Other outstanding examples of Art Deco architecture and architectural decoration that can be found in New York City are the Chanin Building, the old McGraw-Hill Building, the Empire State Building, and the Daily News Building by Raymond Hood. Other, less impressive buildings such as department stores, schools, theaters, banks, apartment and office buildings, and even prisons were designed or decorated in the new style.

## Architecture

Smaller cities felt the impact of the new style as well, in new bridges, train depots, silos, warehouses, and similar commercial structures. Soon suburban banks, cinemas, and even churches adopted an Art Deco style. Today these buildings are increasingly recognized as an important part of our design history, and the effort to preserve them is taking place throughout the states.

What many people know about Art Deco architecture they know because of John Eberson and his son Drew, who built Modern-style movie theaters all over the world. Born of the nickelodeons in 1906, the movie houses adopted the gaudiest of opera house architecture, with gold gilt, marble, and cut-glass chandeliers. In the early 1920s the "Atmospheric" style predominated, and movie theaters looked like palaces with plaster and ornamental wrought iron. The 1930s brought stepped-back facades and Deco murals, mirrors, and lighting. The few remaining original Ebersons, Fox, Lowe, and Paramount theaters are finding new advocates, and preservation efforts are more vigorous than ever before.

We have already emphasized the impact of Frank Lloyd Wright on Art Deco and Art Moderne, and perhaps nowhere is this more apparent than in home design of the 1930s. His influence, along with that of Le Corbusier, Walter Gropius, and Marcel Breuer, is felt in Modern-style homes around the country. Various regional styles of Modern architecture can be found in America.

For example, "Long Island Modern" was coined to describe the many modern Long Island homes built mostly during the 1930s, with outside spiral staircases in metal, decks, and flat or geometric roofs. Beach homes seemed to be the perfect place to experiment with the new Modern style, and the design was well suited to furnishings by Donald Deskey, Paul Frankl (1878–1962), and Walter von Nessen.

Of other regional styles of Art Deco architecture in this country, the most notable are Pueblo Deco and Tropical Deco.

Pueblo Deco is the name given to the Deco-inspired architecture of the Southwest, which was also heavily influenced by Native American design, ornamentation, and color palette. The pueblos, or Indian towns, were like large terraced apartment buildings built from adobe bricks. After 1900 hotels and office buildings began to spring up in such places as Tucson and Albuquerque. The motifs of Indian pottery, jewelry, and basketwork soon appeared on storefronts and city halls throughout the Southwest and Texas.

Tropical Deco is the name given to the architectural design and later to the furnishings and decorations of Florida (especially Miami Beach) and other southern states, as well as to some of the Deco in southern California. With its own stylistic integrity as an architectural style, Tropical Deco used sunny yellow, turquoise, sea green, and flamingo pink. Its motifs included many of the same symbols as other Deco styles—zigzags, and stylized patterning—but it added native plants, birds (such as flamingos, herons, and pelicans), ocean waves, and sea grass. Stepped parapets and facades and geometric-patterned friezes and moldings abound. The 1920s revived sunbathing, and the radiating sun became a favorite Art Deco motif just as Florida was becoming a favorite vacation spot.

Tropical Deco materials include terrazo—floors made from embedding granite or marble chips in concrete—the glass block, and the glass tile, which often was sold under the trade names of Vitrolyte and Carrara. The Art Deco district of Miami Beach, largely built from 1930 to 1945, epitomizes the Tropical Deco style, and its numerous Deco hotels display typical Tropical stylings such as rounded corners, banding or "racing stripes," and etched glass.

## THE ART DECO PRESERVATION MOVEMENT

The Miami district of Art Deco and Mediterranean Revival styles, primarily built from 1930 to 1945, has been renovated to its original splendor. A unique concentration of almost 650 significant buildings, including dozens of small and large hotels off Ocean Drive, this one-square-mile area was placed on the National Register of Historic Places in 1979. Six of the hotels—the Cavalier, the Cardozo, the Carlyle, the Victor, the Senator, and the Waldorf Towers—with a total of eight hundred rooms, have been restored and furnished in the original Tropical Deco style of the 1930s and 1940s. It is the largest architecturally and stylistically coherent block of buildings in the world.

Although the district is on the National Register, its future is not guaranteed. Political and economic pressures on prime oceanfront property are difficult to keep at bay, and the struggle continues. Like Art Deco architecture in many cities, the buildings are threatened by developers who want to replace them with buildings of greater capacity. People immediately think of the Chrysler Building or the Empire State Building when they speak of Art Deco architecture, but most of the structures were relatively small by today's standards.

Leading the fight is the Miami Design Preservation League (MDPL). The league completely opposes any demolition of Art Deco architectural design in the area. Barbara Baer Capitman, who founded the league in 1976 and still serves on its board, was one of the pioneers of the Art Deco preservation movement in this country—a movement that has grown rapidly, with other cities now rediscovering their Art Deco banks, theaters, cinemas, schools, and stores.

Miss Capitman and Leonard Horowitz, another early advocate for preservation, literally drove across the country in the early 1970s to rally support for the preservation of Miami's rich Deco heritage. Their work, and the work of dozens of other committed citizens of the Miami area, resulted in the National Register status and helped fuel the fires of Deco awareness, not only among preservationists but among dealers and collectors.

The 1976 Bicentennial also deserves some credit for awakening Americans to their heritage in Art Deco as well as in other fields. Under the Carter administration, cities and towns were given tremendous support for their renovation and preservation efforts in the inner cities.

Miss Capitman is also the founder and president of the Art Deco Societies of America, located in Miami Beach. One of the purposes of this organization is to encourage the creation of Art Deco societies in other parts of the country by networking interested parties on a local level. She has thus been involved in the creation of numerous other Art Deco societies.

The MDPL's most recent battle is over a small hotel in the Deco district called the Senator. The Senator was designed by L. Murray Dixon, a prominent Miami Beach architect, in 1939. It is a unique example of the best features Tropical Deco has to offer: pelican sculptures, bas-reliefs, etched-glass windows with flamingos, portholes, cantilevered window shades called "eyebrows," pipe railings, and dyed keystone. In 1987 a development group proposed demolition of the hotel to build a parking garage, and the MDPL called for a moratorium on all demolition until a parking plan could be developed that ensured the preservation of significant structures.

Everywhere in this country and in Europe preservationists are struggling to save buildings that incorporate Art Deco design and motifs. Some are small organizations with no paid staff, while others—in New York, Chicago, San Francisco, Los Angeles, and Washington, DC—are well organized in both the battle for preservation and in educating the public about Art Deco through seminars, walking tours, festivals, and publications.

San Francisco has a number of good architectural designs in the Art Deco style, notably by architect Timothy Pflueger (1892–1946), creator of the Oakland Paramount, which was restored in 1978 as a civic center. Pflueger also created many of the buildings at the Golden Gate International Exposition of 1939, as well as I. Magnin's, the Castro and Alhambra theaters, and the San Francisco Stock Exchange with its colorful murals by Diego Rivera.

Washington, DC, has more Art Deco detailing on government buildings than people usually imagine, although the style has been called "Greco Deco" or "Federal Art Deco." Other buildings in Washington also display Art Deco motifs: apartment and office buildings, stores, restaurants, and churches. Recently, the Art Deco Society of Washington was engaged in fights to save a Drew and John Eberson Deco cinema in Silver Springs, Maryland, and the downtown Greyhound Bus Terminal.

**The Senator.** *(Photo by Bob Keubler; courtesy of the Miami Design Preservation League)*

In Boston the stepped-back United Shoe Tower was named a landmark in 1980 by the Boston Landmarks Commission. Boston wasn't building as much during the heyday of Art Deco, and this building is its biggest and best example of Art Deco architecture. The completely renovated office building, now called "The Landmark," was built in 1930 by the firm of Parker, Thomas and Rice. Almost 10 percent of its brickwork had to be restored, and most of the eighteen hundred cast-stone panels in thirty-four different designs had to be replicated.

Also headquartered in Boston, the Society for the Preservation of New England Antiquities (SPNEA) maintains many properties throughout the region. While most of these tend to be "historic" American homes and mansions, the society also owns and maintains the Walter Gropius House in Lincoln, Massachusetts. The Gropius family home was the first house he designed when he arrived in the United States. Today the house is on display, complete with furnishings made in the Bauhaus workshops as well as objects acquired in this country.

Numerous other cities hold rich and interesting Art Deco architecture. Seattle is an important city for architecture, and the art museum there is housed in an Art Deco–style building. In Spokane, Washington, the city hall is now housed in a rehabilitated Art Deco Montgomery Ward building. Indianapolis, Indiana, has notable Art Deco architecture. The Union Terminal in Cincinnati, Ohio, is another fine example of a building that has been saved and restored. The Art Deco

# Architecture

**The Gropius House.** *(Photo by J. David Bohl; courtesy of the Society for the Preservation of New England Antiquities)*

architecture of Kansas City includes the Kansas City Power & Light Building, and the interior of the Kansas City Municipal Auditorium. Treasures of Tulsa, Oklahoma, include Bruce Goff's Boston Avenue Methodist Church, the Warehouse Market, and the Tulsa Fire Alarm Building. (See photo in our color section, "An Art Deco Portfolio.")

Drawing together people who share their interests, other Art Deco societies have been created in Philadelphia, San Diego, and Kansas City, in Texas, Ohio, and California's San Joaquin Valley, even as far away as Napier, New Zealand. The Art Deco Trust of Napier concentrates on preservation of the buildings in the center of the city. Much of the city was destroyed during an earthquake in 1931 and rebuilt in the Deco style. Art Deco treasures here include the fire station, the municipal theater, the Ministry of Transport, the Daily Telegraph Building, and many others.

It almost doesn't matter where you live; when you really start looking, you will find many examples of Art Deco architecture everywhere. Recognizing the motifs, design styles, materials, and sensibilities of Art Deco in architecture will help train your eye for the collecting field. Many of the architects' names you've seen in this chapter will reappear when you read about the furniture, clocks, glass, and other household and decorative objects they also designed.

## Special Focus: Architectural and Interior Design Components

In the United States the new architecture allowed for the increased use of glass by providing stronger structural support from steel and concrete. Glass roofs came into being, and in southern architecture the glass block achieved an increasingly important status. Sand-blasted glass murals, brightly lit from behind, appeared in cinemas and other public gathering places, depicting Jazz Age themes. Mirror, black enamel, and chrome became the color theme of every "chic" cocktail lounge.

Often the architect was also the interior designer, creating mirrors, lamps, lighting fixtures, rails, gates, metalwork, and terra-cotta friezes as part of the unified vision.

Architectural and interior design elements are attracting new and important attention on the collecting market. One of the hottest items on the New York market in the fall of 1987 were the aluminum spandrels removed from the Barbizon Plaza. The spandrels, relief panels used in the design of the building's facade between floors, make imposing Art Deco sculpture when framed and mounted on a base.

Many office and apartment buildings in this country, notably in New York, Philadelphia, Washington, and Chicago had Art Deco lobby and hallway lighting fixtures and wall sconces, mailboxes, door grates, or sidewalk gates. These kinds of elements are today being salvaged by knowledgeable dealers and collectors for their design and historic value. The same is true of theaters and cinemas, with their ornate Deco doorframes, lighting fixtures, and mirrors.

Salvage companies are doing a stronger business in Art Deco elements than in previous years, when many pieces rusted on a back lot. Although the demand in this country is still very high for Victorian weather vanes, stained glass, pillars, and doorknobs, more people are effectively integrating Art Deco components into the building of new houses.

Some household interior design components, such as Art Deco plaster and electric fireplaces, are true kitsch; they look great in a room where Bakelite radios and Chase Chrome predominate. The electric fireplaces, usually made of painted plaster, have streamlined or geometric designs, sometimes with horizontal brass "speed stripes."

They could be leaned against any wall, as long as there was an outlet to plug in the lights that created the effect of fire in the plaster logs. We've seen these at flea markets for under $150, but those in better condition and somewhat more tasteful can retail for up to $1,800. The nicest ones have an overall marbleized look with geometric patterns. No matter how small your modern apartment, you could still have a fireplace!

# Architecture

Again, it is Frank Lloyd Wright who leads the market in American architectural and interior design elements. A Frank Lloyd Wright "Prairie Window"—long thin panes of leaded clear and colored glass in a geometric pattern or with abstracted plant designs—can bring tens of thousands of dollars today.

Wright-designed homes are sought after, and expensive. For example, the California home of Dr. John Storer by Frank Lloyd Wright was purchased in 1984 by Hollywood producer Joel Silver, at a reported cost of $790,000. One of nine Wright homes in Los Angeles, the house was renovated for a rumored $2 million, and Silver completely refurnished it with period furniture. It has been called the most perfectly restored Wright house in the world.

But the Art Deco architectural component of the year is "Diana and the Deer," a pair of Art Deco gates by Edgar Brandt that once graced the 1925 Paris Exposition. They sold at William Doyle Galleries for $80,000 in June 1987. (See the photo in our color section, "An Art Deco Portfolio.")

## PRICE LISTINGS

*Gates, "Diana and the Deer,"* by Edgar Brandt, French, 1925. Gilt-bronze mounted wrought-iron gates, reeded frames, elaborate filigree door in a design of ginkgo leaves, with central gilt-bronze figure depicting Diana and a deer amid lacy foliage; flanked by conforming rectangular side panels, painted gray. Prominently displayed in Brandt's own exhibition at the 1925 Paris Exposition. Each door, 6'10" tall x 3'3" wide; each side panel, 5'9" tall x 2' wide. Pair. (For illustration see color insert.)

**$88,000 (1987)**

*Panel,* by Rene Chambellan, American, c. 1935–1939. In aluminum, design depicts parakeets against a stylized background. Signed by artist on front. Molded on back: "Alcoa U.S. Aluminum Co. Patent #4406". Chambellan was the designer of the Chanin Building and Radio City Music Hall murals. 12" tall x 10" wide.

**$1,050–$1,200**

*Clock,* designed by George W. Maher, American, for the Winona State Bank, Winona, MN, c. 1914. In white marble, the circular face featuring reticulated hands and surmounting double volutes with foliate devices and resting on a marble plinth. 36" wide x 28" high x 6" deep.

**$3,520 (1986)**

*Theater masks,* designed by Jo Meilziner for Billy Rose, installed in Ziegfeld Theater, New York City. Made from gilt-plaster, depicting the faces of comedy and tragedy with flamboyant bow topknots. 39" tall, mask only. Pair.

$2,000–$2,500

*Spandrels,* designed by Murgatroyd & Ogden, 1928, for the Barbizon Hotel on West 58th Street, New York. In cast aluminum, designs have highly stylized figures of artists' faces, paint brushes, palettes, and musical instruments. Framed in black lacquered maple for display as sculpture. In all, 30 relief panels were salvaged from the upper facade.

| | |
|---|---|
| Smaller size (without faces), 54" tall x 40" wide | $8,500–$9,000 |
| Larger size, 70" tall x 40" wide | $12,500–$14,000 |

*Gates,* by Eliel Saarinen, American, 1928, for the Cranbrook Academy of Art's Museum. In wrought iron, the interior with stepped skyscraper design surmounted by a foliate motif. 48" tall x 36" wide. Pair.

$5,500 (1986)

*Lighting fixtures,* by Sabino, French, c. 1930, for the Grand Salon of the *Normandie* ocean liner. Molded white frosted glass, square geometric forms in two tiers. First tier, 16" x 16" square; second tier, 10" x 10" square. Each.

$660–$750

Spandrel from the Barbizon Hotel. *(Photo by R. Four; courtesy of Lost City Arts)*

## Architecture

*Escutcheons* (covers for mailbox slots), designed by Louis H. Sullivan, executed by Yale and Towne Manufacturing Co. for letter slots at the Guaranty Building, Buffalo, NY, 1894–1895. Made from cast iron, rectangular, cast with an ornate scrolled and stylized floral design, two with springed doors cast "Letters," each cast Y & T. 8¾" long (two pairs).

$1,540 (1986)

*Leaded glass windows,* by Frank Lloyd Wright from the Avery Coonley house, Riverside, IL, 1908. Geometric vertical designs and squares in clear and colored glass. 44" long x 16¼" wide. Pair.

$90,000–$95,000

*Leaded glass window,* designed by Frank Lloyd Wright for the B. Harley Bradley house, Kankakee, IL, c. 1900. Vertical, elongated form with white, textured, and clear glass, in some instances with encased gold foil. Restoration to leading and replacement of some clear-glass sections. 62½" high x 14" wide.

$2,420 (1986)

*Lighting fixture/sconce,* by Frank Lloyd Wright from the Avery Coonley house, Riverside, IL, 1908. Two lights, framed in copper with a square geometric design, rectangular mica panels and glass globes. Carbon filament bulbs cast a yellow light.

$25,000–$27,000

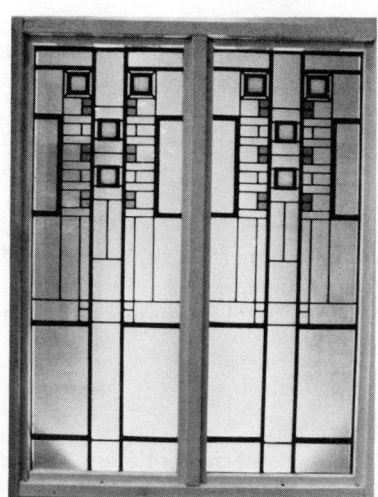

Leaded glass windows by Frank Lloyd Wright. *(Photo by R. Four; courtesy of Struve Gallery)*

*Doorframe section,* anon., American. In cast bronze for the entryway of the Strand Cinema in New York City. Stylized design similar to designs on the Chanin Building at Radio City Music Hall. 52" long section.

$550–$750

*Fireplace,* anon., American, 1930s. Marbleized plaster in white and black with geometric line designs and stepped-back capstone. "Glowing ember" effect is generated when plugged in. Approx. 4½' tall x 5' long.

$1,500–$1,800

*Light fixture,* anon., American. Hanging store fixture with chrome chain and stepped fitter, milk-glass shade with black decoration. 22" from top of fixture to bottom of shade, 11½" diameter.

$300–$315

*Marble blocks/decorations,* anon., American. Depicting eagles and griffins, from the entranceway to a bank in Trenton, NJ. Stylized animals in Italian veined brown, white, and gray marble. 24" square, 5" thick. Pair.

$4,800–$5,000

*Mirror,* anon., American, c. 1930, designed for the Roxy Theater, New York City. Blue peach and clear mirror set in two semicircular bands of blue and peach glass tiles. 54" tall.

$770 (1986)

*Mirrored panel,* anon., American, 1939. Two rectangular blue mirror panels, depicting etched scene of two figures, a Greek male figure in toga and a lithe female nude, holding comedy and tragedy masks, stamped "SHGW" within a diamond and the date "Jul 17 1939." Each panel 44" x 36".

$1,320 (1987)

*Mirrored panel,* anon., as above, 1939. Two rectangular blue mirror panels, depicting a nude maiden running with a deer, stamped "SHGW" within a diamond and the date "Jul 17 1939." Each panel 44" x 36".

$990 (1987)

*Panels,* anon., American, c. 1925. In bronze and wrought iron with foliate and geometric motifs and figural designs of dancing women, champagne glasses, and couples toasting. Perhaps commissioned for a

## Architecture

Manhattan bar or cocktail lounge. Three panels, a companion pair and one other. Tallest, 108″ tall x 16″ wide.
$2,000–$4,000

*Screen,* anon., designed for the Beach Hotel, Monaco. Three-panel silvered and black-lacquered screen, each panel trimmed in silver leaf with rounded edges. 93″ tall x 15½″ long. Each.
$2,530 (1987)

*Wall bracket,* anon., American, c. 1930, from the Beach Theater in Miami, FL. In aluminum, rectangular frame enclosing three central vertical supports intersecting a row of four circles, unmarked. 64″ tall x 18″ wide.
$440 (1986)

*Wall sconce,* anon., American, c. 1935. In copper and glass, stylized skyscraper form with clear and frosted glass wings projecting from tops, frosted glass panels at front centering translucent glass rod, unmarked. Perhaps used in an apartment or office building. 34½″ tall.
$880 (1986)

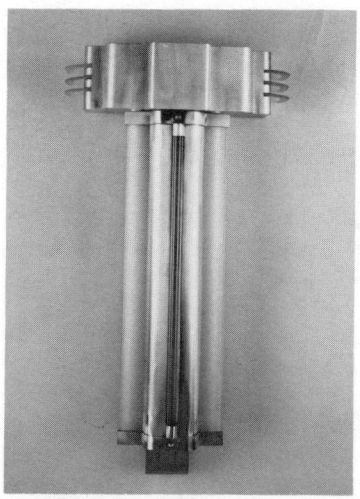

**Wall sconce by an unknown designer.** *(Photo courtesy of Christie's East)*

*Wall sconces,* anon., American, c. 1930, from the Beach Theater in Miami, FL. In bronze and Lucite, each with a bronze beaded acanthus leaf finial supporting a seven-sided shade; seven curled Lucite panels above seven butterfly-wing Lucite panels, unmarked. 36" tall x 26¼" high. Pair.

$2,000–$3,000

# FURNISHINGS

Perhaps more than any other area of decorative arts, furniture and furnishings reflected the profound changes in fashion, style, and society in the 1920s and 1930s. Furnishings were transformed not only by new life-styles but by technical advances, new materials, and new inventions. The interior designer was first and foremost concerned with furniture. Later, architects too became concerned with furniture design and used their talents to create architecturally fine design on a smaller scale.

In France at the beginning of the Art Deco period, as we have noted elsewhere, furniture was created in more of a continuum of past styles than as a revolution.

Tradition-loving French *ébénistes*, or cabinetmakers, while abandoning the overly ornamental Art Nouveau still used highly refined materials. Woods such as *ébène de macassar*, or Macassar ebony, Brazilian palissandre, rosewood, palmwood, zebrawood, mahogany, amboyna, amaranthe, violet wood, sycamore, and elm were popular. Other materials such as lacquer, silver, copper, *bronze doré* (gilt bronze), ivory, mother-of-pearl, and tortoiseshell were also frequently used.

Another favorite material was *galuchat*, the skin of a dogfish, specially treated to be tooled and glued to desk tops and other furniture. Today you'll often hear *galuchat* called sharkskin, and it is also substituted as a term for *peau de chagrin*, which translates as shagreen. In metalwork, wrought iron surpassed bronze in popularity, no doubt in part because of the talents of the artists who chose the medium.

The work of many artists of the period is notable, highly prized, and highly priced today. For the most part, they created their furniture for a wealthy clientele and were often commissioned to design unique pieces.

The artists of the deluxe Art Deco era who have been popular on the market in recent years include Armand-Albert Rateau (1882–1938); Jacques-Emile Ruhlmann (1879–1933); Jules Leleu; Louis Süe (1875–1968) and André Mare (1887–1932), who founded the Compagnie des Arts Français in 1919 and are today better known simply as Süe et Mare; the company Dominique, created by Andre Domin and Marcel Genevrière; and the master lacquer artist who worked for many designers, Jean Dunand.

Other well-known artists of this era include Maurice Dufrène (1876–1955), Paul Vera, Clément Mère, Léon Jallot, Paul Follot (1877–1941), and Paul Iribe (1883–1935).

One outstanding figure in Art Nouveau furniture, Louis Majorelle (1859–1926), created some less ornate works in his latter years, but he is not often represented on the Art Deco market.

Although works by other artists have brought higher prices at times, Jacques-Emile Ruhlmann remains the undisputed master of the Art Deco furniture market, and his pieces are bought up by both collectors and museums.

Ruhlmann's furniture has elegant lines, discrete curves, or slightly bombé fronts. The plinth, a base on which furniture may rest, is a favorite Ruhlmann motif; it added more majesty to his already sumptuous pieces. He was also the master of modern veneering in exotic woods. Veneers were laid down with grains in opposition to the wood below them, to lessen warping. This allowed Ruhlmann to create his broad flat surfaces for doors, cabinets, and other furniture.

Armand-Albert Rateau really was an independent artist who followed no particular movement. Influenced by Oriental art, he often used lacquers and preferred to work in solid oak. In 1920 he was commissioned to design the apartment of fashion-setter Jeanne Lanvin, for whom he created bronze furniture.

Of the more traditional Art Deco designers, Süe et Mare were perhaps the most traditional and were influenced by provincial styles. Their gilt-bronze clocks with flowery ornamentation and the dignified carved tassels on their furniture make them highly sought after today for their refinement and restraint.

Jean Dunand perfected the art of lacquer, especially eggshell lacquer. Other artists were influenced by Japanese art during this era, but the lengthy lacquering process of layer upon layer requires extreme skill and patience to achieve a high-quality finish. Léon Jallot also created lacquered screens and furniture. But by the 1930s traditional lacquer was giving way to industrial, fast-drying lacquer. The use of enamel extended right down to designs on cheap cigarette cases.

## Furnishings

The fashion of the day strongly affected furniture design. Just as the previous generation's hoopskirts and crinolines needed certain proportions for chairs and sofas, the new fashion meant new furniture. To wear an Oriental-inspired robe or long stylish dress with casual slinkiness, one needed a low-slung couch or *chaise longue* (literally "long chair") to go with it. And to go with low chairs, tables became low cocktail or coffee tables.

The impact of the Ballets Russes on early Deco furniture was an Orientalism that some have called a "boudoir style." There was a trend for colored, patterned textiles and cushions with long tassels. Furniture was redesigned for comfort, including deeper armchairs and dining room tables with a single pedestal instead of legs.

Paul Iribe, known for his work in the fashion world, produced refined, comfortable, and elegant furnishings. His work was often embellished with beautiful materials and carved or encrusted ornaments. His "Escargot Chair," designed in 1913, with its low seat and high back, has carved arms in the shape of snail shells.

Interior designers paid as much attention to tapestry, curtains, chair covers, and wall hangings as they did to furniture. Fountains, flowers, and multicolor brocades were typical designs.

Paul Follot used abstract shapes and stylized flowers in textiles to create a rich effect. Follot liked "beautiful" materials and techniques such as marquetry, lacquer, and bronze work. In 1923 he took over the management of Pomone, the workshop for the department store Au Bon Marché, and he was in charge of its pavilion at the 1925 exposition. He defended deluxe tradition and opposed mass-produced furnishings.

Maurice Dufrène, who in 1904 had been a founding member of the Salon des Artistes Décorateurs, became the director of La Maîtrise, the workshop for the department store Galleries Lafayette. He designed a multitude of furnishings, ceramics, and decorations that were executed by numerous companies.

Often artists also made carpet designs as part of their interior design work. These were sometimes inspired by painters such as Picasso, the Cubists, and most of all, Mondrian. Exhibitions of Moroccan art in Paris just after World War I brought the thick handmade woolen piles and brown and red geometrical patterns of Berber carpets to public view. They inspired a style of which the leading practitioner was Bruno Da Silva Bruhns, whose work is largely held by museums today. Other notable carpet designs came from Robert Mallet-Stevens (1886–1945) and Jacques Doucet. In England, Marion Dorn (1899–1964), the wife of poster artist E. McKnight Kauffer, became one of the most notable European rug designers.

Many noted lamp designers were glassmakers, such as Daum Nancy, led by Auguste Daum (1853–1909) and his brother Antoine (1864–1930), Sabino, and René Lalique (1860–1945). Edgar Brandt worked with Daum to create stunning torchères (literally "torches"), or floor lamps. Today they are sought after by glass collectors as well as by Brandt collectors.

Figural and sculptural lamps also increased in popularity. Another noted artist was Jean Goulden, who was influenced by Byzantine enameling and who created stunning geometric and abstract designs for lamps, as well as other furnishings.

In metalwork there is no question that the dominant artist of early Art Deco is Edgar Brandt (1880–1960). Brandt's work is remarkable for the combination of traditional skills and the use of new technology. He used autogenous welding, a process that permits two different metals to be welded together, and the new power hammer; these tools allowed for greater production and lower costs. Today his lamps, andirons, wrought-iron-mounted tables, fire screens, and other work bring thousands of dollars.

Whereas metalwork was reserved for such accessory furnishings as these in the early Art Deco period, in 1927 metal furniture was exhibited for the first time at the Salon des Artistes Décorateurs.

The new furniture designers, influenced by Cubism, the Wiener Werkstätte, and social and economic changes in the world, rejected past forms and design. Sometimes called the "moderns," these artists often regarded furniture as "interior architecture" or "household equipment" and emphasized the use of metal. They further simplified the lines, volume, and decoration of furniture as well.

The furniture of the Viennese Secessionists inspired many French artists. Today Viennese Secessionist furniture is in high demand, and Josef Hoffmann, one of the founders of the Wiener Werkstätte, commands the highest prices.

The Wiener Werkstätte's rectilinear design lent itself to sophisticated, restrained furniture. Generally speaking, this furniture was made in very small quantities. It is virtually unavailable outside top-of-the-line dealers and the best auction houses, although certain designs by Hoffmann have been reissued.

More affordable today is the large production of the Thonet company, which started production around 1832 in Vienna and continues in Pennsylvania today. The name has almost become synonymous with bentwood furniture. Some classic designs, such as its café chairs, are still in production. Early Thonet bentwood chairs still show up at antiques fairs and country auctions. They can sometimes be identified by a paper label by the maker on the bottom of the seat. The quality of the lacquer and its finish will help determine the price.

A few French artists remained loyal to traditional materials, but many began using metal, especially painted, hollow metal tubes that could be mass-produced. Thonet began to mass-produce tubular steel frames in 1928. Restaurants and other commercial establishments were quick to realize the practicality of the new stacking chair.

Especially after the Wall Street crash of 1929, which affected the entire world, the demand for fine furnishings was not as great as the demand for less costly, mass-produced furnishings created with lower-middle-class families in mind.

In 1930, inspired by the Bauhaus and the theories of Le Corbusier, a number of artists created the Union des Artistes Modernes (U.A.M.) and declared a radical departure from the style of their contemporaries. The artists included Jacques Adnet, René Prou, Francis Jourdain, R. Block, Raymond Templier, and architects René Herbst, Robert Mallet-Stevens, André Lurçat, Pierre Chareau (1883–1950) and others. Other French "modern" designers, whose work came into prominence later, are André Arbus and Lyon furniture maker André Sornay. Many of these artists are popular and somewhat expensive today.

Two others who are often called "modernist" in their designs but who were actually more independent of the movement were Pierre Legrain and Eileen Gray.

Le Corbusier set the philosophical tone of the Modern Movement, declaring that furnishings should be made in the service of man, not of art. We have already described the reaction to his pavilion at the 1925 exposition. In 1927 he designed chairs and tables of various types that were manufactured by Thonet in tubing, metal, and glass. The chair coverings were simple pieces of canvas held taut by spring fastenings. However, his best-known chair uses pony skin stretched between metal tube supports.

René Herbst was one of the main instigators of the split that led to the Union des Artistes Modernes. He was openly hostile to all decoration and made prolific use of metal, steel, aluminum, and other new materials. Robert Mallet-Stevens also made use of chromed and painted metal tubing. He attracted attention as a decorator as early as 1913 with his use of color and straight-line design.

Francis Jourdain was one of the first to face the problem of smaller living spaces with the design of his furniture. He was determined to produce low-priced furniture for the masses. Like Pierre Chareau, he looked at furniture with the eye of an architect. Chareau, however, still preferred to use fine materials. His work is very popular on the Art Deco market right now.

Eileen Gray, who was Irish but worked in Paris, created floor lamps, benches, and tables using asymmetrical designs that echo Cubist patterns. Her lacquer work was extremely well executed, and her work in general has a sculptural dimension that raises it far above the ordinary. We suspect that there will be a renaissance of interest in her work very soon, although it is already generally very high priced.

By the 1930s even Süe et Mare were creating furniture in metal and other modern materials. Times had changed.

Modernist design became an international movement, as the entire world came to terms with the Wall Street crash and the rise of fascism, the growth of urban centers and the need for mass-produced furnishings.

In France, Décoration Intérieur Moderne (D.I.M.), founded by René Joubert in 1919, a few years later became one of the first French companies to start producing chrome furniture. In 1931 Practical Equipment Limited (PEL) opened its showroom in England, obviously influenced by the idea of furniture as "equipment."

It should be remembered, however, that at the time these companies were still producing furniture for a fairly wealthy clientele, one that considered itself "modern" and "progressive" enough to buy metal furniture.

In America designers were more influenced by these "modern" artists and by the Wiener Werkstätte and German Bauhaus than by Ruhlmann and Süe et Mare. Americans would adopt more of the Germans' principles than they would those of the early French. Many Modernist designers, in fact, had emigrated to the United States early in the century and had established themselves mainly in New York City.

Furniture designers such as Bruno Paul came to America because they felt their ideas would be readily accepted in the country that was moving the fastest toward industrialization. Paul's work was particularly praised at the 1928 Macy's exhibition.

The Bauhaus, which had been founded by Walter Gropius in 1919, found its way to the United States along with Gropius himself. Ludwig Mies van der Rohe (1886–1969) and Marcel Breuer also came to America. Many of their designs have been reissued by Kroll International, founded by Hammond Kroll, and are popular today.

Another designer who is making waves on the collecting market is Alvar Aalto of Finland. Known for his simple, streamlined designs for chairs, armchairs, and tables, he typifies the influence of Scandinavian Modern design, which was beginning to be felt in furniture, glass, and other production at the time.

Eliel Saarinen (1873–1950), who emigrated to America from Finland, is also highly collectible. As the first director of the Cranbrook Academy of Art in 1922, he influenced an entire generation of American designers. His work was amply represented at the 1970 Finch College Museum exhibition by a dining room table and chairs, coffee table, cabinets, and more. His "Blue Chair," designed in 1929, is now being manufactured again.

America really had no strong native style of furniture since the Colonial style. Many movements had had their heydays—Chippendale, Tudor, Victorian Gothic, Rococo, Eastlake, and Mission among them—but none of these could serve as inspiration for the new Modernism. However, when the new European design reached America,

## Furnishings

the forces of the Prairie School and Frank Lloyd Wright (1867–1959) were already at work, transforming the shape of both architecture and furnishings in America.

Another architect, Joseph Urban (1872–1933), who emigrated from Vienna, had a strong influence on both architecture and American decorative arts of the period. He was director of the short-lived Wiener Werkstätte Gallery in New York, where he displayed a variety of furniture.

It is Paul Theodore Frankl (1878–1962) who stands out clearly as the first major Modernist in America. Born in Vienna, he studied in Berlin and Copenhagen before coming to America in 1914. He noted that the 1925 exposition in Paris would have been markedly different if America had been able to display a skyscraper or two.

Skyscrapers provided the inspiration for his extraordinary desks, wardrobes, and bookcases in the stepped style of the day, custom-made at Frankl Galleries, Inc., in New York. Generally made of California redwood with nickel-plated steel or laquered trim and interiors, these met with immediate acclaim, and they sell for thousands of dollars today—on the rare occasions when they can be found on the open market.

Even his chrome and Bakelite "Telechron" mantel clock now sells for up to $1,200. His Skyscraper furniture can bring $20,000 for a single piece, even though only one small piece was on display at the Minneapolis Institute of Arts revival exhibition in 1971.

Although some criticize Frankl's work for its use of cheaper materials and sometimes less than elegant finishing and enameling, his conceptual strength shows through. Frankl was also a great spokesperson for the Modern movement—a prolific writer who spread his design ideas by example and by the written word.

Eugene Schoen was another early Modernist designer in America; he established an architectural practice in New York in 1905. Although modern in some materials and in style, he produced only one-of-a-kind items that have traces of both French and German influences. His work has been compared to Ruhlmann's in that it is monumental and unadorned and often relies simply on the grain of the wood for its design.

Changes in urban living spaces and the American life-style called for furniture to change dramatically once again. Built-in closets and cupboards eliminated the need for wardrobes and kitchen stands. Sofa beds made their appearance. Dining room center tables were given drawers for silverware. Even baby grand pianos were designed by Chickering, Steinway, and others in the new Modern style.

Fireplace chairs disappeared with fireplaces, and washstands disappeared with hot running water. Metal and glass increasingly replaced wood. Upholstered "easy chairs" and sofas became popular.

Also, a host of synthetic materials came into use, known by trade names such as Formica and Bakelite. Thin wood veneers became popular in hiding furniture's metal frames. With the end of Prohibition in America, liquor cabinets, bars, and all of the paraphernalia associated with smoking and alcohol consumption—cocktail shakers, ashtrays, smoking stands, and cocktail trays—proliferated.

For design pioneers in America like Donald Deskey (b. 1894), the use of plastics, steel, and aluminum to create low-cost, comfortable furnishings that could be easily mass-produced was a way to satisfy the twin goals of quality *and* quantity.

Donald Deskey is a giant of American design who started by designing on private commissions and then went to work for large manufacturers such as Ypsilanti Reed Furniture Company. More than four hundred pieces of his work were put into production in the four-year period 1930 to 1934. The Widdicomb Company also manufactured Deskey designs in tubular chrome.

He is known not only for his furniture but also for textiles, metalwork, glasswork, and even packaging and corporate image-making for companies like Johnson & Johnson. He led his own international design consulting firm. His use of modern materials was sometimes shocking: the aluminum-foil wallpaper he used in 1932 in the Men's Lounge, the so-called "Nicotine Room," in Radio City Music Hall raised more than a few eyebrows.

Ruth Reeves (1892–1966), one of the leading modern carpet and fabric designers, is sought after for her block-printed "Manhattan" and other designs on cotton and cotton velvet. She designed jazzy rugs for Donald Deskey for Radio City Music Hall.

Known for his metalwork in a more traditional way was William Hunt Diederich. Born in Hungary in 1884, Diederich emigrated to America, as did so many of his contemporaries. Noted for his weathervanes, fireplace screens, and other metalwork, Diederich worked primarily on Long Island. He died in 1953.

Kem Weber (1889–1963) was born Karl Emmanuel Martin Weber in Berlin, where he studied under Bruno Paul. Settling in the Los Angeles area, he also adopted the skyscraper style, as did many imitators. A proponent of Streamline style in furnishings and other designs, he even streamlined his own name, taking his initials, KEM, as a first name. Weber preferred wood over metal and often lacquered it in more typically California colors of sage green, orchid, rose, or bluegray.

Other important American furniture designers of the 1920s and 1930s include Ilonka Karasz (1896–1981), who is also noted for graphic and textile design; Gilbert Rohde (1894–1944), mentioned later in this chapter for his clocks and mass-produced furniture designs; and Wolfgang Hoffmann (1900–1969), the son of Josef Hoffmann, who designed metal, enamel, and glass furniture for the Howell Company. One of our contacts reports that Josef tried to dissuade the younger Hoffmann from designing furniture but to no avail.

Norman Bel Geddes (1893–1958) is another towering figure in the world of American design of the era. He began as an advertising illustrator for the first major advertising agency in America, J. Walter Thompson in New York. His talents were applied to furniture by Simmons and other companies, and he went on to design cars, railroad engines, the giant General Motors "Futurama" exhibit at the 1939 New York World's Fair, and much more.

Streamlining as a design style was promoted by Bel Geddes in his book *Horizons* in 1932. He claimed that *everything* should be redesigned, and some credit him with coining the term "industrial designer" to describe the trade of designing for everyday mass-produced goods and appliances.

Walter von Nessen (1889–1943) studied in Berlin under the progressive architect Bruno Paul of the Bauhaus. He settled in New York in 1925 and within two years had opened an office there. He received commissions for architectural lighting as well as doors, vestibules, and elevator cabs. Known for his many chrome creations, he was very frequently commissioned by Chase Chrome, who actively promoted his work. He created many small metal furnishings, drawing on Bauhaus prototypes for chairs, tables, mirrors, desk sets, and other furniture in tubular metal. His furniture designs are still manufactured and sold today.

Von Nessen is also noted for his lamp designs, in some of which he used aluminum, glass, and Bakelite. Lamps and lighting fixtures had undergone a change. With the perfection of Edison's incandescent bulb in the 1920s, lighting had become more of a science. The form of the lamp depended more on the type of lighting desired than on the shape of a lamp as sculpture.

Other lamp designers of the day include Donald Deskey, Walter Dorwin Teague (1883–1960), Kem Weber for Miller Lamp Company, Kurt Versen (b. 1901) for Lightolier, and Carl Sorensen. Through the 1920s and 1930s dozens of companies produced decorative and commercial lighting fixtures. A new term, "illuminating engineer," came into being, and many unique designs were created. Lamps and lighting fixtures of this era not only have collectible value but contemporary, useful value when integrated into a 1980s "Eclectic Urban" apartment.

Russel Wright (1904–1976) created a wealth of designs for furniture, ceramics, chrome, fabrics, and floor coverings. He worked for the Heywood-Wakefield furniture company, among others, and created the "Flexible Modern Line" for that manufacturer. He was perhaps the first to introduce sectional sofas.

## Special Focus: Clocks

We've singled out clocks as a special focus because they make an interesting category of furnishings for collectors of Art Deco. One can trace the evolution of the Art Deco style by looking at the clocks that were always a part of the furnishings. From key-wound models to later electrified alarm clocks, they capture the passing of time in more ways than one.

Viennese clocks by Josef Hoffmann, Joseph Urban, and others are very highly priced today. Their geometric designs show the influence of this early Modern design movement on later production.

In the early Art Deco period, French clocks were often made of gilt bronze and marble and designed with fruit, flowers, and stylized birds or veiled nudes. Albert Cheuret emerged in the early Art Deco period as a leading designer of lamps and clocks, such as his 1930 silvered bronze and onyx clock that was so reminiscent of a Cleopatra headdress.

Luxurious glass clocks were made by Lalique, Daum Nancy, and other glassmakers, and fabulous jeweled bedside and mantel clocks were made by Cartier and other leading jewelers. (See "Silver, Jewelry, and Fashion.")

In France in the 1920s and 1930s many manufacturers produced Art Deco mantel clocks with garniture. Literally translated as "garnish," these were two additional pieces placed on either side of the central clock to decorate the mantel. Clock garnitures had been made previously, but the Deco style made use of marble or onyx set in geometric patterns.

In addition, the clock may feature bronze or brass figures. Some had figures of Cleopatra, Amazons, and animals, with distinctive Art Deco angles and faces and the stepped-temple look. These clocks are decidedly "bourgeois" and were produced in great quantities for middle-class French households of the day—as were so many of the objects treasured by Art Deco collectors today.

American manufacturers of Art Deco clocks which are now sought after are Seth Thomas; Manning Bowman, which still produced clocks in wood and/or marble before switching to chrome; J. E. Caldwell, and others.

In the 1930s in America, clock designs reflected the Modern style. Clock faces changed dramatically as designers replaced numerals with simple chrome balls or squares of plastic.

Kem Weber's digital clock designs for Lawson Time, Inc., such as his "Zephyr" clock, are among the most notable of the era. Gilbert Rohde, who designed many everyday objects, was one of the leading clock designers; he created several designs for Herman Miller Clock Company of Zeeland, Michigan.

At the time these clocks—in chrome, Bakelite, mirrored blue glass, and other materials—could be bought in department stores for as little as $5. Today they are bringing hundreds of dollars, and sometimes more than $1,000, on the market, and they seem to be gaining by leaps and bounds.

## MASS-PRODUCED FURNITURE

There were numerous American furniture manufacturers in the 1930s, and so many of the designs look alike that unless there is a company mark or label, it is often hard to tell the difference.

The industry centered mostly in Grand Rapids, Michigan, where it had the resources of numerous European immigrant cabinetmakers and workers who had settled in the Midwest. Among the most collectible furniture makers of the era are the Herman Miller Furniture Company; the Howell Company of Geneva, Illinois; Widdicomb Furniture Company; Simmons Furniture Company, which employed the talents of Norman Bel Geddes; Boston's Heywood-Wakefield; S. Karpen Company, which sponsored an early design competition in this country; Lloyd Manufacturing Company; and smaller firms like Donald Deskey's Deskey-Vollmer, where the designer became the manufacturer. Warren MacArthur (1885–1961) also designed for his own manufacturing corporation, which used spun aluminum extensively in furniture.

Much of this furniture survives, but since it was for everyday use, it is often in need of refinishing when found today. It is growing in popularity and price on the Art Deco collecting market. In addition, more of it is coming onto the market directly from the households where it has been used (or stored) since the 1930s.

It is usable, functional furniture, and although it is bought by serious collectors, it is also popular with urbanites who want to bandy a name at a cocktail party or furnish their houses or apartments in the style of the era. It is still relatively inexpensive compared to other Art Deco furniture, but that may not be the case a few years from now, as growing documentation of mass-produced design leads to new interest.

However, at a recent auction we attended, a nice, signed five-piece Heywood-Wakefield bedroom set with bed, bureau, vanity, and two matching chairs in blond wood sold for a measly $400. (Bear in mind that it depends on who comes to the auction, but you can hardly buy new furniture in the stores for prices like that, and what was mass-produced in the 1930s often is still better than what is being mass-produced today.)

Heywood-Wakefield commissioned Gilbert Rohde and Russel Wright, among other noted designers. Rohde also designed tubular steel and glass furniture for the Troy Sunshade Company of Ohio and for Herman Miller.

One of the most common types of anonymously mass-produced American Art Deco furniture used blue mirrored glass for tops of tables, coffee tables, bars, and the like. Much of this production is unidentifiable, and in the late 1960s and early 1970s numerous cheap reproductions using blue mirrored glass were manufactured.

Mass-produced English furniture of the 1930s was also sold in this country, and the most notable examples on the market are the bar cabinets, armoires, and other furnishings designed by Ray Hille. Again, this production is largely bought by those desiring a little style in their homes and is rarely considered an investment. However, well-designed, anonymously made English furniture of the era is today a very good buy.

Of course, the most valuable collectible furniture and decorations will always be those of recognized designers. However, more and more people are seeking to furnish their homes in "Blue Collar Deco"—a name sometimes given to the overstuffed American mohair furniture that was popular during the Depression. Today this furniture is being refinished and reupholstered for sale to many who find that it is functional, comfortable, and durable—the very reasons it was popular in the 1930s.

## PRICE LISTINGS

### Furniture

*Armchair,* by Alvar Aalto, Finnish, 1937, for Artex. Deep back and seat joined by low doughnut-shaped bent blond wood supports, original brown upholstery, marked. 26" tall.
$1,500–$2,000

*Armchairs,* by Alvar Aalto, c. 1925. In bentwood, the seats and backs one continuous piece of molded plywood, the arms and legs also of one continuous piece. Stenciled "Alto Designs made in Finland." 26¼" tall. Pair.
$1,980 (1986)

## Furnishings

*Armchairs*, by Alvar Aalto for Finmar Ltd., c. 1929. In birch with molded plywood back and seat, plastic Finmar tag. 27¾" tall x 19¾" wide. Pair.

$1,000–$1,500

*Chair*, by Alvar Aalto, c. 1925. In bentwood, the webbing in a natural fiber and dyed navy blue. 38¼" tall.

$1,100 (1986)

*Stools*, "Stool 60," by Alvar Aalto for Finmar Ltd., c. 1933. In birch, each with three bent plywood legs, one with a Finmar Ltd. tag. 14¾" diam, 17¼" tall. Pair.

$330 (1986)

*Table*, by Alvar Aalto for Finmar Ltd., the bent birch plywood legs of U-form supporting a square top, with a metal Finmar Ltd. tag. 24" square top, 27" tall.

$700–$1,000

*Table*, by Alvar Aalto for Finmar Ltd. In birch, rectangular with four legs, Finmar Ltd. metal tag. 45" wide x 28" deep x 28¼" tall.

$600–$800

*Desk-vanity*, by Jacques Adnet, French, c. 1930. In sycamore, rosewood, and chrome, with beige parchment top. Solid U-shape sides, geometric drawers, and stepped top, with chrome pulls and trim. 47" wide x 23" deep. With matching chair.

$11,000–$11,500

*Armchairs*, in the style of Jacques Adnet for Hermes. Leather-covered chrome chairs, the tall shaped rectangular back fastened with leather straps and buckles to arched arm over curved leather seat, impressed "VB." 37" tall. Pair.

$1,650 (1986)

*Center table or partner's desk*, in the style of Jacques Adnet for Hermes. Leather-covered brass and chrome, the replaced plywood rectangular top inset in conforming mount supported by four legs joined by two arched sides stretched at center (missing glass top). 28" tall x 84" long x 44" wide.

$330 (1986)

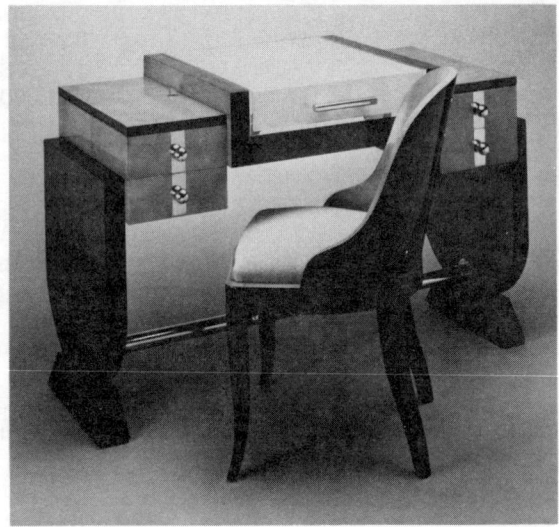

Desk by Jacques Adnet. *(Photo courtesy of Bob Aibel, Moderne)*

*Coffee table,* in the style of Jacques Adnet for Hermes. Leather-covered brass, chrome, and glass, the rectangular glass top suspended on four-legged, leather-covered stretcher with movable wicker magazine racks. 18" tall x 46" long x 20½" wide.
$418 (1986)

*Corner table,* in the style of Jacques Adnet for Hermes. Leather-covered brass, chrome, and glass, the square glass tabletop with second-tier glass half-shelf on leather-covered, four-legged mount with arched side stretchers joined at center. 29" tall x 37" long x 37" wide.
$275 (1986)

*Commode,* by André Arbus, French, c. 1935. In parchment and ivory, low form with small drawers flanking larger central ones, on gently curving cabriole legs. 26¼" tall x 59¾" wide x 18¾" deep.
$5,280 (1986)

*Baby grand pianos,* American, 1930–1945, by Baldwin, Chickering, Steinway, and other companies. Pianos with Art Deco styling. Legs and piano stools may have fluted styling in wood, or silver-painted repetitive lines. Overall shapes are often in Streamline Deco style, which worked well acoustically.
$16,000–$40,000

*Furnishings* 119

*Bedroom suite*, by Norman Bel Geddes, American, for Simmons Furniture Co., 1936. In black-lacquered and chromed steel, comprising a five-drawer tall dresser; a four-drawer low dresser; a one-drawer nightstand; two single beds with headboard, footboard (no rails), and a rectangular mirror. Dresser 45½" tall x 33" long x 19" wide.

$1,000–$1,200

*End table*, by R. Block, French, c. 1930. In walnut. Circular overall with three tiers, top and second tier "pie-cut" to create interesting shelf spaces. 22" tall, 24" diameter.

$2,500–$2,750

*Center table*, by Edgar Brandt, French, c. 1929. In marble, wrought iron, and bronze, the rectangular top of variegated marble surmounting an elaborately worked base of repeated scrolling devices, the center panel featuring two bronze fans, stamped "E. Brandt." 30½" tall x 63" wide x 33½" deep.

$35,000–$45,000

*Side chairs*, by Marcel Breuer, German, for Thonet, 1930s. Rectangular caned back set on chrome side supports joining wide squared seat continuing to arched U-shape leg support, impressed "Thonet made in Germany." 31" tall. Pair.

$400–$600

**Bureau by Norman Bel Geddes for Simmons.** *(Photo courtesy of Christie's East)*

*Stools*, by Marcel Breuer. In chrome and cloth, the rectangular, tubular chrome base stretcher with black hopsacking seat. 18″ tall. Pair.
$165 (1986)

*Articulated nest of tables*, by Pierre Chareau, French, c. 1924, "MB106." Nest of rosewood wedge-shape tables with rounded edges opening from the apex of their triangular shapes. 21¾″ tall x 24¼″ wide x 15″ deep.
$18,700 (1986)

*Bérgères* (large, deep armchairs), by Pierre Chareau, c. 1923. Macassar ebony chairs, stamped on leg when they were confiscated by the Germans in World War II. 26″ tall. Pair.
$100,000–$105,000

*Bookcase table*, by Pierre Chareau, c. 1930. French walnut and chromed metal/steel with dark gilt finish. 25″ tall.
$125,000–$132,000

*Gueridon* (small, round table), by Pierre Chareau for the clubhouse at Beauvallon, c. 1943. The circular mahogany top is set on a wrought-iron pedestal base. 23¾″ tall, 21¾″ diameter.
$8,000–$12,000

*Table*, by Pierre Chareau for the Grand Hotel at Tours, c. 1928. In metal, the shaped top with inset white metal cup for cigarettes. 28″ tall.
$16,500 (1987)

*Table*, by Pierre Chareau, of wrought iron and mahogany, the base of L-form with two additional rods for support in the front. 19½″ wide x 19″ deep x 18½″ tall.
$13,200 (1986)

*Tables*, by Pierre Chareau, French, c. 1928. Modern-style tables with steel bases and wood tops in sycamore or ebonized wood. Steel bases have three flat legs joining in T-shape on floor. Branded with monogram underneath. Each.
$10,000–$15,000

*Vanity*, in the style of Pierre Chareau. In palissandre, with rectangular top and central door flanked by side doors, semicircular drop shelves, supported on two pedestals. 30″ tall x 39½″ long x 20″ deep.
$600–$800

*Furnishings*

Tables by Pierre Chareau. *(Photo courtesy of Maison Gerard)*

*Vanity*, by Décoration Intérieur Moderne (D.I.M.), French, 1930s. In bird's-eye maple and mahogany, central high, rectangular chrome-banded mirror, in low conforming mount with rounded shelf unit and open bays at sides, supported on mahogany stretcher. Ivory knobs. 62" tall.

$880 (1987)

*Desk*, by D.I.M., 1930s. In palissandre (Brazilian wood), burl walnut, and glass, with glass top and two small shelves at the back right, two drawers on left, unsigned. 34¾" tall x 40¾" wide x 25½" deep.

$900–$1,300

*Coiffeuse* (a type of vanity for hair brushing), by Debacq and Pascal, French, c. 1928. In mahogany with slab sides resting on a plinth foot, the top with sections of shagreen separated by ivory stringing forming the top, flanked by two signed compartments, unsigned. 35" tall x 40¼" wide, 21" diameter.

$3,850 (1986)

*Table*, by Donald Deskey, American, for the Seligman house, c. 1929. The two U-shape supports are of chromed metal, the upper and lower tier of lacquered wood. 18" tall x 20" wide x 12" deep.

$1,430 (1986)

*Tub chair*, by Donald Deskey for the Seligman house, c. 1929. The low U-shape back and arms upholstered in black fabric, the feet of silvered metal. 24¼" tall x 24" wide.

$2,420 (1986)

**Desk by D.I.M.** *(Photo courtesy of Christie's East)*

**Table in the style of Donald Deskey.** *(Photo courtesy of Christie's East)*

## Furnishings

*Side table*, attributed to Donald Deskey. Black-lacquered, rectangular top with rounded corners and four bent chrome legs joined at X on bottom. 27" tall x 11" long x 24" wide.

$418 (1987)

*Center table*, in the style of Donald Deskey, c. 1930. Two U-shape aluminum supports joined by stretcher and surmounted by a black glass top. 29¼" tall x 60¼" wide x 26¼" deep.

$2,420 (1986)

*Console*, by Dominique, French, 1931. In mahogany, the cabinet in the form of a heavily molded frame, the two doors with African genre scenes carved in liqueur wood, the whole set on carved turned feet, with marble top, unsigned. 43" tall x 88" wide x 21" deep.

$2,750 (1986)

*Side table*, by Dominique, French, c. 1927. In palissandre with sharkskin marquetry. Solid sloping support to semicircular base, and top completely covered on all sides with sharkskin.

$40,000–$46,000

*Bérgère*, by Maurice Dufrène, French. Covered in green satin with a gauffraged sunburst design.

$18,000–$21,000

*Bed/bateau*, by Jean Dunand, French, and André Arbus, c. 1937. In lacquered wood and galuchat (sharkskin), gondola-shaped, with caramel lacquer, on a galuchat-covered plinth, branded "Arbus." 18½" tall x 94¾" long x 60" wide.

$45,000–$65,000

*Table*, by Jean Dunand. Wooden, the top and four legs with hand-hammered surfaces, lacquered red and heightened with gilt, branded "Jean Dunand Lacquer." 19" tall, 25½" diam.

$11,000–$13,000

*Games table*, attributed to Jean Dunand, c. 1934, for the first-class lounge on the *Normandie*. Orange lacquered-wood table with flip top decorated with eggshell lacquer chessboard. 28" square.

$3,200 (1987)

*Parsons tables*, attributed to Jean-Michel Frank, French. In burled wood, one slightly smaller than the other. The larger, 17" tall, 17½" square; the smaller, 16" tall, 16½" square. Pair.

$990 (1986)

*Armchairs*, by Paul Theodore Frankl, American, c. 1930. In lacquered wood, red and black with detailing in gold, featuring Chinese squared volutes (scrolled designs) on the backs and arms and cloud lift frets beneath the seats. With metal tag "Skyscraper Furniture, Frankl Galleries, 4 East 48th Street, New York," and branded "CFC 2739." 35" tall. Pair.
$5,000–$7,000

*Chairs*, by Paul T. Frankl, c. 1930, same as above but with original damask fabric on the drop-in seats. Set of 6.
$5,000–$7,000

*Bookcase*, in the Skyscraper style, by Paul T. Frankl, American, c. 1927. Three modules in skyscraper form, with shelves, compartments, and bookshelves. Painted black with painted-silver edging.
$17,000 (1987)

*Coffee table*, by Paul T. Frankl, c. 1927. Overall triangular shape with flattened corners and three tiers. Painted black with silver edging.
$3,000 (1987)

*Coffee table*, by Paul T. Frankl. Rectangular cork top with curved ends on four short rectangular wooden legs, unmarked. 13½" tall x 70" long, 20½" diam.
$770 (1986)

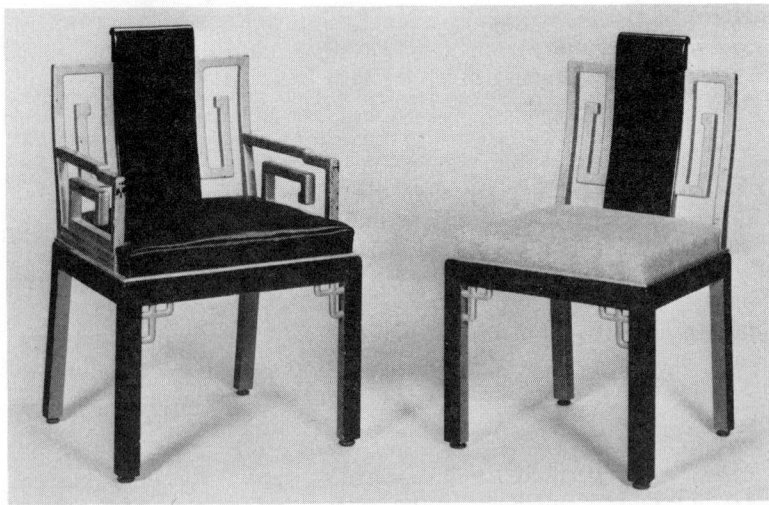

**Chairs by Paul Frankl.** *(Photo courtesy of Christie's East)*

# Furnishings

"Skyscraper" bookcase by Paul Frankl. *(Photo courtesy of Phillips)*

*Dressing table and stool,* by Paul T. Frankl, c. 1927. Table of silvered wood with the heads of llamas supporting the circular mirror. Gondola-form stool of black lacquered and silvered wood with a cutout below the seat. Metal tag "Skyscraper Furniture Frankl Galleries 4 East 48th St New York." Dressing table, 65" tall x 56" wide.

$13,200 (1987)

*Telephone desk,* by Paul T. Frankl. In gray lacquer with black Bakelite top and handles of satin chrome over brass. Matching chair reupholstered in black leather. 30" tall x 27" wide.

$17,500–$19,500

*Vanity,* by Paul T. Frankl. Mirrored glass top over two triangular gray-lacquered side doors divided by vertical silver borders with central undershelf, unsigned. 29" tall x 42" long x 18" wide.

$3,500–$4,000

*Couch and chair,* attributed to Paul T. Frankl, c. 1927. Steel frame in aerodynamic design. Two-seat couch has sloping arms from top of back to back to floor. Covered in gray leather.

$15,000–$17,000

*Console table*, by George Fry, for the G. Fox Department Store, c. 1937. In polished and gilded wrought iron and zebra wood, the central section lined with wood veneers, the outer sections with buttressing and squared volute terminals. All three sections with mirrored tops. 24" tall x 29¼" wide x 52" deep.

$5,000–$8,000

*Desserte boisée* (small wooden side cabinet), by Albert Guenot, French, c. 1925. In carved mahogany, rectangular form, the three hinged doors carved in geometric bas-relief. 61" tall x 86" long x 21½" deep.

$550 (1986)

*Table*, by Eileen Gray, Irish, worked in France, c. 1922. Black lacquered wood with tortoiseshell brown and dark brown panels in a geometric design set with gold particles. Long, low. 14⅛" tall x 51⅝" long x 12¼" deep.

$50,000–$53,000

*Coffee table*, by Heywood-Wakefield, American, c. 1935–40. In blond mahogany, the circular top supported by four curved legs joined by cross stretcher, stamped "Heywood-Wakefield, Platinum, M1578G." 15¼" tall, 38" diameter.

$165 (1986)

*Double chest of drawers*, by Heywood-Wakefield, c. 1935–40. Black-lacquered eight-drawer low dresser, each drawer having curved handle in silver leaf. Rectangular top. 34" tall x 53" long.

$700–900

*Mirrored vanity*, by Heywood-Wakefield, c. 1935–40. Black lacquered, with central circular mirror set on low curved base, deep kneehole with protruding two-drawer sides, silver knobs. 64" tall x 49" long x 18" wide.

$660 (1986)

*Vanity*, by Heywood-Wakefield, 1930s. Huge semicircular mirror reaches between cabinets almost to the floor. Maple side cabinets are curved, with curved drawers. Glass makeup shelf is suspended between cabinets and curved to allow chair closer access to mirror. 59" tall overall, side cabinet 17" deep.

$750–$950

*Bookcase nightstand*, Heywood Wakefield, matching above. 33" tall x 32" wide x 12" deep. Paper label intact.

$250–$285

## Furnishings

*Cocktail cabinet,* by Ray Hille, English, 1930s. U-base with fluted pale burl walnut veneer front, curved doors, and Bakelite handles. Main cabinet opens into a two-tiered mirrored bar. 65" tall x 55" wide.

$3,800–$4,300

*Bedroom set,* attributed to Ray Hille, English, 1930s. Six pieces: two armoires, vanity with mirror, two nightstands, and double bed in burl walnut veneer.

$1,400–$1,795

*Chair,* by Josef Hoffmann, Austrian, 1905. In unrefinished beechwood. Combines straight lines and bentwood to achieve a modern geometric look. Chair reclines. Manufactured by Jacob & Joseph Kahn. Paper manufacturer label intact.

$35,000–$36,500

*Settee* (sitting table set), by Josef Hoffmann, c. 1910, produced by Mundus. Bench, center table, two armchairs, and four side chairs. In beechwood with Wiener Werkstätte–designed fabric.

$19,950–$21,000

*Settee,* designed by Josef Hoffmann, c. 1908, produced by Mundus. Bench, two armchairs, four side chairs, center table, and side table in blond beechwood with Wiener Werkstätte–designed fabric.

$21,500–$23,000

*Rocking chair,* by Josef Hoffmann, c. 1903. In stained bent beechwood, saddle seat with original caning. Footrest is raised or lowered by use of a wooden bar support.

$35,000–$36,500

*Suite of furniture,* by Josef Hoffmann for Thonet. In black-painted bentwood, with a settee, a pair of tub armchairs, and a circular table. Paper labels intact.

$6,600 (1987)

*Vanity,* by Josef Hoffmann for J. & J. Kohn, 1906. In elm with square swinging mirror on curved bentwood frame, joined with wide sides to single drawer on tall straight legs, U-shape stretcher. 53" tall x 23½" long x 19" deep.

$330 (1986)

**Settee by Josef Hoffmann.** *(Photo courtesy of Gallery Vienna)*

**Bentwood rocker by Josef Hoffmann.** *(Photo by R. Four; courtesy of Galerie Metropol)*

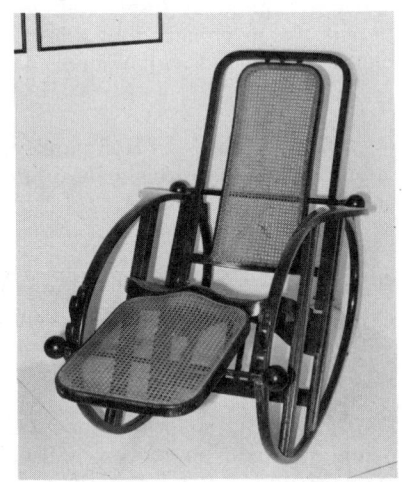

*Coffee table,* by Wolfgang Hoffmann, American (son of Josef Hoffmann), 1932, for Howell Manufacturing. In black-lacquered wood and chromed steel, rectangular with two tiers. 20″ tall x 20″ wide x 12″ deep.

$1,200–$1,400

*Desk and chair*, by Wolfgang Hoffmann, for Howell. Black-lacquered rectangular top supported by rectangular chrome sides joined in back by two struts and flanked on right side with two-drawer bay, chrome and ball handles, with an upholstered black-velveteen and chrome spring-back armchair. 30" tall.

$660 (1986)

*End tables*, by Wolfgang Hoffmann, American, c. 1935–40, for Howell. In black lacquer and chrome with three-tier rectangular open shelves joined by U-shape chrome support, unsigned. 22¼" tall x 30" long x 12" wide. Pair.

$330 (1986)

*Lamp table*, by Wolfgang Hoffmann, 1930s, for Howell. High-gloss black lacquer and tubular steel. Circular base and top with three legs. 26" tall, 20" diameter.

$650–$800

*Sofa*, by Wolfgang Hoffmann for Howell, c. 1935–40. Three-seat sofa with ebonized chrome armrests. 28" tall x 65" long x 34" wide.

$132 (1986)

*Armchairs*, by Wolfgang Hoffmann for Howell, c. 1935–40, same as above. Pair.

$110 (1986)

*Armchair*, by Paul Iribe, French, 1913. In French walnut, with high back and circular snail design on the sides of the armrests. Sometimes called the "Escargot Chair" because of this. Signed "Paul Iribe 1913." 42" tall.

$75,000–$78,000

*Chair*, by Marcel Kammerer, Austrian, 1906, manufactured by Thonet. Bent beechwood with inlaid lemonwood and circles of bird's-eye maple.

$3,500–$3,750

*Cabinet*, by Jules Leleu, French. In Macassar ebony with glazed central two-door vitrine, over two drawers with round knobs, flanked by two tall doors trimmed in gilt bronze. 63" tall x 83" long x 15½" deep.

$3,850 (1986)

*Cabinets*, by Jules Leleu, c. 1939. Ebonized cabinets with extensive ivory and mother-of-pearl inlay in the shape of flowers and feathers, and on trim. Signed. 51½" tall x 31" wide x 15" deep. Pair.

$20,000–$22,000

"Escargot Chair" by Paul Iribe. *(Photo by R. Four; courtesy of French and Company)*

**Coffee table by Jules Leleu.** *(Photo courtesy of Nancy McClelland, Christie's)*

*Coffee table,* by Jules Leleu. Mirrored top supported by a four-section pedestal base also faced in mirror, resting on four feet, with the firm's ivory tag. 20¼" tall, 35½" diameter.

$2,800–$3,400

*Coffee table*, by Jules Leleu. In mahogany with circular green marble top in conforming dish-shaped mount, set on three saber-shaped legs. 18" tall, 32" diameter.

$715 (1986)

*Cocktail table*, by Jules Leleu. Circular, with reverse-painted mirror top and gilt bronze frame on wooden tripod with gilt bronze sabots (foot covers). 20½" tall, 30½" diameter.

$3,500–$5,000

*Commode*, by Jules Leleu, c. 1925. In satinwood, the slightly bombé (curved) front inlaid with mother-of-pearl and various woods to depict Diana and Actaeon among scattered flower blossoms, heavy curved cabriole legs edged in brass. 73" wide x 19" deep x 36¼" tall.

$8,800 (1987)

*Console*, by Jules Leleu, French, c. 1925. In rosewood with distinctive U-shape styling and streamlined form. 30" tall x 25" wide x 13" deep.

$2,700–$2,850

*Sideboard cabinet*, by Jules Leleu, with lacquered top by Jean Dunand. In palissandre with caramel-color lacquered top and inlaid mother-of-pearl flowers, gilt-bronze trim and fittings. With the firm's ivory tag. 9' long.

$56,000–$60,000

**Console by Jules Leleu.** *(Photo courtesy of Bob Aibel, Moderne)*

## ART DECO

*Tabouret* (stool or footstool), by Jules Leuleu, c. 1927. African influence is apparent in this Macassar ebony piece with curved seat, a circular base, and octagonal terminals on the two legs. 23½" tall.
$25,000–$27,000

*Table*, by André Lurçat, French, c. 1930. Two-tiered, in glass and chromed metal, both tiers supported by chromed tubular steel supports. 24" tall, 31½" diameter.
$935 (1986)

*Armchairs*, by Warren MacArthur, American, c. 1935. In ebonized aluminum with horizontal arched slat back joined by end posts, ebonized armrests, and overlarge black leather-covered seat. Four legs, joined by stretcher. 35" tall. Pair.
$600–$800

*Bar stools*, by Warren MacArthur, 1930s. In spun aluminum with MacArthur's recognizable double-circle couplings. Seat and back in black vinyl. 38" tall. Pair.
$1,800–$2,000

*Chairs*, by Warren MacArthur. In spun aluminum, with rubber feet. Re-covered in beige leather. 31" tall x 22" wide. Set of eight.
$3,800–$4,000

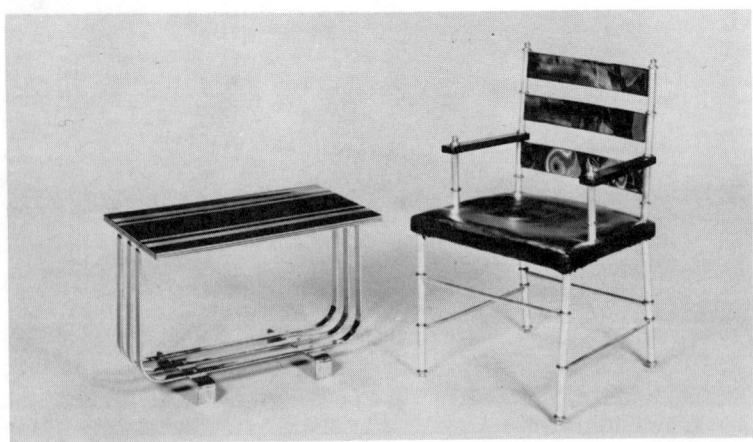

Armchair by Warren MacArthur and table by Kem Weber for Lloyd Manufacturing. *(Photo courtesy of Christie's East)*

## Furnishings

*Chair*, by Warren MacArthur. In spun aluminum, re-covered in mohair. 31" tall.

**$1,350–$1,500**

*Lamp table*, by Warren MacArthur. In spun aluminum, circular. 19½" tall, 16½" diameter.

**$1,350–$1,500**

*Tub armchair*, by Warren MacArthur, c. 1930. Blue leather-upholstered backrest joined to curved padded arms and circular seat. Four aluminum supports joined by curved stretcher at midpoint. Paper label intact. 33½" tall.

**$1,760 (1986)**

*Chairs and ottoman*, by McKay Company, American, late 1930s–1940s. Set of four chrome chairs and matching ottoman, with suspended seats of colorful striped canvas.

**$800 (1987)**

*Armchairs*, by Ludwig Mies van der Rohe, German (later worked in America), in the "Wassily" style, for Knoll Associates. Horizontal black leather strips form backrest and similar vertical seat, supported on rectangular chrome armature. 28½" tall. Pair.

**$165 (1987)**

*Armchairs*, by Ludwig Mies van der Rohe, 1926. Chrome "Mr." chairs upholstered in black leather. 32" tall. Pair.

**$400–$600.**

*Chairs and ottomans*, by Mies Van der Rohe, c. 1927. Pair of chairs with X-frames upholstered with leather straps and loose, tufted, brown-leather cushions, matching ottomans with leather seats and cushions (lacks three cushions). Chairs 29½" tall x 29½" wide.

**$1,540 (1986)**

*Hall stand*, by Nic Frères, French. In wrought iron and frosted glass, the basket-form hat rack over the large glass panel enclosed by vertical panels bearing hooks on both sides, flanked by columnar ends and having protruding umbrella stands. 73" tall x 55" long x 16" deep.

**$1,500–$2,000**

*Stereo cabinet*, by George Nelson, American, for Herman Miller. In walnut, rectangular top with four long drawers butting a two-door bay at right, on slender chrome legs with mushroom-shaped ends; original, white enameled waisted metal knobs, metal tag. 33¼" tall x 67½" long x 18½" deep.

$440 (1986)

*Modular vanity,* by George Nelson for Herman Miller. In walnut with two low four-drawer cabinets joined at sides by hinged desk top, opening to reveal a mirrored, lighted interior with frosted-glass divider. Metal tag, model 4661. 27" tall x 78" long, 18½" diameter.

$1,650 (1986)

*Sideboard,* by Parsinger. White-lacquered, the rectangular white glass top over double three-drawer chest with horizontally ribbed front and sides, horizontal chrome pulls, and raised ends on chrome-banded stretchers. 33" tall x 72" long, 20" diameter.

$495 (1987)

*Cabinet,* by Jean Pascaud, French, c. 1930. Outer case in ebony, interior in sycamore, doors veneered in sharkskin and set with bronze plaque and handle. Overall rectangular shape on plinth.

$25,000–$30,000

*Low table,* attributed to Bruno Paul, German, c. 1929. In walnut, square top with rounded corners. 3' square.

$1,500 (1987)

*Chairs,* by René Prou, c. 1933. Upholstered seats and backs. 34½" tall. Set of 6.

$1,760 (1986)

*Desk and chair,* by René Prou, c. 1933. Double-pedestal piece with four drawers in each undulating pedestal, the swivel chair en suite. 29" tall x 86½" wide x 39¼" deep.

$4,000–$6,000

*Coffee table,* by René Prou, c. 1933. The pedestal base of double and reversed ogee form set on a plinth. 17¾" tall x 47" wide x 31¼" deep.

$3,000–$4,000

*Coiffeuse,* by Armand-Albert Rateau, French, c. 1920–1922. In bronze, marble, and ivory, the mirror surrounded by three stylized marguerites (daisies) separated by butterflies and supported by two finely feathered pheasants with undulating foliage. Tabletop of black and white marble with bronze drawer featuring an ivory pull, surmounting finely cast reeded legs further enhanced by borders of flower blossoms,

stamped "A. A. Rateau Indu" twice and "Paris 1211 343C." 60½" tall x 35½" wide x 20¾" deep.
$110,000 (1987)

*Table*, by Armand-Albert Rateau, c. 1921–22. Rectangular top of cream marble, base of red-lacquered bronze in elaborate foliate designs, stamped "A. A. Rateau Paris." 30½" tall x 18½" wide x 10½" deep.
$55,000 (1987)

*Armchair*, by Gilbert Rohde, American, 1930s, for Herman Miller. Black-lacquered steel, with cushion in white vinyl with black piping. 33" tall x 23" wide.
$1,500–$1,750

*Chair*, by Gilbert Rohde, 1934, for Troy Sunshade Company. In tubular steel with black leather cushion and armrests. Spring base.
$1,800–$2,000

*Desk*, by Gilbert Rohde, for Herman Miller. In mahogany, central drop front with large knob, opening to reveal black pigeonhole interior, framed on all sides by shelved bookcase divided by glass and wood, on base composed of two long drawers. 47" tall x 60" long x 17" deep.
$2,500–$3,500

*Games table*, by Gilbert Rohde, 1930s, for Herman Miller. In inlaid fruitwood with inlaid chess/checkerboard and circular tapered legs. Inset in the table at each corner is a chrome ashtray with mesh screen.
$900 (1987)

*Planter end table*, by Gilbert Rohde. In blond mahogany, glass, and chrome, the clear rectangular glass top ending with two copper-lined planters, over open bay having long lower shelf with chrome pull, on black lacquer U-shaped supports. Model 4745. 22¼" tall x 34" long x 18" wide.
$198 (1986)

*Dining room suite*, by Charles Ross. Rectangular table on four tapering legs, four highback side chairs with wood seats with tapering legs. Table 30¾" tall x 73¾" long x 30¾" deep.
$1,000–$1,200
$330 (1987)

## ART DECO

*Manicurist's desk,* manufactured by Royal Chrome, 1920s. Black painted-wood desk with chrome-plated tubular legs, one drawer, and glass-door compartment. 31" tall x 30" wide x 15" deep.
$275–$350

*Armchair and ottoman,* by Jacques-Emile Ruhlmann, French, c. 1927. In Macassar ebony, leather, and bronze, the deep chair upholstered with brown leather, the frame outlined in Macassar and resting on rounded bronze feet. The ottoman same as above, unsigned. Chair 29¾" tall x 23" wide x 32¾" deep.
$13,200 (1986)

*Chiffonier* (kind of chest of drawers), "Fontane," by Jacques-Emile Ruhlmann, c. 1923. In Macassar ebony and ivory, of slightly bombé form, the double doors with ivory escutcheons opening to a shelved interior. Ivory stringing rising from the legs onto the cabinet and terminating in volutes, the top of the cabinet in stepped design, branded "Ruhlmann." 53¾" tall x 35½" wide x 15½" deep.
$37,400 (1986)

*Desk,* by Jacques-Emile Ruhlmann, French, c. 1924. This remarkable desk in palissandre, green-tinted galuchat, silvered bronze and ivory was the ambassador's desk in the Ambassade Française at the 1925 Paris Exposition. The top, with a geometric sunburst design worked into the sharkskin, was executed by Ruhlmann's top craftsman, Adolphe Chanaux. Documented. Signed/branded "Ruhlmann Atelier." 28¾" tall x 70¼" long x 45¼" deep.
$350,000–$370,000

*Salon suite,* "Ducharne," by Jacques-Emile Ruhlmann, c. 1928. Giltwood frame with beaded motif, the front legs of fluted design, comprising a settee and two armchairs, each branded "Ruhlmann." Settee 75½" wide, armchairs 35¾" tall.
$29,700 (1986)

*Bérgères,* by Jacques-Emile Ruhlmann, Paris, c. 1928. Same as the above. Pair.
$18,700 (1986)

*Sideboard cabinet,* by Jacques-Emile Ruhlmann. In palissandre, slightly bombé front with gilt-bronze fittings and two 3"-diameter medallions with stylized faces. 8½' long.
$15,000–$18,000

## Furnishings 137

*Side chair,* by Jacques-Emile Ruhlmann. In palissandre with wide, 1"-thick arms, terminating in a squared volute, grain running vertically down the arm to accentuate the lines of the chair, leather-upholstered.

$18,000–$21,000

*Side chair,* "Drouant," by Jacques-Emile Ruhlmann, c. 1924. In Macassar ebony and ivory, suede-covered back and seat, the legs terminating in sabots of ivory. 33" tall.

$2,860 (1986)

*Side chair,* by Jacques-Emile Ruhlmann, c. 1925. In Macassar ebony, with fluted back in a gondola form, drop-in seat, branded "Ruhlmann." 37¾" tall.

$5,500 (1986)

*Table,* by Jacques-Emile Ruhlmann for François Ducharne's l'Hotel Ducharne, Paris, c. 1928. In palissandre and giltwood, the top of rosewood, its grain radiating from the center. Three gilt-wood legs of slight cabriole form, the gilded apron of scalloped sections carved with muguet (lilies of the valley) and with the inscription "Sculpté pour la Famille Ducharne/Ruhlmann Le Bourgeois 1929," and branded "Ruhlmann" with the insignia of the atelier. 29" tall, 37" diameter.

$28,600 (1986)

*Twin beds and bedside cabinet,* by Eugene Schoen, American, c. 1929, executed by Schmieg, Hungate & Kotzian. In harewood and rosewood, each of simple rectangular form, together with a dressing unit. Headboards 30" tall, cabinet 2' long.

$1,500 (1987)

*Card table,* by Eugene Schoen, 1930s. In elm, walnut, and black ebony. Top laid so that wood grains are squares-within-squares and disappear to a point in the center. Numbered, perhaps commissioned. 28" tall, 35" square.

$10,000–$12,000

*Dining room table,* by André Sornay, French, 1934. Modernistic, angular design in palissandre veneer. Probably a special commission. 8'7" long x 3' wide. (For illustration see color insert.)

$40,000–$44,000

*Center table,* by André Sornay. In African mahogany, with his trademark design created by simple lines of inset brass nails. Two tiers. Overall 23" tall x 59" long x 25" wide.

$8,700–$8,900

*Armchair*, by Thonet Industries, German (but relocated to America), c. 1929. With bent, laminated plywood arms, legs, and back supports; armrest, back, and seat in yellow vinyl.

$325–$375

*Armchairs*, by Thonet. Bentwood chairs with arched back with pierced slat enclosing triangle design, joined to circular seat, stamped "Thonet." 32" tall. Pair.

$200–$400

*Armchairs*, by Thonet. Bentwood upholstered chairs with curved rectangular cushioned backrest suspended by red lacquered arched support, shaped sides in black vinyl. 33½" tall. Set of 4.

$660 (1986)

*Armchairs*, by Thonet. Tall padded backs with square seats joined by blonde wood bent arms, upholstered in black hopsacking. Paper label intact. 41" tall. Set of 3.

$308 (1986)

*Settee*, by Thonet. Bentwood settee with arched backrail enclosing three ovals, the center oval framed by curving tendrils, over the kidney-shaped seat on cabriole legs joined by high stretcher (no caning). 42" tall.

$462 (1987)

*Chair*, by Thonet, for Cafe Daum. In bentwood elm and cane, spoon back with heart-shaped design over caned circular seat on four slightly tapered legs joined by ring stretcher, stamped "193." 36" tall.

$100–$200

*Cradle*, by Thonet. In bentwood elm, the U-shaped support on twin legs supporting rectangular cradle, arched fronts with inverted U-shape bands, tall overhead crook. 43" tall x 41" long x 21" deep.

$275 (1986)

*Side chair*, by Thonet, c. 1935. Molded laminated plywood, back and seats in natural color, legs and back support made of wood painted to look like anodized aluminum.

$175–$225

*Table*, by Thonet. In bentwood elm, oval top of the center table supported on four curved legs joined at center and strongly arching to four turned legs, stamped "XIII." 30" tall x 32½" wide, 23" diam.

$660 (1986)

*End table,* by Kem Weber, American, for Troy Sunshade Company, c. 1935. Black lacquer and chrome, square top set on double carved chrome supports, arched to form handle, remnants of paper label. 2¾" tall x 15¾" long x 17¾" wide.

$330 (1986)

*Side tables,* by Kem Weber for Lloyd Manufacturing Company, c. 1935. Two-tier table, double chrome arched sides, with paper label; two-shelf sofa table, unsigned. Both in black lacquer and chrome. Table 25" tall x 22" long x 12" wide; sofa table 22" tall x 17½" long x 28" wide.

$308 (1986)

*Table,* by Kem Weber for Lloyd Manufacturing Company, c. 1935. Silver-inlaid ebonized and chrome table with rectangular top, two horizontal bands on three-pedestal arched base, joined by inverted side struts. Paper label. 18" tall x 27" long x 16" wide.

$770 (1986)

*Writing desk and chair,* by Kem Weber for Lloyd Manufacturing Company, c. 1935. In chrome, rectangular top with canted corners and one drawer, on four curved legs, joined as pairs and with stretcher, relacquered in red; black vinyl and chrome desk chair with label. Chair 33½" tall; desk 29" tall x 33" long x 21" deep.

$300–$400

*Cabinet/bookcase,* attributed to Kem Weber, American, c. 1935. Series of stacked designs in black and red lacquer. Some compartments have doors. Front edges are fluted and lacquered silver. Lower unit, 34½" tall x 41½" long x 12" deep. Three upper units in varying sizes; tallest adds 37½" to overall height.

$13,000–$15,000

*Vanity and stool,* Widdicomb Furniture Company, American. In walnut and mahogany, low rectangular top with sloped sides and long drawer at left, two drawers at right with ebonized-chrome handles. Long rectangular stool with leather padded seat and wood sides. Impressed manufacturer's tag. Vanity 23" tall x 47" long x 18" wide.

$700–$900

*Vanity and stool,* Widdicomb Furniture Company. In mahogany, ebonized vanity with low rectangular top over long drawer at right and two drawers at left with long, horizontal, lacquered and chrome handles. Tan upholstered circular stool on circular wooden stretcher. Vanity 26" tall x 46" long x 17" wide.

$550 (1987)

## ART DECO

*Chair*, by Frank Lloyd Wright, American, 1903. High-back chair from the Warren Hickox house in Kankakee, IL. Straight back with ten square spindles. Original dark brown finish.
$80,000–$84,000

*Side chair*, by Frank Lloyd Wright, c. 1916–22, for the Imperial Hotel, Tokyo. In oak, with the hexagonal back and the seat covered in yellow oilcloth. 37¾" tall.
$20,900 (1986)

*Spindle side chair*, by Frank Lloyd Wright, for the Ward W. Willits House, Highland Park, IL. In oak, with a broad crest rail surmounting vertical spindles that join the stretcher below the seat, the feet and the terminals canted slightly backward, the drop-in seat covered in leather and secured with screws. Original dark brown finish. 56¼" tall.
$198,000 (1986)

*Armchair*, anon., American, 1930s. Inlaid and stuffed, curved back with sleigh-like wooden design in scrolled and geometric patterns. Original yellow upholstery.
$550 (1987)

*Bar*, anon., American, 1930s. Black lacquered, gilt, and airbrushed. Triangular form, divided in sections by "skyscraper" side relief; original gilt and airbrush design of repetitive circles. 49" tall x 59" long.
$1,650 (1987)

Chair by Frank Lloyd Wright.
*(Photo by R. Four; courtesy of Struve Gallery)*

## Furnishings

*Bar*, anon., American, 1930s. Custom design, both bar and back wall in lacquer, blue mirror, glass, and chrome, with chrome footrest that runs the length of the bar. Fully restored. (For illustration see color insert.)

**$12,000–$13,000**

*Bar/cabinet*, anon., American, late 1930s. In polished walnut, two-door storage with shelves below, upper portion opening to reveal mirrored bar with light, ashtray, and toothpick holder. 44" tall x 73" wide x 14" deep.

**$375–$450**

*Bar cabinet and pair of stools*, anon., American, 1930s. Mahogany and ebonized cabinet of shallow rectangular form, with four-bay grid enclosing silver and black Deco design. Two matching round stools with silver seats. 48" tall x 57" long x 13" wide.

**$500–$700**

*Cabinet*, anon., American, 1930s. In mahogany and walnut, rectangular, two-part cabinet with open bay on right, three-quarter door and open bay on left, supported on long rectangular three-door plinth raised on ebonized sled base. 60" tall x 51" long x 15" wide.

**$300–$500**

*Chair*, anon., American, 1930s. May have been designed to be shown at the World's Fair furniture exhibit in Chicago. Circular seat and spiral-design back that spirals down in front below seat level. Upholstered in new mohair with a feather cushion and hand-tied spring units.

**$1,700–$1,900**

*Chairs*, anon., American, late 1930s. Probably designed for an office or a nightclub. In original leather, with solid, rounded dark brown arms, and rounded backs and seats in burgundy or tan leather. Pair.

**$900–$1,000**

*Coffee table*, anon., American, 1930s–1940s, or a 1970s reproduction. Stained blond wood in need of refinishing. Top has slight curve and inset blue mirrored glass in fair condition. Legs are vertically banded. Two tiers. 17" tall x 32" long x 17" wide.

**$75–$100**

*Coffee table*, anon., American. Circular glass top supported on tripod walnut stand joined by circular brass armature. 17" tall.

**$500–$700**

Chairs from an American nightclub, designer unknown. *(Photo courtesy of Paul Fuhrman, The Warehouse)*

*Console,* anon., American. In composition material with mirrored rectangular top over clamshell support on rococo base, painted white. 33" tall x 37½" long, 14" diameter.
$400–$600

*Console,* anon., American. Triangular mirror set in conforming chrome link mount, and console having opaque black glass top with canted sides, trimmed with brass diamond band, over triangular and diamond stretcher. 35" tall x 40" long, 10" diameter.
$2,000–$3,000

*Daybed,* anon., American, 1930s. In mahogany and metal, the cushioned sofa with long, low wood back flanked by D-ends, one with shelf and underdrawer, gilt chrome accents. 30" tall x 94" long x 24" wide.
$220 (1987)

*Desk/cabinet,* anon., American, 1920s. In bird's-eye maple and walnut, drop front, with desk at left and glass vitrine at right, supported on four-door base. 67" tall x 70" long x 16" wide.
$400–$600

*Display bookcase,* anon., American, 1930s. In black-painted wood with three shelves, two central dividers. 36″ tall x 41″ wide x 9½″ deep.
**$250–$350**

*End table,* anon., American, 1930s–1940s or a 1970s reproduction. Stained blond wood, in need of refinishing. Top has slight curve and inset blue mirrored glass in fair condition. Legs are vertically banded. 25″ tall x 21″ long x 12½″ wide.
**$75–$100**

*End table,* anon., American, 1930s. U-shaped with stepped-back designs on base in walnut. Rectangular with inset blue mirrored glass in excellent condition. 24″ tall x 22″ long x 14″ wide.
**$350–$400**

*Living room chairs,* various anon., American, late 1930s. Living room chairs with deep seats, wide arms. Overstuffed look, with rounded edges and occasionally with wood veneer trim.
Unrefinished and unrestored **$500–$600**
Restored and reupholstered **$1,500–$2,000**

*Living room set,* anon., American. Including a sofa and a pair of tub chairs, upholstered in maroon velveteen, of low shape with tufted vertical divisions.
**$275 (1986)**

*Living room set,* anon., American, 1930s. Three-piece mohair set with deep seats, curved cushioned arms, and stylized wooden feet. In need of repairs.
**$600 (1987)**

*Parlor set,* anon., American, 1930s. In split reed rattan with geometric-pattern leather cushions in orange and black. Includes couch, two chairs, and lamp table.
**$3,300 (1987)**

*Side table,* anon., American, c. 1930. Black-lacquered with frosted glass pedestal, hexagonal form, fitted for electricity. 26½″ tall.
**$154 (1986)**

*Side table,* anon., American, c. 1940. In chrome, rectangular top with canted corners inset with tinted blue mirror above an ebonized frieze raised on a chrome base. 31″ tall x 37″ wide.
**$2,090 (1986)**

*Sofa*, anon., American, late 1930s. High back and overstuffed cushions. Central cushion is higher than others, which are vertically cut in three sections each. Rounded edges and wood veneer trim. Deep-seated.
Unrefinished and unrestored $700–$800
Restored and reupholstered $2,500–$2,750

*Vanity*, anon., American, c. 1935–40. In blond wood, with large circular glass mirror set on long pedestal, flanked on left with four-drawer dresser with glass knobs. Overall 58½" tall x 59½" long x 18" deep.
$330 (1986)

*Vanity and pair of nightstands*, anon., American. Lacquered black, white, and gray, the large circular mirror flanked by low doors, joined by stretcher, including a pair of matching lighted, one-door nightstands. 54" tall.
$495 (1987)

*Vanity and stool*, anon., American, 1930s. In walnut, the rounded low stretcher supporting two drawers at left with white glass top, and at right a circular stand inset with revolving rectangular chrome mirror having white-upholstered, three-legged stool. 44" long x 16½" wide; 12" mirror.
$605 (1987)

*Bar cabinet*, anon., French. In mahogany, rectangular form with burled front doors, geometric rays. 35" tall x 18" long x 14" deep.
$400–$600

*Cabinet*, anon., French, c. 1920. Rectangular black marble top over wider, two-door, green-stained mahogany cabinet with horizontal curved molding and brass piping on sled base, two pedestals. 42" tall x 99" long x 23" deep.
$1,800–$2,500

*Chauffeuses* (fireplace chairs), anon., French, c. 1930. Probably a special commission. Upholstered in beige leather with ebony back reinforcement on base, designed to show triangular ebony design from side. Pair.
$30,000–$31,500

*Corner cabinet*, anon., French, late 1920s. Special commission in Macassar ebony. Side hutches have tall doors, central piece has two panel doors bleached and set so that grain runs in angular pattern to central rectangle in nickel. Nickel fittings and keys. 6' overall.
$5,400–$5,800

## Furnishings

*Dining room suite,* anon., French. In elm, with a dining table resting on U-shape sled base, joined by brass stretchers (one 15" leaf); 30" tall x 56" long x 39" wide; six matching side chairs, 33" tall; and two demilune sideboards, one with bar area above two doors, the other with two doors. 39" tall x 45" long x 18" wide.
$308 (1987)

*Dressing mirror/vanity,* anon., French, c. 1922. In burl walnut, with inlaid squares of ivory and onyx pulls. Drawers, one on each side, are almost circular and are surrounded on three sides by the curve of the back. Elongated oval mirror. 78" tall x 57" wide.
$1,250–$1,350

*Music cabinet,* anon., French, 1920. In mahogany with *coquille d'oeuf* (eggshell) lacquer. Small gallery with curved sides, supported on rectangular top with volute ends on waisted rectangular one-door stand, centering rectangular blue enamel plaque lacquered silver and red, inlaid with eggshell in stepped geometric motif, artist-initialed "M.H.," opening to reveal four bays. 55" tall x 28" long x 16½" deep.
$1,210 (1986)

*Pedestal desk,* anon., French, 1930s. In mahogany, rectangular top supported on pedestals, each having three drawers with chrome handles. 30" tall x 55" long x 30¾" wide.
$600–$800

French dressing mirror/vanity, designer unknown. *(Photo courtesy of Bob Aibel, Moderne)*

*Secretary,* anon., French, c. 1930. In walnut with sharply triangular pulls in onyx. Open bookshelf surmounted by three drawers and secretary. Fronts have geometric designs within the wood grain. Sides have a stepped-back pattern in three layers of wood. Marble top. Approx. 46" tall x 26" wide x 18" deep.

$4,500–$4,800

*Side chairs,* anon., French, probably 1920s. In Macassar ebony, the upholstered tapering back joined to wide seat set on cabriole legs. 33" tall. Set of 4.

$440 (1987)

*Sideboard,* anon., French, c. 1930. In exotic woods and metal, a smaller stepped rectangular tier above the rectangular top with bombé two-door front flanked by two outer doors, all having lighter marquetry square on front with gilt-bronze circular hardware, on undulating pedestal base. 40" tall x 118" long, 26" diameter.

$1,000–$1,500

*Sideboards,* anon., French, c. 1930. Studio production or special commission. Painted black with sanded glass panels with brass frames and crosshatch designs. Mirrored tops. 4' tall x 5' long x 16" deep. Pair.

$35,000–$36,500

*Smoking table,* anon., French, c. 1935. In Macassar ebony with sharkskin top. Octagonal top with drawer on pedestal base, ball feet. 22" tall, top 20" wide.

$7,500–$8,000

*Armoire,* anon., English, 1930s. In walnut veneer, two doors with Bakelite handles, fitted interiors. Inside compartments with glass doors have metal labels marked "Shirts," "Collars," "Sportswear," "Pajamas," etc. 70" tall x 46" wide x 20" deep.

$600–$800

*Bedroom suite,* anon., English, 1930s. In bird's-eye maple and walnut, including three-door armoire, two-door armoire, pair of end tables, mirrored vanity, and headboard, all rectangular with three horizontal bands of walnut veneer.

$1,500–$2,000

*Bookcase,* anon., English. In burl walnut, glass, and brass, rectangular top with rounded corners over two sliding glass doors housed in case with rounded sides and four protruding horizontal divisions, supported on sled base trimmed in brass, with one blond mahogany shelf. 38½" tall x 48" long x 16½" deep.

$1,045 (1986)

*Chair*, anon., English, 1930s. Maple framework with black lacquer. Seat depth 27", and arms in four horizontal planes from back to arm support. Two cushions, restored in original pink satin.

$1,500–$1,650

*Chairs*, anon., English, 1930s. Gondola or tub style, with curved backs and tapered legs in burl walnut. Set of 4.

$800–$1,000

*Chairs*, anon., English, 1930s. Bird's-eye maple veneer shell back with tan plaid velveteen upholstered front and slat on four straight legs. 34" high. Set of 6.

$300–$500

*Cocktail cabinet*, anon., English, 1930s. "Hollywood" style, in burl walnut. Flat front swings out to reveal two semicircular bar trays in peach mirror glass and two built-in drawers. Interior is veneered in ash. 55" tall x 36" wide x 17½" deep.

$2,700–$3,100

*Curio case*, anon., English. Curved walnut glass-front case with mirrored back, glass shelves, painted decorated glass-front doors. 45" tall x 40" wide x 14" deep.

$525–$750

*Curio case/secretary*, anon., English, 1930s. "Moon"-style cabinet in walnut veneer with glass shelves and glass painted to appear etched. Fabric-lined interior. 48" circular cabinet on 6" plinth.

$500–$700

*Curio case/secretary*, anon., English, 1930s. In walnut with glass doors on side hutches, and drop-front desk. Interior woods blond. Approx. 3½' tall x 3' wide x 1' deep.

$1,200–$1,300

*Love seat and chair*, anon., English, 1930s. In original cut mohair. Brown, orange, and beige with both straight lines and contrasting large stylized triangles.

$1,200–$1,400

## ART DECO

*Side chair*, anon., English, 1930s. Mahogany framework, refinished and upholstered in original green leather with white-and-red leather trim and piping.
$975–$1,050

*Table*, anon., English, 1930s. Walnut table with bombé legs. 72" long x 36" wide.
$800–$1,000

*Bedroom suite*, anon., Italian. In amboyna, with mirrored vanity and stool, mirrored dresser, mirrored armoire, pair of end tables, and pair of twin bedsteads including rails.
$1,100 (1987)

*Mirror and hall rack*, anon. Hat shelf above marble rack, the central square mirror in conforming sunburst, geometric wrought-iron mount with low black marble shelf and seven coat hooks. 29" tall x 39" long x 12" wide.
$385 (1987)

*Ship's cocktail table*, anon. Upright bar in square mount swings with the movement of the ship, fitted with a central cocktail shaker flanked by four matching glasses hanging vertically in separate swinging holders, the far ends with transparent glass panels. 27½" tall x 25" wide.
$500–$700

*Sofa*, anon. Upholstered, with low padded back over deep seat, rounded pillow arms, on encurvate walnut trim base. 28" tall x 80" long x 38" wide.
$440 (1987)

### Lamps and Lighting

*Torchères*, by American Rubber Products, American, 1930s. In chrome, the clover molded circular base and circular stem supporting two-part trumpet lamp etched with floral design, marked. 74" tall. Pair.
$600–$800

*Floor lamp*, by Edgar Brandt, French, c. 1925. In wrought iron and glass, the mottled polychrome glass shade supported by a shaft of numerous intricately worked sections, the base of in-turned cushion form, stamped "E. Brandt." 74" tall.
$28,600 (1986)

*Floor lamp*, by Edgar Brandt. Flared cylindrical four-section alabaster shade on a wrought-iron base with six slender notched columns, separated by beading and rings, raised on a spiraled and domed six-sided base, impressed "E. Brandt." Restoration to one section of shade. 73″ tall.

$6,000–$8,000

*Table lamp*, by Edgar Brandt and Daum. In wrought iron and glass, the six plum- and orange-mottled translucent glass shades on six slender curved arms continuing to a banded column, forming a ginkgo tree, raised on a domed, hammered, six-sided base, impressed "E. Brandt," shades inscribed "Daum Nancy." 25½″ tall.

$13,200 (1986)

*Torchère*, attributed to Edgar Brandt, c. 1925. In wrought iron and alabaster, silvered base with openwork floral and geometric motifs raising a flat circular shade. 6′ tall.

$2,000–$4,000

*Floor lamps*, "La Religieuse," by Pierre Chareau, French, c. 1928. Cuban mahogany, sliced, sharply triangular alabaster and painted metal. The alabaster gives the impression of a French nun's habit, thus the name. 73½″ tall. Pair.

$250,000–$260,000

*Chandelier*, by Albert Cheuret, French. Scalloped and curved patinated bronze arms support two tiers of fitted alabaster sections, impressed "Albert Cheuret." 32″ tall x 33″ wide.

$33,000 (1986)

*Floor lamp*, by Albert Cheuret, c. 1924. Silvered bronze and alabaster. Stylized leaf motif of pyramid base and square support leads to flowerlike fixture in diamonds of white alabaster. Shown at the 1925 Paris Exposition.

$50,000–$60,000

*Chandelier*, by Daum Nancy, French. Domed shade of clear glass, etched with radiating columns and random ovals, on a trumpet-shaped column etched with vertical bands, both impressed "Daum Nancy France." 24″ tall, 15⅞″ shade diameter.

$3,850 (1986)

*Lamp*, by Daum Nancy, 1930s. Rounded base and mushroom-shaped top in white frosted glass with pink staining. Acid-cut geometric design. Original electrification. Approx. 14″ tall.

$18,500–$20,000

## ART DECO

*Lamp*, by Daum Nancy, c. 1925. In frosted, colorless glass with silvered shade support, inscribed "Daum Nancy France" with the cross of Lorraine, firm's mark. 15½" tall.
$3,000–$5,000

*Lamp*, by Daum, c. 1930. Domed shade and matching ovoid base of clear glass, deeply etched with radiating columns and random circles, shade and base etched "Daum Nancy France." 21" tall, 18¾" shade diameter.
$8,250 (1986)

*Lamp*, by Donald Deskey, American, c. 1932, for Radio City Music Hall. In chromed metal and Bakelite, with dome-shaped up-lighter, base circular with four cylindrical supports. 67½" tall.
$3,300 (1986)

*Table lamp*, by Donald Deskey, c. 1929, for Deskey-Vollmer. In chrome-plated metal and wood. Dome-shaded adjustable reading lamp with semicircular support that rests on curved wooden base. 15¼" tall, 8¾" shade diameter.
$2,000–$2,500

*Lamp/sculpture*, by Jean Goulden, French, c. 1925. Composed of alternating geometric forms in silver, turquoise blue enamel, and frosted glass panels on the lights. Goulden was inspired by Byzantine enameling and taught by Jean Dunand. Some cracks on glass. Approx. 14" tall.
$85,000–$89,000

*Lamp*, "Paons" (peacocks), by René Lalique, French, c. 1921. Square-sectioned stem tapering from spreading base with bracket-type feet. Each face molded in etched glass with a peacock with elongated tail feathers. Molded "R. Lalique." 15½" high.
$7,000–$10,000

*Sconce*, by Jules Leleu, French. Two-arm gilt-bronze and glass, the circular mount supporting two gently curved arms, each with a glass disk ending in a pleated cream shade, stamped "LELEU, Paris, Made in France, PZ78846." 13" tall.
$250–$300

*Luminaires*, after Louis Majorelle. In patinated bronze and etched glass, the cylindrical shade with etched geometric design on circular martelé green-patinated base with four pierced oval insets. 11" tall. Pair.
$600–$800

**Lamp/sculpture by Jean Goulden.** *(Photo courtesy of Audrey Friedman, Primavera Gallery)*

**"Paons" lamp by René Lalique.** *(Photo by Frank Cooper, from a private collection)*

*Table lamp,* by Gilbert Rohde, American, c. 1933, executed by Mutual-Sunset Lamp Manufacturing Co., Inc., Brooklyn. Long, cylindrical, chrome-plated shade on a tubular C-shape arm, continuing to form a base flanked by two cylindrical tubes, unsigned. 14" long.
$2,860 (1987)

*Lamp*, by Sabino, French. In smoked, frosted glass, geometric teardrop shape, molded with three levels of circles, mounted as a lamp. 13" high.

$300–$600

*Luminaire*, by Sabino. In gilt and lacquered metal, footed trumpet form, the silvered gray ground with borders of gilt and brown lacquered leaves, incised "Sabino, Paris." 17" tall.

$462 (1986)

*Table lamp*, by Schneider, French. In glass and silvered metal, the circular foot molded with stylized overlapping blossoms, flaring cylindrical standard with similar vertically striped decoration, holding a white-to pink-flecked glass shade with shaped metal border, shade etched "Schneider." 21" tall.

$800–$1,200

*Torchère*, by Carl Sorensen, Swedish (worked in America), 1930s. In bronze, the fluted trumpet-form light supported on columnar pedestal, impressed "Carl Sorensen." 64" tall.

$825 (1987)

*Luminaire*, attributed to Süe et Mare, French. In carved alabaster, domed oval shade carved as a profusion of overlapping rose and poppy blossoms with leafage, pierced in places for light emission, overhanging the oval base carved with ribbed stylized petal on lobed foot housing the lighting element, unsigned. 11½" tall.

$8,000–$10,000

*Desk lamp*, by Walter Dorwin Teague, American, c. 1939, for Polaroid Corporation, Cambridge. In brown Bakelite and aluminum with brown hood shade, supported on conical shaft with circular base, paper label. 12¾" tall x 11½" wide.

$1,500–$1,750
$825 (1986)

*Floor lamp*, by Kurt Versen, American, 1930s. In keeping with Versen's style, lamp top can flip on its hinge from torchère position to reading lamp position. 61" tall.

$450–$600

*Desk lamp*, by M. G. Wheeler Company, Inc., American. In black-painted metal and brass, the lamp on square black platform with spherical brass knob, pivoting arched arm, and flat, layered circular black shade. Paper label intact.

$55 (1986)

Furnishings 153

Polaroid desk lamp by Walter Dorwin Teague. *(Photo courtesy of Christie's East)*

*Desk lamp,* anon., American. Rectangular polished-steel base with curved arm supporting a faceted rectangular shade applied with buttresslike clips on foot and around the rim, unmarked. 19" tall.
$700–$900

*Sconces,* anon., American, 1930s. Vertical chrome mounts with skyscraper stepped finial, holding seven vertical panels of frosted glass to form a faceted vertical shade, interesting switch system for controlling color and intensity of lighting, unmarked. 23" long. Pair.
$2,090 (1987)

*Table lamp,* anon., American, c. 1935. Triangular stem formed of three aluminum rods issuing from cylindrical black knob on circular aluminum base, unmarked. 24" tall with shade.
$55 (1986)

*Torchères,* anon., American. In chrome, the circular foot supporting tall stem with inverted trumpet lamp. 70" tall. Pair.
$880 (1987)

*Boudoir lamp,* anon., French. With floral frosted shade, buffed wrought-iron base with leaves and berry decoration, signed "France." 12½" tall.
$175–$200

*Torchère,* anon., French, c. 1930. In walnut and brass, with flaring cylindrical wood standard on circular base, surmounted by a decorative carved spherical wood knob, raising a flared brass shade, unmarked. 70" tall.
$650–$800

*Torchère,* anon., French. Black and red lacquered, on square black base, the red stem divided by a black square surmounted by a transparent glass knop, silvered shade with winglike projections of clear and frosted glass. 74" tall.

$770 (1986)

*Floor lamp,* anon. In alabaster, in the form of a stork standing on a pedestal. 61" tall.

$1,800–$1,890

*Lamp,* anon., 1920s. A nude holding crystal-gazing ball, seated on alabaster stepped base with two columns supporting flame shades. 14½" x 6¾"; base 21½" tall.

$2,000–$2,100

*Lighting fixture,* anon. The square chrome framework hung from the ceiling by four rods, holding a square panel of frosted glass, unmarked. 29⅝" long from ceiling.

$242 (1987)

*Mounted globe,* anon. In wrought iron, the spherical shade of frosted glass, molded with foliate panels, on a footed, encircling, wrought-iron mount, unmarked. 11¼" tall.

$198 (1987)

## Other Furnishings

*Andirons,* by Edgar Brandt, French, c. 1928. In wrought iron with almost square bases from which a pair of serpents rise and intertwine to a face-to-face position on the top of each andiron. Approx. 17½" tall. Pair.

$38,000–$42,000

*Andirons,* by Donald Deskey, American. In gilt bronze, each of flat-sided rectangular form tapering to forward-slanting top, on cast-iron base. 19½" tall. Pair.

$880 (1987)

*Andirons,* anon., American. In gilt bronze, cast to resemble stylized feathers, unsigned, pair. 12½" tall.

$176 (1986)

Andirons by Edgar Brandt. *(Photo courtesy of Audrey Friedman, Primavera Gallery)*

*Ashstand*, "Climax Cocktail Smoker," by W. J. Campbell, American, 1934, for Climax Machinery Co., Indianapolis. In steel and aluminum with circular base, five tubular steel legs on a horizontal plane; and circular stand. 26½" tall, 16½" rim diameter.

$800–$1000

*Ashstand*, anon., American, c. 1930. Painted cast iron, cast as a long-legged Black waiter in red tailcoat, holding tray with ashtray and covered cigarette box, unmarked. 32" tall.

$286 (1986)

*Floor ashtray*, anon., American, 1930s. In bronzed metal, handle across the top surmounted with leaping gazelle.

$75–$125

*Ashstand*, anon., 1930s, probably American. In iron, with black, triangular base with raised painted gold triangles, triangular top with raised gold section for ashes, and 5" standing scottie. 19" tall.

$125–$175

*Carpet,* attributed to Marion Dorn, English. In wool with two vertical bands of staggered yellow rectangles on tufted beige ground, unsigned. 128" long x 109" wide.

$825 (1986)

*Carpet,* by Ruth Reeves, American, c. 1932, for Donald Deskey for Radio City Music Hall. In wool, depicting abstract guitars and banjos in alternating rectangular repeats in shades of salmon, gray, cinnamon, and tan, woven reverse "Radio City Music Hall." 143" long x 109" wide.

$2,860 (1986)

*Carpet fragment,* by Ruth Reeves, c. 1932, for Donald Deskey for Radio City Music Hall. In wool, depicting abstract guitars and banjos in alternating rectangular repeats in shades of salmon, gray, cinnamon, and tan, pieced. 38" long x 24½" wide.

$352 (1986)

*Carpet,* anon., French, c. 1920. Hand-loomed, incorporating floral design in salmon, lime, and ivory bordered by gray, ivory, and brown. 216" diameter.

$1,000–$1,500

*Carpet,* anon., French, c. 1929. Machine-made wool carpet in cocoa, with cream and dark brown geometric design. 93½" long x 66" wide.

$150–$225

*Carpet,* anon. In wool, machine-made carpet with allover colorful decorative motif similar to the Deco frieze of the Chanin Building. 9'11" long x 8'8" wide.

$605 (1987)

*Carpet,* anon. In wool, gray ground with bronze rectangle encircled by orange stepped, geometric framework. 139" long x 98" wide.

$2,000–$2,500

*Fire screen,* by Edgar Brandt, c. 1925. In gilt-bronze-mounted wrought iron, the central section depicting a dancing figure, impressed signature "E. Brandt." 33½" tall.

$6,750 (1987)

*Fire screen,* attributed to Wilhelm Hunt Diederich, America, c. 1925. In wrought iron with stylized matador and bull. 3'6" long.

$2,000–$2,500

## Furnishings

Fire screen by Edgar Brandt. *(Photo courtesy of William Doyle Galleries)*

Fire screen by Wilhelm Hunt Diederich. *(Photo courtesy of William Doyle Galleries)*

*Fire screen,* anon., French. In wrought iron and frosted glass, the rectangular geometric etched-glass panel inset in conforming black-painted wrought-iron mount. 35″ tall.

**$715 (1987)**

*Hall stand,* anon., French. In wrought iron, the canted rectangular mirror inset against two horizontal planks, with shelf hat rack on top and protruding umbrella stand at base. 71″ tall x 25″ long.

**$350–$500**

*Mirror,* anon., American, c. 1935. In blue glass, the circular mirror center set in conforming octagonal blue glass frame, on four Lucite ball rests. 24″ diameter.
$77 (1986)

*Mirror,* anon., French, c. 1920. The oval mirror set in wrought-iron frame with conforming foliate sides. 39″ diameter.
$700–$900

*Mirror,* anon., French, c. 1920. In peach glass and chrome, the circular mirrored plate set in conforming chrome mounts. 71″ diameter.
$1,210 (1986)

*Mirror,* anon., French, c. 1920. In oval wrought-iron frame with fan-shaped sides flanked by branches. 34″ tall.
$200–$300

*Mirror,* anon., German, c. 1935. Cheval swivel rectangular mirror with rounded edges on low, squared mount. 70″ tall.
$400–$525

*Mirror,* anon., 1930s. Circular blue glass with silver-colored plaster sailing ship mounted on center bottom. 24″ diameter.
$85–$135

*Panel,* by E. Paul Sain, French. Rectangular, painted gold leaf depicting two stags in a stylized landscape with trees at right side, painted signature. 74″ tall x 72¾″ wide.
$800–$1,200

*Pedestal,* by Clément Rousseau, French, c. 1923. In Macassar ebony, each side of the base with stepped triangular device, inscribed on the top "Clement Rousseau Sc." and inside in pen, "Clement Rousseau Sc 1923." 47⅜″ tall.
$6,600 (1986)

*Scatter rug,* by Jules Leleu, French, c. 1920. A woven work rug with rectangular lime and forest green ground and three stepped geometric areas. 68″ long x 35″ wide.
$2,090 (1986)

*Scatter rug,* by Marion Dorn, c. 1930. In woven wool, rectangular, the beige ground with entwined three-swirl design in green, peach, and red. 70″ long x 36″ wide.
$1,210 (1986)

*Screen,* by Léon Jallot, French, c. 1925. Wooden screen, carved and lacquered, the two hinged rectangular panels finely carved and lacquered on the obverse and reverse with underwater scenes of tropical fish, shells, plants, and other marine life in shades of brown, green, and red on a metallic green ground; inscribed signature, 67" tall x 72" wide. Offered with four original pencil and watercolor sketches by Jallot of the fish on the screen and a fifth drawing in pencil of the entire screen, each with Jallot's monogram.

$14,000–$18,000

## Clocks

*Mantel clock,* by Bond Electric, American. The circular clock face, in black diamond-shape Bakelite frame held in flared rectangular tortoiseshell Bakelite mount with silver feet, marked. 7" tall.

$44 (1986)

*Table clock,* by J. E. Caldwell, American, c. 1934. In green onyx with arched casing and rectangular plinth. Wood inset to complete design at angle of base and casing. 7" tall x 9" long. Working.

$125–$150

*Mantel clock,* "*Telechron,*" by Paul T. Frankl, American, for Warren Telechron Co., c. 1929. The rectangular face, of radiating brush-burnished brass, set in a chromed and black-enameled metal housing raised on a black Bakelite base, face painted "Telechron" with firm's applied tag. 7¾" tall. (For illustration see color insert.)

$1,100–$1,200
$770 (1987)

*Mantel clock,* "*Telechron,*" designed by Paul T. Frankl for Warren Telechron Co., c. 1929. The rectangular face, of radiating brush-burnished brass, set in a chromed and black-enameled metal housing raised on a black Bakelite base, engraved "Presented to Dr. Felix E. Held by the Business Men's Economics Discussion Club, Akron, Ohio May 12, 1931," with firm's metal tag. 7¾" tall.

$528 (1986)

*Table clock,* by Josef Hoffmann, Austrian, c. 1906, executed by Alfred Meyer for the Wiener Werkstätte. In silver, the circular face with stylized Arabic chapters, in a rectangular latticework silver body raised on a domed rectangular base, base engraved with crest and "Et Si Ostendo Non Jacto," impressed "WW" with Austrian punch mark, firm's *rosenmarke,* designer's mark, and silversmith's mark. 11" tall, 63 troy oz.

$60,500 (1986)

Clock by Josef Hoffmann. *(Photo courtesy of Nancy McClelland, Christie's)*

*Clock*, by Josef Hoffmann, c. 1913. In silvered metal, square clock bridges two rectangular bases. Front of clock is square-within-a-square pattern, and sides and bases are fluted vertically. Approx. 14" tall.
$85,000–$87,000

*Oven timer and clock*, "Telechron," by Hotpoint, American, 1930s. Curved triangular shape and triangular numerals on face. Marked "Telechron" and "GE" on face. Mounted on black base at a later date. 8" tall.
$145–$165

*Mantel clock*, by E. L'Adrin, French, c. 1930. In onyx and silvered bronze, the ziggurat-form clock in white onyx alternating with striated red/brown marble cut to form rays, and housing diamond-shape face above a silvered bronze relief cast as two polar bears in craggy arctic wasteland, impressed "E. L'Adrin." 17½" tall x 19¼" long.
$1,000–$1,500

*Glass clock*, "Deux Figurines," by René Lalique, c. 1925. Metal-mounted clear and frosted glass clock/luminaire of arched form, molded with two maidens flanking a floral garland centered by a clock face. The tabular glass surround inscribed "R. Lalique France," on polished chrome metal base. 14¾" tall.
$6,000–$8,000
$6,250 (1987)

# Furnishings

*Glass clock*, "Le Jour et la Nuit," by René Lalique, c. 1930. In clear and frosted blue glass, the circular black face, with white Roman chapters, in a circular blue glass frame, intaglio-molded with a frosted nude male and relief-molded with a nude female, raised on a bronze base, etched "R. Lalique," face enameled "Made in France." 14¾" tall.
$52,800 (1986)

*Glass clock*, "Le Jour et la Nuit," by René Lalique, c. 1930. Same as above with clear frosted glass and circular frosted dial with white enameled chapter ring on a white truncated pyramidal base, molded "R. Lalique." 14¾" tall.
$20,000–$30,000

*Glass clock*, "Quatre Perruches" (four parrots), by René Lalique, French. In frosted glass, square with birds at each corner among flowerheads centering glass dial, inscribed "Lalique, France." 7¼" tall, on original illuminated mount.
$1,870 (1987)

*Glass clock*, by René Lalique. Yellow frosted glass, demilune shape, the clock face framed by pairs of small birds, molded "Lalique." 6½" tall.
$1,100 (1986)

*Table clock*, by A. L'Emeraude, Swiss, c. 1925. Onyx and wrought iron, the rectangular face set into variegated mustard-colored onyx case, raised on hammered wrought-iron side supports spanned by an

"Le Jour et la Nuit" clock by René Lalique. *(Photo by Frank Cooper, from a private collection)*

arrangement of openwork holly leaves and berries, on onyx plinth, marked "A. L'Emeraude Lausanne." 7⅜" tall.
$350–$400

*Mantel clock,* by Manning Bowman, American, c. 1930. In pyramid style with three colors of wood veneer inlaid in geometric patterns. Rectangular face with stylized Roman numerals. 10" tall. Working.
$250–$350

*Mantel clock,* by Manning Bowman, c. 1928. Square chrome casing with semicircular feet. Face has pattern of repetitive arrows in alternating directions. Mounted on a chrome and green onyx base. Clock case: 9" x 9". Onyx base ½" thick.
$875–$950

*Mantel clock,* cast from a model by Menneville and Rochard, French. In patinated metal and ivorene with central figure of a woman standing flanked on the left by her greyhound and on the right by a domed clock, the base and clock in various stone veneers. Inscribed "Menneville et Rochard." 19½" tall x 23½" long.
$500–$700

*Table clock,* cast after a model by J. Merlot, French, 1922. Silvered bronze, pyramidal form, cast obverse and reverse with Japanese-style cloud form, pine branches with fanned needles in which nestle a pair

**Manning Bowman mantel clock.** *(Photo by R. Four)*

Mantel clock by Menneville and Rochard. *(Photo courtesy of Christie's East)*

of embracing birds forming apex above trapezoidal clock face, impressed "J. Merlot 1922." 10" long.

$660 (1986)

*Mantel clock,* by Vincent Mettier, French. In frosted glass and gilt bronze, the cathedral-shaped case has black enamel dial with gilt numbers, over long clear and frosted panel depicting woman holding floral garland overhead, flanked by stylized semicircles, with dentil molded border (fitted for electricity). 15¾" tall.

$1,870 (1986)

*Table clock,* by New Haven, American, 1930s. In white onyx with square case surmounting a rectangular white onyx plinth. A triangular piece of green oynx forms an accent in the angle created by the case and base. 6" long x 5" tall overall. Not working.

$55–$80

*Alarm clock,* by Gilbert Rohde, c. 1932–1933, for Herman Miller Clock Co. The circular blue mirrored glass face, with chromed-metal hands and 12 balls for hour marks, raised on a rectangular brushed-chromium base, unsigned. 6½" tall. (For illustration see color insert.)

$605 (1987)

*Table clock*, by Gilbert Rohde, c. 1932–1933, for Herman Miller. As above, the circular blue-mirrored glass face, with polished chromium hands and balls for hour marks, raised on a rectangular brushed-chromium base, unsigned. 10½" tall.
$143 (1986)

*Table clock*, by Gilbert Rohde, c. 1932, for Herman Miller. The square face, with black Arabic chapters, in a rectangular bird's-eye maple case, with rounded right side, intersected by three chromed-metal bands, face painted "Herman HM Miller Herman Miller Clock Co. Zeeland, Mich. USA." 13⅛" long. (For illustration see color insert.)
**$1,045 (1987)**

*Clock*, attributed to Jacques-Emile Ruhlmann, French, c. 1925. In gilded carved wood with overall triangular shape. Clock casing is octagonal and decorated with random square designs bordered by flowing lines. Originally key wound, electrified at a later date.
**$5,000–$6,000**

*Clock*, by Süe et Mare, French, c. 1925. In gilt bronze, with overall triangular shape composed of grapes, pears, flowers, and other designs surmounted by two doves. Scrolled side stands. Designed by Paul Vera and sculpted by Poisson, signed by both. Sunburst design on clock face. Approx. 18" tall.
**$65,000–$68,000**

**Clock attributed to Emile-Jacques Ruhlmann.** *(Photo courtesy of Maison Gerard)*

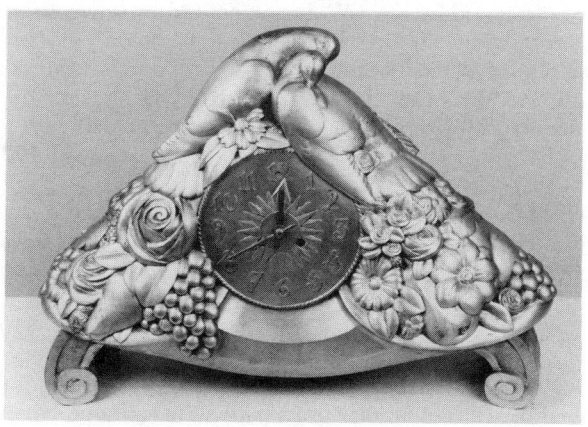

Clock by Süe et Mare. *(Photo courtesy of Audrey Friedman, Primavera Gallery)*

*Mantel clock,* by Josef Urban, Viennese, c. 1906, for the Paul Hofner restaurant, Vienna. The circular ivorene face, with hinged convex glazing, having chapter ring formed as circular convex silver-plated disks enameled in green with Arabic numerals within green enameled ring borders, the silver-plated arms with staggered heart-shaped bands, raised on two agate columns and "draped" in burl walnut–veneered surround flaring at either end and decorated with mother-of-pearl inlay of tiered triangular section, the whole raised on burl walnut–veneered plinth set with a narrow silver-plated band with egg-and-dart motif, unsigned. 22⅝" tall x 20⅛" wide x 7¼" deep.
$44,000 (1986)

*Wall clock,* by Warren Telechron, American, late 1930s–1940s. In chrome with green Bakelite face. Square, 5" x 5".
$50–$60

*Table clock,* "The Zephyr," by Kem Weber, American, 1933, for Lawson Time, Inc. Rectangular face, with digital dial, in a rounded and curved rectangular brass body with an applied long, slender, chrome-plated ribbon on top and a short, curved, chrome-plated section on front, impressed "Lawson Time Inc. Los Angeles, Calif. W.4V.110 CYC. 60 Model No. 304." 7½" long. (For illustration see color insert.)
$605 (1986)
$990 (1987)

*Table clock*, designed by Kem Weber, executed by Lawson Time. The rectangular digital face set in a brass housing flanked by ribbed rectangular clear plastic blocks in chromed metal mounts raised on a white onyx plinth, face painted "Lawson," with firm's applied metal tag. Working order. 12⅞" long. (For illustration see color insert.)
$1,100 (1987)

*Table clock*, by Kem Weber for Lawson Time. Burnished brown metal body of rounded rectangular form on brass sled foot with streamlined brass decoration on either side of the digital display, marked. 7¼" long.
$400–$600

*Table clock*, by Kem Weber, for Lawson Time Inc. Rectangular face with digital dial in a rectangular brass body with rounded edges, raised on twin rectangular chrome-plated ribbed feet, face painted "Lawson," with firm's applied metal tag. 7" long.
$330 (1986)

*Mantel clocks*, various anon., French, 1920s–1930s. In marble or onyx with distinctive angles in design achieved through layering different colors. A wide variety of colors and designs of the same basic style, sometimes surmounted with a reclining female figure, a greyhound, or other figure. Statue sometimes in brass but more often in base metal. Often called "clock garnitures," literally translated as "garnish," which means a pair of decorative pieces in the same design and materials comes with the clock to decorate the mantel on either side of the clock. Generally 12"–14" tall x 16"–20" wide
Not working $200–$300
Working $400–$600

*Mantel clock and garniture*, anon., French, 1920s. As above but surmounted with a reclining girl in brass, with a bird perched on her finger in white marble. Working.
$650–$800

*Mantel clock and garniture*, anon., French, c. 1930. As above, in variegated inlaid marble with standing green-painted iron leaping gazelles.
$750–$950

*Mantel clock and garniture*, anon., French. As above, the center piece of stepped rectangular form flanked by spheres, with black and red variegated marble panels and gilt-metal applications of stylized floral design; with matching triangular side garnitures. Center clock 11" tall.
$650 (1987)

*Mantel clock and garniture,* French, c. 1930. As above, with the central clock piece decorated with the huntress Diana pursuing a leaping antelope in polychromed metal, the side pieces of trumpet form, on black and beige marble bases, clock marked "Diedsheim" and "Nantes." Center clock 21¾" long.

$700–$900

*Table clock,* anon., French, c. 1930. Octagonal glass clock with rectangular chrome pieces to mark the numbers. Set on a four-tiered rectangular chrome base. 10" tall.

$750–$900

*Mantel clock,* anon., French, c. 1925. The circular silver-plated metal face, with stylized openwork Arabic chapters, on a circular green onyx body with triangular and rectangular projections raised on a tiered rectangular black onyx base, unsigned. 12¼" long.

$165 (1986)

# SCULPTURE AND STATUES

Affected by the same forces that shook the world of painting—Cubism, Fauvism, and Futurism—sculpture itself took on new forms. Fine art and monumental sculpture attracted numerous talented artists in the Art Deco era, in both Europe and America.

In Europe artists working in several mediums, such as Alexander Archipenko (1887–1964), Gustav Miklos (1888–1967), Italian Rembrandt Bugatti, and Josef Csaky, a Hungarian who worked in France, translated into sculpture the new dimensions that Cubists were portraying on the two-dimensional plane.

Early fine sculpture of the period was also inspired by African masks and motifs from other ancient cultures as the Western world became more exposed to new influences. Jean Puiforcat (1897–1945), most often noted for his silver, also created dramatic bronze sculptures. Edouard Marcel Sandoz was particularly noted for his sculptures of animals. Some of the finest European bronzes of the period were cast by the Valsuani Foundry.

Today the work of these artists is very expensive and handled only by the finest galleries and auction houses. Because many of the bronzes created by artists such as these were produced in very small editions, prices are correspondingly high. For example, Archipenko usually made bronzes in editions of no more than twelve, and many of his works sell for over $150,000 today. Miklos, who sometimes made editions as small as four, has recently brought prices near the $100,000 mark.

## Sculpture and Statues

In America, many fine sculptural artists were commissioned for public monuments of the period. One of the best, Lee Lawrie, has already been discussed in the chapter on architecture. Other distinguished artists would become well known during the period, among them Paul Manship (1885–1966), Anna Hoyt Huntington (1876–1973), Carl Milles (1875–1955), Carl Paul Jennewein (1890–1978), Sydney Waugh, Elie Nadelman, John Storrs, William Hunt Diederich, Boris Lovet-Lorski, William Zorach, and Waylande Gregory.

Some of these artists are known to collectors of other Art Deco items; for example, both Waylande Gregory and Paul Manship designed ceramic pieces for Cowan Pottery of Ohio, while Sydney Waugh designed glass for Steuben.

One work by Manship sold for over $200,000 on the auction market in recent years. His well known "Europa and the Bull," in a casting 9⅜ inches high, brought $34,000 at Christie's, New York, in 1985. "Days and Hours," a Manship sculpture from 1916 cast by Roman Bronze Works in New York in an edition of ten, brought $26,000 the same year. Manship's style and influence can be seen in the work of many other artists.

Artist Carl Milles, who taught at the Cranbrook Academy of Art, also had a sculpture entitled "Europa and the Bull," which he created in 1951. In 1985 it went for $47,300 at auction.

Roman Bronze Works was one of the foremost bronze foundries in America and executed both fine art and monumental sculptures for many of the leading artists. In many ways it helped place the bronze sculptures of America in the same rank as those of Paris and Rome.

The Art Deco era saw a closer rapprochement, or coming together, of the fine arts and the decorative arts than ever before. In consequence, or as part of that process, decorative bronze sculpture came into greater demand, building on a popularity that had started in the 1890s.

Talented European artists created works that would satisfy the new markets, the advent of which also happily coincided with advances in bronze casting. Artists such as Belgian Claire Jeanne Roberte Colinet began in the tradition of fine arts and were later commissioned for works produced in larger quantities.

After World War I decorative bronze sculptures were being produced for and distributed through the major department stores. Pomone at Au Bon Marché commissioned artists to create works specifically for their stores. Etling, known to many for its imitations of Lalique glass, entered the statuary market with works by such artists as Demetre H. Chiparus, Joé (Jean) Descomps, and Maurice Guiraud-Rivière.

In statuary the Modern style did not follow the lead of the Viennese perhaps as much as in other decorative arts. With its emphasis on functionality, the Secession did not produce many decorative sculptures for their own sake. However, one Austrian name does stand out on the collecting market: Atelier Hagenaur. Sculptures by this workshop, mostly from the late 1920s and early 1930s, were often retailed through department stores and at times were commissioned by the Wiener Werkstätte. But as if to underline the lesser importance placed on statuary by the Viennese, much of this work, though well executed, is knickknack size.

Fine artists most often did not paint the bronze beyond overall patination in green, brown, or black, but many of the new decorative statues were polychromed in bright colors and mounted on bases of marble or onyx.

Art Deco sculpture reflected the new design style with lithe nude maidens—often dancing, sometimes flying through the sky. The female figure was the most popular subject for decorative statues, and often the subject was a well-known singer, actress, or personality, such as Josephine Baker and Sarah Bernhardt.

Not far behind women in popularity was the *animalier* movement in sculpture. Art Deco's favorite animals—greyhounds, gazelles, and wild cats—were perfect subjects for the sleek new look. Some of the best decorative bronzes of animals are by Max Le Vérrier, but other artists executed fine examples as well.

Other outstanding artists in bronze include Marcel Bourraine, Fayral, Pierre Traverse, Pierre le Faguays, Gilbert Privat, Paul Phillipe, Gustav Gillot, Alexander Kelety, and the Italian artists Gerdago and Gambogi.

Americans too saw an upsurge of decorative bronze production, much of it through the Gorham Company. Known for its silver, Gorham opened bronze foundries in Providence, Rhode Island, in the 1920s. Its production was sold in fine New York stores. Among the most notable Art Deco artists is Harriet W. Fishmuth, who created statues and electroplated bronze car radiator ornaments of nude women, their hair streaming behind them as they flew through space.

Yet by far the most active of American companies producing decorative sculpture was Frankart, which is discussed later in this chapter. Frankart took its cue from the works of artists such as Le Vérrier and the Austrian Lorenzl and created mostly figural but functional lamps, ash stands, and the like. In addition, it substituted base metals for bronze, which both lowered the cost and increased the output.

### *Special Focus: Chryselephantine Statues*

By far the most popular statues of the Art Deco era are chryselephantine, or bronze-and-ivory statues. Many of the artists named above were also well known for their designs in bronze and ivory.

Chryselephantine statues were popular for at least two decades before the Art Deco period, but their production reached its peak during the late 1920s and 1930s.

Bronze-and-ivory statues are often mounted on onyx or marble bases. The most popular and numerous portray slender women in a variety of roles, as dancers, singers, cabaret girls, medieval maidens, winged goddesses, and nymphs. Animals, too, make their appearance, especially greyhounds, borzois, and birds.

Many Art Deco chryselephantine statues mirror the gaiety and high style of the era. Others are cast as figures of children, jesters, schoolmasters, and other characters. Still others are golfers, swimmers, and ice skaters, dressed in sporty clothes.

These statues, along with many decorative bronze-only pieces, were ignored for many years, but there was a strong resurgence of interest in the early to mid-1970s. At that time, leading scholars and dealers such as Brian Catley, Victor Arwas, and Alain Lesieutre renewed the collecting market's interest in them.

Prices rose dramatically until about 1983, when a flood of reproductions created both in the United States and abroad hit the market. (See "Fakes, Forgeries, and Reproductions," and "Today's Market" for more about reproductions.)

Today prices seem to be making something of a comeback. However, even though at least one company has ceased its production of the chryselephantine statues, the reproductions are still fairly easy to find and cost no more than a few hundred dollars. Bronze-only statues have also been reproduced in quantity. Because many of these statues are not protected by copyright, a modern manufacturer can simply cast a mold from one and start production.

For example, we spotted a bronze figure by Demetre Chiparus called "Hindu Dancer" at an antiques show recently, selling for $225. The dealer claimed it to be a real French bronze. In 1987 "Hindu Dancer" sold at auction at Christie's, New York, for $6,600. The dealer said it was a French bronze. She didn't say when it was cast.

Sometimes well executed, these reproduction statues are deceptively tempting to collectors who want to think they have made a "find." Remember: a very low price with a claim of originality is a clear warning. Because the signatures are more often on the bases than on the statues, collectors should also be aware that signatures are easily faked and also that a fake statue can be put on a signed base.

Sun Foundry in California issues what they feel are high-quality bronze reproductions of Chiparus and other artists at a fraction of the cost of the originals. Some individuals purchase them purely for their decorative value. But authentic early-20th-century castings of bronze-and-ivory figures can easily command thousands of dollars, or even tens of thousands of dollars, in today's Art Deco market, depending on the design, the size, the materials used, the artist, the subject, and the workmanship.

The best auction houses and dealers use standardized language to indicate the casting of bronze and bronze-and-ivory statues. When a bronze is made from the artist's original model and was cast during the artist's lifetime or shortly thereafter, it will read "Cast *from* a model by." When it is a later casting it will read "Cast *after* a model by."

The term "chryselephantine" was first used to describe the statues that used both gold and ivory in ancient Greece. During the Art Nouveau era the Belgians, the most prolific producers of bronze-and-ivory statues, extended the meaning to encompass any statue fashioned in combination with ivory.

Ivory has always held the interest of sculptors for its beauty and ease of carving. Ivory also ages, yellowing in attractive ways. In the middle of the 19th century, however, ivory was being used primarily for everyday items like brushes, doorhandles, piano keys, and the like.

When the Congo was conquered by the Belgians, ivory tusks were shipped back to Europe in quantities that far exceeded household needs, and in 1894 the secretary of state for the Congo Free State called on Belgian artists to use more ivory. The use of ivory was further encouraged by government-sponsored commissions and competition exhibitions.

However, the basic materials that were used—bronze, ivory, and marble—changed as the market for the statues grew. Cheaper metals—such as spelter, a type of zinc that is more akin to pewter and that molds more easily—came into use; and a composition plastic—ivorene, which only sometimes actually contains powdered ivory—replaced the real thing.

The bases, which were once of high-quality marble and even lapis lazuli and which had increased the status of the statues as precious objets d'art, changed to cheaper marble and finally seamed onyx or other marble-like stones. The best onyx came from Brazil and was a favorite material for other decorative objects as well.

Again, good dealers will distinguish to the best of their ability the materials used. This affects the market value of the work, and it also helps in dating it.

Even early Art Deco bronze and ivory statues do not tend to be one of a kind. Although they were not exactly mass-produced, castings *en série* were possible when talented carvers were hired to execute the artist's design in the ivory. For this reason, no two are exactly alike.

The Ballets Russes and the cinema had an influence on the chryselephantine sculptures. Exotic entertainers frozen in theatrical attitudes, with highly stylized costumes and polychromed patination, were typical. Demetre H. Chiparus, a prolific sculptor, is best known for theatrical performers who strut and fret their hour upon the stage. Chiparus is also the most often forged signature on modern marble bases. Chiparus went to study in Paris from his native Rumania and exhibited at the Salon des Artistes Français from 1914 to 1918. His works sold in major department stores and jewelry shops. Chiparus figures include nudes, women in beaded cloche hats, adorable children, and little clowns.

Very often the artist also designed the base, and Chiparus designed many using elaborate stepped pyramids and decorated with mosaics or inset bronze. Marble of different colors might also be used in geometric combinations.

Claire Jeanne Roberte Colinet, already mentioned, also designed in bronze and ivory. A native Belgian, she also moved to Paris and was elected to the Société des Artists Français in 1913. She exhibited at the Salon des Indépendants from 1937 to 1940.

A German, Ferdinand (or Fritz—his first name is not really known) Preiss, was just as popular as Chiparus, and his work was widely distributed by the Phillips and MacConal Gallery of Arts in Great Britain, as well as by others. Preiss created ivory-only sculptures as well as bronze-and-ivory, and these are highly priced on today's market. However, he is best known for his sportily clad men and women who mirrored modern life. He often used a cooler color palette of blues, silvers, and grays. He also created figures from the world of entertainment, such as Brigitte Helm as the heroine of Fritz Lang's *Metropolis* and as the Bat Dancer from the Hollywood film *Flying Down to Rio*.

Preiss influenced many other sculptors. Another German, Professor Otto Poerzl, copied Preiss so closely that some suspected "Poerzl" was just a pseudonym for Preiss. An Austrian artist named Joseph Lorenzl or K. Lorenzl also imitated Preiss, signing some of his works "K. Lor" and "Ronr." Lorenzl is a highly collected artist, and his nudes may have inspired the American Frankart company designs.

Joé Descomps, also already mentioned, is another talented artist in bronze and ivory. Born at Agen in southwest France, he exhibited his work as early as 1903 and 1904 at the Société des Artistes Français. In the 1920s the noted French artist Pierre Le Faguays also exhibited his work there.

German Bruno Zach, who worked mostly in Austria, designed some truly erotic sculptures in bronze and ivory. He often depicted his women in leather trousers, smoking cigarettes, or wearing garters. His designs influenced other German artists in the medium. Zach also designed a few bronzes with American Western designs, such as cowboys and Indians on horseback, sleekly galloping across plains he had never seen—except in the movies.

Alexander Kelety, a Hungarian who went to live and work in France, and Roland Paris, born in Vienna, are two other noteworthy sculptors. Roland Paris's works are like none of the above—often funny, sometimes satirical. He created bronze-and-ivory jesters, caricatures, and clowns, both as statues and as more functional objects like bookends.

A host of other talented artists worked in bronze and ivory, and because of this we feel that the market may yet recover from the wave of early 1980s reproductions as the high quality and styling of the original works become better known and as collectors learn to spot the forgeries and avoid them.

## FRANKART

Generally easy to identify, Frankart was everyman's Art Deco statuette and plainly molded its name and usually a patent number, or "Pat. Pending" or "Pat. Appld. For," into each piece. Sometimes pieces are also dated, and a reprinting of a major Frankart catalog in 1981 gave serious collectors a very fine guide to work from.

Collectors should be aware and "beware," however: the patents on several Frankart statues, ashstands, and lamps have been bought by contemporary manufacturers and are being reissued in some quantity. If the pieces are not impressed with the name of the new firm, it is up to scrupulous dealers to at least leave the tag from the current manufacturer on the piece. (For more on reproductions see "Fakes, Forgeries, and Reproductions," and "Today's Market.")

In some ways it's a shame. Good-quality Frankart lamps, for instance, are real beauties, and pioneer collectors have been gathering them up for years. However, imitations have weakened the market for authentic Frankart.

Frankart was art and functionality combined. Few except the earliest pieces are purely decorative. Bookends, ashstands and ashtray holders, vase stands, and lamps were the basis of Frankart's widespread popularity in this country. It was inexpensive art for everyday use.

Some of the pieces produced by the Frankart Company in New York City are quite stunning. "The Spirit of Modernism" lamp, for example, had a parchment shade, and for the base, tall abstract rectangular shapes suggested skyscrapers with irregular towers or a cluster of skyscrapers as a city unto itself, culminating in the figure of a slender muse. This piece rarely appears on the market, and it seems that fewer of these were produced than most other Frankart lamps.

## Sculpture and Statues

As far as is known, Frankart's first figure was introduced in 1921. It was a sleek figural nude candleholder, appropriately called "Flame," with a somewhat Art Nouveau base. In the years following its immediate success, more than one hundred other pieces were sculpted by the chief designer, Arthur von Frankenberg. In 1923 stepped or pyramidal bases were introduced, perhaps influenced by the discovery of the tomb of Egyptian pharaoh Tutankhamen, while the skyscraper style was used on both bases and glass lamps.

Von Frankenberg did not design elaborate costumes or headdresses for his sculptures, which were usually of nude women. In this way, his work is often similar to that of Lorenzl. Early Frankart lamps also resemble works by Max Le Vérrier's company in Paris.

Frankart copyrighted its designs, but competing firms still copied them, changing only minor details. The imitators also relied on the popular nude and often green-painted women, nicknamed "greenies." The companies Nu-art and Eckart produced designs of poorer quality, which can still be found in some flea markets.

Frankart lamps have risen in value to hundreds of dollars recently. At a show not too long ago we were almost shocked to hear a dealer asking $400 for just the base of a Frankart lamp, and that in relatively poor condition. Many of the best Frankart designs for lamps are today selling for $800, $900, and up to as high as $2,000. However, Frankart is relatively weak in many parts of the country and in recent years on the auction market as well.

The most popular Frankart items today are still the lithe nude lamps and ashstands, but Frankart also issued a bucking donkey lamp and bookends shaped like scotties and bears; these bring lower prices on the auction and retail market.

After about ten years of production, the company closed its doors, one of the many Deco victims of the Depression. In the mid-1940s most of the original molds were hauled out of storage and melted down as scrap. In theory, the numbers of good Frankart pieces are therefore somewhat limited, and there is a broad enough market among noncollectors to support good retail prices in some cities.

The collecting market situation may change in the years ahead, but one company, which owns many of the Frankart patents, has plans to continue issuing them. Because in some cases the company can work from original molds, it is hard to tell the difference. For someone who is seeking only to decorate a room, there really is no difference, and of course the new pieces are much less expensive.

The makers of Frankart reproductions feel that they are serving a lower-end market that enjoys the Deco style but cannot afford the originals. Ironically, this was exactly Frankart's own appeal in its day.

# ART DECO

## PRICE LISTINGS

*Figure of a winged woman,* cast from a model by A. Bazzoni, French, c. 1937, executed by Barbedienne. Bronze in stylized posture symbolizing speed, rich green-brown patina, inscribed "A. Bazzoni/Paris, 1937" with foundry mark. 32" long.

$2,000–$4,000

*Figure of a woman warrior, "Amazon,"* cast from a model by Marcel Bourraine, French, early 20th century. In gilt bronze, the nude woman kneeling, preparing to throw her spear, her hair and robes streaming behind her, inscribed "M. Bourraine" on angled white onyx base. 24" long.

$2,000–$3,000

*Figure of a young deer,* cast from a model by Rembrandt Bugatti, Italian, early 20th century. In bronze, with dark brown patina, inscribed "R. Bugatti," and impressed with the Hegrard foundry seal. 13¼" tall.

$8,800 (1987)

*Figure of a baby deer,* cast from a model by B. Butzke, German, c. 1925, in bronze with green patina, impressed "B Butzke/Bildgesserei Kraas/Berlin S A," octagonal marble plinth. 24" tall.

$1,000 (1987)

*Figure of a dancer, "Anita,"* cast and carved from a model by Mme. Callender, French, early 20th century. Standing polychromed bronze figure draped in black shawl decorated with silver studs. Hands, arms, and face in ivory, inscribed "Callender." 16½" tall.

$6,000–$8,000

*Figural group, "Accident de Chasse"* (Hunting Accident), by Demetre H. Chiparus, French. In bronze, the young woman seated binding the paw of her wounded dog, on bronze base set on marble base, inscribed "Demetre Chiparus." 7¼" tall x 17" long.

$2,500–$3,000

*Figure of an exotic dancer, "Dourga,"* cast from a model by D. H. Chiparus, early 20th century. A cold-painted bronze and ivory figure of woman in exotic, fitted body suit, arms raised above her head, standing with legs crossed, including elaborate brown and beige onyx base, signed "D. Chiparus." 24⅞" tall.

$7,920 (1986)

## Sculpture and Statues

*Figure of a young girl, "Flower Gatherer,"* cast from a model by D. H. Chiparus, early 20th century. In gilt bronze, the girl carrying a basket of flowers, her hands and face of ivory, standing on bronze base, inscribed "Chiparus." 11″ tall.

$3,000–$3,750

*Figure of a dancing girl, "Hindu Dancer,"* cast from a model by D. H. Chiparus, early 20th century. In parcel-silvered bronze, including veined black marble plinth, signed "D. H. Chiparus" and inscribed "Etling Paris," golden patina, with traces of cold-painting. 23½″ tall.

$6,600 (1987)

*Figural group, "Les Amis de Toujours"* (Friends Forever), cast from a model by D. H. Chiparus, c. 1925. In gilt bronze and carved ivory, figure of a woman in medieval robe and cap touched with red and silver, with her two dogs, raised on a shaped, stepped onyx plinth, inscribed "D.H. Chiparus," inlaid foundry mark "LN/JL." 24″ tall.

$10,000–$15,000

"Les Amis de Toujours" by Demetre Chiparus. *(Photo courtesy of William Doyle Galleries)*

*Figure of a child, "Little Clown,"* cast from a model by D. H. Chiparus, early 20th century. Bronze figure in clown costume, the face ivory, on round marble onyx base, inscribed "Demetre Chiparus." 9" tall.
$2,000–$2,750

*Figure of a clown boy, "Pierrot,"* cast from a model by D. H. Chiparus. In bronze and ivory, on brown Italian marble circular base, front of clown outfit has animated carving of the sun, back has face in crescent moon. Pointed clown cap painted silver; hands and face in ivory with meticulous detail, stepped marble base is inscribed "D.H. Chiparus." 12" tall.
$4,500–$5,500

*Figure of a young girl, "The Little One,"* cast from a model by D. H. Chiparus, early 20th century. Gilt-bronze and ivory figure of young girl drying her tears with her drapery, on veined marble base signed "D.H. Chiparus" and inscribed "Etling Paris." 6⅝" tall.
$3,520 (1986)

*Figure of a woman, "Top Hat,"* cast from a model by D. H. Chiparus, early 20th century. In cold-patinated bronze and ivory, the young woman with top hat and cane standing on her toes in dancing position, poised on a shaped, stepped onyx base. Base with bronze plaque inscribed "Demetre Chiparus." 19½" tall.
$14,000–$17,000

*Figural group,* cast from a model by D. H. Chiparus, early 20th century. A cold-painted bronze of a harem dancer cuddling a lion, green marble base. Inscribed "D.H. Chiparus." 14" tall x 23⅛" long.
$8,250 (1986)

*Figural group,* cast from a model by D. H. Chiparus, French, early 20th century. Gilt-bronze and ivory statue of three girls huddling under an umbrella on pink alabaster and metal base, inscribed "Chiparus 4551." 9⅝" tall.
$2,090 (1986)

*Figural group,* cast from a model by D. H. Chiparus, French, 20th century. In bronze and ivory, three children with green coats huddled together under purple umbrella, on self bronze base, inscribed "Demetre Chiparus." 8" tall.
$2,750–$3,500

*Figure of a woman,* cast from a model by D. H. Chiparus, c. 1930. In polychrome spelter set on rectangular stone base, the woman in sitting position, wearing beaded cloche hat and holding small dish from

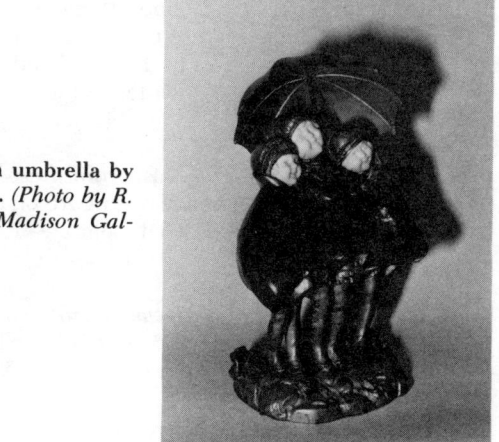

Children under an umbrella by Demetre Chiparus. *(Photo by R. Four; courtesy of Madison Galleries)*

which two parakeets are feeding. Inscribed "D. H. Chiparus." 11¾" long.

$2,000–$3,000

*Figural group,* cast from a model by D. H. Chiparus, in cold-painted parcel-gilt spelter and ivorene. A maiden in medieval costume holding garland, being pulled by goats at her sides, inscribed "D. H. Chiparus" on brown marble base trimmed in green onyx. 34" long.

$1,320 (1986)

*Figure of a nymph,* cast from a model by D. H. Chiparus. In polychromed spelter, the reclining woman in harem costume, holding a cluster of grapes overhead, with a single bird alight nearby, inscribed "D.H. Chiparus" on rectangular green onyx and black marble base. 12¼" long.

$1,800–$2,200

*Figure of a schoolgirl,* cast from a model by D. H. Chiparus. A bronze figure of a young girl carrying her books and wearing a cloak and hat, the face in ivory, on onyx base, inscribed "Demetre Chiparus." 8" tall.

$1,800–$2,000

*Figure of an Oriental dancer,* by D. H. Chiparus. In polychrome patinated bronze, a dancing woman on one knee in exotic costume and jewelry. Base in onyx and marble in yellow, red, and black with geometric design. Inscribed "D. H. Chiparus." 23" tall x 26" long.

$13,000–$15,000

*Figure of a snake charmer,* "*Dance of Carthage,*" cast from a model by Claire Jeanne Roberte Colinet, Belgian, early 20th century. A cold-painted gilt-bronze and white-marble group of a man wearing sandals, with a snake slithering around his neck and arms, inscribed "Cl. J. R. Colinet." 22¼" tall x 23¾" wide.

$13,200 (1986)

*Figure of a woman juggler,* cast from a model by Claire Jeanne Roberte Colinet, c. 1935. The bronze figure on one foot, balancing three balls, onyx base, inscribed "CJR Colinet." 19¼" tall.

$1,000–$1,200

*Figural group of woman with two parrots,* cast from a model by Claire Jeanne Roberte Colinet, c. 1925. The bronze figure nude, verde-antico marble plinth, inscribed "CJR Colinet." 30¾" tall, including base.

$1,600 (1986)

*Figural group,* "*Adam and Eve,*" cast from a model by Josef Csaky, Hungarian, but worked in France, early 20th century. Monumental bronze of stylized man and woman standing side by side, naked, with their arms around each other, in a rich brown patina, inscribed "Csaky AC ⅜, Blanchet-Fondeur." 61¾" tall.

$22,000 (1986)

**Statue by Claire Jeanne Roberte Colinet.** *(Photo courtesy of William Doyle Galleries)*

*Sculpture and Statues* 181

*Head of a young woman, "Tête de Jeune Fille,"* cast from a model by Josef Csaky, early 20th century. Stylized, Cubist-influenced head of silvered bronze, inscribed "Csaky." 13¼" tall.
$3,000–$4,000

*Figure of a nude woman,* cast from a model by F. David, French, 1902. In bronze, standing holding a bowl in upraised arms, inscribed "Fdavid I.H.F. Fondeur Paris/Copyright by David 1902," brown patina on self base. 19¼" tall.
$330 (1986)

*Figure of a nude girl,* by A. Davmiller. In silvered bronze, nude girl with arms partially extended, standing, inquisitive expression on her face, on marble base. Inscribed "A. Davmiller." 13" tall.
$900–$1,000

*Figural group,* cast from a model by Decour, French. Two menacing panthers in silvered bronze, on black onyx base trimmed in green onyx. Inscribed "Decour." 19½" long.
$1,320 (1986)

*Figure of a maiden,* cast from a model by Joé Descomps, executed by Etling, c. 1925. The bronze nude figure raising a garland, inscribed "Joé Descomps" and with foundry mark, onyx plinth. 21" tall
$800 (1987)

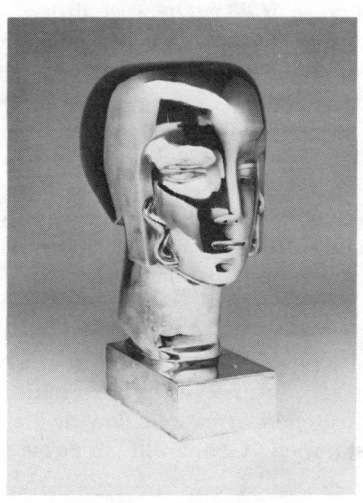

"Tête de Jeune Fille" by Csaky.
*(Photo courtesy of Nancy McClelland, Christie's)*

**Panthers by Decour.** *(Photo courtesy of Christie's East)*

*Figure of a woman,* cast after a model by Joé Descomps, French, 20th century. Bronze statue in which the overall body is swathed in beaded and chased suit, the helmet-form hat with cross bands, cape flowing from her shoulders, on stepped onyx base inscribed "Joé Descomps." 20½" tall.

$13,000–$16,000

*Figure of a nymph,* cast from a model by Fayral, French. In bronze, the lithe nude holding a scarf at her hips, and a large mirrored tambourine at her right shoulder, inscribed "Fayral" on green marble base. 23" tall.

$1,200–$1,800

*Figure of a gazelle,* cast after a model by Fayral, in bronze, the sleek animal lying down, his long horns curving back over his body, inscribed "Fayral" in greenish brown patina on stepped black base. 14¾" long.

$495 (1987)

*Figure of an exotic kneeling dancer,* cast from a model by G. Gambogi, in gilt bronze, the dancer scantily clad in Egyptian bra, short slit skirt, and turban headdress, inscribed "G. Gambogi" on stepped, light brown onyx base. 15" tall x 15" deep.

$935 (1986)

*Figure of a nymph,* cast from a model by A. Gennarelli, Italian, early 20th century. Gilt-bronze nude woman on marble column with outstretched arms and flowing hair, balancing a pigeon on her hand, stamped "Gennarelli" in circle. Overall 34" tall.

$3,500–$4,500

# Sculpture and Statues

Exotic dancer by Gambogi. *(Photo courtesy of Christie's East)*

*Figure of a dancer,* cast from a model attributed to Gerdago, Italian. In cold-painted bronze and ivory, dressed in scarlet, turquoise, and black floral suit, on green onyx base. 10½" tall.

$770 (1986)

*Figure of a dancer,* in the style of Gerdago. In gold-painted gilt bronze and ivory. Dancer resting on one foot in tight fitted suit with green-painted armature in side profile, her arms upheld in the Egyptian manner, on green onyx videpoche. 12" tall.

$1,760 (1986)

*Figure of a goddess,* cast from a model by Gustave Gillot, French, executed by Pomone, c. 1935. The bronze figure draped in starry robe with fruit-laden garland, green patina, inscribed "G. Gillot/Edition Pomone." 20½" tall.

$1,200 (1986)

*Figural group of a woman and ocelot,* cast from a model by Gustave Gillot, executed by Pomone, c. 1935. Bronze reclining nude figure, inscribed "G. Gillot/Edition Pomone." 16½" long.

$1,000–$1,200

*Figure of a young girl,* by Gregoire, French. In parcel-gilt bronze and ivory, the girl standing barefoot on a rocky step, her apron held out to form a basket, inscribed "Gregoire." 8¼" tall.

$1,320 (1986)

*Figure of a nymph, "The Comet,"* cast from a model by Maurice Guiraud-Rivière, French, early 20th century. Parcel-silvered bronze allegorical figure on stepped Belgian marble plinth. Inscribed "Guiraud-Rivière, Etling Paris." 24¾" long.

$13,200 (1986)

*Figural group of Diana and a deer,* cast from a model by Maurice Guiraud-Rivière, executed by Etling, c. 1925. In silvered bronze, verde-antico marble plinth inscribed "Guiraud Rivière/Etling Paris." 19½" tall.

$1,200–$1,800

*Figure of a kneeling nymph,* cast from a model by Maurice Guiraud-Rivière. In bronze, the stylized woman kneeling, loosely wrapped in a robe, arms raised to hold a ball, inscribed "Guiraud-Rivière" (ball missing). 17⅜" tall.

$2,000–$3,000

*Figure of a dancer,* by Hagenauer, Austrian, for Wiener Werkstätte, retailed by Rena Rosenthal. In chrome and walnut, the bare-breasted coquette in short swirled wooden skirt, on circular base, marked. 6" tall.

$880 (1986)

"The Comet" by Maurice Guiraud-Rivière. *(Photo courtesy of Nancy McClelland, Christie's)*

*Figure of a horse,* by Hagenauer, retailed by John Wanamaker's. In wood and metal, the sleek animal rearing, stamped "Atelier Hagenauer Wien, John Wanamaker, Made in Vienna Austria" (ear repaired). 15¾" tall.
$660 (1987)

*Figure of a boxer,* by Hagenauer. In bronze with black finish, the stylized pugilist mounted on bronze ring base. Head lowered and throwing a left hook. Stamped "Hagenauer Wien" and "Made in Austria" on feet. Hagenauer touchmark on left foot. 9" tall.
$950–$1,200

*Figure of a polo player,* anon., but in the style of Hagenauer, Austrian, c. 1930. In bronze with nickel finish, the sleek Etruscan-style horse mounted by rider holding crop, restrained, stylized features. Stamped "Made in Austria" and trade-marked "Cross." 6" tall.
$450–$650

*Figures,* in the style of Hagenauer. Two slender stylized bronze nudes standing with hands raised, black patina on green onyx mounts. 9" tall.
$200–$300

*Figure of a nymph,* cast from a model by Alexandre Kelety, French, early 20th century. In silvered bronze, the nymph running through a hoop of coins, formed as a luminaire. Inscribed "A Kelety" and

**Boxer by Hagenauer.** *(Photo by Dennis Galloway; courtesy of Ed Forcum, Rosebud Gallery)*

stamped twice. Wired for electricity, including hollow gray marble base. 19⅛" tall.
$8,800 (1986)

*Figure of a scarf dancer,* cast from a model by Alexandre Kelety, early 20th century. In gilt bronze, inscribed "A. Kelety" and stamped twice, on Belgian marble base. 13¼" tall.
$1,320 (1987)

*Figure of a crouching tiger,* cast from a model by Georges Lavroff, French, early 20th century. In silvered bronze, the snarling animal preparing to pounce, inscribed "G. Lavroff" and stamped 8591, including shaped Belgian marble base. 24⅛" long.
$12,100 (1986)

*"Diana,"* figure cast from a model by Pierre Le Faguays, French, early 20th century. The bronze figure of an archer with right leg raised, on tiptoe, aiming bow toward the sky, having just released an arrow. The figure green patina, the base black patina, inscribed "Le Faguays, Susse F(es) Ed(TS) Paris," stamped "B" with the Susse Freres foundry seal. 26½" tall.
$1,500–$2,000

*Figure of a woman, "Nais,"* cast from a model by Pierre Le Faguays, c. 1925. In gilt bronze and ivory, the woman standing, holding a puppet in each hand. Originally issued complete with illuminated theater scene stage in marble and alabaster. (Without theater scene.) 19" tall.
$3,000–$5,000

*Figure of a nude bearing a dove, "Message of Love,"* cast from a model by Pierre Le Faguays. In bronze, the tall, slender nude on very tall base with arm stretched straight up, gently cradling a small dove. Brown patina. Inscribed "Le Faguays," on black marble base. 30" tall.
$2,090 (1986)

*Figure of a nymph,* cast from a model by Pierre Le Faguays, early 20th century. The silvered bronze nude stretching on her toes, her arms crossed above her head, stamped "78," including veined black-marble plinth signed "Le Faguays." 28⅞" tall.
$2,860 (1986)

*Figure of a walking lion,* cast from a model by Max Le Vérrier, French, early 20th century. In metal with black patina. 11¾" tall x 22⅝" long.
$10,000–$15,000

"Nais" by Pierre Le Faguays. (Photo courtesy of William Doyle Galleries)

*Figure of an archer*, cast after a model by by Max Le Vérrier. In bronze, with Cubistic black marble base in two steps on which the archer is kneeling. Action is implied through the lines of the archer's loincloth with streams behind. Signed. 10¼" tall x 9" long.

$600–$750

*Figure of a man and a lion*, cast after a model by Max Le Vérrier. A man striding with a lion by his side in green-patinated metal. Impressed "M. Le Verrier Paris," on a black marble base. 23" tall.

$1,980 (1986)

*Figure of a panther*, cast after a model by Max Le Vérrier. In patinated metal, the lithe animal on the prowl, in green patina on variegated black marble base, unmarked. 26" long.

$500–$700

*Figures of dancers*, cast after models by Max Le Vérrier. In patinated metal; the first, stylized nude woman with one knee raised, her hands extended outward, each holding a marble-like ball; the second, lithe nude figure swinging two hoops about her upper body; both impressed "LeVerrier" in green patina on rectangular stone mounts. 10½" tall.

$990 (1987)

Man and lion by Max Le Vérrier. *(Photo courtesy of Christie's East)*

*Figure of an exotic dancer,* cast from a model by Lipchytz. In polychromed bronze and ivory, the dancer seated with one leg outstretched, the other drawn up, her arms raised, holding a tambourine in her right hand. Inscribed "J Lipchytz," on rectangular green onyx base. 11" tall.

$2,800–$3,200

*Figure of a dancer,* cast from a model by Lorenzl, Austrian, c. 1925. The bronze figure on one foot, in green patina, inscribed "Lorenzl" and impressed "Austria" on onyx plinth. 22½" tall.

$850 (1986)

*Figure of a dancer,* cast from a model by Lorenzl, after F. Preiss, c. 1925. Polychromed bronze figure standing on her right foot, balanced on cone-shaped dome, her arms outstretched, ivory feather in headdress, on onyx base. Inscribed "Lorenzl."

$8,000–$9,000

*Figure of a dancer,* cast from a model by Lorenzl. In bronze, the lithe figure with arms outstretched and one knee drawn up toward her chest, her hair streaming behind her. Brown patina on green onyx block base. Inscribed "Lorenzl." 13¾" tall.

$1,870 (1986)

Statue by Lorenzl. *(Photo courtesy of Christie's East)*

*Figure of scarf dancer,* cast from a model by Lorenzl, early 20th century. Polychrome bronze of nude woman, gracefully posed on tiptoe, one leg raised and bent at the knee, holding a scarf with two hands, one arm extended, on green onyx octagonal plinth. Inscribed "Lorenzl," stamped "21" underneath. 28½" tall.
$8,000–$12,000

*Figure of a snake dancer,* cast from a model by Adolf Marcuse, early 20th century, executed by Gladenbeck. In bronze, in Secessionist taste, the nude figure with inscribed signature and foundry mark, onyx plinth. 21½" tall.
$1,100 (1987)

*Figure of a muse, "L'Inspiration,"* cast from a model by Eugène Marioton, French. The bronze winged nymph standing with lyre in her raised left arm, inscribed "Eugène Marioton" on self bronze base with ribbon inscribed "L'Inspiration" (lyre broken). 36¼" tall.
$1,320 (1986)

*Head of a goddess, "Divinité Solaire,"* cast from a model by Gustav Miklos, French, 20th century. Very stylized, polished-bronze head of a woman, inscribed "G. Miklos 4/4," and stamped with the Valsuani Foundry seal. 25⅝" tall.
$38,500 (1986)

*Figure of a dancer,* L. Morelli, Italian, 20th century. In carved white marble. An Egyptian dancer, nude except for stylized loincloth and sandals, gracefully leaning backward with one hand raised to her face. On a black stone base inscribed "A. Frilli Ltd./L. Morelli, Florence." 30" tall.

$1,300 (1987)

*Figure of a ballerina girl,* cast from a model by Omerth. In gilt bronze and ivory on alabaster base, inscribed. 8½" tall.

$550 (1986)

*Figure of a child,* cast and carved from a model by Omerth. In gilt bronze and ivory, figure in peasant dress, on green onyx, inscribed. 6½" tall.

$385 (1986)

*Figure of a clown boy,* cast and carved from a model by Omerth. In gilt-bronze and ivory, on green onyx base, inscribed. 8" tall.

$462 (1986)

*Figure of a Dutch boy,* cast and carved from a model by Omerth. In bronze and ivory, inscribed on base "L'Ollandais" and "Made in France," in gold brown patina on yellow onyx base. 6½" tall.

$750–$800

*Figure of a skater,* cast from a model by Omerth, in bronze and ivory. The child in knickers, one leg held back and arms outstretched, holding a cane, inscribed "Omerth" on white onyx rectangular base. 7⅞" tall.

$528 (1987)

*Figure of a skater,* cast from a model by Omerth, in bronze and ivory. The little girl in skirt, holding an upraised hockey stick, inscribed "Omerth" on rectangular white onyx base. 7¼" tall.

$800–$1,000

*Bookends,* cast from models by Roland Paris, born in Austria. In bronze and ivory, one bookend of a seated gentleman in top hat with a bird perched on his knee; the other of a jester with an owl, on black marble mounts. Inscribed "Roland Paris." 7" tall.

$1,210 (1986)

*Bust of a jester,* cast from a model by Roland Paris. In bronze and alabaster, the jester's alabaster face cocked to one side, smiling slyly, framed by red-patinated jester's cap, inscribed "Roland Paris." 10" tall.

$485 (1986)

## Sculpture and Statues

*Figure of a Pierrot*, cast from a model by Roland Paris. In polychromed bronze and ivory, the clown in blue cape and pantaloons, holding a sword in his left hand, with his right hand to his heart, on octagonal black base, inscribed "Roland Paris." 10½" tall.

$1,200–$1,800

*Figure of a schoolmaster*, cast from a model by Roland Paris. In bronze and ivory, the schoolmaster with blue enamel suit with silvered collar and hose, holding book and baton. Inscribed "Roland Paris" on square green onyx base. 10" tall.

$825 (1986)

*Figure of an exotic dancer*, cast from a model by Paul Phillipe, French, 20th century. The standing figure with arms aloft in gilt-bronze halter and swirling skirt, the arms, head, and legs of ivory, on circular two-tier green onyx base, inscribed "Phillipe." 23½" tall.

$9,000–$12,000

*Figure of a modern señorita*, cast from a model by Paul Phillipe. Smiling figure wearing a broad-brimmed hat and shawl, her left hand on her hip, her right hand holding an opened fan. Inscribed "P. Phillipe made in France" on domed red marble base. 18½" tall.

$7,700 (1987)

*Figure of a butterfly dancer*, cast from a model by Prof. Otto Poertzel, German. In gilt bronze, the dancer on tiptoe, with arms outstretched, her short tunic with full sleeves draped from her arms, resembling butterfly wings. Inscribed "Prof. Poertzel" on square, black, faceted marble base. 24" tall.

$2,000–$3,000

*Figure of an acrobat, "Balancing,"* cast from a model by Ferdinand (Fritz) Preiss, German, early 20th century. A cold-painted bronze and ivory figure, in metallic gold and green, inscribed "F. Preiss" and stamped with the Preiss-Kassler foundry seal, including marble base. 15⅜" tall.

$7,700 (1986)

*Figure of Ada May, "Beach Dancer,"* cast and carved from a model by Fritz Preiss, early 20th century. In cold-painted bronze, ivory, and glass, on Belgian marble and green onyx pedestal, signed "F. Preiss." 14⅜" tall.

$7,700 (1987)

*Figure of a dancer, "Cabaret Girl,"* cast from a model by Fritz Preiss, early 20th century. In cold-painted bronze, on triangular green onyx socle, inscribed "F. Preiss." 15" tall.

$12,000–$18,000

*Figure of a musician, "Flute Player,"* by Fritz Preiss, c. 1930. In bronze and ivory, a young man walking and playing his instrument, his trousers, vest, and shirt poloychomed bronze, face and hands well-carved ivory, on marble base. 17½" tall.

$12,000–$15,000

*Figure of a woman, "Lighter Than Air,"* cast from a model by Fritz Preiss, early 20th century. In cold-painted bronze, ivory, and glass, stamped with the Preiss-Kassler foundry monogram, on Belgian marble and green and brown onyx base, with brass tag inscribed " 'Lighter than Air' Ada May by F. Preiss." 13½" tall.

$6,600 (1987)

*Figure of a skater, "Skater,"* cast from a model by Fritz Preiss, early 20th century. The cold-painted bronze and ivory skater, on one leg with her other leg and arms extended and head tilted back, on black and green onyx base signed "F. Preiss." Inscribed with the Preiss-Kassler seal. 13⅛" tall.

$3,850 (1986)

"Cabaret Girl" by F. Preiss. *(Photo courtesy of Nancy McClelland, Christie's)*

## Sculpture and Statues

"Flute Player" by F. Preiss. (Photo by R. Four; courtesy of Madison Galleries)

*Figure of a dancer,* cast from a model by Fritz Preiss, early 20th century. In parcel-gilt cold-painted bronze and ivory, including green onyx base, inscribed "F. Preiss." 14¼" tall.

$12,100 (1987)

*Figure of a nymph,* by Fritz Preiss, early 20th century. Ivory figure standing on her toes, her arms extended overhead, on shaped green and black onyx plinth, signed "F. Preiss." 17⅜" tall.

$9,680 (1986)

*Figure of a nude,* cast from a model by Gilbert Privat, French, c. 1925. Bronze statue of a standing nude woman holding a drape in her hands as she looks down. 27" tall.

$2,400 (1985)

*Figure of a black panther,* cast from a model by M. Prost, German. In bronze, the stylized cat, in dark patina, creeps forward stealthily on a black, inclined base. Inscribed "M. Prost." 14¾" long.

$1,210 (1987)

*Figure of a dancer,* cast from a model by Marcel Claude Renard, French, executed by Valsuani Foundry, c. 1928. The bronze, draped figure with rich brown patina, stepping forward with one foot and holding drapery in her hand. Sculpture rests on drapery and dancer's toe. Inscribed artist's signature, date and impressed Valsuani Foundry mark. 27½" tall.

$3,400 (1987)

# ART DECO

*Figure of a woman dancer*, by Rischmann, French, c. 1925. In bronze, the woman with one leg extended wears a wide flaring skirt and in her outstretched hand holds a tiny Buddha. On a veined marble base. Inscribed "Rischmann." 25½" tall.

$1,650 (1986)

*Figure of a young woman*, by G. Rigot, French, 20th century. In bronze, the woman standing demurely with hands held behind her back, her patterned dress with silver and gold inlay, on black-gold marble base with green onyx band. 14" tall.

$4,000–$6,000

*Figure of a monkey*, by Edouard Sandoz, French. In bronze, figure of a marmoset monkey with long tail wrapping over head and back, in rich black patina, signed and stamped "Ed. M. Sandoz." 8" tall.

$5,000–$5,500

*Figural group of a couple*, "Rhytmi Vitea," cast from a model by A. Sciortino, Italian. In bronze, the couple standing back to back with outstretched, intertwined arms, in reddish brown patina on self base, inscribed "A. Sciortino 1927 Roma." 21" tall.

$3,300 (1986)

Statue by Rischmann. *(Photo courtesy of William Doyle Galleries)*

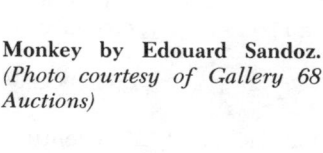

Monkey by Edouard Sandoz. *(Photo courtesy of Gallery 68 Auctions)*

*Figural group*, cast from a model by Pierre Traverse, French. In bronze, the stylized nude maiden running alongside a prancing gazelle, her arm around the animal's neck, inscribed "Pierre Traverse" and "La Stelle." Green patina on a variegated marble base. 12⅞" long.

$1,430 (1987)

*Figure of a smoker*, cast from a model by J. Ulrich, Austrian. In green-patinated bronze and ivory, the languid maiden draped over a chair, holding a cigarette in her right hand, with a blanket across her lap that lifts to reveal her bare midsection as well as a compartment for matches. Impressed under the chair, "Austria" and "J. Ulrich," on green onyx videpoche or ashtray base. 6¼" tall.

$1,100 (1987)

*Figural group*, by J. Wasey, American, bronze sculpture of two stylized roosters in cubistically hieratic composition on gray marble base, signed "J. Wasey." 8¾" tall.

$500–$750

*Figure of a man, "Mephistopheles,"* by Waldmuller, German, c. 1925. Dramatic bronze hooded and cloaked figure with hands clutching at cloak, the face and hands in ivory, scrolls on rectangular bronze base, bronze inscribed "Waldmuller B.K." 22¾" tall.

$6,500–$8,000

*Standing figure, "The Riding Crop,"* cast from a model by Bruno Zach, Austrian, early 20th century. In bronze and ivory with reddish brown patina, the bare-breasted woman standing with feet apart, hands clasped behind her back, eyes closed, with smile on her face. Inscribed "Zach." 11" tall.

$4,620 (1986)

*Figural group,* by Bruno Zach, 20th century. In bronze and ivory, the woman astride a prancing horse, her figure in gilt semidraped dress, a javelin in hand. The head, body, arms, and legs of ivory, on oval onyx base, inscribed "Zach." 15" tall.

$7,000–$9,000

*Figural group,* cast from a model by Bruno Zach, early 20th century. Cold-painted black bronze of horse with cowboy on his back, the cowboy trying to subdue his rearing mount, lasso in hand, on veined marble base. Inscribed "Zach." 16⅝" tall.

$1,430 (1986)

*Figure of a dancing girl,* cast from a model by Bruno Zach, early 20th century. In bronze and ivory, figure wears a sleeveless and shoulderless dress and over-the-elbow gloves. Shoulders and head in ivory, with hair in ribbons. Inscribed "B. Zach," brown patina. 15⅜" tall.

$6,600 (1987)

Statue of a dancer by Bruno Zach. *(Photo courtesy of Nancy McClelland, Christie's)*

## Sculpture and Statues

*Figure of a girl,* cast from a model by Bruno Zach. In cold-painted and parcel gilt, with head tilted back and dress held out to the sides, inscribed "Zach" and "Made in Austria," on stepped base. 7" tall.

$1,500–$1,750

*Figure of Paavo Nurmi,* cast from a model by Bruno Zach. Polychromed, bronzed running figure breaking the finish line tape. Inscribed "Zach, Argentor Vienna, Made in Austria" on veined white marble base. 11¼" tall.

$1,800–$2,200

*Antelopes,* anon. In bronze, the stylized animals standing with noses raised, their curved horns touching their dark brown patina on self rectangular bases. 6¾" long. Pair.

$300–$400

*Figure of a girl,* anon. In bronze, profile of girl facing right with flowing hair, on marble base, unsigned. 8½" tall.

$275–$325

### Frankart

*Ashstand,* by Frankart, American. In silvered metal and brass, silvered nude standing on tiptoe on a glass ball, arms raising circular dish (missing ceramic liner) on square platform, stamped "Frankart, Pat. Des. 80059." 23½" high.

$275 (1986)

*Ashstand,* by Frankart. Three stylized nudes standing, holding pottery insert. 24" tall.

$850 (1987)

*Ashtray holder,* by Frankart, 1927. In green-patinated metal, the prancing stylized nude holding arms out to one side for circular green-glazed ceramic ashtray, on octagonal self base, impressed "c. Frankart '27." 10" tall.

$330 (1986)

*Bookends,* by Frankart. In white metal, each formed as a standing mother bear, flanked by twin cubs on self-shaped triangular base, gold/brown patina. Impressed "Frankart Inc. Pat. Appld. For." 6¾" tall. Pair.

$33 (1986)

## ART DECO

*Bookends,* by Frankart. In silvered metal, modeled as busts of scottie dogs with wispy curled whiskers, unmarked. 5½" tall. Pair.
$110 (1986)

*Figure of a woman,* by Frankart. Slender figure in cast white metal, painted black, holding blue glass dish. Molded "Frankart, Inc. Patent Pend." 14" high,
$250–$300

*Figure of a woman,* by Frankart. Kneeling figure in cast white metal, painted black, holding integrated metal dish, molded "Frankart, Inc. Patent Pend." 12" high. This model was also issued as a lamp.
$175–$225

*Head of a woman,* by Frankart, in the style of Modigliani. In white metal, with long curved neck and highly stylized facial features. Approx. 8" tall.
$100–$150

*Lamp,* by Frankart. Modeled as two stylized kneeling nudes protecting an amber crackle-glass globe, in green patina, molded "Frankart Inc., Pat Appl'd For." 9½" tall.
$800–$1,200

**Head of a woman by Frankart.**
*(Photo courtesy of Peter Boehm, Dualities Gallery)*

## Sculpture and Statues

Kneeling woman by Frankart.
(Photo by R. Four)

*Lamp*, by Frankart, 1927. Two green-painted metal figures holding a shade of clear and frosted stepped glass. 20½" tall, marked "Frankart, Inc. c 1927."

$350–$500

*Lamp*, by Frankart. Two silver-black painted nude figures of women kneeling back to back, holding an 8" orange crackle-glass globe, marked "Frankart, Inc. U.S. Des. Pat. 82400."

$500–$700

*Lamp*, by Frankart. In patinated metal and glass, square base with bucking donkey, white glass stepped shade.

$300–$500

*Lamps*, by Frankart, 1927. The base of each metal lamp modeled as a pair of lithe nudes on tiptoe, standing back, holding overhead a skyscraper-stepped amber glass shade, each impressed "c. Frankart '27," in Roman green patination. 21" tall. Pair.

$1,200–$1,800

*Lamp and ashtray*, by Frankart. In black-painted metal, base decorated with a nude kneeling, holding a black glass ashtray, molded "Frankart Inc." 15" tall.

$99 (1986)
$330 (1986)

## ART DECO

*Lamp*, possibly by Nuart. Brown patinated metal base cast as two lithe figures on tiptoe standing back to back, arms raised overhead to support an amber glass spherical shade, unmarked. 19¾" tall.

$150–$200

*Smoking stand*, by Frankart. White metal, painted silver-black, female figure holding a hoop atop which is an opaque green glass ashtray with three cigar rests. 27" tall, molded "Frankart, Inc."

$400–$600

*Statue/pen tray*, by Frankart, cast in white metal with original green paint, woman standing on rectangular base, molded with pen trays and small stylized skylines. Her arms are spread wide to hold angular frosted-glass panel behind her in the manner of a luminaire. Molded "Frankart, Inc. Pat. Pending." Approx. 8" tall.

$260 (1987)

*Vase with figural nude*, by Frankart. Cast in white metal, woman in dance position holding floral wreath that encircles and supports a fluted amber glass vase. Molded "Frankart" on octagonal base. Overall 15" tall, 8" vase rim diameter.

$385 (1987)

Statue with vase by Frankart.
*(Photo courtesy of Savoia and Fromm Auction Services)*

# GLASS

The pharaohs may have been the only ones to own glass in Egypt, but by the Art Nouveau and Art Deco periods both art and functional glass were in high demand by the middle classes.

Glass is usually made from powdered flint or fine sand, ashes or another alkali, salt or metallic oxide, and lime. The type and proportion of its ingredients give it its color, transparency, opacity, ability to distort light, and so on. Lead crystal has at least 24 percent lead oxide. Other metallic oxides are what give color to glass.

Cameo glass was one of the first major types of glass to gain popularity and was revived in England in the 1870s. Cameo glass has two or more layers of superimposed glass; then the top layer is cut away to create designs in the lower layer. At first glass was carefully cut by hand, but soon glassmakers were using hydrofluoric acid and cutting wheels. Cheaper and faster methods were devised, ultimately resulting in a glass in which an enameled design was added to simulate the look of cameo. Much production came from Czechoslovakia, where labor was cheap and raw materials abundant. It became one of the two major centers of European glass production. The other was along the border of Germany and France near the city of Nancy in Alsace-Lorraine, where the rich forests fired the furnaces.

With the emergence of the individual decorative artist in the mid-1800s, artists and designers began working in glass. Emile Gallé and another Alsatian glassmaker, Daum, etched and carved flowered designs mainly on the surface of the glass—a style and technique that provided the standard for the form. Gallé was also one of the first artists in glass to sign his work.

Art Nouveau iridescent glass is best known from the works of Tiffany and Steuben in the United States and Loetz in Czechoslovakia. Tiffany brought the United States unrivaled preeminence in stained and iridescent glass during this period. Tiffany lamps are commanding astronomical prices on today's market and are perhaps the best-known American furnishing.

Art Nouveau styles continued to be made into the 1930s, although the designs became repetitive or degenerated from the originals. In addition, because mass-produced glass was needed to meet the demand of middle-class households, artistic production increasingly became economically unfeasible. Schneider glassworks in France succeeded in bringing industrial techniques to the styling of cameo designs in their Verre Francais, greatly popularizing it. But by then the love affair with cameo and iridescent glass had all but ended.

Like all decorative arts, Art Nouveau glass design was challenged by the Vienna Secession and Deustcher Werkbund, which searched for functionality and simplicity of style and line. In Vienna, Josef Hoffmann, Koloman Moser, Ludwig Moser (1833–1916), and other artists were creating innovative designs in glass, some based on geometric patterns and shapes.

In France three separate design styles and movements in glass had been emerging since the turn of the century.

The first was led by Francois Decorchement (1880–1971), the leading artist of the *pâte-de-verre* method. Blown glass is given its shape while still molten. Afterward surface decoration may be added. In contrast to to this method, *pâte-de-verre* can be molded in its cold state.

*Pâte-de-verre*, or "glass paste" as it literally translates, is finely crushed crystals of glass mixed with a binding agent to make it malleable, plus different metallic oxides for color. The paste can be sculpted like clay and shaped as figures, plaques, bowls, or vases. The glass is then fired to revitrify the crystals. The result is a glass that can be decorated or colored throughout its mass, not just on the surface.

The finished product can be eggshell thin or very thick and chunky. Decorchemont also produced eggshell-thin *pâte-d'email*, a porcelain of which little has survived. His *pâte-de-verre*, however, was thicker, heavier, and translucent rather than transparent. It was often cut with geometric motifs. His work is equal to that of the leading artists in other decorative arts of the period and is therefore both difficult to find and generally very expensive. Others re-created *pâte-de-verre* using more industrial, commercially viable methods.

Notable *pâte-de-verre* artists who are sought after on today's market include Gabriel Argy-Rousseau (1885–1953) and Alméric Walter. These artists produced a great many different types of glass: bowls, vases, and other vessels; candlesticks and utilitarian objects; glass sculptures; and *videpoches*—"empty pockets"—a decoratively sculpted glass dish one kept on a dresser to hold coins, pins, and the like.

Alméric Walter set up his own company and commissioned several other artists to produce work for him. However, only a few glassmakers ever used the *pâte-de-verre* method. Daum produced a few fine examples, but Gallé and Lalique never adopted it. The work of all *pâte-de-verre* artists is fairly high priced on today's collecting market but still within reach.

The second movement in glass was in handcrafted glass, inspired by Maurice Marinot (1882–1960). The artist and perhaps one or two assistants created the works, as opposed to the Lalique method, which produced glass as an industrial process. Artists Jean Sala, Henri Navarre (1885–1971), and André Thuret (1898–1965) are other notable individuals who had the same philosophy and employed techniques similar to Marinot's. Marcel Goupy, another noted French glass designer, at least personally supervised the blowing of his pieces at the glassworks.

Marinot is the most sought after, but he is also the hardest to find, as his work was bought up by collectors and museums from the start of his career as a glassmaker. Marinot began as a Fauve artist, with such painters as Matisse, Dufy, and Braque. He was the first fine artist to undertake ma' ...g glass himself, and from 1923 he blew his own glass. One of his hallmarks was the way he captured the air bubble in the glass. Marinot's glass is often deeply etched, and the color effects are subtle.

His patterns are mostly geometric; even natural motifs such as flowers are stylized geometrically. He used many methods for cutting the glass, using flint, a cutting wheel, or etching with acid. Typical patterns are series of triangles or circles in bold relief.

Marinot's art soon gave way to an increasingly industrialized glass manufacture using molds and power presses. However, it is interesting to note that the success of some of Marinot's design creations—especially the deep, acid-etched geometric patterns—inspired the Daum Nancy company to create more Modernist designs to meet changing tastes and increasing demand.

Although this connection was observed some years ago by author Katherine Morrison McClinton, Daum is still essentially collected by connoisseurs of Art Nouveau. Auguste Daum (1853–1909) and his brother Antoine (1864–1930), and their company, Daum Nancy, were important Art Nouveau glassmakers who managed to make the transition to Art Deco with their new designs. Very recently, Daum vases and lamps of this later design have been finding more buyers and higher prices in the Art Deco field.

The third and certainly the best-known design style in glass was led by René Lalique, the master of decorative, industrially molded glass. His imitators included Sabino, Etling, Hunebelle, Genet and Michon,

Edouard Cazaux, Henri Dieupart, Verlys, Jobling, and many other glass houses in the United States and Europe that turned out Lalique-like glass in the 1920s and 1930s.

Generally lower priced than Lalique on the market, often very well executed, these works can confuse collectors. Fortunately, many pieces are well marked: "Etling France," "A. Hunebelle," "Sabino," and so on. Unfortunately, many collectors pass up a real value simply because it does not come with the name "Lalique." Too often dismissed as "imitators," none of the above should be overlooked, for all produced very fine pieces.

Etling, for example, was one of the most important makers of glass, statues, bronzes, and other ornaments in France during the period between the two wars. Andre Hunebelle was a leading designer of table glass in the same period, and his designs tend to be more abstract than Lalique's. Marius Ernest Sabino was a talented designer who exhibited at the 1925 Paris Exposition.

In the United States, Consolidated Lamp and Glass Company and Phoenix Glass, both located in Pennsylvania, copied Lalique and Nouveau styles for their molded vases and lamp bases. It is often impossible to distinguish the work of these companies. Typical patterns are dragonflies, grasshoppers, birds, flowers, and nudes, molded in relief on a frosted background to give the appearance of cameo or Lalique-type glass.

Many Phoenix glass pieces are actually handsome, but it is usually easy to distinguish them from Lalique as they tend to be less well executed, both in color and quality, and somewhat heavier. However, Phoenix vases in this style are bringing anywhere from $80 to $500 on today's market and are highly collectible. Phoenix gained a popular market at about the time Lalique's works were selling at fine department stores.

From the Scandinavian countries came the best of yet another design movement: clear cut crystal in Modernist design. Companies such as Orrefors, Leerdam, Kosta, and Boda led the way. (See "Fakes, Forgeries, and Reproductions.")

French *crystalleries* offered some competition to the leaders, most notably the Baccarat crystal factory. Founded in France in 1764, it continues today. In the 1920s it was known for its perfume flasks and tableware in both glass and crystal, especially designs by Georges Chevalier.

Swedish Modern had a great deal of influence in household furnishings with its strong, clean lines and use of natural materials. Scandinavian Modern furnishings of the 1920s and 1930s are increasingly showing up on the Art Deco market.

The most collected is Orrefors, which until World War I was a little-known company in the forests of southern Sweden. Orrefors was the first crystal company to commission artists, such as Simon Gate (1883–1945), Edvard Hald, and Vicke Lindstrand, in 1915 and 1917.

It also developed a stunning type of glass called *graal,* a cased glass in which colored relief decorations are covered with clear, smooth crystal. Even today Orrefors advertises crystal that is "devoid of intricate cutting patterns" but also "devoid of flaws." This 250-year-old company continues to be recognized for its glass artistry.

There are comparatively few examples of fine Art Deco American glass from 1925 to 1939. Artists were certainly aware of designs by Lalique, Daum, and others being imported in large quantities to this country in the 1920s and 1930s. Still, a Deco style in glass failed to materialize over here.

Some say that Tiffany's overwhelming control on American decorative arts was the force that blocked a transition in glass in America. Like the stubborn French Art Nouveau glass companies, Tiffany was faced with bankruptcy by 1930.

Frederick Carder (1863–1963) established the Steuben Glass Company, absorbed by the Corning Glass Works in 1918. Carder's incredibly beautiful iridescent designs wound up gathering dust on the shelves, as they were strongly challenged by the Scandinavians, and Steuben was forced to make a transition to a new style.

Some of Steuben's designs before 1930 fall broadly into the range of Art Deco style, such as its "jade glass" vases with "alabaster" handles, of opaline glass, made around 1925. The best Modern designs from Steuben came much later, when Walter Dorwin Teague designed a series of crystal stemware patterns such as Riviera, Spiral, Blue Empire, Winston, and St. Tropez. Teague was the firm's design consultant for only a short period of time, and his work for Steuben is highly collectible.

In 1933 Steuben commissioned John Gates and Sidney Biehler Waugh to create clear-glass objects in Modern design that could compete with the Scandinavians. Waugh created massive vases with bold facets. He also used stylized mythological motifs carved into crystal, such as his "Europa" bowl in 1935. His "Gazelle" bowl, also created in 1935, is one of the best known examples of quality Art Deco glass in America. Among other things, John Gates designed the World's Fair Cup for the 1939 New York World's Fair, which incorporated the design of the trylon and perisphere on top.

## PERFUME BOTTLES

In the fall of 1987 Elizabeth Taylor introduced her new perfume "Passion," with much fanfare. One ounce of perfume retailed at $165. It should be no surprise that the bottle and packaging were distinctly Deco in style: rich purple glass in a stepped-back design with sharp angles, stylized fanlike stopper, gold banding at the neck, and a gold diamond in the center, and boxes to match. For seven decades the Art Deco/Art Moderne style in perfume bottles has maintained its air of sophisticated elegance.

The perfume bottle is currently the least expensive and most available category of early Art Deco glass collecting, but that may not last for long. One event that may affect prices is the major exhibition being organized by the Fragrance Foundation in association with the Smithsonian Institution for the fall of 1988.

Perfume bottles were made by several well-known early glass designers, most notably René Lalique. In general, Lalique perfume bottles command the highest prices, especially earlier bottles and those with beautiful fanlike stoppers of flowers and fruit.

Gaston Vuitton, Baccarat, and many fashion companies created perfume bottles, cologne bottles, atomizers, and other toiletry bottles. Some are influenced by Cubism, and others have repetitive patterns or motifs of shells, the French fleur-de-lis, bees, and of course flowers. Some have stoppers that are more elaborate than the bottle itself, and others are decorated with designs in black enamel.

Perfume bottles were also made in Germany, Sweden, Czechoslovakia, and other countries in both clear and colored glass. Many of these were manufactured in great quantities for retailing through department stores. Because the Art Deco style has persisted in perfume bottles to the present day, it is difficult to tell 1920s and 1930s works from later pieces.

Look for those that are wheel-cut or etched "Czechoslovakia" at antiques shows and flea markets. They can still be found priced as low as $50 to $65, and on up to $300 or more. The price depends on the design of the glass and/or the enameling and the condition of the bottle and stopper. Bottles without stoppers can be very cheap, but don't expect to find a stopper that fits at a later date.

A beginning collector may even want to start with bottles that were designed in the Art Deco period but are still on the market. "L'Air du Temps," with its two frosted doves, was originally designed by Marc Lalique. Other modern examples are "Shalimar" from Guerlain and of course Elizabeth Taylor's "Passion."

## MASS-PRODUCED GLASS

In England several companies produced cheap glassware that was influenced by the Modern style in the 1930s. English berry bowl sets are decorative and often have a Modernist look. In America these might be called salad sets or dessert sets—one large bowl and four to six smaller bowls. Generally speaking, not a lot of English "Thirties" glass makes its way to American antiques shows and flea markets, and most of what does is impossible to tell from the American production of the same era.

In America one successful company, already mentioned, was Consolidated Lamp and Glass Company, which produced "Ruba Rombic" tableware, a cased, blown glass with irregular geometric planes and angles. It is very popular and growing in value on the Art Deco market today.

Libbey Glass Company was the leader of Modern design for everyday glassware in the 1930s, and, like Steuben, employed the design talents of Walter Dorwin Teague.

Between the two world wars Carnival and Depression glass flourished in America. Carnival, as it is called because of its use as prizes at carnival shooting booths, comes in a wide variety of styles, shapes, patterns, and manufacturers. Basically, all Carnival is molded glass enhanced with a metallic surface finish—the Tiffany of carnival-goers.

Depression glass refers to low-quality glasswares created for the masses by numerous American companies in the late 1920s and through the 1930s. Generally crystal (clear), amber, pale blue, or pale green transparent glass, whole sets of this everyday kitchenware were given away as premiums with the purchase of a refrigerator or stove. Among the companies that produced it are Indiana Glass Company, Anchor Hocking, Westmoreland, Hazel Atlas, and Federal.

Most Depression glass is not in the Deco style, but a few patterns are and have become more popular on the Deco market in recent years, notably Indiana Glass Company's "Pyramid" and "Tea Room" designs in pink, green, or clear and Anchor Hocking's "Manhattan" in clear and pink.

Depression glass is a collecting field unto itself, with many collectors, clubs, and newsletters. However, in general, the few Deco styles seem to bring higher prices with Art Deco collectors than they do with collectors of Depression glass.

"Pyramid" is most often seen in clear pink with a repetitive triangular pattern. A "Tea Room" tumbler looks like several smaller glasses stacked one inside the other, each larger than the next, and it has a stepped base as well. We've spotted these in flea markets for about $15 to $20.

The "Manhattan" style in particular is enjoying popularity in the Art Deco collectibles market. A press-mold glass, "Manhattan" pieces have repetitive horizontal ribbing, which extends onto the handles. Feet and knobs may be clear glass balls.

A good strong molded glass, "Manhattan" is often put to utilitarian use by its collectors. As the household wares of the 1930s show up frequently in flea markets and used furniture stores, "Manhattan" bowls, sugar and creamer sets, butter dishes, and other service pieces can still be found in perfect condition. However, prices for these are easing upward, and dealers now ask $15, $50, $100, and up for a single service or decorative piece of "Manhattan."

Flea markets and low-end antique shows abound with Deco-style glasswares, both American and others, while some of the best representative pieces find their way into posh showrooms. Much of the production is anonymous, and many companies copied one another's designs. If you are interested in collecting this Deco-style glass, look only for perfect pieces. In addition, serving and decorative pieces are more valuable than plates, saucers, and the like, and sets or subsets can bring good prices.

## *Special Focus: René Lalique*

René Lalique (1860–1945) is the most noted of Art Deco glassmakers, both because of his tremendous design talents and because he was the first really to accept and develop industrial mass-production of glass, which helped lower prices and open up new markets.

Generally, the shapes of his bowls, vases, and other vessels are simple, and the glass may be tinted in a variety of different colors, frosted, or enameled. His molded designs can be in low, medium, or high relief. Motifs range from gods and goddesses to geometric patterns to insects and fish, but most of his designs were drawn from nature. Especially popular are his figures of draped or nude women, which have been imitated by many since then.

Apart from vessels, Lalique created an incredibly wide range of glass objects that expanded his market and his popularity: picture frames, inkwells, glass table services, clocks, statuettes, jewelry pendants, candelabra, wall panels, lamps and lighting fixtures, car radiator ornaments, and perfume and toiletry bottles. He even made public fountains and dining room tables in glass.

As an Art Nouveau jeweler, he had his first exhibition in Paris in 1890. His use of glass enamels, rock crystal, and precious metals was immediately recognized for its genius and brought him clients such as Cartier, Boucheron, and Sarah Bernhardt.

But after about ten years he needed a new challenge, and somewhere around 1900 he started to create seriously in glass. At first his designs were molded in a *cire-perdu*, or "lost wax" method, and retained naturalistic motifs of humans, animals, and foliage in an Art Nouveau style. As he moved from this handcrafted style to a more industrial production, his designs also changed to reflect the newer styles. His real genius was in staying ahead of the times.

In 1907 and 1908 Lalique was commissioned by Coty perfumes to design a line of scent bottles. Roger Coty was an entrepreneur with a great idea. Until then customers had to bring their own bottles to the stores to be filled with perfume. What if, Coty thought, the perfume was sold in its own special bottle? For one thing, it would mean that perfume could be sold everywhere instead of in just a few places.

For Lalique, it was the right idea at the right time. Already very interested in glass, he now truly committed himself to it by founding a factory for glass production near Paris in 1909. Since that time the bottle itself has been almost as important as the perfume inside in terms of making a sale.

Lalique immediately saw the value of mass-producing glass, especially since the market for household objects and furnishings was expanding so quickly. In 1920 he acquired the company's present glassworks in Alsace, right in the center of glass production in France, with its abundant natural supply of wood for the furnaces.

Continually increasing his market, his production, and his line of goods, Lalique made his later models available in quantity in both American and European department and jewelry stores. Vases, sculptures, and other decorative objects were popular gifts for weddings, anniversaries, and holidays. By 1933 he had produced more than fifteen hundred different items.

In today's collecting market, rarer Lalique pieces can easily command thousands of dollars. However, some pieces can still be purchased or acquired at auction for under $1,000. The market base for Lalique has expanded, which means there are more people seeking to assemble collections. In most cases, serious, knowledgeable collectors of vases seek particular designs and pattern numbers identified through Lalique's catalogs.

Lalique car radiator ornaments, too, have found dedicated, passionate collectors today and are commanding the highest prices ever, especially in rare colors. (See the photo in our color section, "An Art Deco Portfolio.")

Prices for some of his vases have skyrocketed. The "Bacchantes" vase, for example, sold at $4,600 at auction in 1985, and in 1987 it brought $15,400. A "Cluny" model vase sold in 1987 at Christie's Monaco for $170,000. Although he has gone in and out of favor with collectors and dealers in the past twenty years, his work is now at its highest level of demand. America is the strongest market worldwide for Lalique, but it has also become very popular in Japan. All of his tremendous output has great value on the market today. (For more about the Lalique market see "Today's Market.")

After René Lalique's death in 1945, the family's artistic tradition was carried on by his son Marc. He reconditioned the factory, which had closed in 1939 because of the war, and revived many of his father's designs as well as creating his own. He also created perfume bottles, such as the well-known "L'Air du Temps" for Ricci. Marc also changed the production from glass to lead crystal. Crystal has a content of at least 24 percent lead oxide, giving it greater weight and sparkle.

When Marc Lalique died in 1977, he left the direction of the factory to his daughter Marie-Claude, who today designs a third generation of Lalique sculptures, vases, and other items for exclusive distribution.

The newer Lalique is sold under the trade name "Cristal Lalique" and is engraved "Lalique France." Works by René Lalique are identified by the inscription "R. Lalique" or "René Lalique." The company inscription has changed several times, which helps to date a piece easily. For serious collectors the best resources for information and documentation are books by Katherine Morrisson McClinton, the Lalique catalogs themselves, and *Lalique par Lalique*, published by the Société Lalique in 1977. However, the book is now out of print and therefore difficult to find.

Although we have not yet seen the newer Lalique creations on the secondary market, we feel that it is just a matter of time. René Lalique's work is becoming very costly, while the newer work can be bought off the shelves of the stores with distribution agreements with the French company. Already some of the Cristal Lalique has seen high increases. Six years ago a pair of angel-wing champagne glasses, sold as the perfect wedding gift, were priced at $70 a stem. Today the price is $130 a stem.

A recent five-city tour of the United States by Marie-Claude Lalique to promote her work resulted in sales of close to $100,000 at Saks Fifth Avenue and of more than that amount in an Indianapolis store. Cristal Lalique sells for considerably more than did the original Lalique, but it is crystal, not glass, and each piece is treated to an extensive process of hand finishing. Small decorative pieces are still under $100, but figural pieces can run as high as $1,000, and larger vases range from $700 to $2,300. The company also has a Cristal Lalique dining room table that sells for $44,000.

Today there are many collectors of Cristal Lalique. Knowledgeable collectors know that they will find a catalog number on a piece, not a price tag. In fact, prices and price increases on contemporary Lalique are set by the company, which has exclusive contracts with its distributors, of whom it requires significantly large orders. The catalog number of each piece refers to the established price the dealer must charge.

Until now, Cristal Lalique has been white-frosted or clear, but in 1987 it began to introduce pieces that combine crystal with amber, blue, and green opalines. Marie-Claude Lalique has already indicated that in the future she may produce Lalique jewelry—a full-circle return to her grandfather's original art.

## PRICE LISTINGS

### Other Glass Designers

*Covered box*, by Gabriel Argy-Rousseau, French. Circular, in *pâte-de-verre* (glass paste), the cover cast with central Bacchanalian mask in dark red ringed by mauve ivy leaves and scalloped border marked with stars, the base with purple ivy leaves framed by arches and stars, on frosted ground mottled with mauve. Impressed "G. Argy-Rousseau," two small chips to base rim. 6" diameter.

$5,280 (1986)

*Table garniture*, by G. Argy-Rousseau, c. 1925. In *pâte-de-verre*, in Egyptian taste, comprising center bowl and four candlesticks in "tortoiseshell" glass molded with ibises, molded signatures on each. Bowl 14" long (5 pieces).

$4,250 (1987)

*Vase*, by G. Argy-Rousseau. In *pâte-de-verre*, cup-shaped, in purple and green molded with pink flowerheads. Signed. 2¾" tall.

$400–$600

*Vase*, by G. Argy-Rousseau. In *pâte-de-verre*, with waisted, flaring body, cast with a band of berried and leafy branches in ambers, greens, and cinnamon on frosted ground, lightly mottled with yellow, impressed "G. Argy-Rousseau France." 3½" tall.

$2,640 (1986)

Table garniture by Gabriel Argy-Rousseau. *(Photo courtesy of William Doyle Galleries)*

*Car ornament,* after Red Ashay. In chrome-mounted frosted glass, woman's head in profile, her hair streaming back behind her, unmarked. 5" long.

$100–$200

*Stemware set,* by Baccarat, French, c. 1937. In glass, with 10 champagne, 10 water, 10 liqueur glasses, set of 4 candlesticks, pair of decanters, and a water pitcher, each bowl raised on slender rectangular stem and cut on underside with semicircles at juncture, the stem continuing to faceted rectangular foot, unsigned. Decanter 10⅝" tall. 47 pieces.

$8,800 (1986)

*Olympic trophy,* designed by Constantine Brancusi, 1936. In glass, formed as a colorless stylized athlete standing with arms upraised, curving backward, on cylindrical black glass base, with bronze plaque reading "1936 Olympic Games," figure inscribed "Brancusi." 19⅞" tall.

$990 (1987)

*Vase,* by Edouard Cazaux, French, for Gueron. In clear and frosted glass, square vase molded on both sides with circular relief panels of the huntress Diana with bow, inscribed "Gueron Cazaux." 8¾" tall.

$500–$550
$275 (1986)

*Vase,* by Cogneville, French. In clear and frosted glass, bulbous shape with inverted rim, molded with two angelfish surrounded by rippling outlines, molded "Modele Dep de R. Cogneville France" (chips). 8¾" tall.

$660 (1986)

*Vase,* by Andries Dirk Copier, Swedish, for Leerdam. Oviform, the thick, yellow-tinted, transparent glass body encasing large air bubbles in the shape of stylized doves, etched with maker's mark. 8" tall.

$1,200–$1,500

*Lamp shade,* by Daum Nancy, French. Conical, the frosted glass with vertical ribs and circles against acid-etched ground, unsigned. 16" in diameter on an original wrought-iron mount with contemporary bulbous base of similar design; 16" tall overall.

$825 (1987)

*Vase*, by Daum Nancy, c. 1930. Etched, footed vase in dark olive glass cut with squares staggered above thin vertical rectangles, inscribed "Daum Nancy France" with the firm's cross of Lorraine mark. 4⅜" tall.

$495 (1986)

*Vase*, by Daum Nancy, c. 1930. Cylindrical glass vase, thick transparent olive ground deeply etched on the obverse and reverse, inscribed "Daum Nancy." 5½" tall.

$700–$900

*Vase*, by Daum Nancy, c. 1930. Conical, the thick transparent olive ground deeply etched with a wide central band of stylized flowers and stems, inscribed "Daum Nancy France." 12" tall.

$2,200 (1987)

*Vase*, by Daum Nancy, c. 1930. Spherical, the thick transparent green-gray glass ground deeply etched with arches filled with V-shapes, inscribed "Daum Nancy France." 15½" tall.

$3,300 (1987)

*Vase*, by Daum Nancy, c. 1925. Large etched, footed vase, bulbous, in peach glass, inscribed "Daum Nancy France" with cross of Lorraine. 12" tall.

$2,000–$3,000

*Vase*, by Daum Nancy, c. 1930. In olive etched glass with geometric motif, inscribed "Daum Nancy" with cross of Lorraine. 6" tall. (It is designs such as these that were inspired by the smaller studio production of Maurice Marinot.)

$375 (1986)

*Vase*, by Daum Nancy, c. 1930, of flattened and tapered cylindrical form, the obverse and reverse of the thick transparent amber glass ground deeply etched with three bands of dots, the sides with columns of semicircles, inscribed "Daum Nancy France." 10½" tall.

$1,100 (1986)

*Vase*, by Daum Nancy, c. 1930. In cast iron and etched glass, ovoid with twin semicircular handles, the thick transparent amethyst ground deeply etched with stylized leaves and flowers, the handles etched with an angular design, inscribed "Daum Nancy France." Electrified, triple-tiered, silvered-iron base with removable ball supports, unsigned. 17" tall.

$770 (1986)

## ART DECO

*Left.* **Vase by Maurice Marinot.** *(Photo courtesy of the Corning Museum of Glass) Right.* **Vase by Daum Nancy.** *(Photo courtesy of William Doyle Galleries)*

*Vase,* by Henri Dieupart, French. Cream-colored opaque glass vase of bulbous form molded in relief, with nude female striding through a field of textured patterns, molded "Dieupart, France." 8¼" tall.
$605 (1986)

*Vase,* by H. Dieupart. As above but with frosted and black stained glass. Molded "Dieupart, Edition Simonet." 8¼" tall.
$1,000–$1,200

*Vases,* by H. Dieupart. In frosted glass, of tapered conical form in milky white frosted glass molded with a honeycomb pattern, each molded "H. Dieupart" and etched "Made in France Exclusively for Paris Decorations." 12" tall (pair).
$825 (1986)

*Figure of harem girl,* by Etling, French. The opalescent, slender, barebreasted woman in blossoming overshirt, molded "Etling." 11" tall.
$440 (1986)

*Figure of nude holding drapery,* by Etling. In opalescent glass, translucent blue on clear base, molded "Etling." 9" tall.
$220 (1986)
$400–$500

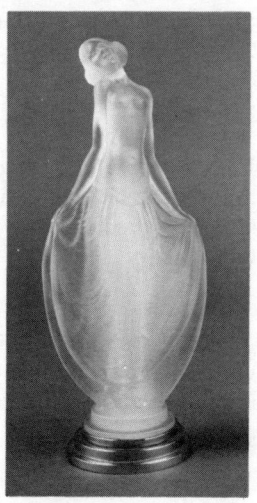

Harem girl by Etling. *(Photo courtesy of Christie's East)*

*Vase*, by Etling. In clear and frosted glass, the ovoid body molded with medallions enclosing fronds of foliage and berries, molded "Etling 35 France." 11" tall.

$495 (1986)

*Pitcher*, by Marcel Goupy, French. Rounded body with large handle and flat, circular base. In smoky glass with stylized enameled flowers. 9" tall.

$475–$550

*Vase*, by Hunebelle, French. In clear and frosted glass, the globe form molded with diamond shapes, molded "A. Hunebelle & R. Cogneville, France." 8" tall.

$825 (1986)

*Vase*, by Hunebelle. In opalescent glass, conical, with five opalescent vertical ribs, etched with snowflake design, molded "HuneBelle (sic), France." 9¼" tall.

$990 (1987)

*Decanter set*, by Ludwig Möser, Möser & Sons, Bohemian but worked in Vienna. In amethyst glass, optically interesting with vertical fluting, including stoppered decanter with six glasses, signed. Decanter 9½" tall.

$350–$500

ART DECO

*Vase,* by Möser and Sons, c. 1930. In amber glass, with applied gold band displaying Bacchanalian classical figures, signed "Moser Carlsbad." 9¾" tall.

$900–$1,200

*Vase,* by Orrefors, Swedish, designed by Edvard Hald. In *graal* glass, the clear ovoid body with green internal decoration of fish swimming amid seaweed, inscribed "Orrefors, Graal No. 1245, Edvard Hald." 5" tall.

$165 (1987)

*Vase,* by Orrefors, designed by Vicke Lindstrand, c. 1937. In clear glass, rectangular form tapering to base, engraved with a woman playing tennis and a monogram. Inscribed bottom, signed "Orrefors Lindstrand 1937." 8¾" tall.

$330 (1986)

*Vase,* by Orrefors, designed by Ingeborg Lundin. An ariel glass piece of cylindrical form, the clear glass internally decorated in dark blue with six striped panels, inscribed "Orrefors Ariel Nr. 535K Ingeborg Lundin." 5½" tall.

$286 (1986)

*Vase,* by Orrefors, designed by Edwin Ohrstrom, 1938. In *graal* glass, massively walled body with amorphic figures engaged in games, inscribed "Orrefors 1938 Graal 781 E. Ohrstrom." 8¾" tall.

$6,600 (1987)

*Vase,* by Orrefors. In cut lead crystal, with thick base and geometric rectangular designs. Inscribed "Orrefors." 4½" tall.

$120–$150

*Vase,* by Phoenix Glass Co., American, 1930s. In white glass with molded relief of wild roses. Gold and black Phoenix sticker intact. 11" tall, 4½" rim diameter.

$65–$75

*Vase,* attributed to Phoenix Glass Co. In white glass with molded relief of dragonflies and cattails. 7" tall, 3" rim diameter.

$40–$50

*Vase,* attributed to Phoenix Glass Co. Molded in translucent glass with nude female figures. 11½" tall.

$125–$150

*Graal* vase by Orrefors. *(Photo courtesy of Nancy McClelland, Christie's)*

*Bud vases,* by Sabino, French. In frosted glass, squat ovoid form with everted rim, molded with overlapping leaves and berries, both inscribed "Sabino, France." 4" tall (pair).

$242 (1986)

*Vase,* by Sabino. In blue glass, pear-shaped body molded with two rows of faceted ovals, inscribed "Sabino France." 5" tall.

$440 (1986)

*Vase,* by Sabino, c. 1925. In molded opalescent glass, with design of standing and kneeling women carrying baskets of fruits and flowers. Molded "Sabino." 9" tall. (This piece is a particularly good Sabino and could pass as Lalique were it not for the signature.)

$500 (1986)

*Vase,* by Sabino, c. 1935, French. In amber glass with raised cube and geometric decoration, signed "Sabino." 6" tall, 6½" diameter.

$300–$350

*Goblets,* by Steuben, American. In green jade glass, model #5154, the conical bowl descending to alabaster twist stem on circular foot, unmarked. 7" tall. Set of 13.

$880 (1987)

Vase by Sabino. *(Photo courtesy of William Doyle Galleries)*

Green jade vases by Steuben. *(Photo courtesy of William Doyle Galleries)*

Vases, by Steuben, c. 1925. In green jade glass with alabaster-colored glass handles. 13" tall. Pair.

$1,600 (1987)
$1,300 (1987)

Vases, by Steuben, c. 1925. As above but 10½" tall. Pair.

$1,100 (1987)

Vases, "American Ballad," by Sidney Waugh, American, 1942, for Steuben. In clear glass, the cylindrical bodies supported by a broad column encasing a band of air bubbles; one engraved with an Indian, one with a guitar-playing cowboy; both inscribed "Steuben." 6½" tall (one with restored finial).

**$495 (1986)**

*Vase, "Ganymede,"* by Sidney Waugh, 1938, for Steuben. Footed conical body in clear glass engraved with a standing nude man being carried aloft by a large eagle, inscribed "Sidney Waugh." 13⅝" tall.

**$7,700 (1986)**

*Shallow bowl, "Mariners,"* by Sidney Waugh, 1937, for Steuben. In glass, the transparent ground of the circular bowl engraved with a compass bordered by a nude woman reclining beneath a palm tree, a nude bearded man and two seahorses, inscribed "Steuben 1937." 15½" diameter with stand.

**$2,000–$2,500**

*Vase,* by Verlys, French. In frosted glass, the ovoid body molded all over with bees in flight against a grassy background, signed. 5⅜" tall.

**$1,430 (1986)**

*Vase,* by Verlys. In blue glass, the footed ovoid form molded in relief with heads of wheat, brilliant blue glass, molded "Verlys." 9¾" tall.

**$3,520 (1986)**

*Plate,* by Verlys, in clear and opalescent glass, molded with birds and bees, etched "Verlys." Approx. 8" diameter.

**$400–$500**

*Figure of a pheasant,* by Alméric Walter, French, modeled by A. Houillon. In *pâte-de-verre,* bird's lime-green head shading to emerald-green in the body and tail, on a streaked dark green ground, molded signatures "A. Houillon, A. Walter, Nancy." 7½" long.

**$1,054 (1986)**

*Figure of a seal,* by A. Walter, modeled by H. Mércier, c. 1925, in lime green *pâte-de-verre,* inscribed "A Walter/Nancy/h Mercier." 7" tall.

**$850 (1987)**

*Figural videpoche* (a small dish for "emptying pockets" into), by A. Walter. In *pâte-de-verre,* figure of Buddha in lime green mounted on the oval tray, inscribed (small chips in reverse). 4" tall.

**$550 (1986)**

Figure of a seal by Alméric Walter. *(Photo courtesy of William Doyle Galleries)*

*Tray,* for A. Walter, by Henri Bergé. In *pâte-de-verre,* six-sided green and opalescent ground molded with ochre and dark blue flowers at the corners and a large central green and dark blue dragonfly, molded "A. Walter Berge." 7" long.

$4,620 (1986)

*Vase,* for Wiener Werkstätte, Austrian, design attributed to Josef Hoffmann. Clear balustered glass vase with black-enameled vertical stripes, flared rim with border decoration of dots, unmarked. 3⅝" tall.

$198 (1987)

*Candy dish,* anon., late 1920s. Covered, made in glass, reverse-painted in desert scenes, palm trees, and camels, with knob handle. 4" tall, 4" diameter.

$35–$50

*Decanter,* anon., probably American, 1920s. Clear molded glass with geometric black-enameled designs of half-circles and parallel lines; stopper. 10" tall.

$150–$200

*Liqueur set,* anon., English. In blue glass, skyscraper shape, stoppered decanter with six glasses. Decanter 9½" tall.

$200–$350

*Perfume bottles,* various anon. designers, Czechoslovakian, 1920s, 1930s, and 1940s. In various sizes in clear or translucent colors. Many designs were produced with both stoppers and bottles cut in regular

## Glass

or irregular geometric faceting. Generally identified by wheel-cut or inscribed "Czechoslovakia" on bottom. In perfect condition, depending on size, color, and detail of faceting, each:

$75–$400

*Perfume bottle,* anon., wheel-cut "Czechoslovakia" on bottom. Blue glass cut in geometric pattern, with stopper. 5" tall.

$150–$175

*Perfume bottle,* anon., French. In cranberry cut crystal, with stopper. Stopper design has stylish angel "wings" of cranberry glass with angular repetitive pattern. 7" tall.

$400–$450

*Perfume bottle,* anon., French. Of red glass with black stopper in skyscraper style, marked "France."

$275–$425

*Perfume display bottle,* anon., French. Designed for Chantilly perfume, in flattened bottle with flared cylindrical stopper, marked "Houbigant." 11⅛" tall.

$300–$400

*Perfume display bottle,* anon., designed for Norell perfume, American. Rectangular glass bottle with designed edges, tall stopper of hexagonal form, unmarked. 8¼" tall.

$300–$400

*Plaque,* anon., in the manner of René Lalique. In frosted glass, oval, molded with four cavorting dancers and Pan under leafy trees. 12" long x 8" tall.

$400–$500

*Salad or berry bowl set,* anon., probably English, 1930s. In clear and dark blue glass, with blue square geometric patterns. Large bowl, 9" diameter. Four small bowls, 4" diameter. Set of 5.

$200–$225

*Vase,* anon., 1930s. In green malachite glass, three nudes with grapes and vines, unsigned. 8⅝" tall, 4½" diameter.

$450–$500

*Vase,* anon., Swedish. Globe-shaped in black amethyst glass with red and silver enameled swirling designs, marked "Sweden."

$200–$275

# ART DECO

## Mass-Produced Glass

*Candy bowl,* "Manhattan," by Anchor Hocking, American, 1930s. In pink glass with horizontal, repetitive ribbing and three ball feet. 6" diameter.
$8–$15

*Cup and saucer,* "Manhattan," by Anchor Hocking, in clear glass.
$12–$18

*Serving dish,* "Manhattan," by Anchor Hocking, in clear glass, with ribbed, stepped handles. 9" diameter.
$15–$20

*Vase,* "Manhattan," by Anchor Hocking, clear glass. 8" tall, 5" rim diameter.
$30–$35

*Cookie jar,* "Manhattan," by Anchor Hocking. In clear glass with cover. 9" tall.
$30–$35

*Cookie jar,* "Manhattan," by Anchor Hocking. Pink, with cover. 9" tall.
$100–$125

"Manhattan" bowl by Anchor Hocking. *(Photo by R. Four)*

*Bowl, "Ruba Rombic,"* by Consolidated Lamp and Glass Company, American, late 1920s. Geometric, asymmetrical bowl of cased, blown gray/lavender glass. Approx. 4½" high, 8" diameter.

$150–$250

*Drink glasses, "Ruba Rombic,"* by Consolidated Lamp and Glass Company, late 1920s. Cased, blown pink glass. 2¾" tall, 2" diameter. Set of 5.

$225–$300

*Glass, "Ruba Rombic,"* by Consolidated Lamp and Glass Company. In cased, blown brown/gray glass. Approx. 4" tall.

$40–$50

*Footed tumbler, "Ruba Rombic,"* by Consolidated Lamp and Glass Company. In cased, blown brown/gray glass. Approx. 7" tall.

$75–$80

*Bottle/decanter,* by Frigidare, American, 1930s. In green semifrosted glass, with stopper. Horizontal repetitive ribbing similar to "Manhattan," stopper somewhat geometric in shape. Marked "Frigidare." 11" tall.

$20–$35

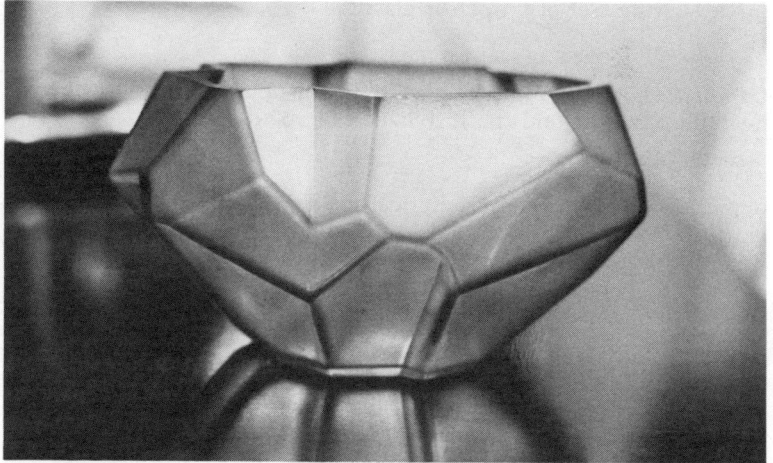

"Ruba Rombic" bowl by Consolidated. *(Photo by R. Four)*

*Bowl, "Pyramid,"* by Indiana Glass Co. American, 1930s. In clear pink glass with repetitive triangular design and stepped-back handles. 6" diameter.

$28–$35

*Salad or berry bowl* set, *"Pyramid,"* by Indiana Glass Co., American, late 1920s–1930s. Pink pressed glass with triangular repetitive pattern. Large bowl, 8½" diameter; 6 small bowls 4½" diameter.

$250–$400

*Tumblers, "Tea Room,"* by Indiana Glass Co. In pink, green, or clear glass with an inverted stepped-back pattern. 7" tall.

$20–$25

*Serving bowl, "Tea Room,"* by Indiana Glass Co. In pink glass. 9" diameter.

$50–$60

*Salt and pepper shakers, "Tea Room,"* by Indiana Glass Co. In clear glass. 3" tall. Pair.

$35–$40

*Creamer and covered sugar bowl, "Tea Room,"* by Indiana Glass Co. Green, with carrying tray with handle. 6" tall.

$30–$35

*Wine glasses, "Embassy,"* by Libbey Glass Co., American, designed by Walter Dorwin Teague, 1939. Stems are flat and vertically ribbed. Approx. 1" wide. Set of 6 in clear glass.

$200–$250

*Candy dish,* anon., American, 1920s. Green opaque glass with clown's head for a handle and three stylized feet. 6" diameter.

$20–$25

*Refrigerator bottle,* anon., American, 1930s. Shaped like a lidless tea kettle in clear glass, with chrome screw-on cap over spout. Molded design of horizontal lines at base and top, with diagonal "speed lines" around the body. 7" tall.

$45–$65

*Vases,* anon., American, 1930s. In opaque pale green glass, triangular, press-mold glass with relief of Deco-style nudes on each panel and cross-hatch backgrounds. Squared corners and three square, flared feet. Pair.

$100–$140

*Vase*, anon., probably American, 1930s. U-shaped in pink glass with flared base, shape repeated three times in a stepped-back motif on front and back. 8" tall.

$75–$125

## René Lalique
### Car Mascots (Radiator Ornaments)

*"Archer,"* by R. Lalique, French. In clear and frosted glass, circular, molded with a nude male archer, molded "R. Lalique." 5" tall.

$1,650 (1987)

*"Canard"* (duck), by R. Lalique. In smoked glass, inscribed "R. Lalique." 2½" tall.

$600–$800

*"Coq Nain"* (dwarf rooster), by R. Lalique. In frosted and clear glass with molded signature. 8" tall.

$1,320 (1987)

*"Chrysis"* (daughter of the priest of Apollo), by R. Lalique. In opalescent glass, etched "R. Lalique/France," with wooden mount. 4¾" tall.

$12,100–$14,000

*"Faucon"* (falcon), by R. Lalique. In clear and frosted glass, molded "R. Lalique" and etched "France no. 1124." 6¼" tall.

$605 (1986)
$1,430 (1987)

*"Faucon,"* by R. Lalique. In clear and frosted purple glass, molded as a falcon, molded "R. Lalique." 6¼" tall.

$26,400 (1987)

*"Grande Libellule"* (large dragonfly), by R. Lalique. In clear and frosted purple glass, inscribed "R. Lalique France." 8¼" tall.

$33,000 (1987)

*"Hirondelle"* (swallow), by R. Lalique. In clear and frosted glass, molded "R. Lalique France." 5¾" tall.

$1,540 (1987)

*"Sanglier"* (wild boar), by R. Lalique. In gray frosted glass, inscribed "R. Lalique France" and indistinctly numbered. 2¾" tall.

$990 (1986)

# ART DECO

"Victoire" car mascot by René Lalique. *(Photo courtesy of Nancy McClelland, Christie's)*

*"Victoire,"* by R. Lalique. In clear and frosted glass, head of a woman with hair flying straight back in linear design. Used on Chrysler and Bugatti cars from 1932 to about 1935. 10" long.
$13,500–$14,500
$7,700 (1987)

## Lighting

*Luminaire, "Gros Poisson Vagues"* (Big Vague Fish), by R. Lalique. In clear glass and bronze, cast as a massive carp with curved dorsal fin and tail, inscribed "R. Lalique," on bronze illuminating base cast with stylized aquatic vegetation. 15" long x 15¼" tall overall.
$4,000–$5,000

*Lighting fixture, "Nanking,"* by R. Lalique. Triangular faceted, frosted glass globe molded "R. Lalique" and inscribed "France R. Lalique" (chip to fitter rim). 15" long.
$2,000–$3,000

*Luminaire, "Oiseau de Feu"* (Firebird), by R. Lalique. In clear and frosted glass, semicircular, intaglio molded on the reverse with a large mythical firebird, probably inspired by Stravinsky's music of the same name. Molded "R. Lalique," with electrified square bronze base cast with moths or butterflies. 17" long.
$6,000–$8,000

*Luminaire, "Oiseau de Feu,"* by R. Lalique. In purple glass, semicircular, intaglio molded on the reverse with a large firebird, molded "R. Lalique" and inscribed "France," with electrified square bronze base cast with butterflies. 17" long. (For illustration see color insert.)

$14,000–$18,000

*Chandelier, "Stalactite,"* by R. Lalique. In frosted glass, the shallow bowl molded with hanging stalactites, inscribed "R. Lalique France." 10¾" diameter with mounts.

$1,100 (1986)

*Statue/luminaire, "Suzanne au Bain"* (Suzanne Bathing), by R. Lalique. In frosted yellow glass, molded as a standing nude woman with a robe draped over her outstretched arms. Molded "R. Lalique," the original electrified patinated bronze base unsigned, with original price tag. 9" tall.

$8,250 (1986)

*Lamp, "Suzanne au Bain,"* by R. Lalique, c. 1925. As above but in amber glass, attached circular lampshade with molded glass finial. Molded "R. Lalique." Sculpture 9" tall.

$9,000–$11,000

*Chandelier,* by R. Lalique, c. 1925. In glass panels molded with sparrows flying around a bramble molded cup, molded "R. Lalique." 24" diameter.

$3,400 (1986)

*Chandelier,* by R. Lalique. In frosted amber glass, the domed bowl molded with overlapping fruit and beech leaves, with gold silk cords and gilt metal ceiling cap cast "France." 15" diameter.

$1,800–$2,500

*Wall sconces,* by R. Lalique, c. 1925. Four-light, in clear and frosted glass, each molded as leaf-clad branches issuing from base with chromed-brass wall mount, terminating in petaled tulip-form shades. Unsigned, small chips to edges and large chip to one shade base. 17¾" tall. Pair.

$2,420 (1986)

**Chandelier by R. Lalique.** *(Photo courtesy of William Doyle Galleries)*

## Perfume and Toiletry Bottles

*Perfume bottle, "Amphytrite"* (a sea goddess), by R. Lalique. In brown-stained glass, the bottle molded as a shell, the stopper molded as a kneeling nude woman. Inscribed "R. Lalique France, no. 5764," stopper inscribed "82." 4" tall.

$1,650 (1987)

*Perfume bottle, "Amphytrite,"* by R. Lalique. In brown-stained glass, the bottle molded as a shell, the stopper molded as a kneeling nude woman. Inscribed "R. Lalique France No. 514" and molded "Lalique." 3¾" tall.

$1,760 (1986)

*Perfume bottle, "Dans la Nuit"* (In the Night), by R. Lalique. In clear glass, molded "R. Lalique French Bottle." 5" tall.

$300–$400

*Stoppered bottle, "Fleurette,"* by R. Lalique. In brown-patinated glass, tapered rectangular bottle with circular stopper, the edges with floral molded border, molded "Lalique." 6¼" tall.

$300–$400

# An Art Deco Portfolio

Boston Avenue Methodist Church, Tulsa, Oklahoma. Bruce Goff, architect. *(Courtesy of "TourLink")*

"Diana and the Deer," one of a pair of gates by Edgar Brandt. *(Courtesy of William Doyle Galleries)*

A dining room table by André Sornay. *(Courtesy of Carolle Thibaut-Pomerantz)*

Penguin chromium cocktail shaker, by an unknown German designer. *(Courtesy of George Theofiles, Miscellaneous Man)*

American clocks, designed, from left to right, by Kem Weber, Paul Frankl, two clocks by Gilbert Rohde, and another by Weber. *(Courtesy of Nancy McClelland, Christie's)*

"Les Sauterelles," a sapphire blue glass vase with grasshoppers by René Lalique. *(Photo by Frank Cooper, from a private collection)*

"The Firebird," a luminaire by René Lalique. *(Courtesy of Nancy McClelland, Christie's)*

An oriental dancer by Demetre Chiparus. *(Courtesy of Gallery 68 Auctions)*

*Left to right.* A vase by Boch Frères, a covered box by Claude Levy for Primavera, and a vase by Charles Catteau. *(Courtesy of Morton Abromson Decorative Arts. Photo by R. Four)*

"Archaic" ceramic vases by Clarice Cliff. *(Courtesy of Meisel-Primavera)*

Flowered vases by Boch Frères. *(Courtesy of Morton Abromson Decorative Arts. Photo by R. Four)*

"Jazz Bowl" by Viktor Schreckengost. *(Courtesy of the Cowan Pottery Museum, Rocky River Public Library. Photo by Larry L. Peltz)*

Burlesque dancer and Nubian head by Waylande Gregory. *(Courtesy of the Cowan Pottery Museum, Rocky River Public Library. Photo by Larry L. Peltz)*

"Sunray" pattern ceramics by Clarice Cliff. *(Courtesy of Meisel-Primavera)*

*Left.* **Bracelet in coral, moonstone, lapis lazuli, onyx, diamonds, and platinum.** *(Courtesy of N. Bloom & Son Antiques) Right.* **Bakelite jewelry pins.** *(Courtesy of Frank and Barbara Pollack)*

**Silver coffee and tea service by Jean Puiforcat.** *(Courtesy of N. Bloom & Son Antiques)*

"Secession 49. Ausstellung" by Egon Schiele. *(Courtesy of Nancy McClelland, Christie's)*

"L.M.S. Bestway" by Cassandre. *(From the collection of Pat Kery)*

"Pandorra" by Jan Toroop. *(Courtesy of Bernice Jackson)*

An American blue mirror, glass, and chrome bar. Designer unknown. *(Courtesy of Paul Fuhrman, The Warehouse)*

## Glass

*Cologne bottle, "Marguerites"* (daisies), by R. Lalique. In frosted and clear glass, flat-sided, round, molded with flowerheads heightened with sienna enamel, molded "R. Lalique." 7" tall.

$385 (1986)

*Cologne bottle, "Méplat Sirènes"* (mermaids on the surface), by R. Lalique. In frosted glass, with vertical bands of mermaids about the edge. The stopper is molded in full relief of a kneeling nude woman figure garnished with flowers, inscribed "R. Lalique France." 14¼" tall.

$3,500–$4,000

*Brule parfum, "Sirènes"* (incense burner), by R. Lalique. In opalescent glass, with willowy sirens floating around the circumference, semi-spherical top. Molded "R. Lalique." 6⅝" tall.

$1,760 (1986)

*Perfume atomizer,* by R. Lalique, for Molinard Cushion. In frosted glass, the form molded with frieze of nude figures in rhythmic procession against leafy ground. Impressed "Lalique" and engraved "Molinard, France Lalique." 5½" tall.

$600–$800

*Perfume atomizer,* by R. Lalique. In frosted and clear glass, a squat, bulbous form molded with numerous butterflies and heightened in amber enamel stain, molded "R. Lalique." 3" tall.

$330 (1986)

"Méplat Sirènes" cologne bottle by R. Lalique. *(Photo by Frank Cooper, from a private collection)*

*Perfume bottle*, by R. Lalique. In clear and frosted glass, square bottle with square stopper, the front panel molded with a woven textured pattern, molded "R. Lalique." 3⅛" tall.

$300–$400

## Sculpture

*Sculpture, "Grande Nue Longs Cheveux"* (Tall Nude with Long Hair), by R. Lalique. In frosted glass, young maiden standing. One arm shields her face while her flowing hair falls to her feet, mounted on a wooden base. Wheel-cut "Lalique France." 16½" tall.

$16,000–$20,000

*Sculpture, "Source de la Fontaine"* (Muse of the Fountain), by R. Lalique. Clear glass molded as a standing woman, wearing a clamshell headdress, with water cascading over her body. Inscribed "R. Lalique France," mounted on an electrified wood base. 27" tall.

$6,050 (1986)

*Sculpture, "Tête Penchée"* (head tilted down), by R. Lalique. In clear and frosted glass, cast as a maiden clad in diaphanous drapery, standing on domed base within clear arched glass decorated with frosted florette garlands, trace gray enamel in recesses, inscribed "R. Lalique." 14½" tall.

$2,090 (1986)

"Source de la Fontaine," sculpture by R. Lalique. *(Photo courtesy of Nancy McClelland, Christie's)*

Glass                                     231

## Other Glass Items

*Dish, "Coupe Motif Sirène,"* by R. Lalique. In opalescent glass, circular three-footed dish molded with a central mermaid surrounded by swirling bubbles. Molded "R. Lalique," incised "France" and "No. 376." 14½" diameter.

$800–$1,200

*Picture frame, "Inseparables,"* by R. Lalique. In clear and frosted glass, molded "R. Lalique." 4¼" square.

$500–$800

*Inkwell, "Sirènes,"* by R. Lalique. In frosted glass, circular, with four nude mermaids, molded "Lalique." 6¼" diam.

$550–$700

*Ashtray, "Statuette,"* by R. Lalique. In frosted glass, the small dish with central standing figure of a maiden with lotus, inscribed "R. Lalique France No. 288." 4¾" tall.

$2,090 (1986)

*Inkstand, "Three Sirens,"* by R. Lalique. In gray-stained, frosted yellow glass and silver, the domed circular body molded with three sirens, the silver collar with a domed frosted-glass cover and a glass inkwell. Molded "R. Lalique," collar with French poincons, inkwell with chips in rim. 9½" diam.

$2,200 (1986)

*Covered box, "Trois Graces,"* by R. Lalique. In frosted glass, molded "R. Lalique France" and "D'Orsay." 3¾" diam.

$275 (1987)

*Charger,* by R. Lalique. In opalescent glass, the circular piece molded with numerous fish against wavy ground, stamped "R. Lalique." 11½" diam.

$495 (1986)

*Menu holders,* by R. Lalique. Three frosted glass holders in demilune shape molded with fruit-filled baskets. Inscribed signatures, one with brown patination. 2⅛" long.

$300–$500

*Paperweight,* by R. Lalique. In frosted glass, formed as an elk with large stylized rack, etched "R. Lalique France." 3⅝" tall.

$748 (1987)

*Set of stemware,* by R. Lalique. Four wines and four cordials, each with clear-glass foot and conical bowl, the swelled cylindrical stems molded with overlapping leaves (one with repaired stem). 5¾" and 4⅞" tall. Set of 8.

$400–$600

## Vessels

*Vase, "Alicante"* (a French province), by R. Lalique. In frosted and clear glass, shouldered ovoid form molded with pairs of parrots with finely detailed plumage, inscribed "R. Lalique France." 10" tall.

$1,980 (1986)

*Vase, "Archers,"* by R. Lalique, c. 1925. In molded, cased yellow glass, molded "R. Lalique." 10½" tall.

$2,250 (1986)

*Vase, "Bacchantes"* (priestesses of the god Bacchus), by R. Lalique. In gray-stained opalescent glass, with nude women encircling the vase, dancing arm-in-arm, and standing from base to rim. Etched "R. Lalique France." 9⅝" tall.

$15,400 (1987)

*Vase, "Bias"* (oblique lines), by R. Lalique. Molded brown-enameled vase in low relief showing intertwining berried vines, molded "R. Lalique." 10½" tall.

$11,000–$15,000

"Bacchantes" by R. Lalique. *(Photo courtesy of Christie's East)*

"Bias" by R. Lalique. *(Photo by Frank Cooper, from a private collection)*

Covered vase and bowl, *"Cariatides Couvert"* (priestesses of the temple of Diana), by R. Lalique. In frosted and clear glass, shouldered ovoid form, molded with eight figures of women against foliate ground, trace green enamel patination. Inscribed "R. Lalique France No. 924," 7⅝" tall, lacking cover; the bowl molded on the underside with overlapping stylized leaves, brown enamel patination, etched "R. Lalique France." 12¼" diameter.

$880 (1986)

Bowl, *"Coquilles"* (shells), by R. Lalique, in clear glass, molded with four scallop shells. Molded "R. Lalique," 9⅓" diameter.

$600–$700

Vase, *"Danaides"* (daughters of Danaos, king of Egypt), by R. Lalique, c. 1930. In low relief topaz, molded with a frieze of nude women pouring water from urns on their shoulders, molded "R. Lalique, France." 7¼" tall.

$2,500–$4,000

Vase, *"Davos"* (city in Switzerland), by R. Lalique, early 1930s. Graduated spheres decorate the vase in a geometric pattern, similar to an arrangement of snowflakes or frosty glass; made of alexanderite, stenciled "R. Lalique." 11½" tall.

$4,000–$6,000

Vase, *"Dentelé"* (toothed, like a saw), by R. Lalique. In smoky clear glass, gourd-shaped with ridged vertical rims, inscribed "R. Lalique France No. 943." 7½" tall.

$550 (1986)

Vase, *"Escargot"* (snail), by R. Lalique. Flattened ovoid contour with short flaring neck, in deep red glass, low-relief pattern shows a coiling snail shell, etched "R. Lalique." 8¾" tall.

$2,000–$4,500

Vase, *"Esterel"* (a mountainous area of Provence in France), by R. Lalique. In brown-patinated frosted glass, the squat baluster form molded with overlapping leafy branches, inscribed "R. Lalique." 6⅜" tall.

$500–$700

Decanter, *"Faverolles,"* by R. Lalique. In clear and frosted glass the balustered body on circular foot, the stopper molded with roosters; with two matching cordials, stenciled signature. Decanter 9¼" tall.

$500–$700

Vase, *"Férrières"* (a city in France), by R. Lalique, c. 1925. In green molded glass, shaped in a tiered pattern, inscribed "R. Lalique No. 1897." 6½" tall.

$2,000 (1987)

Center bowl, *"Gui"* (mistletoe), by R. Lalique, c. 1925. In clear molded glass with mistletoe design, broad-shouldered piece with short neck, molded "R. Lalique." Widest diameter, 9½".

$700–$900

"Férrières" by R. Lalique. *(Photo courtesy of William Doyle Galleries)*

## Glass

Vase, *"Gui,"* by R. Lalique. In opalescent frosted glass, bulbous, molded with berries against stems, unsigned. 7" tall.

$495 (1987)

*"Laurel,"* vase, by R. Lalique. In opalescent glass, cylindrical, molded with long slender leaves and berries. Molded "R. Lalique," incised "France." 7" tall.

$600–$800

Vase, *"Luxembourg,"* by R. Lalique. In frosted brown-stained glass, molded with eight standing nude women between stylized leaf arches, etched "R. Lalique." Largest of Lalique's mass production of vases. 18" tall.

$16,000–$20,000

Vase, *"Margaret,"* by R. Lalique. In clear and frosted glass, the massive rectangular-section body with canted corners and flanked by rectangular D-form handles molded with plump parakeets amid berried branches, trace brown-patinated enamel, inscribed "R. Lalique." 8⅝" tall.

$1,870 (1986)

Centerpiece, *"Marguerites"* (daisies), by R. Lalique. In clear and frosted glass, the broad shallow bowl encircled by wide rim cast with daisy heads, the underside of the cavetto and well molded with stylized stems, etched "R. Lalique." 14¼" diameter.

$440 (1986)

Centerpiece, *"Martigues"* (a port city in France), by R. Lalique. In opalescent glass, the circular shallow bowl heavily molded on the underside with a shoal of fish forming the feet, molded "R. Lalique," wheel-cut "France." 14½" diameter.

$1,540 (1986)

Bowl, *"Nemours"* (a city in France), by R. Lalique. In frosted glass, enameled and orange-stained bowl, impressed with rings of black-eyed susans, stamped "R. Lalique France." 10" diameter.

$418 (1986)

Vase, *"Ormeaux"* (young elms), by R. Lalique. In frosted gray glass, spherical, with narrow neck and everted rim, molded with overlapping leaves, inscribed "R. Lalique, No. 984" (minor flake in rim). 6¾" tall.

$550–$750

*Vase, "Palastre,"* by R. Lalique, c. 1922. In frosted glass, oviform, molded with 12 standing nude men in various poses, shoulder to shoulder. Etched "R. Lalique France." 16¼" tall.

$22,000–$24,000
$20,900 (1986)

*Vase, "Palissy"* (a French artist), by R. Lalique. In gray glass, of globe form, molded with snail shells, molded "R. Lalique," inscribed "R. Lalique France." 7⅝" tall.

$1,000–$1,400

*Vase, "Palissy,"* by R. Lalique. In frosted gray glass, molded over its entirety with clusters of snail shells, inscribed "R. Lalique France." 6½" tall.

$605 (1986)

*Vase, "Périgord"* (a region of France), by R. Lalique. In frosted glass, a squat spherical form with six curved protruding ribs, etched "R. Lalique," inscribed "France 1002." 6" tall.

$500–$700

*Bowl, "Pérruches"* (parakeets), by R. Lalique. In opalescent glass, with blue staining of the 1920s, molded with a frieze of perched parakeets on blossoming branches, stenciled "R. Lalique." 10" diameter.

$2,500–$5,000

*Vase, "Pérruches,"* by R. Lalique. In frosted green glass, shouldered ovoid body below short cylindrical neck molded with pairs of parakeets perched on blossoming quince branches, inscribed "R. Lalique." 10" tall.

$6,000–$7,000
$4,400 (1986)

*Vase, "Pierrefonds"* (a city and chateau in France), by R. Lalique, c. 1925. In butterscotch molded glass with polished outer edges of scrolled thorny strap handles, inscribed "R. Lalique." 6¼" tall.

$5,720 (1986)
$6,050 (1986)

*Vase, "Pierrefonds,"* by R. Lalique, c. 1925. In colorless molded glass with frondlike curling handles on either side, inscribed "R. Lalique/France." 13" long, over handles.

$1,350 (1987)

"Pierrefonds" by R. Lalique. *(Photo by Frank Cooper, from a private collection)*

"Poissons" by R. Lalique. *(Photo courtesy of William Doyle Galleries)*

*Vase, "Poissons"* (fish), by R. Lalique, c. 1925. In molded, cased yellow glass, inscribed "R. Lalique France." 9¼" tall.

**$1,900 (1986)**

*Vase, "Poissons,"* by R. Lalique. In frosted red glass, spherical, molded with large fish, inscribed "R. Lalique France No. 925," molded "R. Lalique." 9⅝" tall.

**$5,500 (1986)**

*Vase, "Rampillon,"* by R. Lalique. In clear, frosted, and opalescent glass, with birds and floral design in high relief. Molded "R. Lalique." 5" tall.

**$440 (1986)**

*Vase, "Sauterelles"* (grasshoppers), by R. Lalique. In blue- and green-stained clear glass, ovoid, molded with grasshoppers among blades of grass enhanced with blue and green enamel, inscribed "R. Lalique." 11" tall.

**$2,200 (1986)**

*Vase, "Sauterelles,"* by R. Lalique. Tall and medium relief on sapphire blue molded glass, depicting grasshoppers perched in undulating grasses. Signed "R. Lalique." 10⅝" tall. (For illustration see color insert.)

**$3,000–$4,000**

*Vase, "Serpent,"* by R. Lalique, c. 1924. In rare violet frosted glass, curled serpent makes form and structure of vase, showing its fangs. Molded "R. Lalique." 10¼" tall.

**$15,000–$17,000**

*Vase, "Serpent,"* by R. Lalique. As above but in frosted gray/amber glass, molded "R. Lalique." 10¼" tall.

**$9,350 (1986)**

"Serpent" by R. Lalique, in rare violet glass. *(Photo by Frank Cooper, from a private collection)*

*Vase, "Serpent,"* by R. Lalique. As above but in frosted and clear glass, molded "R. Lalique." 10¼" tall.
$2,000–$2,500

*Vase, "Thistles,"* by R. Lalique, 1925. Modeled with thistles, in clear and frosted glass. Etched "R. Lalique France No. 979." 9" tall.
$600–$800

*Vase, "Thistles,"* by R. Lalique. In clear frosted glass, with traces of yellow stain, molded "R. Lalique." 8½" tall.
$242 (1986)

*Vase, "Thistles,"* by R. Lalique. As above but in gray frosted, orange-stained glass, inscribed "R. Lalique France 21:979." 9" tall.
$935 (1986)
$1,045 (1986)

*Vase, "Thistles,"* by R. Lalique. As above but in amber glass. Inscribed "R. Lalique France No. 979." 8½" tall.
$1,210 (1986)

*Vase, "Tourbillons"* (whirlwinds), by R. Lalique. In frosted amber glass, oviform, deeply molded with spiked spirals, inscribed "R. Lalique France No. 973." 8" tall.
$4,620 (1986)

*Vase, "Tournesol"* (sunflower), by R. Lalique. A cased, opalescent glass vase, tapering ovoid body, molded with stylized sunflower heads in geometric configuration. Inscribed "R. Lalique France No. 1007." 4⅝" tall.
$550–$650

*Carafe,* by R. Lalique. In pink-stained and clear glass, pear-shaped, stopper molded as a fan-shaped flower, handle modeled as a satyr's mask. Signed "R. Lalique pour Censier." 9¾" tall.
$605 (1986)

*Vase,* by R. Lalique. In opalescent gray-patinated glass, spherical with narrowed neck, molded with overlapping fern fronds, signed "R. Lalique France." 7⅜" tall.
$700–$900

*Vase*, by R. Lalique, early 20th century. Clear glass molded with the *cire-perdu* or "lost wax" method, with figural decoration of dragonflies around the rim. Shows the transition of Lalique's style from Art Nouveau to Art Deco. 6½" tall.

$9,000–$12,000

*Cire-perdu* vase by R. Lalique. *(Photo courtesy of William Doyle Galleries)*

# CERAMICS

## EUROPEAN CERAMICS

Ceramics were among the major materials of decorative arts in both the Art Nouveau and Art Deco periods. The entire range of ceramics—earthenware pottery, porcelain, and china—provides some fine examples of the Art Deco style.

In the late 19th century ceramic designers reacted against the traditional French styles of painted porcelain and faience, which, however, remained popular. Faience, which looks something like porcelain, is not baked at as high a temperature. Even today craftsmen in tiny southern French villages like Moustiers turn out quality reproductions of once popular faience styles. By the turn of the century, however, people had tired of the traditional designs.

Art Deco brought a breakthrough in form, color, and subject. Not only were potters no longer limited to traditional vessels, jugs, bowls, tea sets, and the like, they could experiment with incised or painted decoration, angularity, and subject matter as sculptors were doing.

Decorative pieces explored a wider range of subjects, and figural pieces could be sleek or geometric instead of frilly or provincial. All of the favorite Art Deco exotic creatures can be found: wild cats, deer, sleek dogs, even elephants, and giraffes. One piece from Primavera is in the shape of a bison or buffalo, created at a time when the American West was also considered exotic in Paris.

Decorative or functional, Art Deco ceramics represent a huge field, with lots of quality and lots of fun for the collector—and many times at lower cost than other areas.

Typically, bone china, china, and porcelain cost more than pottery, as they are more difficult to make and cost more when they are produced. In pottery, studio pieces—that is, individually crafted, glazed, or enameled pieces—are generally more expensive than manufactured work, but there are exceptions. For example, the work of Clarice Cliff, which lies somewhere between the two extremes, as it was mass-produced but hand-painted, can be much more expensive than fine works by early French studio potters.

As painters had found inspiration in African art, potters found inspiration in exotic Japanese and Chinese cultures, both for simplified design and for glazing techniques. In addition, the influence of Vienna and the Wiener Werkstätte was also felt on vessels and figural ceramics, perhaps even more in America than in Europe.

Susi Singer and Vally Wieselthier are among the most notable Austrian Wiener Werkstätte ceramists, but Michael Powolny (1871–1954), Berthold Löffler, and Herta Bucher also had strong reputations. Both Singer and Wieselthier came to America when the Werkstätte closed in 1932, and for many years they had exchanged trips with Midwestern American ceramists, especially those working for Cowan Pottery in Ohio.

The two figures who are most highly regarded in the world of pottery in France were Emile Decoeur (1876–1953) and Emile Lenoble (1876–1940). It has been said that Decoeur would smash a piece of his work if it did not, in the end, meet his high standards. Decoeur is known for his glossy, monochromatic glazes. Lenoble, on the other hand, was inspired by Chinese T'ang dynasty pieces and produced granular and matte finishes. The work of Decouer and Lenoble is not often found on today's Art Deco market, as it is often purchased by museums.

Many famous fine artists, such as Joan Miró, Pablo Picasso, and Marc Chagall, were offered and accepted commissions to create ceramic decoration. Such pieces also have been largely acquired by wealthy collectors and museums and only rarely make an appearance on the open market. They are generally executed in the artist's own style and are not necessarily Art Deco as much as they are art.

Suzanne Lalique, daughter of René, produced painted porcelain for Theodore Haviland at Limoges, as did artists Edouard Marcel Sandoz and C. Tharaud. Limoges also commissioned Jean Dufy to design tableware.

The National Manufacture at Sèvres also commissioned artists such as Henri Rapin, Jacques-Emile Ruhlmann, and the Martel brothers. Many notable artists were exhibited in the Sèvres pavilion at the 1925 exposition in Paris. Sèvres produced both porcelain and pottery. Today their later, larger manufacture is produced for the department store trade and often available on the market.

Numerous fine studio artists worked in pottery and porcelain. The most collectible of these today include Lemanceau, René Buthaud, Robert Lallemand, Jean Luce, André Mourier, Jean Mayodon, Georges Serré, Zsolnay, Raoul Lachenal, and André Méthey (1871–1921). Raoul Lachenal worked in sandstone and created enameled geometrical decoration. Robert Lallemand created, among other things, geometric stepped vases and Cubist-inspired candlesticks. Zsolnay's bold sculptures of eagles shine with iridescence.

Morton Abromson, a collector and dealer who specializes in European studio pottery and ceramic manufactures of the era, comments, "French studio pottery by Raoul Lachenal, Edouard Cazaux, Lallemand, and others has a very small but sophisticated market in this country, and is actually more sought after abroad."

He adds, "In America there is more interest in the ceramics manufactured by Boch Frères and Longwy. People are discovering that they can buy fine, beautifully designed pieces at far more reasonable prices than the most ordinary glass of the period. Pottery and ceramics are now catching on, and collectors are becoming more numerous."

Studio pottery can be acquired very reasonably as well, with many studio pieces costing no more, or bringing no more at auction, than many industrially produced pieces.

In the Art Deco era, department stores increased the popularity of the new ceramics through their commissions to artists and manufacturers to create pieces or execute designs, just as they had done with furniture and other decorative arts.

The directors of the department store design studios often created the design, which was then executed for them by the manufacturer. Both Maurice Dufrène (1876–1955), head of La Maîtrise, the workshop of Galleries Lafayette, and Claude Levy of Primavera, the workshop of Le Printemps, created some excellent designs for manufacture by Boch Frères, Longwy, and other leading companies.

Etling too seized on the popularity of ceramics to produce pieces in the crackled finish and glossy style of Longwy. Etling was a prolific company that produced a great volume of decorative and functional glass, bronzes, and statues for the department stores.

## *Special Focus: Boch Frères and Longwy/Primavera*

Two manufacturers who received many of the commissions for ceramics for the department store trade were Longwy in France and Boch Frères Keramis in Belgium. Both of these are generally easy to identify, as the vast majority of their pieces are stamped on the bottom. (See the photos in our color section, "An Art Deco Portfolio.")

Longwy is noted for its high luster and crackled glazes. It produced enameled pottery with rich shades of greens and blues as well as gold and silver. The company was often commissioned to produce vases, tea services, bowls, containers, and trinket boxes for Primavera. Many of these were designed by Claude Levy. The company produced so often for Primavera that we've listed the two together in our Price Listings for this chapter, even when the maker of a Primavera piece is unknown. However, as you'll note in the listings, Longwy also designed pieces for Pomone, a rival workshop directed by Paul Follot (1877–1941) at Au Bon Marché.

Among the favorite collectible items, besides vases, that Longwy produced were small, circular, covered boxes. Sometimes called pin boxes or trinket boxes, they were popular enough to be collected in their own time. The boxes are colorfully enameled and designed with stylized flowers, cactuses and other plants, or geometric motifs. Today they range in price from $100 to $250 depending on the design, the quality of the enameling, and whether or not the designer is known.

Boch Frères was perhaps not commissioned by the department stores as often as Longwy, but it did receive commissions from Maurice Dufrène for La Maîtrise. Boch Frères designed and produced its own successful lines of high-luster pottery similar to the Longwy style, as well as a stoneware with a matte glaze.

Their ceramics are difficult to date precisely, and little is known about the quantities in which its pieces were produced. The factory was severely damaged during World War II, and much of the documentation of production was destroyed. In addition, it is believed that pieces signed "Boch Frères," "Boch Frères Keramis," "Keramis," and "Gres Keramis" are all by the same maker, but nothing is known as to why the name was changed.

In many cases Boch Frères pieces will also have a stamped signature: "Ch. Catteau" for Charles Catteau, their major designer. Catteau's designs are immediately striking. His somewhat geometric patterns are sometimes in high-luster blues and greens against a matte glaze. His depictions of sleek deer and other animals are sought after today.

Another designer for Boch Frères, Jan Windt, is also collected. Windt's designs of birds and flowers are more abstract than those of Catteau, with long curling tail feathers, and sometimes stepped forms are used on the vase bodies themselves.

Other works by Boch Frères are colorful floral patterns, abstract shapes and designs, and stylized animals such as giraffes, birds, and even polar bears.

Generally speaking, larger pieces command higher prices, and those with stylized figures and representations bring up to $1,000 or more. The largest pieces can bring $3,000 to over $6,000, especially if rare, like the stylized 23-inch squirrel-motif vase, first displayed at the 1925 Paris Exposition. Many vases by Boch Frères can still be purchased for under $500, however. This is especially true of colorful floral motif vases with their high-luster crackled finishes and bright enameled designs.

## OTHER EUROPEAN FIGURAL CERAMICS

In Paris, another manufacturer, Robj, is best known on the market for its liquor decanters representing people from all walks of life. Robj also produced statuettes, lamps, bookends, ashtrays, and candy dishes. The company made about ten different decanters, including a coachman, a witch, a monk, a sailor, a Russian cossack, and a woman with an armful of flowers.

These are usually clearly stamped "Robj" and "Paris. Made in France." Stylized, but with a country rather than a city feeling, these decanters are a distinctive collecting area and are fetching prices from $200 to more than $800 for rarer designs, such as the Scotsman.

Figural porcelain and ceramics mirrored what was happening in the world of decorative bronze statues. The German company Rosenthal produced porcelain figures that are sometimes influenced by this design style. One piece depicts a beautiful woman astride an ostrich. Rosenthal pieces are also almost always identified by the factory stamp. Rosenthal made porcelain figures of Pierrots, entertainers, and women in modern dress.

An Austrian firm that also commissioned several artists to create figural statues was Goldscheider. Among their figures in the Deco style were Pierrettes and sleek wolfhounds. The company's production after the 1930s was more traditional, and in the 1940s the family left Austria and established themselves in New Jersey.

## ENGLISH CERAMICS

England, which had picked up on the Modernist idiom by the 1930s even though early Art Deco had somewhat passed it by, gave rise to a host of talented ceramists. Their works are being bought and sold on the American Art Deco market with increasing frequency.

In fact, from what we have seen, it is in this area in Art Deco that English collectibles have made the biggest inroads in the American market. This is in part because as English production increased, more of it reached our shores. We feel that the resurgence of interest in English 1930s ceramics will lead to new interest in other English Modern design as well.

Bernard Leach (1887–1979) is perhaps the best-known studio potter working in England at the time. Other collected English studio ceramists include Michael Cardew and William Staite Murray (1881–1961). Their work is becoming better known in this country.

English ceramics of the 1930s is often somewhere between art and industrial production. England was long known for high-quality porcelain and china. At first, mass-produced pieces in Modern designs were hand-painted. By the mid-1930s, however, most manufacturers had switched to a transfer-printed process.

Ceramic designers working in Modernist idioms included Susie Cooper (b. 1902), Keith Murray, and Eric Slater (b. 1902). Several of the best-known ceramists studied at Burslem School of Art in Burslem, Staffordshire.

Keith Murray, who created glass designs for Stevens & Williams, also designed ceramics for Wedgwood, starting in 1933. Wedgwood needed a competitive edge in the 1930s market, and Murray provided it with simple shapes and solid, light-colored glazes, often with horizontal banding.

Susie Cooper designed numerous dinner, coffee, and tea sets, among other things. In 1931 she rented a building from Doulton and started her own firm, Crown Works. She worked at first in painted wares but switched to transfers in about 1933.

Foley Potteries & China Works, later renamed Shelley Potteries Ltd., also produced porcelain tea sets with geometric decorations and angular handles.

Eric Slater came from a long line of ceramic designers. He took over the position of art director at Shelley in 1928, a position once held by his father. He produced some of the best Modernist designs for that company throughout the 1930s. In 1937 and 1938 he was commissioned to produce tablewares for Imperial Airways.

English manufacturers that produced Deco and Modern designs include Ashtead Potters, Bretby Art Pottery, Carlton Ware, and George Clews & Co.

### *Special Focus: Clarice Cliff*

By far one name in English ceramics stands out, especially for her individuality and daring use of color and patterns: Clarice Cliff (1899–1972).

Cliff attended Burslem and signed on with A. J. Wilkinson in the city of Burslem between 1916 and 1920. She began experimenting in decorating old stock at the nearby Newport Pottery Company, which was later bought by Wilkinson.

The most popular and priciest of her pieces today are her Art Deco geometric and scenic styles. In all, she created and directed the creation of about 250 shapes and over 200 different paint designs, and prices vary greatly according to both shape and design.

Clarice Cliff pottery was first exhibited in this country at the groundbreaking revival exhibition at the Minneapolis Institute of the Arts in 1971. It occupied a good portion of the ceramics section, awakening new interest in her work in this country. It has bold designs, with brilliant color in motifs often borrowed from Cubism, and brightly painted fantastic scenes with blobby trees inspired by Matisse and the Fauves.

Prices for Cliff have been on something of a roller coaster in recent years. A few years ago Cliff received a lot of exposure, and her prices jumped. At auction a 13-inch wall plaque with her "Inspiration" matte glaze of greens and blues sold for $2,420. A 12-inch "Inspiration" lotus vase in the "Persian" pattern sold for an all-time high of $7,700 to a first-time collector. Four "Age of Jazz" centerpieces, depicting tuxedoed band members and ballroom dancers, sold for $3,300 each at the same auction.

Initially, the market was driven higher by a small group of collectors and dealers who recognized Cliff as an outstanding artist and began buying and promoting her work. However, following these sales auction houses began reporting a softening of the prices on Cliff. In the past two years the "Persian" pattern lotus jug may have gained only half of the $7,700 price at auction.

However, prices for Clarice Cliff are once again on the rise, so much so that some of the auction and retail prices from 1986 and 1987 could double in the next few years.

Much of the new excitement about Cliff is due to two committed and passionate dealers and collectors, Louis and Susan Meisel, owners of Meisel-Primavera Gallery in New York. In addition to being the leading collectors of Cliff for many years, for the past five years they have also been the leading dealers in her work.

Louis Meisel first got excited about Cliff when he saw her work at the Minneapolis Art Institute revival exhibition in 1971. Cliff died a year later. The Meisels purchased much of Cliff's work through newspaper ads in New Zealand and Australia, where her work had been very popular in the 1930s and 1940s.

Their book on Cliff, co-authored by Leonard Griffin and entitled *Clarice Cliff: A Bizarre Affair*, just published in 1988, is causing another surge of interest in this artist, who has come to epitomize the Art Deco style in English ceramics.

As with many areas of Art Deco collecting, the publication of this work is broadening the public's interest in Cliff, and there is a corresponding response in the marketplace. We predict that prices on Cliff will rebound and exceed the earlier highs, and we can only recommend that those captivated by her style buy early in the upward trend.

Cliff's greatest production was for A. J. Wilkinson during the years 1928 to 1938. Some of her designs were originally created to be retailed through Woolworth's in the 1930s.

In 1929 her Bizarre ware, designed for Wilkinson, was growing in popularity, and the company devoted the entire production of Newport Pottery Company to its manufacture. Bizarre has several patterns, such as "Crocus," "Appliqué," and "Latona." Two well-known painters who designed for Cliff in 1933 and 1934 were Vanessa Bell and Laura Knight. Knight produced the "Circus" pattern.

Although more collectors of Cliff today are asking for items by pattern name, all of the patterns of the Newport line are still referred to by some simply as Bizarre. Another Cliff line that has several pattern names is Inspiration.

The vivid colors that were, and still are, the source of her popularity were also the tragic cause of her death. The bright orange color used in many of her pieces—such as her most important Deco pattern, "Sunray," with its sunburst geometric design—was toxic and probably contributed to her death from emphysema. The bright red color of the popular American ceramic Fiestaware was also found to be irradiated and toxic, and it has been recalled several times by the Food and Drug Administration. Today artists are fighting for laws to ensure that manufacturers clearly label toxic art materials.

Favorites with collectors are both her large balustered vases and her one-handled lotus jugs. Prices depend on the design pattern. For example, a 12-inch Lotus Jug in a flowered pattern like "Crocus" may cost only $200 to $300, while a geometric design for the same style and size can bring a price of $2,000 to $3,000. The same Lotus Jug in a "scenic" design or the "Tennis," "Sunray," or "Persian" patterns can run from $3,000 all the way up to $7,000. Her "Archaic"-pattern vases, direct steals from the capitals of Egyptian columns, can bring up to $5,000, depending on the size. (See our color section, "An Art Deco Portfolio," for some dazzling photos of her work.)

Other high-ticket Cliff designs include large 18- and 24-inch umbrella stands, which can run from $6,000 to $8,000. Her 14-inch balustered vases now cost between $2,500 and $5,000—again depending on the design—and 18-inch chargers can fetch up to $4,000.

Tea for two Clarice Cliff-style can cost as much as $3,000, and tea for four will run as high as $4,000—for the teapot, creamer, sugar, cups, and saucers. The tea itself is still a bargain.

One of the few categories of items still selling consistently today for under $100 is ashtrays, though some go as high as $150. Other smaller items, such as short candlesticks and smaller bowls and plates, can cost from $200 to $500 or so. Most often it is Cliff's floral patterns that bring lower prices, while her geometric and scenic patterns are soaring.

Modernist bone china services from Shelley Potteries, a contemporary of Cliff's, can still be purchased for around $500, overturning the general principle that china and porcelain are always more expensive than pottery.

Yet, seeing these amazing, colorful designs by an obviously gifted woman, one can begin to understand the excitement and the prices. She was an original in an original time; and though her medium, pottery, may be considered more common, her work is as good as gold on today's market.

## AMERICAN CERAMICS

At the 1900 Exposition Universelle in Paris, the American ceramics industry established its reputation and won many prizes. Rookwood, Van Briggle, Grueby, and Newcomb were some of the ceramic producers who were represented. But while some of these had set fine examples for the Arts and Crafts style, after 1900 innovative ceramics were produced by only a few. Rookwood and Van Briggle did produce some pieces in a more sculptural Art Nouveau style, but on the whole, the American ceramics industry before World War I was not keeping pace.

Studio potters experimented with form and glaze, notably Mary Chase Perry, the founder of Pewabic Pottery, and Adelaide Alsop Robineau of Syracuse, New York, who worked in porcelain.

Some of this early production has been called "proto-Art Deco." For example, John Warham's 1898 bottle vase for Rookwood Pottery in Cincinnati, Ohio, which has black abstract decoration on a white background; or the stylized alligators of Mazie T. Ryan's vase for Newcomb Pottery in New Orleans sometime before 1907.

In Chicago, Teco pottery was producing a line of green pottery vases and urns, mostly between 1903 and 1912. Some of these have handles and designs reminiscent of Art Nouveau, while others have the straight lines of the Prairie School and Frank Lloyd Wright. Teco pottery pieces are now generally bringing prices as high as $500 and even up to $1,500.

Fulper Pottery also exhibits some of the simplified lines of Art Deco and later, around 1930, would more wholeheartedly adopt Deco motifs. However, all of these more accurately belong to the American Arts and Crafts Movement, from which early Modernist designers borrowed what they could.

Manufacturers such as Roseville and Weller continued to produce mostly predictable styles for their own markets. But some companies saw their appeal decline. Grueby, for example, closed its doors before World War I.

By 1910 the foundations for a modern ceramics movement were strong in America. Colleges and universities had established ceramics departments, and studio artists were experimenting with glazes and shapes. However, the arrival of World War I slowed down ceramic development.

Between the two wars American ceramics underwent dramatic changes, especially in Cleveland, Ohio. Students at the Cleveland Institute of Arts came under the influence of a Viennese teacher, Julius Mihalik, who exposed them to the thinking of the Wiener Werkstätte.

Outstanding students of the school included Thelma Frazier Winter (1904–1977), Paul Bogatay, and Edris Eckhardt, all of whom would later design for Cowan Pottery Company, located in a suburb of Cleveland. Many other young ceramists from the Midwest, including Russel Aitken and Viktor Schreckengost, traveled to study in Vienna.

These Cleveland artists started a renaissance in American ceramics. Even though many had won prizes in the annual exhibitions that began in 1919, the New York market overlooked them. In 1926 the Metropolitan Museum of Art in New York had a show that consisted largely of French ceramics.

However, by 1928, when the Metropolitan hosted the International Exhibition of Ceramic Art, the work of the Wiener Werkstätte and many Americans came to the fore. The artists recognized in this exhibit are also those most popular on today's market: Henry Varnum Poor, William Zorach, Carl Walters, Wilhelm Hunt Diederich (1884–1953), and Viktor Schreckengost. Another important ceramist was Maija Grotell, who was associated with the Cranbrook Academy of Art.

In the following years, more exhibitions featured American ceramics. Exhibits in Syracuse brought New Yorkers and Ohioans together on a more neutral ground, furthering the cause.

### *Special Focus: Cowan Pottery*

Cowan Pottery was founded by Reginald (Guy) Cowan in Lakewood, Ohio, and later moved to Rocky River, now an affluent western suburb of Cleveland. Cowan was born in East Liverpool, Ohio, one of the centers of the ceramics industry in that state. He was a successful studio ceramist and in 1917 was awarded first prize for pottery in the international show at the Art Institute of Chicago. A few years later, in 1921, he hired a business manager and set up commercial production in Rocky River.

## Ceramics

Cowan drew together talented young artists to produce both limited editions and larger series of decorative and functional ceramics that have become prized in the collecting world.

The firm lasted about twelve years. At its largest it had about fourteen hundred dealer outlets nationally, including Marshall Field in Chicago, John Wanamaker's in Philadelphia, and Halle's in Cleveland. Commercial production increased, but smaller editions of ceramic sculptures continued to be made.

Cowan attracted such artists as Russel B. Aitken, Arthur E. Baggs, Alexander Blazys (1894–1963), Waylande DeSantis Gregory, Paul Manship, A. Drexel Jacobson, Margaret Postgate, and Vicktor Schreckengost, many of whom had won prizes in exhibitions. At Cowan Studios they created stylish figurines, centerpieces, candlesticks, bookends, plates, tea sets, and vases.

From 1927 to 1932 the company produced some of the most outstanding examples of American Art Deco ceramics. Then financial difficulties caused by a slow market for its more artistic works, coupled with unpopular response to a new commercial line called Lakeware, forced Cowan Pottery into receivership in 1930, and it closed its doors in bankruptcy in 1932. It is interesting to note that many great stylish pieces were created in 1930 and 1931, when the artists were finally free from the pressures of commercial production.

Works by Cowan himself are difficult to find. Starting with his arrival in Cleveland in 1908, he made studio pieces, including ginger jars and vases. His most popular creation was the figural flower frog, small ceramic stylized women and animals rising from lily pads and grasses, to be set in a shallow bowl of water. Loops in the drapery of the figures and holes in the base make it possible to arrange flowers in the piece. He designed numerous pieces for Cowan Pottery Studio, but many are not signed. A number of companies imitated these designs for years.

One of the most prolific of Cowan's Modernist artists was Waylande D. Gregory, who joined Cowan Studios in 1928. His influence there was second only to Cowan's. When the firm closed, Gregory continued producing ceramics under his own name from his studio at the Cranbrook Academy of Art.

For Cowan, Gregory often took subjects from mythology and history, usually women, such as Persephone and Salomé. He even depicted "Radio" as a woman, in white ceramic with hair blowing at right angles in the wind and with the famous Deco zigzag bolt emanating from her fingertips.

He also designed a stylized flamingo centerpiece, figural flower frogs of lithe women, and sleek animals in ivory and jet black. During Prohibition the favorite Gregory design was "Alice in Wonderland" decanters in black trimmed with gold, disguised as bookends.

Gregory also designed the "Fountain of Atoms," a monumental ceramic sculpture for the New York World's Fair, with twelve figures, each weighing over a ton. The work was commissioned by the WPA under its Welfare Arts Program. The ceramics division of this program was set up in Cleveland.

Viktor Schreckengost (b. 1906) is another notable artist who designed for Cowan, joining the firm in 1930. His originality was immediately apparent in the design of his 1930 punch bowl called the "Jazz Bowl."

The Jazz Bowl was 11½ inches high and 16½ inches wide, in porcelain with an "Egyptian blue" glaze developed by Arthur Eugene Baggs, chief chemist for Cowan. It has black "jazz age" designs of skyscrapers, neon signs, cocktail glasses, records, streetlamps, and Stop-and-Go signs. It was created in the sgraffito or graffito technique, which Schreckengost perfected, etching into the blue overglaze to reveal the design in a black underglaze.

Only about fifty of the bowls were made, and each was slightly different. The original was created as a special commission anonymously placed for Eleanor Roosevelt as a gift to her husband, who was then governor of New York. The original design was reissued the following year in a tulip shape created by Cowan himself in two sizes, nine inches high and eight inches high, and decorated by Schreckengost.

The original Jazz Bowl retailed for $50. A Cowan punch bowl was sold a few years ago at $3,250, but it was a restored piece in Cowan's 1931 tulip-shaped form. The price that an original Jazz Bowl in perfect condition would bring on the market today is anyone's guess. (See photos of the Jazz Bowl and works by Waylande Gregory in the color section, "An Art Deco Portfolio.")

Other pieces by Schreckengost that are sought after today include designs for punch bowls, plates, sculpted figures of Danish circus performers, and painted vases. Much of this production has disappeared from the market; some pieces are held in private collections.

The only 1930 Jazz Bowls we've ever seen were in the Rocky River Public Library collection and in the private collection of John Axelrod of Boston that was on view at the Museum of Fine Arts. The Rocky River Public Library in Ohio has the world's largest collection of Cowan pottery, totaling more than eight hundred pieces. In addition, the library has collected the history and catalogs of the company.

Cowan Pottery is receiving wider exposure than ever before on the Art Deco market, and consequently, many of its prices have leaped. Again, as with many ceramic companies and even with potters like Clarice Cliff, the highest prices are fetched by those pieces that are truly Art Deco or Modern in style.

Not all of Cowan's production is terrific, and not all of it is Deco or Modern. Many pieces still sell for under $100. However, Alexander Blazys' "Bird on a Wave" figure can bring as much as $800. Comical black-glazed bookends by Drexel Jacobson, shaped like big-beaked pelicans, can bring $600 or more. Originally priced at $7.50 when it was produced in 1931, an eight-inch vase incised with squirrels and plant motifs can bring over $400, and many other vases bring $200 to $500.

As the production of this important Art Deco pottery company continues to be rediscovered, we predict that prices will continue to rise steadily.

## OTHER ART DECO AMERICAN CERAMICS

American Art Clay Company of Indianapolis—or AMACO, as its pieces are often signed—produced Art Deco–style figural and decorative statues in the 1920s. Not frequently found on the market, its best pieces often command $300 or more. AMACO is notable for the quality of its glazes, which are often finely crazed.

Frankoma Pottery, which started in the mid-1930s in Oklahoma and is still in operation today, created some Modernist designs in their single-handled, lidless water pitchers. Decorative glazing techniques included a brushed glaze in green and copper color, sometimes called "prairie green," and high-luster black glazes with metallic tones. It is difficult to date Frankoma, as its most popular glazes are still being used today.

Roseville Pottery Company of Zanesville, Ohio, annually produced lines of ceramics, usually with flowered patterns in relief, such as "Freesia," "Peony," "Magnolia," and dozens more. However, two Modernistic designs that the company produced are actively collected on the Art Deco market today. These were Futura, introduced in 1924, and Moderne, introduced in 1938. Futura is the more distinctive of the two, with odd-angled and geometric vases with angular handles, stepped-back forms on necks and bodies, and interesting glazes in brown and tan, green and orange, and green and pink combinations.

Futura vases can bring as much as $1,000 on today's market, but most prices fall in the $200 to $600 range and some are still below $150.

Moderne was essentially a spherical and conical style but often had angular handles and Deco line motifs on the body. Vases and bowls in this style bring $50 to $150 today. Although the streamlined styles were successful, Roseville did not continue making Modern-idiom ceramics. When the company closed in 1954, it was still making flowered vessels.

In 1937 Russel Wright was commissioned by Steubenville Pottery Company to create a line of tablewares, which he called American Modern. This style reflects the Streamline design that was being produced in the late 1930s. It was the most popular and widespread line of household ceramics ever produced.

First designed in a beige and bean brown, the line was produced over the years in a variety of colors: powder blue, chutney, green, yellow, camel, and gray. It is widely found on the collecting market, occasionally in full sets. Wright designed other lines of ceramic tableware, such as Iroquois. These ceramics were broadly distributed, often by Hall China, both spreading the acceptance of Streamline and watering down its impact.

In 1904 Robert T. Hall became president of the family company, Hall China in East Liverpool, Ohio. He developed a single-step glaze that could withstand kiln-firing at high temperatures, and this brought down the price of functional ceramics dramatically. Durable and practical, it was first sold to the restaurant and hotel trade and later retailed in department stores.

Among the most collectible Hall items from the Art Deco era are the so-called refrigerator-ware leftover dishes and water pitchers designed by Hall for appliance manufacturers and given away as premiums with the purchase of a new refrigerator. Also popular are streamlined teapots such as "Aladdin," "Surfside," "Airflow," and those with whimsical forms such as "Basketball," "Doughnut," and "Football" styles.

The most highly prized colors are Chinese red and cobalt blue. Chinese red teapots can bring up to $400 or more, although many, in more common glazes, are still under $100. These styles were made largely in 1938, 1939, and 1940. Hall withdrew from the retail market in the 1950s, due to low sales caused mostly by cheaper Japanese ceramics, and returned to producing for the restaurant trade.

However, perhaps in part because of the popularity of Art Deco today, in 1984 Hall reintroduced many of its styles to the public and even included a new line of plates and platters for microwave ovens. All of the molds for the 1,100-plus pieces Hall ever made were still in storage, and many are being reissued—in over one hundred colors.

Among the reproduced Art Deco styles to be aware of are "Aristocrat," designed in 1935 as a Westinghouse giveaway, the common Ball Jugs, and the "Doughnut" and "Airflow" teapots.

These new reproductions are good quality, but they hurt the ceramic collectibles market, where in many cases prices had reached over $100. Dealers find it hard to convince the uninitiated that a pitcher purchased for $75 at an antiques show is better than an exact duplicate purchased in a housewares store for $14.99 to $19.99.

Consequently, there has been a flattening of the market in this area, although avid collectors will pay high prices for pieces they "need" to complete a collection of the fifty or so teapot styles.

Like the Midwestern firms, the New Jersey ceramics industry also adopted many of the Modern forms. Lenox, which was founded under another name in 1889 in Trenton, produced interesting figural and functional Art Deco ceramics. The company is still in operation today.

Another notable company was Trenton Art Pottery, which operated in the 1930s and into the 1940s. Generally, Trenton pieces are geometric in shape and unadorned, with pastel glazes in yellows, blues, greens, and pinks. Trenton vases can bring up to about $200 today.

Cheaper and cheaper ceramics with Deco stylings were produced, including the swarms of pink flamingos that flew home from Florida in tourists' baggage. Much of this kitsch production can still be found in flea markets and fairs, and some of it is interesting, decorative, and functional. However, the spreading of the style in cheap ceramics helped sound the death knell for Deco. As a final blow, Russel Wright's American Modern tableware was ultimately produced in plastic.

McCoy pottery is one of those that included Deco-style pieces in the declining years. There were actually two McCoy pottery companies, both located in Roseville, Ohio. McCoy ceramics continued to use modified Deco motifs through the 1950s, but we call these "Rural Post-Deco." While sometimes incorporating Deco pattern motifs and angular handles, the overall shape is often traditional, and in general the glazes are of very poor quality.

It is interesting to note that neither of the two most important Art Deco revival exhibitions in this country—"Art Deco" at the Finch College Museum of Art in 1970 and "The World of Art Deco" at the Minneapolis Institute of Arts in 1971—included American potters and ceramists.

At the Finch College exhibition, glass and pottery were lumped together with enamel, and notable artists such as Clarice Cliff, Emile Lenoble, and Emile Decoeur were represented, along with the Wiener Werkstätte, but no Americans, except perhaps in anonymous kitsch production, were shown.

At the Minneapolis exhibit, which treated ceramics separately, French, German, English, and even Japanese works stood side by side, but the only identifiably American company represented, and then by only a single piece, was American Art Clay Company.

What happened to reawaken interest in American design perhaps started with the Bicentennial in 1976 and continues today. The resurgence of interest in things American has been greatly felt in collecting ceramics.

As we continue to find out more about the designers and products of our own ceramic industry, it is certain that other great examples of American Art Deco ceramics will be uncovered.

## PRICE LISTINGS

### European Ceramics

*Bowl*, in the manner of René Buthaud, French. Interior painted with people seated around a table drinking, unmarked. 6" diameter.
$300–$400

*Vase*, by Edouard Cazaux, French, c. 1925. Pottery vase of ovoid form decorated in brown and yellow with nudes milking a goat and blue and green foliage on an ivory washed ground, inscribed mark. 9" tall.
$550 (1987)

*Vase*, by E. Cazaux, c. 1925. Pottery vase of squared sections decorated in orange and green wash on white and gilt with classical nudes, inscribed mark. 5" high.
$650 (1987)

*Large urn*, by H. Chaumeil, French. Wide trumpet form, glazed aqua with a gray-green band of stylized Deco motif below the rim, white-glazed interior, painted with artist's signature (drilled, chip in foot). 16½" tall.
$352 (1987)

*Coffee service*, by Susie Cooper, English, c. 1930. In porcelain, comprising six cups and saucers, covered coffeepot, creamer and sugar bowl, in bittersweet with white trim, with grafitto design of whirls and dots, marked. Coffeepot 9½" tall.
$450–$650

*Figure of a gazelle*, by Susie Cooper. Decorative figure of a graceful gazelle with long horns, leaping through tall, swaying grass. Signed. 8" tall.
$85–$135

*Vase*, by Maurice Dufrène, French, executed by Boch Frères, for the shop La Maîtrise at Galleries Lafayette. Ovoid, in greens and pinks with abstract design of polka dots within circular motif and dotted lines running vertically against a dark green body. Stamped "La Maîtrise" and "Fabriqué à Keramis La Louvière (Belgique)." 9½" tall.
$750–$900

Vase by Maurice Dufrène. *(Photo by R. Four; courtesy of Morton Abromson Decorative Arts)*

*Vase*, by Etling, French, c. 1930. With crazed beige matte finish and high-luster black handles in the shape of wings. Stamped "Etling, France." 12" tall.

**$600–$750**

*Figure of a wolfhound*, by Goldscheider, Austrian. Sleek white and gray-spotted animal standing on self base, inscribed "Gemignano" and with firm's stamped marks. 12" long.

**$165 (1987)**

*Figure of Pierrette with guitar*, by Goldscheider, 1920s. A very modern-looking Pierrette with long trousered legs and colorful frock standing on a stepped square base and pensively holding her guitar in front of her. Signed "Dakon," and "Made in Austria." 13½" tall.

**$750–$1,000**

*Coffee service*, by Josef Hoffmann, Austrian, c. 1925, executed by Augarten. In porcelain, comprising coffeepot, creamer and covered sugar, the coffeepot of lobed gourd form, the sugar and creamer, with lip, of lobed melon form, all on splayed lobed feet, underglaze firm's mark. Coffeepot 6⅞" tall. 3 pieces.

**$800 (1986)**

*Bowl*, by Raoul Lachenal, French, c. 1925. Pottery bowl decorated in the Islamic taste, with blue and olive geometric motifs on a green washed ground, inscribed mark. 6½" diameter.

**$200 (1987)**

*Center bowl,* by Lachenal, c. 1920. Modeled as a conventionalized blossom with petals of olive, striated orange, and charcoal, the reverse with a rich pooling ivory glaze with allover crackled glaze, inscribed "Raoul Lachenal." 11" diameter.

$225 (1987)

*Vase,* by Lachenal, c. 1894. Earthenware ovoid form with crazed turquoise body decorated with dark green and black bamboo leaves in relief, the handles in the form of bamboo branches, painted "Lachenal." 12½" tall.

$3,300 (1986)

*Vase,* by Lachenal. Bulbous body formed of three wide-mouthed frogs seated on their haunches, in a brilliant blue crazed glaze, painted "Lachenal." 7½" tall.

$1,045 (1986)

*Vase,* by Simone Larieur, French, c. 1935. Balustered with stylized elephant and tall grasses, the shape of the elephant echoing the shape of the vase. 14" tall.

$2,600–$2,800

*Bowl,* by Bernard Leach, English. Footed, with gently flared rim, the salmon body glazed a powdery chocolate on the exterior with bands of incised decoration, the interior glazed off-white, the bowl's center incised and painted with a bird in flight, with BL stamp. 11½" diameter.

$88 (1987)
$300–$400

*Figural group,* by Lemanceau, French. Maiden and wolfhound in turquoise. 12" high x 20" long.

$325–$450

*Figural group,* by Lemanceau. Two stylized greyhounds running flat out in a cream crazed glaze, self base molded "Lemanceau." 17" long.

$495 (1987)

*Service,* by Jean Luce, French. In porcelain, comprising 11 dinner plates, 23 luncheon plates, 11 salad plates, 19 butter plates, 11 ice cream plates, 12 cream soup bowls, 20 two-handled bouillon bowls with 9 underplates, 11 coffee cups and saucers, 9 demitasse cups with 11 saucers, and 1 vegetable dish; 151 pieces. In pale gray with silver borders, some pieces monogrammed MSD. Stamped "Jean Luce Paris France." Dinner plate 10" diameter.

$165 (1986)

*Plate*, by Jean Mayodon, French, executed by Sèvres. Circular, with gilt-veined cream ground with a central design of three stylized black nudes wearing aquamarine capes, gilded "M 1950 Sevres." 9″ diameter.

$132 (1987)

*Center bowl*, by André Méthey, French, c. 1920. Pottery, decorated with cartouches of lavender quadrupeds on mottled ochre and ground of blue and white stripes, enriched in gilt and with allover craquelure, impressed mark. 7¾″ diameter.

$625 (1987)

*Charger*, by A. Méthey, c. 1920. In the Islamic taste, with ivory flora and lappets on an orange-washed ground, heightened in black and gilt, impressed mark. 10″ diameter.

$200 (1987)

*Vase*, by Moretti, Italian, 1920s. Brown and black stylized archers on a background with blue clouds and green ground. 13″ high, 10″ rim diameter.

$4,000–$4,200

*Compote*, by A. Mourier, French, 1920s. Goblet-shaped, hand-painted and hand-thrown, with classically oriented figural design and gold gilt banding and repetitive semicircular pattern on rim and foot. 7″ tall, 8″ diameter.

$850–$900

*Vase*, by Keith Murray, English, c. 1935, for Wedgwood. Matte-green pottery with horizontal banding, impressed "Keith Murray, Wedgwood, Made in England." 7″ tall.

$400–$600

*Vase*, by Michael Powolny, Austrian, c. 1910. Black and white with a pattern of diamonds and triangles. Stamped "WW" (Wiener Werkstätte) "Keramis." 10″ tall.

$2,300–$2,600

*Maiden figural liqueur bottle*, by Robj, French, 1930s. In porcelain, of a rosy-cheeked maiden in blue dress and yellow apron holding a basket of fruit, the bottle stopper molded as her bonnet, marked. 9¾″ tall.

$385 (1986)

*Scotsman figural liqueur bottle*, by Robj. In porcelain, of a Scotsman in red and white stripes blowing his bagpipe, the bottle stopper molded as his cap, marked. 10¼" tall.
$825 (1986)

*Witch figural liqueur bottle*, by Robj. The bespectacled white-haired figure in peaked black hat and full cloak holding a cane, on circular base, stamped "Robj Paris." 10" tall.
$220 (1987)

*Scholar figural liqueur bottle*, by Robj. Scholar in black academic robe with red details and black tassled hat, molded as the bottle stopper. Stamped "Robj, Paris." 10" tall.
$200–$300

*Cossack figural liqueur bottle*, by Robj. Mustachioed Cossack in red and black with typical Russian fur hat molded as the bottle stopper. Stamped "Robj, Paris." 10" tall.
$200–$300

*Figural lamp bases*, by Robj. In porcelain, of a woman and bearded man in classical white robes each leaning on a gold walking stick, naturalistically colored with gold accents. 11¾" tall. Pair.
$550 (1986)

**Robj decanters of a Scholar and a Cossack.** *(Photo courtesy of Peter Boehm, Dualities Gallery)*

*Porcelain sculpture,* by Ferdinand Lieberman for Rosenthal, German. A pink nude stylized woman astride an ostrich in shades of brown and pink, on a rectangular base. Inscribed "Fred. Lieberman." 21½" long.

$1,400–$1,600

*Vase and cover,* "Tropiques," the shape by Henri Rapin, c. 1925, the decoration by Anne-Marie Fontaine, 1937, executed by Sèvres, 1937. Massive ovoid body painted with continuous tropical landscape with birds and sun setting on blue hillocks, a sailboat glimpsed in the distance between palm fronds, painted in glowing pastel shades of green, blue, mottled rose, and peach impasto, with domed cover in mottled blue. Base printed with firm's mark and incised "16-12-37 PM," vase marked "AM Fontaine 90.37," the cover with painted initials "AMF." 22½" high. Sold with letter from Sèvres with supporting information from company records.

$17,000 (1986)

*Box,* by Sèvres. In porcelain, curved rectangular box of aquamarine sprinkled with navy blue and hints of yellow, in four-footed mount, the lid with central foliate oval cartouche enclosing the figure of cupid, surmounted by a pair of doves, marked. 4⅜" tall.

$308 (1987)

*Sculpture,* by Sèvres, c. 1930. Stalking panther, in shades of gray, black, and white, marked "Sevres France Vinare." 22" long.

$700–$900

*Vase,* by Sèvres. In ormolu-mounted porcelain, bulbous form in mottled oxblood glaze with gilt-bronze Deco applications and four looped "handles" from midsection to rim, marked. 7" tall.

$550 (1987)

*Vase,* by Sèvres. In porcelain, the blue and white body centering an interlocking frieze of birds, inscribed "Sèvres." 24" tall.

$1,100 (1986)

*Table articles,* "Harmony," by Eric Slater, English, 1930s, for Shelley Potteries, Ltd. Each in bright drip glazes comprising two pitchers, pair of covered cheeses, covered butter, open sugar, ashtray, charger, and four luncheon plates, with printed factory marks. 12 pieces.

$250 (1987)

*Tea set*, by Shelley Potteries, Ltd., English, 1930s, possibly by Eric Slater. In bone china, comprising a teapot, sugar, creamer, and two cups and saucers, design in green and black with angular handles and shapes.

$500–$700

*Vase*, by C. Tharaud, French, c. 1925–1930, for Limoges. Spherical with flared rim, depicting stylized flowers and long pointed leaves, repetitive floral outline pattern, decorated in browns, blues, and golds. 9" tall.

$1,100–$1,200

*Candelabra*, by the Wiener Werkstätte, Austrian. Each modeled as a mustard yellow lion supporting a double-nozzle candleholder on his back, stamped with firm's mark. 7½" tall x 8¾" long.

$550 (1986)

*Figural nude*, by Zsolnay, French. The woman standing in contraposto pose leaning on a draped pedestal with urn, in greenish iridescent high glaze, painted mark. 10" tall.

$600–$800

*Figure of a vulture*, by Zsolnay. In porcelain, the bird sitting proudly on his perch in multicolor iridescence, inscribed "Syaetus bellicosus" with red Zsolnay seal. 11½" tall.

$1,000–$1,500

Tea set for Shelley, possibly by Eric Slater. *(Photo by R. Four; courtesy of Historical Design Collection)*

Vase by C. Tharaud. *(Photo by R. Four; courtesy of Morton Abromson Decorative Arts)*

## Boch Frères

*Plate,* by Charles Catteau, for Boch Frères Keramis, Belgium. In navy, turquoise, green, and black on a crackle-glaze background, depicting a grazing antlered deer, with an abstracted floral border pattern. Painted "Ch. Catteau" and "Boch Frères Keramis." 13" diameter.

**$450–$500**

*Vase,* by Charles Catteau, for Boch Frères. In subtle green, gold, and black with a repetitive pattern reminiscent of peacock feathers. Signed "Ch. Catteau" and stamped "Boch Frères." 7" tall.

**$575–$650**

*Vase,* by Charles Catteau, for Boch Frères. Ovoid cream bordered in blue crazed glaze, decorated with vertical stripes enclosing circle blossoms and blue leaves. Signed "Ch. Catteau" and stamped "Boch Frères." 10½" tall.

**$440 (1986)**

*Vase,* by Charles Catteau, for Boch Frères. Earthenware ovoid form, crazed white ground with green-spotted black, navy, and turquoise deer amid stylized turquoise and navy foliage, painted "D943 Ch. Catteau Made in Belgium Fabrication Belge Boch Fès La Louvière." 11½" tall.

**$625–$700**

*Vase,* by Charles Catteau, for Boch Frères. Earthenware ovoid form, crazed white ground with green-spotted black, navy, and turquoise deer amid stylized turquoise and navy foliage, painted "D943 Ch.

Catteau Made in Belgium Fabrication Belge Boch Fès La Louvière." 13¼" tall.

$715 (1986)

*Vase*, by Charles Catteau, for Boch Frères. Earthenware ovoid form, broad central crazed white band with green-spotted turquoise, black, and navy deer amid green and navy foliage, painted "Made in Belgium Fabrication Belge Boch Fès la Louvière D943 Ch. Catteau" and impressed "961." Rare in this size. 19½" tall.

$3,000–$3,500
$1,320 (1986)

*Vase*, by Charles Catteau, for Boch Frères. Same as above but two, sold as a pair.

$6,000–$6,500

*Vase*, by Charles Catteau, for Gres Keramis. Ovoid with abstract black thorny branches rising vertically against an eggshell-white ground. Rim banded with abstract leafy pattern in browns and orange. Marked "Ch. Catteau" and "Gres Keramis." 8" tall. (For illustration see color insert.)

$550–$600

Vase by Charles Catteau and two by Jan Windt for Boch Frères. *(Photo courtesy of Nancy McClelland, Christie's)*

*Vase*, by Charles Catteau. Oviform with stylized squirrels in different poses around the circumference in crackled beige on dark brown rectangles. Body is crackled beige with a band of stylized mountains near the base and stylized suns at the neck. Straight lines of irregular lengths run down from the rim. This design in different colors was shown by Boch Frères at the 1925 Paris Exposition. Signed "Ch. Catteau" and stamped "Gres Keramis." Very rare in this size. 23" tall.
**$6,500–$7,000**

*Vase*, by Jan Windt, executed by Boch Frères. Earthenware in tiered cylindrical form, the central white band with navy, brown, yellow, and turquoise birds on black branches amid brick-red, yellow, and brown flowers, painted "Boch Frères Keramis Made in Belgium W D1130 LD." 14½" tall.
**$550 (1986)**

*Vase*, by Jan Windt, executed by Boch Frères. Earthenware ovoid form, white ground with large yellow, chartreuse, navy, and brown birds on black branches with circular tan, yellow, and brown flowers, painted "WD1130 Boch Frères Keramis made in Belgium" and impressed "961." 20" tall.
**$1,540 (1986)**

*Vase*, by Boch Frères. Footed cylindrical form with slightly flared rim, depicting a stylized archer and sleek hounds running against a mottled red-brown and copper ground that gives the illusion of being in

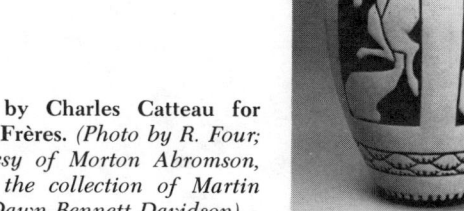

Vase by Charles Catteau for Boch Frères. *(Photo by R. Four; courtesy of Morton Abromson, from the collection of Martin and Dawn Bennett Davidson)*

metallic-colored marble. Stamped "Keramis" and "Made in Belgium." 13" tall.

$650–$750

*Vase*, by Boch Frères. Ovoid with wide rim and abstracted floral and criss-cross design. Stamped "Boch Frères Keramis." 7" tall.

$850–$900

*Vase*, by Boch Frères. Ovoid, with dramatic design of giraffes grazing on stylized palm leaves. Geometric banding at the base. The trees in browns and beiges on a pale yellow high-luster background. Stamped "Boch Frères." 13" tall.

$900–$1,000

*Vase*, by Boch Frères. Designed with long stylized leaves in black and green and flowers in green and orange, against a white crackled ground. Stamped "Boch Frères." 14" tall.

$550–$600

*Vase*, by Boch Frères. Design with stylized red and black flowers running vertically against a crackled white ground. Horizontal banding on rim and foot. Stamped "Boch Frères." 11½" tall.

$500–$550

*Vase*, by Boch Frères. Footed, ovoid form with stylized mountains in orange, yellow, and black against a white crackled ground. Foot is horizontally banded in yellow and black. Stamped "Keramis" and "Made in Belgium." 6" tall.

$150–$200

Vase by Boch Frères with giraffes. *(Photo by R. Four; courtesy of Morton Abromson Decorative Arts)*

*Vase*, by Boch Frères. Crackled red ground with winged horse rearing up on hind legs as if preparing for flight. Banded at base and rim. Made in Belgium, picturing the "Legend of Persée et les Gorgons." 10½" tall.

$450–$750

*Vase*, by Boch Frères. Balustered, the white body painted with stylized grasses reaching from foot to shoulder in black, green, and yellow, in crackled glaze, marked. 13½" tall.

$165 (1986)

*Vase*, by Boch Frères. Ovoid body in chocolate brown with tan border and central panel of orange blossoms and slender olive leaves. Stamped "Boch Frères." 13½" tall.

$132 (1987)

*Vase*, by Boch Frères. Ovoid body with continuous frieze of stylized birds in flight between cloud-form decorated neck with inverted rim and lower portion, in vibrant yellow, blue, and light blue on craquelure ground, printed firm's mark, painted "D 982," impressed "M 951." 13½" tall.

$770 (1986)

*Vase*, by Boch Frères. Balustered, with two squared handles rising above rim, striped in yellow and black with curved vine bearing violet flowers and posy border. Stamped "Boch Frères." 13¾" tall.

$300–$350

*Vase*, by Boch Frères. Tapered cylindrical form, the yellow ground with orange and black polka dots falling amid orange leaves and simple stylized flowers, marked. 12" tall.

$300–$400

*Vase*, by Boch Frères. Balustered, with square handles reaching above rim, the body white with black stripes and oval dots, the shoulder with pink and green flowers, marked. 11⅔" tall.

$250–$350

*Vase*, by Boch Frères. Spherical, the pale gray crazed body incised and painted with triangular panels of yellow, green, and blue abstract foliate motif with green and blue borders, marked. 9⅜" tall.

$500–$600

*Vase*, by Boch Frères. Ovoid body with design of green vertical stripes and black stripes enclosing floral medallions in yellow, orange, and pink, marked. 9¾" tall.

$110 (1986)

*Vase*, by Boch Frères. Balustered body in lemon yellow crazed glaze, incised and painted with sinuous blue trailing vines bearing aqua and red flowers. With firm's stamp. 8¼" tall.

$330 (1987)

*Vase*, by Boch Frères Keramis. Ovoid with cylindrical neck in a crazed cream glaze divided into three decorative panels by blue-dotted borders, each panel with a stylized blue and yellow blossom. With firm's stamp. 8¾" tall.

$440 (1986)

*Vase*, by Boch Frères. Spherical on low black foot, the crazed cream colored bodies incised and painted with panels of yellow leaves and brown rosettes, bordered in black, marked. 9½" tall. Pair.

$800–$900

*Vase*, by Boch Frères. Cylindrical, on short foot and with matching neck, the body molded with wavy horizontal bands, in a bright aqua crazed glaze, marked. 8⅝" tall. Pair.

$600–$800

## Longwy and Primavera

*Bowl*, by Longwy, French. Footed bowl in crazed cream glaze with decorative band of swirls in blue glaze on exterior and central circular panel of same design on the interior, stamped "Atelier Primavera Longwy." 11⅜" diameter.

$440 (1986)

*Charger*, by Claude Levy, French, for Primavera, executed by Longwy. Elegant design with liberal use of colors and gold enameling, depicting a bare-chested mermaid riding through the waves on the back of a fish, with abstract sails and clouds in the distance. Stamped "Longwy" and "Primavera." 15" diameter.

$2,800–$3,000

*Container*, by Primavera, in the style of Longwy, French, c. 1935. Figure of a woman's head, stylized features, elongated nose, smart smile, and curly scalloped hair. White crackle glaze. Ink-stamped "Primavera France." Lid missing. 8" tall.

$150–$250

**Container by Primavera.** *(Photo by Dennis Galloway; courtesy of Ed Forcum, Rosebud Gallery)*

*Covered box*, by Longwy, for Primavera. In navy blue, black, turquoise, and white, depicting a geometrically antlered deer in white with stylized background of trees and flowers. Stamped "Longwy" and "Primavera." Approx. 3½" diameter.

**$150–$250**

*Covered box*, by Longwy. In navy and light blues with overall swirled geometric design. Stamped "Longwy, France." Approx. 3½" diameter.

**$150–$250**

*Covered box*, by Longwy, for the Pomone workshop at Au Bon Marché. In yellow, orange, blue, and green, depicting a stylized nude beneath an exotic tress with yellow fruit. Stamped "Longwy" and "Pomone." Approx. 3½" diameter.

**$150–$250**

*Covered box*, by Claude Levy, for Primavera, executed by Longwy. Circular, in green, gold, and black on a white crackled ground, depicting geometric cactus plants. Signed, and with manufacturer's mark. Approx. 3½" diameter. (For illustration see color insert.)

**$150–$250**

*Figures of cats*, retailed by Primavera, French. In Cubist style with ivory craquelure, impressed marks, 13" tall. Pair.

**$200–$400**

*Figure of a bison,* retailed by Primavera, c. 1925. Glazed in white, brown, and black on unglazed brown ground. Impressed retailer's mark. 22½" long.

$1,400 (1987)

*Plaque,* by Longwy, retailed by Au Bon Marché. Circular with curved rim, decorated with jungle scene of blue elephants and a woman plucking coconuts from palm trees, in shades of blue, brown, green, and mauve on craquelure ground, printed firm's and retailer's marks, incised "1252." 15" diameter.

$1,100 (1986)

*Tea service,* by Longwy. Comprising four teacups and saucers and four octagonal cake plates, with brilliant allover flower design against a lapis ground bordered in royal blue, each marked "Decoré à la Main, Emaux De Longwy France." Cake plate 7¾" diameter.

$200–$300

*Tea service,* by Longwy. Four teacups and saucers and four octagonal cake plates, with brilliant allover flower design against a lapis ground, enamel borders in royal blue, each marked "Decoré à La Main, Emaux De Longwy France." Cake plate 7¾" diameter.

$385 (1987)

**Figure of a bison for Primavera.** *(Photo courtesy of William Doyle Galleries)*

**Vase by Longwy.** *(Photo by R. Four; courtesy of Morton Abromson Decorative Arts)*

*Vase,* by Claude Levy, retailed by Primavera, c. 1925. Stoneware vase of ovoid form decorated with blue, brick, and silver geometric motifs on an eggshell-colored ground, inscribed and impressed marks. 11½" high.

**$750 (1987)**

*Vase,* by Longwy. Ovoid with beige crackled ground and geometric decorations of circles, dots, and horizontal banding, in browns, blues, and beiges, three ball feet, stamped "Longwy." 7" tall.

**$425–$500**

*Vase,* by Longwy, flat-sided circular form featuring blue-bordered decorative panel of a kneeling female nude flourishing green scarf, marked. 11" tall.

**$400–$500**

*Vase,* by Longwy for Primavera. Footed cylindrical form decorated with nudes reclining on beach and birds flying over, crazed yellow glaze with black bordering, marked. 4¾" tall.

**$550 (1986)**

## Clarice Cliff

*Vases,* "Archaic" pattern, by Clarice Cliff. Cylindrical and broadly flared, pattern derived from the ornamentations of Egyptian column capitals. Multicolored, with horizontal banding at foot and stylized repetitive floral and geometric designs on body. In 8", 10", and 12" sizes. All marked. (For illustration see color insert.)

**$4,000–$5,000**

*Tea set*, "Aztec" pattern, by Clarice Cliff. Teapot, creamer, and sugar in geometric, angular design, with triangular handles on teacups. All painted with sharp triangular yellow, red, and orange geometric patterns. Service pieces and cups and saucers for two. All marked.
$2,500–$3,000

*Breakfast set*, Bizarre "Crocus" pattern, by Clarice Cliff. Teapot, sugar bowl, creamer, five cereal bowls and a dish. Set of 9. All marked. Teapot 5" tall.
$1,500–$2,000

*Lotus jug*, Bizarre "Crocus" pattern, by Clarice Cliff. One-handled, central horizontal band decorated with crocus, bordered by orange band at base and yellow neck. Marked. 12" tall.
$350–$450

*Basket centerpiece*, Bizarre "Crocus" pattern, by Clarice Cliff. Designed as a basket with a woven texture and decorated with crocus and orange and yellow abastract triangular sections, on circular foot. Marked. 14" tall.
$700–$900

*Wall plaque*, Inspiration, by Clarice Cliff. With matte glaze of greens and blues. Marked. 13" diameter.
$2,200–$2,600

*Bowl*, Bizarre, by Clarice Cliff for Newport Pottery. The interior of the earthenware bowl decorated with rings of blue, black, and orange, the exterior with decorative band in matched colors. Marked. 8¼" diameter.
$400–$500

*Flower holder*, Bizarre, by Clarice Cliff. Depicting a fantastic landscape painted in yellow, green, brown, and blue. Marked. 5" tall.
$400–$500

*Salt and pepper shaker set*, Bizarre, by Clarice Cliff. Landscape of trees painted in orange, yellow, and brown. Marked. 5½" tall.
$500–$600

*Vase*, Bizarre, by Clarice Cliff. In balustered form, painted with yellow, tan, orange, and brown rings bordering a fantasy landscape in matched shades. Marked. 12" tall.
$2,400–$2,600

*Bowl*, Bizarre "Pansy" pattern, by Clarice Cliff. Painted in lavender, blue, yellow, and green. 7" rim diameter.

**$300–$400**

*Vase*, Bizarre "Pansy" pattern, by Clarice Cliff. Painted in lavender, blue, yellow, and green. 8" tall.

**$1,200–$1,400**

*Bowl*, Bizarre "Snake Tree" pattern, by Clarice Cliff. Depicting a snake tree in bright red, orange, and yellow foliage in a rolling landscape. Marked. 8¾" diameter.

**$600–$800**

*Vase*, Inspiration, by Clarice Cliff. Spherical, depicting a fantasy landscape in lavender, blue, and cream against a green background, painted "Inspiration Bizarre by Clarice Cliff, Newport Pottery Burslem England." 8" tall.

**$1,600–$2,000**

*Lotus jug*, Inspiration "Persian" pattern, by Clarice Cliff. Stamped "Inspiration Bizarre by Clarice Cliff." 12" tall.

**$7,000–$8,000**

*Ashtrays*, by Clarice Cliff. In various patterns. Marked.

**$150–$600**

*After-dinner sets*, by Clarice Cliff. In various patterns with coffeepot, creamer, sugar, and six cups and saucers. 15 pieces. All marked.

**$1,800–$3,800**

*Bowls*, by Clarice Cliff. In various patterns, with 8", 9", or 10" rim diameters. All marked.

**$300–$1,200**

*Candlesticks*, by Clarice Cliff. In various patterns and shapes, such as square-stepped shape "Pansy" pattern, designed with colorful flowers. Marked. 3" tall.

**$200–$400**

*Candlesticks*, by Clarice Cliff. In tapered and geometric forms, various patterns. Marked. 6" to 9" tall.

**$800–$1,500**

*Centerpiece*, in the "Gibraltar" pattern. Stylized Viking ship with colorful medallions and a painted scene of sailing boats. On two triangular feet. Marked.
$2,000–$3,000

*Chargers*, by Clarice Cliff. In various patterns, such as with stylized flowers or geometric designs. Marked.
13" diameter   $1,500–$3,000
18" diameter   $2,000–$4,000

*Head of a woman*, by Clarice Cliff. Stylized face with red lips and floral headdress, painted in green, brown, and blue. Marked. 6¾" tall.
$500–$600

*Jardinieres*, by Clarice Cliff. In various patterns, may be horizontally ribbed with diamond-shaped and triangular color patterns and orange inside glaze.
$1,000–$3,000

*Lotus jugs*, by Clarice Cliff. In geometric paint designs in various patterns. Marked. 12" tall.
$2,000–$5,000

*Lotus jugs*, by Clarice Cliff. In scenic designs in various patterns. Marked. 12" tall.
$3,000–$7,000

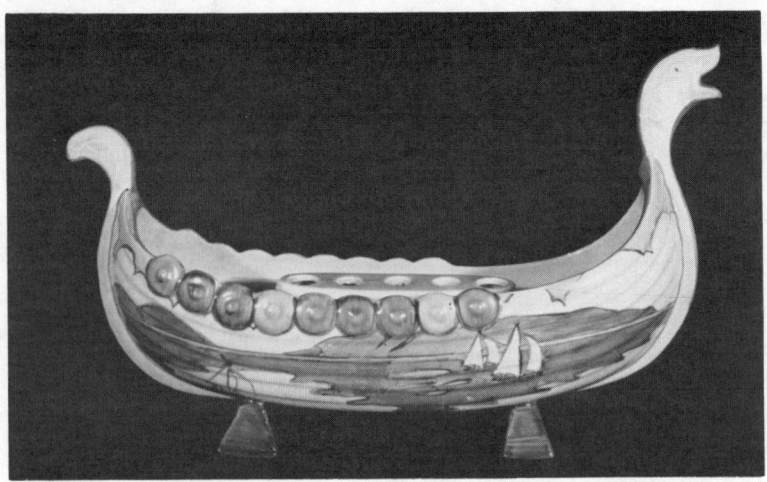

Viking ship centerpiece by **Clarice Cliff.** *(Photo courtesy of Meisel-Primavera)*

*Geometric lotus jug by Clarice Cliff. (Photo courtesy of Meisel-Primavera)*

*Plates,* by Clarice Cliff. In various patterns. 6″–9″ diameter.
$150–$600

*Umbrella stands,* by Clarice Cliff. In various patterns. Marked.
18″ tall $5,500–$6,000
24″ tall $7,200–$8,000

*Vase,* by Clarice Cliff, 1930s. Footed, flared, cylindrical, with repoussé flowers at foot and undecorated body, marked "Newport Pottery Co., England." 12″ tall.
$200–$300

*Vases,* by Clarice Cliff. All marked.
Balustered, various patterns. 14″ tall $2,500–$5,000
Ovoid vases, various patterns. 8″ tall $1,000–$2,000
Ovoid vases, various patterns. 10″ tall $1,500–$3,000

*Vase,* by Clarice Cliff. Ovoid body on flattened conical foot, decorated with a scene of a cottage at the edge of a wood, the flaring trumpet neck with flame streaking carried over to interior, marked. 18″ tall.
$1,430 (1986)
$3,000–$4,000

*Wash basin and pitcher sets,* by Clarice Cliff. In various patterns. Marked.
$2,000–$5,000

Vase by Clarice Cliff. *(Photo courtesy of Meisel-Primavera)*

## American Ceramics

*Bust of a girl*, made by American Art Clay Company (AMACO), American. Finely crazed luminous blue glazing, signed "American Art Clay Company, Indianapolis." 8" tall.

$350–$450

*Vase*, by Fulper, American. Butterfat and goldstone glazing, incised Fulper signature with paper label. (N.B.: A later design, influenced by the Modern movement. Fulper vases are generally considered Arts

Bust of a girl by AMACO. *(Photo courtesy of Peter Boehm, Dualities Gallery)*

## Ceramics

and Crafts pottery.) Marked "Fulper Pottery 125th Anniversary, 1805–1930." 9¼" high.

$150–$300

*Water server,* by Frankoma, American, 1930s. Circular pitcher with stepped-back design where handle meets body and angled spout. Lidless design. In brushed green and copper-colored glaze, sometimes called "prairie green." 6½" tall x 8½" wide.

$25–$35

*Water server,* by Frankoma, American, 1930s. Circular shape with spiral motif and stepped-back design where handle meets body. Lidless design. In deep black glaze with metallic blue tones and finely crazed. 6½" tall x 7" wide.

$60–$75

*Ashtray,* by Waylande Gregory, American. Shaped square brown tray with channel rim and bottom in emerald-colored glaze, inscribed "Waylande Gregory US Patent 2,357399." 2" high.

$550 (1986)

*Vase,* by Maija Grotell, American. Hemispherical body, raised on a dark brown circular base, in an irregular ochre-brown glaze with a dark brown rim, inscribed "Mg CA." 5¼" diameter.

$935 (1986)

**Frankoma water server.** *(Photo by R. Four)*

*Ball jug,* by Hall, American, introduced in 1938. One of the company's most popular and most basic styles for several years, made in a number of different colors and four different sizes: 1½ pts., 2⅓ pts., 2 qts., and 5¼ pts. Still in production today. Overall rounded shape.
$20–$50

*Teapots,* by Hall, introduced in late 1930s. Various styles and sizes including the "Doughnut" (1938), with a hole in the center; the "Automobile" (1938); the "Football" (1938); "Basketball" (1938); "Aladdin" (1939); "Rhythm" (1939); "Surfside" (1939); and "Airflow" (1940). The most popular Hall glazes are Chinese red and cobalt blue.

| | |
|---|---|
| Common styles and colors: | $35–$90 |
| "Aladdin," in various colors | $40–$150 |
| "Doughnut," gold-decorated | $120–$130 |
| "Surfside," in Chinese red | $125–$150 |
| "Rhythm," in Chinese red | $125–$135 |
| "Football," in Chinese red | $400–$500 |

*Leftover covered dishes,* "Emperor" style, by Hall for Westinghouse. One of the 1939 refrigerator ware pieces given as premiums with the purchase of a refrigerator. In "Garden" green, "Canary" yellow, "Sunset" red, and other colors. 6″ long x 4″ deep. Each.
$25–$50

Hall "Aladdin" teapot. *(Photo by R. Four)*

## Ceramics

*Water server,* "Emperor" style, by Hall. In "Garden" green, marked "Made exclusively for Westinghouse by The Hall China Co. Made in U.S.A." 8" tall x 7" wide.

$60–$70

*Water server,* "Patrician" style, by Hall, 1938. In delphinium blue with cover. The first line of refrigerator ware used by Westinghouse. The lid design is an extension of the handle with a stepped-back diamond pattern. Slight tilt gives the impression of speed. 7" tall x 11" long.

$50–$60

*Head of man,* by Lenox, American. In porcelain, glazed in red, signed "Lenox 2672/B391.138."

$450–$550

*Woman's head in profile,* by Lenox, 1930s. In white ceramic, with woman's hair streaming in repetitive lines. Ink-stamped "Lenox." 7" tall.

$100–$150

*Candy dish,* by Reizenstein Son, American, 1930s–1940s. Compote style in beige ceramic with transfer-printed design of Egyptian sailing vessels, and green repetitive pattern of diamonds around the base. Marked "Designed exclusively for the Fort Pitt Hotel" and "Reizenstein Son., Lamberton Company." 7" tall, 7" rim diameter.

$35–$40

Head of a man by Lenox. *(Photo courtesy of Peter Boehm, Dualities Gallery)*

## ART DECO

*Bowl*, Futura style, by Roseville Pottery Co., American, 1928. Angular pattern with stepped-back motif, with an oval stepped base, sharply angular sides, and a brown glaze. 8" rim diameter.

$80–$100

*Jardiniere and pedestal base*, Futura style, by Roseville, in a shaded brown glaze. 29" tall. 2 pieces.

$500–$750

*Vase*, Futura style, by Roseville, with angular handles and stepped-back, conical neck, base green, neck orange. 7" tall.

$100–$125

*Vase*, Futura style, by Roseville. Rectangular with raised *V* decoration on face. Round base. In green and pink. 8" tall.

$200–$225

*Vase*, Futura style, by Roseville, square with inverted triangle design and four half-spheres on square base. In green and tan. 12" tall, 3" rim diameter.

$500–$700

*Vase*, Futura style, by Roseville. Stepped-back circular base. In green and tan, with streamlined curved handles from square vessel to base. 14" tall.

$800–$1,000

*Vase*, Futura style, by Roseville. Rectangular, with stepped-back base and rim, diamond-shaped design on face. In pink and green with handles at right angles from shoulder to base.

$275–$400

*Vases*, Futura style, by Roseville. Six-sided, each side a triangle facing center. 8" tall. Pair.

$250 (1987)

*Vases*, Futura style, by Roseville, round base with stepped conical neck and no handles. In green and orange. 8" tall. Pair.

$110 (1987)

*Bowl*, Moderne style, by Roseville, 1934. Stylized plant motif, turquoise-colored glaze with gold shadings. 5" rim diameter.

$60–$90

Roseville Futura style vases. *(Photo courtesy of Phillips)*

*Vase*, Moderne style, by Roseville. Spherical with angular motifs and stylized handles. White ceramic glaze with pale red accents. 8" tall.
$80–$120

*Leftover dish*, by The Trenton Potteries Company, American. Moss green dish with cover, banding on sides. 8" long x 4" wide x 3" deep.
$150–$175

*"Snufferette,"* by Trenton. Ashtray with holders to stub out cigarettes.
$25–$30

*Vase*, by Trenton, 1930s–1940s. Globe-shaped in mossy blue with banding running vertically on two sides to rim. 6" tall, 2" rim diameter.
$100–$120

*Vase*, Trenton. Light blue, circular, with stepped-back circular motif on face. 6" tall.
$175–$200

*Figural vase*, by Carl Walters. Shaped like a rooster, with a pedestal for legs and the open vase in the tail. Decorated with multiple tiny blue and red abstracted flowers on a white ground. Signed "AAA" (Associated American Artists) and "Carl Walters *c.*" 10¾" high x 8" wide.
$2,000–$2,500

*Set of pottery*, American Modern, by Russel Wright for Steubenville, American, 1930s–1940s. Comprising 12 dinner plates, 12 side plates, 12 bowls, 12 cups and saucers, sugar, creamer, salt and pepper, coffeepot (missing cover), pitcher, covered serving dish, covered serving pot, gravy boat with dish, 2 serving bowls, 3 serving platters of various shapes, demitasse cup and saucer, all in mustard-colored glaze, most pieces impressed "Russel Wright MFG by Steubenville." Largest, 11" high.

$440 (1986)

*Creamer and sugar sets,* American Modern, by Russel Wright for Steubenville. In various colors such as ivory, powder blue, chutney, green, yellow, camel, coral, gray, and bean brown. Stylized design. 5" long x 2½" deep. Set.

$15–$25

*Bowl,* Iroquois, by Russel Wright, ceramic tableware in a brown glaze, 1940s, stamped "Iroquois Casual China" with stamped signature "Russel Wright." 5" rim diameter.

$5–$8
Iroquois cup and saucer, as above $8–$10
Iroquois plates/cakes plates, as above $2–$4

*Pelican planter,* anon. In white ceramic with uneven glaze. Stylized pelican perched on planter. 6" long x 4" wide x 3" deep. Overall 10" tall.

$15–$20

**American Modern by Russel Wright.** *(Photo courtesy of Christie's East)*

*Pink flamingos,* anon., definitely American, 1930s on. Once a dime a dozen, pink flamingos can now be dozens of dollars each. Originally produced for Florida homes, when America discovered Florida beaches in the 1930s, they soon became its most popular souvenir. Flamingos and pelicans adorned glass and ceramic ashtrays, bowls, dishes, hand towels, and other kitchen items, as well as the more collectible planters and lamps. Pink flamingo kitchen planter in pinks, greens, and black with fairly sharp features. 14" tall.

$50–$60

*Pink flamingo statue,* anon. Blurred features. 5" tall.

$12–$15

*Pink flamingo souvenir statue,* anon. Features barely discernible. Ink-stamped "Made in Japan." 3" tall.

$6–$8

*Planter,* anon., 1930s. Panther-shaped kitchen planter in mustard-color ceramic. 12" long.

$14–$20

*Planter,* anon., 1930s. Shaped like a long-legged stylized deer leaping above stylized leafy foliage, in dark green, unmarked. 10" tall x 15" long x 3" deep.

$75–$100

Pink flamingo, designer unknown. *(Photo by R. Four)*

**Decorative planter, designer unknown.** *(Photo by R. Four)*

*Salt and pepper shakers,* anon., 1930s. Designed like bookends in white with stylized "S" and "P" in red. 2½" tall.
$25-$35

*Tea set,* anon. Bright yellow teapot with cover, sugar bowl, and creamer, with an oddly angular design, reminiscent of works in silver by Eric Magnussen.
$750-$850

*Teapot,* anon., a double-spouted ceramic teapot with top handle resting on black wooden stand with candle for heating.
$225-$275

*Teapot,* anon., 1930s. Black crackle-glaze teapot with circular lid and streamlined design. 5½" tall x 9" long.
$100-$125

*Vase,* anon., 1930s. In white ceramic, rectangular, flared, with two stylized parrots in relief, fairly sharp image. 9" tall.
$18-$25

*Vase,* anon., 1930s. Three horizontal parallel bands at neck, semicircular handles also with three bands. In dark pink ceramic, unglazed on bottom or inside. 8" tall.
$12-$25

Tea service, designer unknown. *(Photo by R. Four; courtesy of Helburn & Hoyt)*

## Cowan Pottery

*Ceramic figure,* "Bird on a Wave," by Alexander Blazys, c. 1929 for Cowan Pottery, American. Stylized double wave echoes the shape of a peacock-like bird that seems to be riding the wave. 15" tall.
**$600–$800**

*Bookends,* by Drexel Jacobson, for Cowan. Designed as comical black pelicans with large beaks in a black glaze. 5¼" tall x 4½" long. Pair.
**$600–$700**

*Bookends,* by Cowan. Modeled as small elephants. In Oriental red glaze. 6" tall.
**$800–$1,000**

*Ceramic charger,* by Viktor Schreckengost for Cowan. Depicting a stylized maiden, her hair and skirt blowing in the breeze as she plays with her wolfhound. Yellow figures on turquoise ground, stylized flowers around the border. 15" diameter.
**$950–$1,200**

Bookends by Drexel Jacobson for Cowan. *(Photo courtesy of Peter Boehm, Dualities Gallery)*

*Figure of a woman,* by Cowan. Stylized, cloaked woman kneeling on a rectangular stepped base holding long drapery. In terra-cotta crackle glaze. 10½" tall.

$85–$120

*Flower frog,* centerpiece figure of a woman, by Cowan. Dancing nude woman rising from stylized plants on circular base drilled with holes for flowers, lifting one knee in the air and arm extended upward (without bowl), ivory glaze. 9½" tall x 3¼" wide.

$125–$150

*Flower frog,* figure of a woman, by Cowan. Dancing nude woman on a bulbous circular base with stylized geometric swirls, echoed in the swirling drapery around her, her hair blows in the breeze. Base drilled with holes for flowers, ivory glaze. 7½" tall.

$110–$140

*Plate,* by Viktor Schreckengost, for Cowan. Earthenware circular plate with a Jazz Age stylized scene of a couple dancing among trays full of martini glasses, abstract patterns, and stars. In turquoise and navy, impressed indistinctly "Cowan Pottery." 11¼" diameter.

$1,100 (1986)

*Bookends,* "Introspection," by Cowan, 1920s. Figures shaped like crows, beaks pointed downward in a contemplative pose. In Egyptian blue dark glaze. 8" tall. Pair.

$1,000–$1,200

**Plate by Viktor Schreckengost for Cowan.** *(Photo courtesy of Nancy McClelland, Christie's)*

**Cowan vase.** *(Photo courtesy of Peter Boehm, Dualities Gallery)*

*Lamp,* by Cowan. Green ceramic with rectangular base and winged tiers on either side, with original parchment and decoupage shade. Approx. 18" tall.

$1,200–$1,400

*Vases,* by Cowan. In solid-color matte and high-luster finishes, in "Foliage" (rust), "April Green," "Verde Green," Arabian Night Blue," and other colors. Footed and balustered undecorated shapes, ranging in size from 5" to 10". All marked.

$30–$100

*Vase*, by Cowan. In dark green glaze, depicting a fantastic stylized fish amid bubbles and seaweed, marked. 6½" tall.

$308 (1986)

*Vase*, by Cowan. Flared vase with incised stylized bird below the shoulder and circular base, in finely crackled luminous glazing, signed "Cowan." 1¼" tall x 8" wide.

$350–$450

*Vase*, by Cowan, 1931. Incised, depicting squirrels and leafy branches in "Mother O' Pearl" glaze, a light blue-green. 8" tall.

$400–$425

# SILVER, JEWELRY, AND FASHION

## SILVER

Silver underwent the same transformation of design from Art Nouveau to Art Deco as did other decorative arts. However, silver continued to be produced in traditional styles in great abundance as well.

Long-established French companies such as Maison Laparra, Puiforcat, Tétard Frères, and Christofle (founded 1839) produced Art Deco designs. Although their styles and lines changed and new materials were incorporated—such as ivory, wood, and semiprecious stone for handles—silver still retained its elegance.

The best designers in France were Jean Tétard and Jean Puiforcat (1897–1945), both of whom designed for their family firms. These artists were able to retain the favor of their clientele and still create stunning new forms. One example is Puiforcat's coffee and tea set with quartz crystal handles. (See the photo in the color section, "An Art Deco Portfolio.")

Viennese artists such as Josef Hoffmann and Dagobert Peche influenced the silver design styles of the era, bringing Modern angularity into their work. Often working in hand-hammered silver, they created service sets and pieces, compotes, humidors, clocks, and the like in sterling silver.

However, perhaps the best-known silver artist represented on the Art Deco market today was Danish: Georg Jensen (1886–1935). Jensen had a strong ability to create subtle Modern and Deco decorations in silver. Under his direction, talented designers such as Sigvard

Bernadott, creator of the "Bernadotte" pattern, and Harald Nielsen, creator of "Pyramid" and other patterns, would bring silver into the Modern age. Some of these patterns are still in production today.

Jensen exhibited for the first time in 1913 at the Paris Salon d'Automne, where his work was immediately recognized for its quality. His goal, which he achieved through hand-hammering and other crafts-based techniques, was to revive the art of silversmithy, which was slowly giving way to mass production.

Americans were less ready to accept new forms in silver than were the French. Although they were aware of the new designs in silver, displayed as early as 1922 in the Wiener Werkstätte Gallery in New York, then under the direction of Joseph Urban, the new style had a harder time breaking ground with those who looked to Tiffany as *the* silver maker of the day.

As happened in glass and jewelry, Tiffany's Art Nouveau designs, as well as their more traditional styles, had established a strong market among the privileged classes and were a deterrent to the introduction of new design.

Some of the Tiffany styles may be called Deco or Modern in inspiration, but for the most part it appears that Tiffany was making no more than a weak concession to the new style with designs such as "Hampton." It was only in anticipation of the New York World's Fair of 1939 that Tiffany's would create Modernist designs to compete with those companies who were snapping at its heels as the leading manufacturer of silver in this country.

These other manufacturers engaged leading Modern designers to create silver that would appeal to the new age. Notable designs were produced by Eliel Saarinen (1873–1950), Danish-born Erik Magnussen, and German-born Peter Muller-Munk and Walter von Nessen.

Magnussen designed for the Gorham Manufacturing Company of Providence, Rhode Island, which would emerge as a leader in silver design. One of Magnussen's most intriguing designs was called "The Lights and Shadows of Manhattan," a coffee service designed for Gorham that used burnished silver with gold and oxidized gray panels in an asymmetrical, angular style later to be copied by others in both metal and other media.

Kem Weber (1889–1943) designed for Porter Blanchard Silver among others. Manufacturing companies that worked in the Modern idiom include Towle Sterling, Bernard Rice's Sons, International Silver Company, Revere Brass and Copper, and Reed & Barton.

Under the influence of Modernism, flatware became elongated in some cases and used vertical banding to emphasize the new look. Handles and finials took on new designs, such as the stepped-back sky-

*Silver, Jewelry, and Fashion*

scraper patterns that were popular for a time. Many of these companies returned to creating traditional styles after the Modernist period, but because of the Depression their markets dwindled.

During this time, however, a host of other companies, both French and American, had begun issuing sophisticated Modern designs in silver plate, which was more affordable to the general population and which ate away at the market for sterling.

Companies like Revere Brass and Copper took up chromium and other metals for their housewares in order to compete in the market. (See the section on Chrome and Other Metals in "Modern Living" for more information.) Chrome, nickel, and other cheap metals could be fashioned more easily and could be produced at a fraction of the price of silver.

## PRICE LISTINGS

*Desk set*, by Cartier, French, 1928. In sterling silver. Includes tray, two inkwells, pen and points, and original nib holder.
$3,400–$3,600

*Veilleuse* (nightlight), by Desny, French, c. 1925. In sterling silver. Conical shape with pointed cap. Geometric cuts in the silver allow light to disperse. Electrified, with original cord. 5" tall.
$3,400–$3,600

*Candelabras*, by Tétard Frères, French. In silver, each raised on mahogany rectangular plinth with circular midsection, the long curved silver arm terminating in twin cylindrical reeded nozzles and shallow drip-pans, joined by central section repeating plinth, surmounted by mahogany circular socle and top tier of shorter silver arm with twin nozzles flanking central ring, impressed French "Poincons." 19" long, 87 troy oz. gross weight. Pair.
$1,400–$1,800

*Tray*, by Gorham Manufacturing Company, American, 1930s. Sterling silver, signed "Frankonia pattern, A14115/1." 11¼" diameter.
$650–$800

*Tea and coffee set*, "Winslow," by Gorham Manufacturing Company. In sterling silver, eight pieces, including coffee server, warmer, tea server, water server, sugar, creamer, side dish, and tray. Stamped "Gorham." Tray 25½" long.
$8,750–$9,000

"Winslow" by Gorham. *(Photo by R. Four; courtesy of Perrisue Silver)*

*Vase*, by Josef Hoffmann, for the Wiener Werkstätte. Silver, with lightly hammered ribbed and scalloped oval body supported by a ribbed melon-form column bordered with beaded bands, raised on a scalloped and ribbed domed foot further decorated with small repoussé stars, impressed "900 WW Wiener Werkstätte," with designer's mark, firm's *rosenmarke,* and Austrian punch marks. 10⅝" tall, 19 troy oz.

$6,600 (1986)

*Flatware service,* "Cactus," by Gundorph Albertus, 1930; executed by Georg Jensen Silversmithy, Danish. In silver, comprising 12 dinner knives, 12 luncheon knives, 12 dinner forks, 12 luncheon forks, 12 tablespoons, 12 dessert spoons, 12 teaspoons, 12 demitasse spoons, 6 dessert forks, 6 buillon spoons, 2 jelly spoons, 1 fish knife, pair of salad servers, 1 large serving spoon, 2 medium serving spoons, 3 medium tabletype serving spoons, 1 smaller serving spoon, 2 salts, each impressed with firm's mark. 190 troy oz. net weight. 122 pieces.

$11,000 (1986)

*Flatware service,* "Bernadotte," by Sigvard Bernadott, 1939, executed by Georg Jensen. In silver, consisting of 12 dinner forks, 12 luncheon forks, 12 dessert forks, 12 salad forks, 12 soup spoons, 12 tablespoons, 12 demitasse spoons, 12 dinner knives, 12 luncheon knives, 6 fruit knives, 1 ladle, 1 cake knife, 1 salad serving set, 1 large serving spoon,

1 medium serving spoon, 1 small serving spoon, 1 meat fork, 1 cold cut fork, 1 olive fork, and 1 lemon fork, each impressed with firm's marks from various periods. 223.5 troy oz. gross weight. 125 pieces.
**$8,800 (1986)**

*Serving dish,* "Bernadotte," by Sigvard Bernadott, executed by Georg Jensen. In sterling silver. Two-handled dish with cover and convergent line design to top of handle. Stamped "Georg Jensen." 7" diameter.
**$2,500–$2,700**

*Table service for 12,* "Bernadotte," by Sigvard Bernadott, executed by Georg Jensen. In sterling silver. Parallel lines run length of handles. 139 pieces, including 12 sets of 11 and 8 serving pieces. Stamped "Georg Jensen."
**$11,000–$13,000**

*Candelabra,* by Sigvard Bernadott, executed by Georg Jensen, post-1945. In silver, the circular base bearing six reeded arms riveted to base with pad feet and flaring to S-curve, each terminating in a slender flaring conical nozzle with everted lip, each impressed with designer's signature and "Georg Jensen Denmark Sterling 1050 A." 9¾" high, 82.2 troy oz. net weight (pair).
**$8,800 (1986)**

*Table service for 12,* "Pyramid," by Harald Nielson, executed by Georg Jensen. In sterling silver. Terminals have stepped-back pyramid style. 104 pieces, including 12 sets of 8 and 8 serving pieces. Stamped "Georg Jensen."
**$11,000–$13,000**

*Tea set,* "Pryamid," designed by Harald Nielson for Georg Jensen, 1926. In sterling silver, 4 pieces, including tea server, creamer, sugar, and tray. Handle terminals are in a stepped-back pyramid style. Wooden handle on tea server. Stamped "Georg Jensen." Tray 11" diameter.
**$7,000–$8,000**

*Ashtrays,* executed by Georg Jensen, c. 1925–1932. In silver, oval form supported on flaring leaf clad stem above lobed and paneled foot mounted with small spheres, impressed "Georg Jensen 925 S 42B." 5" long.
**$440 (1986)**

*Cigar lighter,* executed by Georg Jensen, c. 1925–1932. In silver, the compressed hammer body flanked by hinged wishbone-form loose handles with amber beads, supported on lobed and lappet stem above oval base raised on four ball feet; conical cap, applied with four thin beaded straps below amber knop, fitting over lappet ringed onion-form wick support, impressed "Georg Jensen GJ 925 S Sterling Denmark 73." 7″ tall, 7.6 troy oz. net weight.

$4,400 (1986)

*Coffeepot,* by Georg Jensen. Silver ebony-mounted pot with domed top, chased with Neoclassical motifs. 8½″ tall, approx. 16 oz.

$700 (1987)

*Compote,* executed by Georg Jensen, c. 1915–1927. In silver, the deep gently flaring bowl with scalloped and notched lip on drum stem with repoussé design of pods and seeds on leafy ground above circular foot, impressed "Georg Jensen GJ 830 S 105." 6¼″ tall, 12½″ diameter, 11.1 troy oz.

$1,650 (1986)

*Creamer and sugar,* by Georg Jensen. Ebony mounted with unornamented hammered sufaces. Total approx. 10 oz. in all.

$500 (1987)

*Humidor,* executed by Georg Jensen, c. 1925–1932. In silver, rectangular section, the sides with medial horizontal notched band at juncture where upper portion is slightly stepped in; hinged lid with repoussé and engraved bird's-eye view of a Northern European port and bordering urban landscape, with stepped thumbpiece above lock-and-key opening to cedar-lined interior, the whole on rectangular plinth raised on simple bracket feet terminating in foliate scrolls, impressed "Denmark Georg Jensen GJ 925 Sterling G A B F." 6⅞″ tall x 15½″ wide x 12″ deep, 264.5 troy oz. gross weight.

$30,800 (1986)

*Flatware service,* "Parallel," by Georg Jensen. In silver, comprising 12 luncheon knives, 12 dessert forks, 12 dinner forks, 12 soup spoons, 12 tablespoons, 8 luncheon forks, 8 seafood forks, 5 butter knives, pair of meat carvers, pair of salad servers, 1 dessert knife, 1 dessert server, 1 large flat round server, 1 medium ladle, 1 small ladle, 1 medium spoon, 1 small spoon, 1 large serving fork, 1 large serving spoon, 1 medium serving spoon, 2 medium cold cut forks, 1 small server, 1 parfait spoon, 1 salt spoon, 1 bottle opener, each impressed with firm's mark. 224 troy oz. net weight. 101 pieces.

$6,000–$7,000

## Silver, Jewelry, and Fashion

*Tea service,* by Georg Jensen. Silver ivory-mounted three-piece set comprising a teapot, creamer, and covered sugar, approx. total 29 oz. Teapot 8" tall.

$1,000 (1987)

*Bowl,* by Dagobert Peche, for the Wiener Werkstätte, c. 1920. Deep oval with twin curled, fluted handles and two bands of wavy flutes, raised on a flared and fluted circular base, impressed with Austrian punch mark, firm's and designer's marks, a *rosenmarke* and "900 Wiener Werkstätte made in Austria." 11" diameter, 29 troy oz.

$18,700 (1986)

*Centerpieces,* by Jean Puiforcat, French, c. 1925. Comprising a pair of circular glass bowls, the straight sides with triangular faceting, set into stepped gilt-silver ring on octagonal black glass bases, impressed with French punchmarks. 15½" diameter.

$5,000–$7,000

*Covered box,* by Jean Puiforcat, c. 1925. In gilt silver, ivory and square-faceted transparent glass, domed black glass fitted cover planed to corners from central rectangular gilt-silver plaque surmounted with finial formed as a gilt-silver cylinder encircled by twin reeded ivory bands, impressed with French punchmarks. 6½" square.

$1,540 (1986)

Tea service by Georg Jensen. *(Photo courtesy of William Doyle Galleries)*

*Covered tureen,* by Jean Puiforcat, c. 1935. In silver and parcel-gilt, hemispherical bowl with a gilt everted rim and raised on a pedestal foot with angled gilt rim; fitted dome cover with tiered, flared finial, the upper section gilded; bowl and cover impressed with French punchmarks, bowl impressed "Jean E. Puiforcat." 9¼" tall, 80 troy oz.

**$14,300 (1987)**

*Fish service,* by Jean Puiforcat. In silver, comprising six fish forks, six lobster forks, and six fish knives; fish forks and knives impressed with maker's mark, all with French punchmarks. 18 pieces. 33.5 troy oz. net weight.

**$1,540 (1986)**

*Large tray,* by Jean Puiforcat. In silver, oblong form with canted corners curving to stepped rim bracketed at each angle with three ribs, impressed "Jean Puiforcat" and French punchmarks. 25¾" long x 11" wide, 84.5 troy oz. net weight.

**$4,950 (1986)**

*Tea and coffee set,* by Jean Puiforcat, Paris, c. 1928. In silver, with circular tray, rock crystal handles, comprising a teapot, coffeepot, sugar bowl, and creamer. (For illustration see color insert.)

**$19,500–$20,000**

*Tea and coffee set,* by Reed & Barton, American. In sterling silver, handles banded in ivory. Five pieces, including coffee server, tea server, sugar, creamer, and tray. Stamped "Reed & Barton."

**$2,500–$3,000**

*Tumblers,* by William Spratling, American. In sterling silver, cylindrical with three bosses at shoulder, seven horizontal bands at base, impressed "William Sprating Sterling," together with a gilt-bronze quatrefoil ashtray, by Hagenauer, by Weiner Werkstätte. Set of 5. 4¼" long.

**$660 (1987)**

*Creamer/sugar and stand,* by Jean G. Theobold, for Wilcox S. P. Co., 1938. In silver plate, diamond-shaped stand fits triangular creamer and sugar. 3-piece set. 5" tall x 8" long.

**$4,200–$4,500**

*Tea service,* by Jean G. Theobald, 1928, for Wilcox Silver Plate Company. Consisting of a semicircular teapot, covered cream pitcher, and covered sugar bowl fitted in a circular-handled tray, the handles and finials ebony, each impressed "Wilcox S. P. Co. International S. Co. 7036." 4 pieces. 7½" tray diameter.

**$6,600 (1986)**

*Table service for 12,* "Century," by Tiffany & Co., American, 1937. One of Tiffany's most "Moderne" styles. 104 pieces, including 12 sets of 10 plus 8 servers. Stamped "Tiffany & Co."

**$8,500–$9,000**

*Table service for 12,* "Hampton," by Tiffany & Co., American, 1923. A streamlined style with tiered terminals. 101 pieces, including 12 sets of 8 plus 5 servers. Stamped "Tiffany & Co."

**$6,750–$7,000**

*Tea and coffee set,* "Hampton," by Tiffany & Co., American, 1923. Five pieces, including coffee server, tea server, sugar, creamer, and tray. Stamped "Tiffany & Co."

**$4,500–$5,000**

*Salt and pepper,* by Walker & Hall, c. 1936. In sterling silver, in Moderne style. Stamped "Walker & Hall." 3" tall. Pair.

**$1,400–$1,500**

*Sugar bowl with caster,* by Walker & Hall, English c. 1934. In sterling silver, stamped "Walker & Hall" and "Birmingham." 6" long.

**$1,400–$1,500**

*Cocktail service,* anon., American, c. 1930. In silver-plated metal and glass, five pieces, including a cocktail shaker, its cover and handle in the form of a rooster, and four matching cocktail glasses with engraved glass inserts, shaker impressed "Copyright USA 3880 Trade WB Mark" with a dog. Shaker 14½" tall.

**$440 (1987)**

*Cocktail shaker,* anon., American, 1920s. In the form of a rooster. Hand-hammered silver-plate body with pedestal base, surmounted by rooster head whose tongue unscrews to reveal spout. Tail feathers at the base of the container curl into handle. Stamped signed "Trademark W.B." on base. 16" high.

**$950–$1,200**

*Box,* anon., maker's mark "J.G.," French, c. 1925. In sterling silver. 4" square.

**$950–$1,000**

# ART DECO

Rooster cocktail shaker, designer unknown. *(Photo by Dennis Galloway; courtesy of Ed Forcum, Rosebud Gallery)*

*Tea and coffee service*, anon., probably French, c. 1925. In silver plate. Modernistic design with sharp angles and wooden handles. Five pieces, including coffee server, tea server, creamer, sugar, and tray, unmarked. Tray 22" long.
$900–$1,000

*Tea set*, anon., probably French, c. 1930. In silver plate, streamlined shape with softer curves than above. Wood handles stained dark brown. Four pieces, including tea server, coffee, sugar, and tray. Tray 20" long.
$1,550–$1,650

*Tea service*, anon., French. In silver plate, comprising a rectangular tray with two ebonized handles, coffeepot, teapot, milk jug, and covered sugar bowl, all with fluted sides and wooden handles, marked "Gallia, 6118." 20½" high.
$528 (1987)

*Tea service*, anon., French. In silver plate, comprising teapot, hot water pot, covered sugar, creamer, and matching tray with two ebonized handles. Pieces of rounded ten-sided form with angular ebonized wood handles and finials, impressed marks. Tray 24" diameter.
$1,100 (1987)

## Silver, Jewelry, and Fashion

*Tea service*, anon., probably French, c. 1925. In silver plate, barrel shaped, with wooden handles and knobs painted black. Four pieces, including tea server, creamer, sugar, and tray, unmarked. Tray 22" long.

**$1,800–$2,100**

*Tea service*, anon., French, c. 1930. In silver and Macassar ebony, consisting of a teapot, covered sugar bowl, cream pitcher, tea bag strainer with holder, and tray, each piece of paneled form with carved *ebene de macassar* handles, impressed with French punchmarks. Tray 16⅝" diameter.

**$5,500 (1987)**

*Bowl*, anon. In sterling silver, six curved, stylized feet and beaded design, marked "M 1216." 6" tall, 10" diameter.

**$400–$600**

*Candelabra*, anon. In silver, each candelabra on a diamond-shaped base with branching support holding two bobeches, stamped on base "Sterling 950," in gray mock-crocodile case with blue cloth-lined, fitted interior. 4½" tall. Pair.

**$330 (1986)**

French tea service, designer unknown. *(Photo courtesy of Nancy McClelland, Christie's)*

*Tea set*, anon. In silver plate, comprising a tea pot, hot water pot, creamer, and sugar; of compressed cylindrical form, each on circular foot with horizontal banding, curved spouts and scalloped handles, unmarked. Tea pot 5½" tall.

$300–$500

## JEWELRY

Jewelry of the 1920s and 1930s was very different indeed from the fantastic creations of ornate Art Nouveau treasures. Influenced by the same factors that had changed art and design, it became simpler and more restrained overall. (See the photo in our color section, "An Art Deco Portfolio.")

Orientalism in dress brought with it a whole set of jewelry and jeweled accessories. René Lalique (1860–1945) had an international reputation for jewelry in the Art Nouveau period, using colored-glass pastes set in gold mounts.

However, it was during this period that Lalique abandoned jewelry for glass production. Later he would return to jewelry by creating stunning glass pendants with sleek new styling. Other glass artists, such as G. Argy-Rousseau, also created Art Deco glass jewelry.

Many other great Art Nouveau jewelers in Paris, such as Cartier, Van Cleef & Arpels, and Mauboussin, saw their clients return to them to have their precious stones reset in newly designed mounts that were more in keeping with the fashion.

Louis Cartier is far and away the best-known name in the most expensive Art Deco jewelry. His well-heeled clientele included the nobility of many countries, as well as celebrities and even other designers, such as Coco Chanel. His designs were inspiration for other jewelers, in both Europe and America.

He had such a strong impact that many cheaper kinds of jewelry, even costume jewelry in the 1930s, would reflect his design styles. In addition, Cartier's watches, pocket watches, and clocks are as famous as his neckpieces and earrings.

Van Cleef & Arpels jewelry is also sought after by wealthy collectors and admirers. During the Art Deco era the firm's clients came largely from the world of the arts and its wealthy patrons.

Choreographer George Balanchine's inspiration for the full-length ballet *Jewels* came from a meeting with Claude Arpels. The ballet used three different composers for its three parts, with dancers dressed like jewels for each part. Gabriel Fauré composed the "Emeralds" section; Igor Stravinsky, the "Rubies" section; and Tchaikovsky, the "Diamonds" section. No doubt it was the most stunning of premieres, with an opening night gala that glittered with Van Cleef & Arpels jewelry.

## Silver, Jewelry, and Fashion

Van Cleef & Arpels also devised the *serti mystérieux*, or invisible setting, which revolutionized jewelry designs by allowing the stones themselves to create the design rather than merely ornament the setting.

Georges Fouquet (1862–1957) is regarded as the master of Modern jewelry design. He loved fine materials such as black enamel, pearls, diamonds, platinum, onyx, white agate, white gold, ivory, and turquoise.

Fouquet employed designers such as well-known graphic artist A. M. Cassandre (1901–1968) to create astounding jewelry, much of it owned today by museums. Cassandre's jewelry designs are prized on the collector's market, where they appear very rarely.

Fouquet was also on the selection committee for the 1925 Paris Exposition. The works shown included jewelry by Louis Aucoc, Boucheron, Chaumet, and others. Although the selection for the exposition was done anonymously, the entries chosen did include work by Jean Fouquet, Georges' son. Born in 1899, Jean Fouquet carried on his father's reputation for finely designed jewelry.

The Fouquets' competition was largely from Gerard Sandoz, Raymond Templier, and the great lacquer artist Jean Dunand. These artists succeeded in using various materials and colors to give jewelry a new look.

Bold colors and basic geometric shapes dominated the work of this period, which would set a standard for French Art Deco jewelry in the years that followed. Stones and materials were not chosen for their intrinsic value alone but for their impact on the design of jewelry as small pieces of modern sculpture.

Speaking about the market for Art Deco jewelry, Audrey Friedman, owner of Primavera Gallery in New York, states, "People will pay strong prices for unique pieces. A piece has to stand on its own, however, like any piece of sculpture. Often the carat weight of the stones has little to do with the value."

Where early Deco jewelry made use of curves rather than geometric shapes, designers who belonged more to the Modern era created striking black-and-white pieces made of silver, white gold, platinum, black lacquer, black onyx, and other materials. Apart from precious gems, other materials that became popular in jewelry included wood, ivory, tortoiseshell, mother-of-pearl, and semiprecious stones such as amethyst, lapis lazuli, coral, and jade, which give Art Deco jewelry its range of vibrant colors.

The 1922 rediscovery of the tomb of King Tutankhamen had a profound influence on jewelry design, which thereafter was often created with Egyptian motifs. The development of rhinestones, together with the industrialization of jewelry production, extended the wearing of jewelry into the middle classes and into everyday life.

As jewelry became more associated with fashion than with investment, its styles came into and went out of vogue more frequently. Strings of pearls, worn loosely or as chokers, little watches sometimes hung from brooches, and long dangling earrings came into fashion. Brooches and pins were worn traditionally as well as on hats, scarves, and shoes. Another year chunky bracelets and necklaces for plunging necklines would be the trend, or big rings, often with single stones set in platinum. Big hat pins and decorative combs were no longer necessary with short hair.

Coco Chanel capitalized on the vogue for trendy jewelry by producing elegant costume jewelry. Costume jewelry from the era includes pearl necklaces, pins, bracelets, and earrings that today range from $50 to $650 and more.

Until the 1920s Tiffany had been the best-known name in Art Nouveau American jewelry. As in the world of glass, Tiffany's influence was so strong that it continued to dominate the design field well into the Art Deco period.

One notable firm that designed some pieces in the Art Deco style is Black, Starr and Frost, America's oldest jewelry store. Listen closely to the words of the song "Diamonds Are a Girl's Best Friend" and you'll hear their name. In fact, the song is still played on the first day of work for new women employees at the New York company.

A few years ago Black, Starr and Frost started buying back estate jewelry it had created from 1810 to 1950, including many fine pieces of Art Deco design. This jewelry was made from the favorite materials of the era: diamonds, emeralds, brightly colored enamel, and onyx, mainly from Brazil.

Black, Starr and Frost managed to collect several pieces before it abandoned its search, including a diamond, emerald, and platinum watch; a green-and-white enamel compact with a diamond-shaped motif that hung from a gold chain; and an aquamarine pendant set with onyx and diamonds on a platinum chain. Some Black, Starr and Frost pieces have reached the auction market in recent years, and prices of $60,000 and more are not uncommon.

One of the best-known names in jewelry in America is Harry Winston, called "The King of Diamonds." Mr. Winston is also mentioned in "Diamonds Are a Girl's Best Friend." They were certainly *his* best friend. Born in 1896, he worked for his father's small jewelry shop in California. He was obsessed with fine jewels and had a reputation for aggressively going after the estate pieces he wanted.

The material that epitomized the glitziness of Art Deco taste in jewelry was platinum. The rich had money to burn in the 1920s and often purchased such extravagances as diamond shoe buckles and platinum lipstick cases set with precious stones. When articles such as these were no longer fashionable, they often stayed in many families as heirlooms.

One of the techniques used during this period is called "color massing." In this method a large quantity of small colorful stones such as rubies are set with platinum borders or between rows of clear stones to make the colors even stronger.

Stones were often set in *pavé* style. Literally translated, *pavé* means "pavement" and refers to the arrangement of regular square and rectangular stones that were used to create Parisian streets. Lined up in this manner, small square-cut stones could be shaped into geometric designs.

Notable American jewelry companies include J. E. Caldwell and Company in Philadelphia and Spaulding, Gorham in Chicago. Several others produced jewelry in modernist designs later, including Bonner Manufacturing, Walter P. McTiegue, and Hirsch & Leff, all of New York; W. R. Anderson and Company of Chicago; and First and Company of Cincinnati. Pieces of this era are generally not signed or identified in any way and are often represented and sold as French designs, from which they heavily borrowed.

The use of silver and semiprecious materials by even the most talented artists, plus the emergence of women in society, created a higher demand for popular fashion jewelry than ever before. The geometric design in jewelry developed by Fouquet and Templier, combined with the impulse toward costume jewelry was seized on by the manufacturers of less expensive jewelry.

Silver jewelry of the era enameled in the style of Fouquet is relatively easy to find and, when anonymously designed, costs slightly more than new silver jewelry. Pricing often depends on the quality of the enameling. In addition, the more sophisticated the design, the higher the price will be.

Silver jewelry had its masters, too. The Georg Jensen Silversmithy, known primarily for its sterling silver coffee and tea sets and flatware, produced silver jewelry that is popular on the collecting market today, though it is more often seen at jewelry auctions than at Art Deco auctions.

In the United States, William Spratling and others led the way in silver jewelry design. Much of the silver jewelry created for consumption in the United States came from silver-rich Mexico. Soon Mexican artists—such as Margot de Taxco and Antonio Pineda, often referred to simply as "Antonio"—were creating directly for the American market.

During the 1930s numerous designs in Mexican silver made their appearance in geometric motifs, sometimes set with lapis, turquoise, or malachite. Borrowing from native American and Mayan designs, this silver jewelry is still produced and remains a favorite with tourists in Mexico. At the time, however, when pieces did not find a market, they were often melted down for the silver content. Remaining pieces by name designers are commanding high prices.

During the late 1920s and early 1930s, German silver jewelry also was brought into this country, and some was designed there specifically for American markets. German sterling silver jewelry of the period tends to be less geometric and is more often designed as stylized flowers.

The Depression and the 1930s brought new styles in both fine and mid-range jewelry. Popular jewelry often used marcasite, a name given to crystallized iron pyrite when it is set in silver. From a distance, a brooch set with hundreds of small marcasites appears to be shimmering with diamonds. Less expensive stones, such as carnelian and onyx, also became more popular.

Marcasite was even mounted on plastic jewelry of the era. Many marcasite and onyx pieces in geometric styles have been re-created and are widely available. Pins, necklaces, and earrings in geometric designs can be found in many jewelry stores. On much of the new production, however, marcasites are glued in, rather than set in mounts. Older, elaborate pieces are less available, and unique pieces are commanding strong prices.

Both men's and women's watches from the Art Deco era are favorites. Like mantel clocks and table clocks, their faces lent themselves to a variety of shapes and treatments of the numerals. Blending with the sleek style of design, these watches are again sought after as a perfect match to modern, sporty dress. Quality watches in Modern design were produced by many companies in the United States.

No doubt they were in their day influenced by the new outdoor life Americans began to lead when they emerged from dusty Victorian parlors into the modern world: tennis, skiing, water skiing, swimming, horseback riding, polo, golf, and more.

Today both fine and mid-range Art Deco jewelry is not collected as much by Art Deco enthusiasts as by jewelry enthusiasts, and it is sold more often in jewelry stores carrying estate pieces than in antique shops. It still has the same stunningly simple elegance as when it was created, and it goes very well with modern fashion design. The resurgence of popularity of Art Deco has increased the value of original Art Deco fine jewelry on the auction market in recent years.

Deco styling remains a favorite for contemporary jewelry as well. Deco-style jewelry created in the late 1960s and early 1970s is often called "Retro," rather than Deco, but it is sold alongside original Deco designs.

### *Special Focus: Bakelite Jewelry*

The most accessible and collectible jewelry of the Art Deco era today is plastic. The words *plastic* and *jewelry* just don't seem to go together for many people, but they do if you are an avid collector of

Art Deco jewelry in celluloid, Bakelite, Catalin, and other plastics—the colorful fun jewelry that is once again fashionable to wear. (See the photo in our color section, "An Art Deco Portfolio.")

This is the ultimate in costume jewelry—it is worn completely for the effect, to enhance the costume. In fact, we're told that if you're looking for lots of Bakelite jewelry you'll find it in New Orleans, perhaps because of Mardi Gras. Rather than being spurned as it was for many years, it is worn today in the spirit of colorful fun for which it was intended. In addition, on closer look one can find some real examples of great design work in the harder-to-find pieces that have made their happy way to the mid-range collectibles market.

Plastic was a "modern" material, a wonder of the age, and it was treated with a bit more respect than it gets today. Plastic jewelry from many fine designers could be found in good stores, not just Woolworth's.

"The market for Bakelite jewelry has gone up rapidly, especially since the July 1985 cover story in *Connoisseur,*" states Barbara Pollack, who earned the nickname "The Plastic Princess" because of her extensive dealership in plastic jewelry of the era.

"Now it is both fashionable *and* collectible," she says. "You can still find it in flea markets but not to the extent that you could before. I try to buy the best in design, color, and form—polka dots, four-color—anything unusual."

"The best part about wearing it is that you can be very individual and creative in the amount you wear and the colors you combine," she adds. "And it is not just for the young. It really appeals to people of all ages."

In the 1920s most plastic jewelry and plastic boudoir items like powder puff boxes were made from celluloid. In the 1930s and 1940s the two plastics most often used in jewelry were Bakelite and Catalin. Bakelite was generally in plainer colors, more opaque, and heavier. Catalin was more difficult to produce but could be much more colorful, more translucent, and lighter. (See the section on Bakelite in "Modern Living" for more information.) Unlike radio collectors, most people who collect the plastic jewelry of the Art Deco era don't make a distinction between the two plastics.

## PRICE LISTINGS

### Glass Jewelry

*Pendant,* by Gabriel Argy-Rousseau, French. *Pâte-de-verre* oval pierced for stringing and cast with winged insect in black and amber on mauve mottled ground incised with rays, impressed "G-A-R." 2⅝" long.

$990 (1986)

*Pendant,* by G. Argy-Rousseau. *Pâte-de-verre* oval, frosted and molded with a large purple and pink hibiscus bloom with yellow center on a deep green stem, molded "G-A-R," on a rose silk cord. 2⅝" long.

$825 (1987)

*Earrings,* "Fioret," by René Lalique, French. In black-stained frosted glass, each triangular earring molded with a female scarf dancer frolicking beside a tree, each molded "Fioret Paris," with silver floral mounts. Each 2¾" long. Pair.

$550 (1987)

*Pendant,* "Fioret," by R. Lalique. Brown-patinated frosted glass, triangular, molded with a scarf dancer frolicking beneath a tree, molded "Fioret Paris." 1½" long.

$500–$700

*Pendant,* by R. Lalique. In electrice blue glass, of rounded rectangular form, molded with a coiled snake baring his fangs, incised "R. Lalique" with paper "Made in France" label, on blue silk cord. 1¾" long.

$500–$700

### Fine Jewelry

*Bracelet,* by Cartier, French, 1925. Linked pieces in emerald, onyx, and diamonds set in platinum, in a stylized geometric design with a clasp.

$6,500–$7,000

*Brooch,* by Cartier, c. 1930. Overall curved-leaf design in carved amethyst, diamond, onyx bead, and platinum. Twenty-one smaller amethyst leaves on a platinum and diamond stem, interspersed with 18 black onyx beads.

$34,000–$40,000

# Silver, Jewelry, and Fashion

**Cartier leaf brooch and Chaumet circular brooch.** *(Photo courtesy of N. Bloom & Son Antiques)*

*Compact*, by Cartier. In 18-karat yellow gold with blue and white enamel, carved dark Chinese jadeite and assorted small diamonds and rubies.

$5,000 (1986)

*Jeweled clock*, by Cartier. In malachite, jade, and silver. Octagonal chapter ring is surrounded by a circular ring of jade with small cabochon rubies. Clock suspended between column mounts with stepped-back terminals, rectangular base.

$6,500 (1986)

*Jeweled bedside clock*, by Cartier. In onyx and coral, mounted in a square ivory case with mother-of-pearl face. Chapter ring mounted with brilliants. Inscribed "Cartier Paris, 1443."

$5,750 (1986)

*Purse watch*, by Cartier. In 18-karat yellow gold, of rectangular form, case with black enamel Roman numerals and geometric motifs, corners with raised gold knobs, dial concealed by sliding panels operated by black enamel buttons on the sides. Signed "Cartier."

$7,250 (1987)

*Earrings*, by A. Cipulio, 1971. Retro earrings of 18-karat yellow gold, retailed by Cartier, in the shape of Deco-style door knockers, with circular stepped-back and ribbed motif. Signed "A. Cipulio, copyright 1971, Cartier." 30 dwt.

$1,300 (1987)

# ART DECO

A jeweled clock by Cartier. *(Photo courtesy of William Doyle Galleries)*

Purse watch by Cartier. *(Photo courtesy of William Doyle Galleries)*

*Pocket watch,* by European Watch Co., retailed by Cartier. Open face, of 18-karat gold, plain case, matte silvered dial, black-enamel stylized Roman numerals, blued-steel hands, movement signed "European Watch Co."
$1,400 (1987)

*Brooch,* by Chaumet, Paris, 1920s. Circular design in amethyst, with bands and designs of diamonds set in platinum. Platinum and diamond openwork across the diameter, reverse enameled in red.
$51,000–$60,000

## Silver, Jewelry, and Fashion 309

*Pendant, ring, and bracelet set,* by Dusausoy, French, c. 1925. Diamonds set in platinum and onyx. Pendant design is linked circle-shaped pieces, ring is tiered, and bracelet design is linked square-shaped pieces.

$125,000–$130,000

*Pocket watch,* by International Watch Co. 14-karat gold open-face case with a bicolor gold geometric design within borders of scrolling foliage. Matte gold dial, applied gold stylized Arabic numerals, gold hands, subsidiary seconds, signed "International Watch Co., Schaffhausen."

$500 (1987)

*Necklace,* by Georg Jensen, Danish. 18-karat yellow gold, with links of stylized gold approximating the shape of fortune cookies. 41.7 dwt. (For additional Georg Jensen listings see "Silver, Marcasite, and Semiprecious Jewelry," following.)

$1,500 (1987)

*Bracelet,* by Mauboussin, French, 1935. Two-color gold linked circles and rectangles, white and rose gold.

$6,500–$7,000

*Woman's watch,* by Mauboussin, late 1930s. Two-color, white and rose gold, linked rectangle-shaped pieces.

$5,500–$7,000

*Bracelet,* by YARD. In platinum containing three cushion-shape rubies totaling approx. 7.5 carats, 282 round diamonds totaling approx. 26.0 carats, and 36 square rubies totaling approx. 10.0 carats, in overall design of intertwined geometric patterns. Signed "YARD."

$16,000 (1986)

*Bracelet,* anon. Platinum, with round and baguette diamonds in the shape of three stylized bow ties totaling approx. 4.5 carats, and round rubies totaling approx. 3.0 carats, joined by sapphire-set links totaling approx. 10.0 carats.

$6,000 (1987)

*Bracelet,* anon. In platinum, composed of three lozenge-shaped links and smaller geometric links centered by oval cabochon jadeites and containing 42 diamond baguettes and 275 round diamonds totaling approx. 8.0 carats.

$25,000 (1987)

*Bracelet*, anon., French, c. 1925. With diamonds, coral, moonstone onyx, lapis lazuli, and platinum. Design of alternating coral, lapis lazuli, and moonstone onyx bars with geometric square designs of platinum and diamonds. Illegible maker's mark. (For illustration see color insert.)
$59,500–$70,000

*Bracelet*, anon., 1930s or 1940s. Comprising square-cut aquamarine, amethyst, tourmaline, citrine, 18-karat gold and diamond links.
$4,080–$4,800

*Bracelet*, anon. In heavy, linked 18-karat gold, four oval-cut, frosted, and stepped rock crystals.
$4,000–$4,800

*Bracelet watch*, anon. In platinum, rectangular links set with diamond baguettes in a geometric design on a *pavé* diamond ground. Joined by three strands of natural pearls, diamonds totaling approx. 11 carats.
$5,000 (1987)

*Bracelet*, anon., French. In diamonds, approx. 27½ carats, and platinum link, designed in three sections of overall geometric patterns.
$25,500–$30,000

*Brooch*, anon., probably French, c. 1928. Semicircle of raw crystal surrounded by rays of 7.4-karat diamonds set in 18-karat white gold.
$10,750–$11,300

*Brooch*, anon. With diamonds, rubies, sapphires, and 18-karat white gold, in shape of a dragonfly. Body set with alternating semicircles and wings with alternating zigzags of rubies and sapphires.
$5,865–$6,900

*Brooch*, anon. Diamonds and platinum, in bow shape.
$4,590–$5,490

*Brooch*, anon. In platinum, of overall geometric design. Three spiraling curves, graduated cabochon rubies, approx. 5.0 carats, and alternating triangular, round, and baguette diamonds totaling approx. 5.25 carats. One baguette missing.
$4,400 (1987)

*Brooch*, anon. In platinum, with overall shield shape centered by a pear-shaped old-mine diamond approximately .90 carat and containing 22 baguettes and 65 round diamonds totaling approx. 1.25 carats.
$4,400 (1987)

*Brooch,* anon. In white gold, containing two rectangular aquamarines totaling approx. 50.0 carats, 18 assorted small round diamonds and one pear-shaped diamond totaling approx. 1.0 carats, and assorted square rubies. Designed with one horizontal aquamarine from which a vertical aquamarine hangs.

$7,000 (1986)

*Brooch,* anon. In diamonds and platinum, in shape of three leaves mounted on a circular ring.

$3,000–$3,250

*Brooch,* anon. With diamonds, lapis lazuli, and platinum. Composed of two carved lapis lazuli tablets in a floral motif, separated by upturned bars of green enamel. One terminal ends in three stepped-back green enamel bars. Centered by four round and three fancy cut diamonds, set in square, triangular and circular mounts. Approx. 1.5 carats.

$1,900 (1987)

*Cigarette case,* anon. In 18-karat yellow gold, containing 71 fancy-cut blue sapphires, 109 dwt. The sapphires are set in ten elongated triangles along the sides, and the gold has an overall repetitive elongated diamond-shaped design.

$2,800 (1986)

*Cuff links,* anon. Ruby, platinum, and 18-karat gold, square, with rubies bordering two sides.

$2,800–$3,300

*Earrings,* anon., probably American, c. 1925. Circular hoops with a swirl pattern of diamonds set in platinum and onyx.

$8,500–$9,000

*Earrings,* anon. In platinum, the pendants set with pear-shaped Chinese jadeites with diamond terminals.

$1,700 (1987)

*Earrings,* anon. Dangling diamond and platinum earrings with two rectangular-cut aquamarines.

$12,750–$15,000

*Earrings,* anon. Round and baguette diamonds set in platinum in stylized tassel motif with detachable 13½ mm South Sea pearl drops.

$10,100–$11,900

## ART DECO

*Earrings,* anon. Dangling stylized diamond, 18-karat white gold, and cultured pearl drop. Triangular clip with three inverted U-shapes from which pearl hangs.

$3,300–$3,900

*Necklace,* anon. Three strands of cultured pearls, with rectangular emerald center stone from which two diamonds and two pendant emeralds hang. Center emerald approx. 10.0 carats.

$3,000 (1986)

*Pendant,* anon. In platinum, centered by an oval cabochon jadeite in a frame set with 45 round diamonds and 5 baguettes totaling approx. 2.5 carats, surmounted by a kite-shaped diamond approx. 1.1 carats.

$37,000 (1987)

*Ring,* anon. Two demantoid (green) garnets, diamonds, and platinum in squared geometric design with 18-karat gold band.

$3,145–$3,700

*Ring,* anon. Overall diamond shape, with square- and baguette-cut diamonds bordering diamond-shaped sapphire set in platinum.

$5,000–$5,900

*Retro bracelet,* anon., exact date unknown. In 14-karat yellow and red gold, composed of two-tone geometric rectangular and bar links, 37.4 dwt.

$1,000 (1987)

*Retro bracelet,* anon., exact date unknown. In 14-karat yellow and red gold, composed of two-tone geometric triangular and semicircular links, 39 dwt.

$1,200 (1987)

*Ring,* anon., American, c. 1927. In platinum with a *pavé* setting of four stepped-back rows of 4 color-massed cut rubies each, and 16 small diamonds.

$1,800–$1,900

*Ring,* anon., American. In platinum with a *pavé* setting, three circular diamonds set horizontally between color-massed rows of rubies that angle off in different directions from the design. Probably an estate piece. Approx. 16 points of rubies.

$1,965–$2,000

*Ring*, anon. In platinum, of bombé (curved) form, set with 30 round sapphires totaling approx. 3.0 carats, and small round diamonds. The sides have channel-set caliber rubies.

$2,200 (1987)

*Ring*, anon. In platinum, containing an oval cabochon jadeite, flanked by four round diamonds and two tapered baguettes.

$8,000 (1987)

*Watch*, anon., probably French, c. 1925. Rectangular base of diamonds set in platinum, with a floral vine pattern of rubies, sapphires, and onyx winding across the watch base. Face set in the upper right-hand corner of the base and quite small. At the band the watch base is tapered off in a tiered pattern.

$36,000–$40,000

## Silver, Marcasite, and Semiprecious Jewelry

*Brooch*, by Georg Jensen. In silver, amber, and chrysoprase, a large amber cabochon set within openwork scrolling foliate surround set with chrysoprase cabochons, impressed "Georg Jensen 925 S Denmark 78." 2" long.

$300–$400

*Brooch*, by Georg Jensen. Two pod-form flowers with scrolling tendril set with chrysoprase cabochon, hammered finish, impressed "GJ 100 Denmark 8803." 1¼" long.

$300–$400

*Necklace and bracelet*, by Georg Jensen, c. 1919–1927 and 1933–1944. In silver, cast as articulated trios of scrolling leaves and cabochon flanking a berried section with cabochon center, conjoined by twin sets of beaded links, impressed "GJ Sterling Denmark 925 1," 16" long; bracelet impressed "Georg Jensen Denmark 830 3," 7" long.

$550 (1986)

*Pendant necklace*, by Georg Jensen, c. 1919–1927. Silver and amber, cast as an openwork mount with furled leaves surrounding large amber oval cabochon, pendant from bud-form link and simple link chain, impressed "Georg Jensen Denmark 830 54." Pendant 2½" long.

$880 (1986)

*Pin*, by Peter Macchiarini, American, 1930s. Modernist abstract design in hand-hammered copper and sterling silver, set with tiger's-eye. 3¼" long.

$650–$700

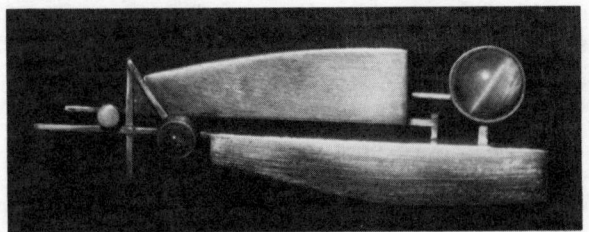

Pin by Peter Macchiarini. *(Photo by R. Four; courtesy of Meisel-Primavera)*

*Necklace,* by Margot de Taxco, Mexican, 1930s. In squared S-form links of black champleve enamel with silver edge, stamped "Margo de Taxco 5404A." 15" long.

$55 (1986)

*Bracelet,* by Antonio Pineda, Mexican, 1930s. In silver, of eight large concave, curved, rectangular hinged sections with angular ends, impressed "Antonio Taxco AAR 925 Mexico." 2.6 troy oz.

$1,200–$1,400

*Bracelet and earrings,* by Antonio Pineda. Of oval obsidian cabochons in winged silver mounts, bracelet impressed "Antonio Taxco Mexico 925." 2.9 troy oz. gross weight.

$500–$550

*Necklace, bracelet, and earrings,* by Antonio Pineda. The necklace of rectangular sections, set with oval moonstone cabochons and bordered on two sides by a curved silver band on a solid concave collar, impressed "Antonio Taxco Sterling." 8.2 oz. gross weight.

$1,200–$1,500

*Necklace and bracelet,* by Antonio Pineda. The necklace of silver angled arches, enclosing spheres of tiger's-eye, on a collar of alternating curved rectangles and spheres, impressed "Antonio Taxco Silver Mexico Sterling HHN 970." 7.2 troy oz. gross weight.

$800–$1,000

*Necklace and bracelet,* by Antonio Pineda, 1930s. Concave rectangular silver sections alternating with cylindrical sections inset with a central onyx band, both with applied tag with artist's mark, necklace impressed "925 Taxco."

$1,100 (1987)

## Silver, Jewelry, and Fashion 315

*Necklace and bracelet,* by Antonio Pineda, 1930s. Both of rectangular sections of silver, each alternating section inset with black onyx, both impressed "Antonio Taxco FRD 970 TR-55."

$2,000–$2,500

*Bracelet, "North Star,"* by William Spratling, American, 1930s. In silver and amethyst, with central amethyst cabochon radiating spiked arms alternating with flowered segments, each topped with a smaller stone, on an incised cuff with amethyst cabochons flanking the center star, stamped "Sterling Mexico."

$495 (1987)

*Necklace,* by William Spratling, made in Mexico, 1930s. In sterling silver in cross-hatch design with inset amethysts.

$1,600–$1,800

*Bracelet,* after William Spratling. In silver and amethyst, with central amethyst cabochon radiating spiked arms, alternating with flowered segments, each topped with a smaller stone, on an incised cuff with amethyst cabochons flanking center star, stamped "Sterling Mexico."

$300–$500

*Bracelet and earrings,* by Taxco, Mexican, 1930s. In Mexican silver, the bracelet formed as two opposing curled leaves, each screw-on earring shaped as a single curled leaf, marked "Taxco."

$198 (1987)

*Bracelet,* anon. In sterling silver, with five linked clusters of flowers. Stamped "Sterling."

$135–$150

*Bracelet,* anon. In sterling silver, with four linked clusters of flowers and stylized ribbons in an asymmetrical design. Stamped "Sterling" and "Patent 23654."

$140–$160

*Bracelet,* anon., Mexican. In sterling silver, with five double-linked stylized roses. Stamped "Sterling" and "Made in Mexico."

$200–$215

*Brooch,* anon., American, c. 1934. In onyx and marcasite, set in sterling silver. Overall circular design within a rectangle, with a black onyx circle and the initials "FF" shadowed in black onyx. Approx. 1½" tall x 2" long.

$600–$800

*316* ART DECO

**Marcasite brooch.** *(Photo by R. Four; courtesy of Flora Friedlander Cohen)*

*Earrings,* anon., probably Mexican. In sterling silver, shaped disk and hoop of different sizes connected vertically. The disk is designed with hammered dots; the hoop is larger and has swirled edges.
$50–$75

*Necklace, bracelet, and earrings* (demiparure), anon., probably American, 1930s. In amethyst, silver, and marcasite composed of flexible rectangular links set with rectangular amethysts. The earrings have tapered pendant form.
$3,200 (1987)

*Necklace,* American, c. 1933. In carnelian and marcasite set in sterling silver. Flexible rectangular links with two square and one central rectangular carnelian. Marcasites set in geometric designs surround central stone.
$300–$350

*Pin,* anon., probably American, c. 1930. Marcasite and amber set in rectangular sterling silver with clasp designed to keep pin from falling forward.
$650–$750

## Silver, Jewelry, and Fashion

*Pin,* anon., German, 1930s. An oval of translucent blue chalcedony, cut with facets and with three cut-out circles. In the center circle a round black onyx surrounded by marcasites. Sterling silver mount, stamped "Sterling" and "Germany." 1½" long.

$565–$590

*Pin,* anon., German, 1930s. Lily of the valley with four ivory flowers on curved stem. Stylized leaves set with marcasites. Stamped "Sterling" and "Germany."

$265–$280

*Pin,* anon, probably American. Shaped as a three-leaf clover in sterling silver and set with marcasites. Each leaf of the clover has a stylized flower design.

$210–$225

*Wristwatches,* European and American, 1930s. Various makers such as Gruen, Waltham, and Bulova, with elongated rectangular faces and stylized numerals.

$300–$600

*Wristwatches,* European and American, 1930s, various makers such as Girard Perregaux, Bulova, and others. Geometric faces and faceted crystals.

$900–$1,800

### Bakelite Jewelry

*Bakelite striped bracelet.* Various colors in four-color combinations. Approx. 1½" thick.

$475–$495

*Bakelite bracelets.* Bow-tie pattern. Approx. 1" thick.
  Multicolored $425–$450
  Black and red $300–$325

*Bakelite hinged bracelets.* Carved designs, in red, black, green, and yellow.

$100–$125

*Bakelite bangle bracelets.* In red, yellow, black, green, and orange with intricate geometric designs.

$95–$139

*Bakelite bracelets.* Bakelite and amber pieces connected by elastic.

$60–$65

*Striped Bakelite bracelets.* In green and red, and yellow, black, and red. Approx. 1" thick.
$60–$65

*Polka-dot Bakelite bracelets.* In green and yellow, and yellow and auburn. Approx. 1" thick.
$60–$65

*Bakelite bracelet.* On three elastics, green round beads on all strings, connected with green rectangular pieces.
$50–$60

*Bakelite bracelet.* On elastic, mustard-colored with broad, 1"-wide rectangular pieces.
$40–$45

*Bakelite bangle bracelets.* Geometric engravings, olive green, yellow, and mustard.
$25–$40

*Bakelite bangle bracelets.* In green, yellow, and other colors molded with stylized floral designs.
$15–$25

*Bakelite bangle bracelets.* Plain, in green, mustard, and other colors.
$10–$25

*Bakelite bangle bracelet.* Brown, with molded circular designs.
$10–$15

*Bakelite hoop earrings.* In marbled orange and green.
$25–$35

*Bakelite earrings.* Plain, circular, or square, in brown, green, and other colors.
$10–$15

*Bakelite necklace.* Black-and-white swirled circular beads.
$35–$40

*Bakelite necklace.* Orange and white beads molded with floral design.
$35–$40

*Bakelite necklace.* Series of nickel-sized yellow disks.
$30–$35

## Silver, Jewelry, and Fashion 319

*Bakelite pendant on a rope chain.* Shield shaped in black with a motif of stylized leaves. Blue glass-paste stones set in asymmetrical arcs.
$90–$100

*Bakelite bar pins.* Four-color, laminated, various colors. Approx. 2″–3″ diameter.
$215–$225

*Bakelite shield pins.* Four-color, laminated, various colors, Approx. 1½″–2″ diameter. (For illustrations see color insert.)
$240–$255

*Bakelite "hat" pins.* Approx. 2″–3″ diameter
| | |
|---|---|
| Red hat with white trim | $275–$295 |
| Mustard hat with red trim | $230–$245 |
| Bonnets, yellow with black polka dots, pair | $210–$215 |
| Red hat with clear rim | $185–$195 |
| Green hat with clear rim | $140–$150 |
| Alpine hat | $140–$150 |
| Olive green hat with clear rim | $125–$130 |
| Pilgrim hats, red and black, pair | $120–$125 |

*Bakelite pin.* Molded in design of bow tie, caramel colored.
$20–$25

**Bakelite "hat" pins.** *(Photo by R. Four; courtesy of Frank and Barbara Pollack)*

*Bakelite pin.* Molded in form of long fish, horizontal bar pin in black.
$18–$20

*Bakelite pins.* Molded with geometric designs, horizontal bar pins in green, yellow, and other colors.
$15–$20

*Bakelite pins.* Plain horizontal bar pins in red, green, and other colors.
$10–$15

*Bakelite rings*
Orange-yellow polka dot $100–$105
Red, with squared crown $95–$105
Yellow, with bulbed crown $60–$70
Carved yellow ring $50–$55
Three-color striped $50–$55

*Bakelite rings.* In solid colors—red, green, mustard, yellow, and other colors.
$15–$20

## FASHION AND ACCESSORIES

The fashion designers of the Art Deco period were not satisfied with just designing clothes. Many were also interior designers and created a wide variety of furnishings and decorations. The foremost of these were Jacques Doucet, Paul Poiret, Coco Chanel, and Jeanne Lanvin, but many others were active in Paris. It has been reported that no fewer than twenty new fashion companies were created in the first quarter of the century.

Prior to the outbreak of World War I, perhaps the two strongest influences on fashion and fashion illustration were the Ballets Russes and Japanese prints. The Ballets Russes (see "Artistic Influences" for more information) created an explosion of color and Orientalism in fashion and the arts from its very first Parisian performances in 1909. Japanese prints in the *ukiyo-e,* or "floating world," style introduced new graphic angles, plain or simply screened backgrounds, sophisticated color palettes, and an uncluttered look—all of which had an impact on fashion illustration.

Fashion design also was influenced by the Cubists and Modigliani. This can be seen particularly in the facial features of illustrated figures.

The war had a strong effect on fashion. First, it speeded up the development of man-made materials and ready-to-wear clothing. Second, it accelerated the emancipation of women, whose active role in society now required a new kind of clothing. Two million young Frenchmen died in the war, and many women found themselves still working for a living even when the war was over.

Skirts became shorter and not as restrictive, and the *rayons*, or aisles, of the department stores were filled with a diversity of fashion never before seen. In evening wear the Ballets Russes was still popular, but the Folies Bergères had become the real trend-setters.

Some of the most successful new fashion houses were managed by women. Supple, lightweight materials were used for straight, free-flowing dresses, and their long line was accentuated by the absence of a waistline. Hemlines went up and down, reaching their shortest length in 1927. Some say that this was an indication that the economy of the time was strong. New fabrics were invented for sportswear. Elegant pajamas were acceptable attire for lounging around the house.

The world was full of trains and cars and other speeding vehicles, and clothes also took on a faster look, with geometric patterns, lines, and angular cuts. Hair was shingled or "bobbed." Women smoked in public and even drew attention to their new freedom with long jeweled cigarette holders and Deco-designed cigarette cases.

For evening wear dresses were styled with low-cut V-shaped backs and designs in gold and silver lamé thread. Accessories included silk scarves and veils. Hats were still de rigueur, but now it was cloche hats, a closer-fitting variety in a wide variety of shapes and colors.

It is a curious historical fact that the first of the grand couturiers in Paris was an Englishman, Charles Frederick Worth. Before Worth's time, clothing for women was largely made by seamstresses, not designed by men. Worth's customers dressed in yards and yards of fabric with lace trim and beadwork. Hats were large and covered by then-plentiful ostrich feathers. The style was designed to suit an elegant, rich society where the women were inactive enough not to worry about flowing trains on their dresses.

It was Paul Poiret who first challenged the Worth empire with his new style of fashion. Of course, Worth thought Poiret's designs were vulgar. However, his styles were popular with women. Many wore clothes that were risqué, which at the time did not mean salacious as much as daring. The new clothes were symbolic of their newly liberated attitudes.

Poiret opened his first shop in 1903. He had been an employee of both Worth and Jacques Doucet and had been influenced by the latter's great talent. He, in turn, influenced younger designers, such as Paul Iribe, and built an interior decorating empire through his firm, Martine.

At the beginning of his career, Poiret promoted an Orientalism in fashion, no doubt influenced by the Ballets Russes, which was the dernier cri, or "the latest rage," but which did not last. Poiret's 1912 collection was highly influenced by the Ballets Russes, however, and established his reputation.

Over the years, Poiret's design changed to a more vertical, slimmer style with bright colors. The song "Anything Goes" could easily be about his designs: it was he who introduced transparent stockings. His short skirts were designed to show off the knee-high Moroccan boots he suggested be worn with them. And as if all that was not shocking enough, he abolished corsets and invented the bra.

Poiret was a truly "modern" fashion designer as we understand the term today. He was one of the first to create his own perfume. In addition, because he also designed interiors, it was possible for someone to become totally absorbed in his style. He made no secret of the fact that he wanted to "fashion" his clients' lives in every way.

Four other designers who also had an enormous impact on fashion in the 1920s were Madeleine Vionnet, Madame Lanvin, Coco Chanel, and Jean Patou. Fashion became one of France's biggest exports, not only because it was appealing but also because many of these designers were skilled at promoting their work and dealing with the press and magazines. They often visited showrooms around the world where their work was sold and always took advantage of "photo opportunities" by being seen in the right places.

Vionnet is credited with the invention of the bias cut which is the slanting or diagonal cut of clothing that became popular as a hallmark of 1920s fashion. So many designers borrowed ideas from one another, which they then claimed as their own, that Vionnet went to the trouble of documenting her designs by photography as a deterrent to that practice.

Coco Chanel is perhaps the best-known name in fashion design of the era, and her work commands high prices at auction. As a celebrity of the time she was extensively written about, and all of her many love affairs were followed in the gossip magazines. She worked for a very established clientele and was the first to introduce costume jewelry.

Her name became well known in the United States, especially after she had the idea to create paper patterns of her dresses for sale to homemakers who couldn't afford her original designs. In 1925, the year of the Paris Exposition, she introduced her famous "Chanel No. 5" perfume. The four previous attempts had not been successful.

Jeanne Lanvin was really the first to introduce an internationally successful perfume, "Arpege," in 1923. Also well known in the United States, she opened the first ready-to-wear boutique for high fashion in Paris in 1929.

The same year Jean Patou opened a ready-to-wear boutique as well. Patou's name is not as recognized today, but he was an important male designer in a woman's world. His sports clothes and white satin evening gowns established him as the designer for café society in the 1920s. He also had a number of celebrities, such as Gloria Swanson, as clients.

Patou is perhaps best known for the *garçonne* style, a word created from the French word for "boy" with a feminine ending added. When he introduced the look at Wimbledon in 1922, worn by a famous tennis player of the day, it was an immediate success. Women seized on the short hair, simple sportswear, and casual "tomboy" look.

The Depression had a devastating effect on the fashion world, which really did not recover until the mid-1930s. By then many of the 1920s fashion designers had lost their appeal or had had to change their designs to meet new tastes.

However, these and other designers of the 1920s had such an impact that there is hardly an area of fashion or accessories that does not reflect their style. Many manufacturers of lesser quality created imitations of Chanel, Lanvin, Patou, and Vionnet dresses, handbags, scarves, shoes, hats, and more.

The fashions of the 1920s are both expensive—a 1984 auction, which had anticipated a price of $1,000 for a three-piece Chanel black-and-white suit, actually brought in $7,150—and difficult for a collector to house and show with ease. The most finely made fashions of the day are still worn, especially dresses by Fortuny, Chanel, Vuitton, and others. However, if damaged, the restoration process requires special skills and specially re-created materials. The clothing is fragile, and easily destroyed unless properly stored, climate-controlled, and protected from ultraviolet light.

There are today several museums in this country that house collections of dresses, gowns, hats, and the like, in which Art Deco designs are represented—the Costume Institute at New York's Metropolitan Museum of Art and the Museum of the City of New York, to name just two.

Many still collect and wear the ready-to-wear and commercially produced fashion of the day. Also, many more recent designers have been inspired by or have directly copied the designs of the era. Art Deco fashion continues to come into and go out of vogue, reflecting the style's tremendous impact on the world of design. Some men's clothes of the era have been translated into women's fashions.

In general, hats, gloves, and scarves of the 1920s and 1930s today sell for $15 to $75 and more in "secondhand but chic" stores in many major cities. Sometimes promoted as "vintage" or "gently worn" clothing, shirts, skirts, blouses, jackets, and other apparel can bring anywhere from $25 to $1,500 for a gold lamé evening dress by an unknown designer.

Handbags of the day in "antelope" (actually a type of cow leather), lamé, Moroccan leather, and Bakelite can easily bring from $100 to $650 or more. Alligator handbags, which were popular in the 1930s, are fetching $200 and up in fine condition.

Mention luggage and the name Gaston Vuitton springs to mind. Everyone traveled—by motorcar, by airplane, by luxury ocean liner. No traveling ensemble was complete without a matching set of Vuitton luggage. But Vuitton went beyond clothing trunks to create specialized cases for fishing gear, typewriters, shoes, and other items.

Like many famous designers, Vuitton was imitated, and his suitcases, handbags, and other creations have been counterfeited from the start. A July 1987 news story from San Jose, California, reported that customs officials had seized a shipment of 6,200 fake Vuitton bags, the largest ever on the West Coast.

At a New York auction in 1984 Vuitton's fitted trunks brought around $1,000, with a top price of $1,250 paid for a trunk especially designed to hold thirty-three pairs of shoes. Today the best Vuitton designs from his early period can easily be twice as expensive on the antiques market. With the new Vuitton trunks selling for as much as $12,000 or more, it isn't hard to love the old ones.

Oshkosh suitcases and steamer trunks are popular collector pieces, as are both Vuitton and Oshkosh men's and women's fitted cases for toiletries and the like.

Many department stores of the day, such as Bergdorf-Goodman, had fitted cases designed especially for them. Men's cases were crafted in heavy cowhide and often have squared-off toiletry bottles in enameled glass. More expensive cases have ivory components, while less expensive models included ivorene. Fitted cases can bring anywhere from $120 to $1,500 and more. The price generally depends on the condition and age of the piece and the designer.

More popular than clothing or suitcases are the innumerable "accessories" and "decorations" of the day. For example, the eggshell lacquer technique perfected by Jean Dunand was also used by goldsmiths and silversmiths for such small objects as belt buckles, hair clips, and vanity cases.

When faster-drying enamels were developed, accessories such as compact cases, cigarette cases, buttons, and cuff links were produced in bright-colored or black-and-eggshell enamel.

Makeup cases and lipstick batons came in a variety of shapes and sizes and are now one of the most easily collectible items of the era.

In addition, cigarette cases and smoking accessories, lacquered boxes and silver-plated coffers, jewelry boxes, and other boudoir decorations are very popular, and many are still inexpensively priced. Other "decorations" often found in antique fashion stores include desk sets, manicure sets, humidors, boudoir lamps and nightlights, powder boxes, bookends, mirrors, letter openers and letter seals—the list seems endless.

As fashion accessories and decorations such as these proliferated, cheap imitations of expensive materials became the norm. Silver was replaced by silver plate, nickel plate, and chrome. Enameling was replaced by transfer printing. And plastic came to look like ivory, tortoiseshell, coral, and jade. What saved this production from being thrown away—and what makes it collectible today—is that although it was cheap, it was also fashionable.

All of these categories of collectibles can vary widely in quality, design, and execution. After all, some were made of precious and semiprecious materials, and others were made of Bakelite. It is up to you to develop an eye for quality workmanship and for what fits your budget and pleases you in this area of Art Deco collecting.

For fashion lovers, some of the greatest collectibles of the period are perfume and toiletry bottles (see "Glass" for more information) and original fashion designs, fashion plates, advertisements, and covers that were produced for the publications of the era, such as *Gazette du Bon Ton*, *Modes et Manières d'Aujourd'hui*, the German *Styl*, and the American *Vogue*, *Harper's Bazaar*, and *Vanity Fair*. (See "Posters and Graphics.")

The influence of Paris as the epicenter of fashion began to wane as some of these new magazines, geared to American women, saw rapidly rising circulations. *Harper's Bazaar* and *Vogue* would seize the imaginations of young urban American women while continuing to promote an essentially French style of fashion.

However, by the end of the 1920s there was a reaction against the fashion that had been popular since the war, and long hair and flowing gowns once again returned to the scene. By 1930 hemlines had dropped all the way down, and skullcaps had replaced cloche hats. In the early 1930s elegant evening and cocktail gowns reappeared. Elbow-length gloves, padding, and oversize coats were added.

As the world trudged through the Great Depression and headed again toward war, a plainer, more serious style of everyday clothing reclaimed dominance. In fact, fashion was looked on as one of the more frivolous aspects of urban society in a world where Hitler had raised the flag of the Third Reich. Toward the end of this era, it was the gold-diggers, collaborators, and even the hookers who were depicted as hanging onto the more dramatic aspects of Deco style, like the ubiquitous exaggerated cigarette holders of the era.

## PRICE LISTINGS

*Belt buckle*, American, 1930s. In butterfly shape in red and black Bakelite.
$295–$325

*Belt buckle*, American, 1930s. In four-color striped-pattern Bakelite.
$295–$325

*Boudoir lamp*, probably American, 1930s. Glass base and shade in milky frost glass with vertical, angular ribbing. Pale green painted highlights have almost disappeared. 12" tall.
$100–$110

*Bookends*. Egyptian Revival in marble and alabaster, each carved as the face of a haughty sphinx, with zebra-striped gray and white hair ornament. Each 9" tall. Pair.
$400–$500

*Box*, probably American, 1930s. Silver-plated box with streamlined leaping deer with elongated horns. Purple felt interior. 5" long x 4" wide x 1/12" deep.
$30–$50

*Box*, American, 1930s. Chromium-plated, rectangular, with wood lining, the top with stylized decoration of crescents and other emblems, unmarked. 8" x 5¼".
$150–$200

*Cigarette case, "Volupté,"* American, 1930s. Chrome cigarette case with geometric pattern in a sunray motif. Some panels varnished to brass color. With felt carrying pouch printed with "Volupte, USA." Stamped "Volupté." 6" long x 4" wide.
$65–$80

*Cigarette case*, probably American, 1920s. Green, black, and eggshell enamel in a diamond-pattern design. 4" x 4".
$400–$450

*Cigarette case*, probably American, 1920s. Red, black, and eggshell enamel in a geometric design. 5" long x 3" wide.
$500–$575

# Silver, Jewelry, and Fashion

"Volupté" cigarette case. *(Photo by R. Four)*

*Cigarette case,* American, 1930s. Cylindrical, of black metal with chrome top with standing scottie design.

$35–$45

*Cigarette case,* Austrian, c. 1910. Rectangular silver case with molded horizontal surface, miniature painting on ivory, opening to reveal vermeil interior with hinged door on interior top, opening to reveal a passionate couple in bed. 3½" long.

$385 (1986)

*Cigarette case,* Austrian. The square silver and enameled case decorated with a scene of a bare-breasted young woman reclining among pillows. 3¼" long.

$550 (1986)

*Cigarette case and lighter,* by Dunhill, American. In silver and black lacquer with diagonal stripes of eggshell-lacquer decoration, the case with monogram, stamped "Made in USA, Dunhill, Sterling," the lighter also marked. Case 3¼" x 3½".

$385 (1987)

*Cigarette case,* English, c. 1935. In green shagreen (a fish skin treated to be used like leather) with brass clasp. Marked "Made in England." 4" long x 3" wide.

$100–$120

*Cigarette case,* English. In silver, the rectangular box divided into two wooden compartments with central handle, blue-enameled script reading "Cigars" on one side, "Cigarettes" on the other, marked. 7½" long.

$385 (1986)

*Cigarette case,* probably English, 1930s. In silvered nickel with geometric pattern of rays of light emanating from sun in lower corner. Marked "W.H. & Co., Ltd." 4" x 4".

$40–$60

*Cigarette case,* possibly French, c. 1920. In brown and tan shagreen. 2" tall x 4" square with hinged lid.

$60–$80

*Cigarette case,* probably French, 1930s. Designed in the Cartier style with stripes in two colors of gold and platinum. The clasp is a small sapphire. Approx. 6" long x 4" wide.

$1,400–$1,700

*Cigarette case,* German, 1930s. In chrome with black enamel design. Stamped "Germany." 5" long x 3½" wide.

$10–$12

*Coat,* by Jeanne Lanvin, French, 1929. Black silk velvet with velvet ribbons sewn individually to cuffs and hemline, giving "feathery" look. Label intact. Size 5.

$3,800–$4,000

*Compact set.* In enameled gilt metal, comprising a flat circular powder compact and a smaller circular compact with powder puff, both mirrored, and a cylindrical lipstick case, all in green enamel with black banding; in fitted green leather case, unmarked. Case 3" x 5".

$40–$60

*Decorative box,* French, 1925. Red, silver, and black lacquered geometric design in the style of Jean Dunand. Possibly used as a jewelry box. Detachable lid. 11" long x 7" wide x 2½" deep.

$1,200–$1,300

*Desk set,* cast from a model by P. Terescsuk. In bronze and ivory, comprising an inkwell with a pen rest, a rocker blotter, and a letter opener all with peacock feather decoration, the "eyes" of each set with a woman's face in ivory; blotter inscribed "P. Terescsuk." Blotter, 5¼" tall. 3 pieces.

$605 (1987)

## Silver, Jewelry, and Fashion

**Decorative box.** *(Photo by R. Four; courtesy of Coram Nobis Antiquarians)*

*Desk set*, anon. Five pieces, with blue Bakelite handles in original case, marbled red and green paper inlay. 9½" by 4".
$135–$150

*Dress*, by Galenca, Italian. (Galenca was the mistress of the famous Italian designer Fortuny.) Black silk with stenciled silver and gold stylized griffins. Signed on fabric. Size 5.
$2,500–$2,800

*Dressing set*, by Pereline Works, American, 1920s. Including tray, clock, cotton box, powder box, hand mirror, comb, brush, scissors, manicure set, and foot buffer. Mustard-color plastic with black, brown, and gold geometric design. Set in original case, oystershell-shaped with fluted edges and mirrors on either side. Case 31" long x 18" wide. 14 pieces.
$1,200–$1,400

*Evening bag*, c. 1930. Chrome-plated with fitted black case including change purse. Bag has interior compact and lipstick compartments.
$20–$45

*Handbag*, probably American, 1930s. Tan-colored suede, with carnelian and marcasite clasp and buckle. Approx. 5" square.
$375–$400

*Handbag*, probably American, 1930s. In "antelope" leather. Black, with strap and clasp set with marcasites. Approx. 5" wide.
$475–$550

*330* ART DECO

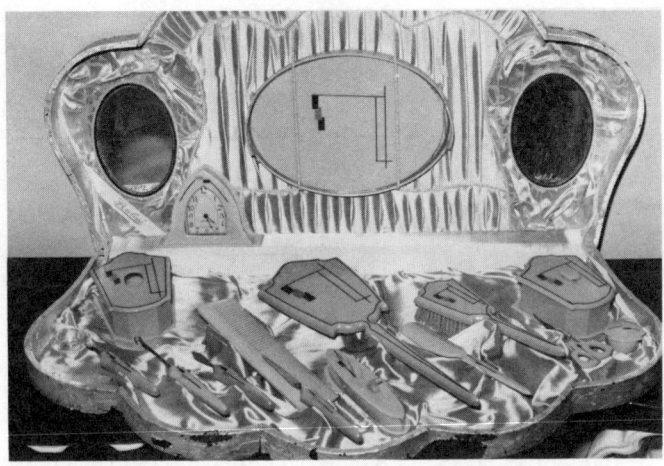

**Dressing set by Pereline Works.** *(Photo by R. Four; courtesy of Norman Crider, A Rose Tree)*

*Hand mirror,* by Hagenauer, Austrian. The handle formed as a stylized female nude, arms raising the circular chrome mirror, marked. 6⅜".
$242 (1986)

*Hand mirror,* probably American, 1930s. In brown plastic designed to look like tortoiseshell. 10" long.
$20–$25

*Humidor,* Austrian. Copper-inlaid rosewood humidor, the circular covered box lined in brass, the exterior of rosewood inlaid with copper, on the sides a procession of ladies in sweeping gowns, and on the lid a design of curving and interlacing forms, unmarked. 4¼" tall.
$300–$500

*Letter opener,* by Georg Jensen, Danish. In sterling silver, the looped handle with openwork, foliate design, Jenson stamp, inscribed "H.M.R. 1922–28 B.S." 9½" long.
$242 (1986)

*Letter seal,* probably American, for use with sealing wax by "BK." In sterling silver with stylized swirl design and beaded outline. Marked "D.C. Sterling." 2" tall.
$40–$60

*Silver, Jewelry, and Fashion* 331

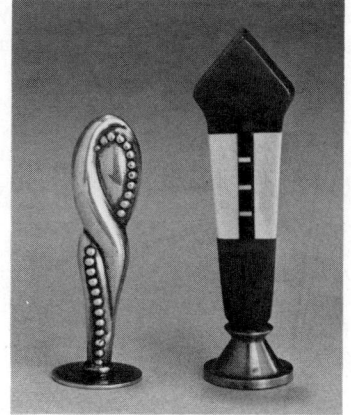

Letter seals show the change from early Deco style to later Modern. *(Photo by R. Four)*

*Letter seal*, probably American, for use with sealing wax by "CD." In green, black, and ivorene Bakelite with brass seal, in a geometric design. Unmarked, 2½" tall.

**$35–$50**

*Manicure set*, probably American, 1930s. Eight pieces, with red Bakelite handles in original case, geometric pattern of purple and gold paper inlay. Case 6½" long x 8" wide.

**$55–$65**

*Mirror, "La Peer,"* American, 1928. Stand-up beauty mirror from the Agnes Moorehead estate. Mirror has built-in light from behind, concealed by a frosted glass shade. Approx 10" tall.

**$425–$500**

*Nightlight*, by Chase Chrome, American. In wood, metal, and polychrome, bulbs with painted faces form heads, one with hat. 9¼" tall.

**$150–$250**

*Opera coat*, American, 1930s. In green lamé with design of ladies and borzois in gold thread.

**$1,500–$1,750**

*Pin tray in pewter holder*, by Wallace Pewter. Insert signed "Jefferson," rests on three squirrels, decorated border, holder signed "Wallace Pewter # P8011."

**$35–$38**

## ART DECO

*Powder box,* American, 1930s. White frosted glass with fluted sides and a chrome cover with green enamel, inscribed "R." 4" diameter.
$15–$20

*Powder boxes,* American, 1920s. Circular, in yellow, brown, maroon, and other colors, of celluloid with hole in lid for removing powder puff. Generally 2½"–3" tall x 4"–5" diameter.
$25–$50

*Powder compact,* by Rex, American, 1930s. Circular compact in black enamel with brown Bakelite decoration with floral design on cover. Powder puff inside has silk ribbon marked "Rex" and "Fifth Avenue." 3½" diameter.
$40–$50

*Purse,* probably American, 1930s. Overall swirled plastic in cylinder design with rectangular clear top and red handles. 4" tall x 6" long.
$30–$50

*Purse,* by Koret, French, 1930s. In snakeskin and plastic, with handles. Lined in red plastic grained as leather, with a small red pouch containing a purse mirror and change purse. Inside stamped with gold ink "Koret," with leaping antelope. Cylindrical. 9" long x 4½" wide x 5" deep.
$100–$150

*Purses,* by Alpacca, German, 1920s–1930s. Mesh "flapper" purses, sometimes with clasps decorated with rhinestones or marcasites. Usually stamped "Alpacca" on the inside of the clasp. Price depends mostly on condition and materials used.
$150–$300

*Purses,* by Whiting & Davis, Co., American, 1920s–1930s. One of the leading makers of chain-mail mesh purses. Usually enameled with geometric or floral designs in green, orange, blue, yellow, and other colors, with chain-linked straps. Often marked "Whting & Davis." Generally 6½" to 7½" long without the chain.
$80–$150

*Scarves,* various and anon. makers, American, 1930s.
    Striped black and blue, peach and navy.
        Silk. 41" long     $30–$40
    Geometric patterns in brown, maroon,
        blue and yellow. Silk. 42" long     $35–$45
    Ivory-colored silk. 42" long     $55–$65

# Silver, Jewelry, and Fashion

Crown Rayon, maroon, with gray geometric designs and long tassles. 42" long     **$40–$50**

*Shoe trunk,* by Louis Vuitton, French, 1930s. With brass fittings, leather strap, wooden reinforcements, and fitted trays inside for shoes. "LV" inscribed on brass. Catalog #174. 19" tall x 35" wide x 15" deep.
**$2,200–$2,400**

*Shoe buckles,* probably American, 1930s. Triangular shape in honey-colored Catalin plastic with silver-plated clasps. Pair.
**$60–$75**

*Skirt suit,* by Coco Chanel, French, 1930s. In white and black, with bold designs, geometric cut, and broad lapels. Label intact.
**$8,000–$10,000**

*Smoker's compendium,* American, c. 1920. In shagreen, the rectangular box covered in shagreen with ivory stringing, opening to reveal cigarette box with separate matching lighter, with tag reading "Patent No. 291,615." 3¾" tall.
**$80–$120**

*Shawl-gown,* American, 1920s. Loosely fitting in the "flapper" style. Egyptian-inspired motif in black silk with gold metallic decoration.
**$110 (1987)**

*Ties,* American, 1930s. Men's ties in silk and rayon. Some are as hideous as when they were made, and others have good geometric designs in contrasting colors.
**$8–$30**

*Traveling vanity case,* French, retailed by Tiffany & Co. Fitted leather, square-handled, fitted with 16 pieces, most with purple enameling over sterling silver case, marked. 5" tall, 12½" long x 11" wide.
**$550 (1986)**

*Traveling vanity case,* retailed by Bergdorf Goodman, American, c. 1931. Square case with seven toiletry bottles and brushes, in olive green.
**$350–$375**

*Vanity mirror,* by Paul Kiss, French. In wrought iron and green marble, the swinging beveled oval mirror held by curved supports with openwork floral design on arched vase terminating in curled feet, on green onyx marble base and wrought-iron base, unsigned, with original paper label from Maison D'Arte, Montparnasse. 19" tall.

**$1,430 (1986)**

*Vanity mirror,* probably Austrian. Silver plate, the mirror of irregular circle shape, the frame incised and cut out with curvilinear patterns and iris motif. 16½" tall.

**$495 (1986)**

# POSTERS AND GRAPHICS

Graphic design had to change to fit the "advertising age," to attract wider markets to the host of new products being offered.

In Europe posters were the most effective way of reaching mass audiences. Art Nouveau posters were too leisurely in delivering their message. In the modern world posters had to be strong enough to be seen and read from passing cars. They had to capture attention with bold lines and colors, short messages, and interesting angles and perspectives. The poster's job was to sell a product in a competitive way.

Magazines, too, would change greatly. Color lithography, which had been perfected by poster artists, was also used to create color covers for magazines. Technical advances such as the rotary press, the linotype machine, and cheaper paper speeded up the changes in the publishing world. Fashion magazines began using *pochoir* printing, a stenciling method, to render multiple copies of color plates of fashion designs. The task of making woodcuts for illustrations gave way to photoengraving.

It has also been argued that, were it not for advertising art and magazines, many of the new artistic movements would not have gained acceptance so rapidly. Many magazines were devoted to the work of certain schools of artists. More important, many fine artists were asked to illustrate both posters and magazines.

The numerous posters, books, magazines, and other graphic-design materials that carried the style of the era to millions are highly collectible today.

## POSTER PRINTING TECHNIQUES

In the 1800s engravings and woodcuts were popular methods of illustration reproduction. Early color lithography was a cumbersome process of applying grease pencil on heavy stones, and one stone was needed for each color to achieve the desired effect.

In the early 1870s, Jules Cheret, known today as one of the foremost Art Nouveau posterists, helped advance the art of color lithography. However, not everyone was pleased with the proliferation of posters. In fact, in 1892 in London the Society for the Checking of Abuses in Public Advertising was set up with the express goal of doing away with postering.

The finest posters of the Art Deco era were also color lithographs; but as time went on, commercial printing moved to a photographic plate process, and magazine-style offset printing became popular. Posters began to be produced photographically in what has been called photolithographic or photomontage designs. These incorporated photographs into the poster with often startling, eye-catching effects. The photographic image finally overcame the illustrated image as the dominant design.

Early lithographic posters will always be more valuable than those printed by the later method, no matter who the artist. When in doubt, look at the poster under a magnifying glass. Photographic printing is really achieved by a series of lines and dots, which can be discerned on close inspection.

## TYPOGRAPHY

Hand-lettering gave way to typography during the Art Deco period, except as practiced by a few artists. The German Bauhaus did as much to revolutionize typography as architecture. In the late 1920s and 1930s lettering in the Art Deco style became as sleek as the women in the fashion magazines.

Often elongated and condensed, the new typography lent itself to the sense of speed that dominated graphic design. Many of the new typefaces were sans serif, that is, the letters did not have little feet. Other decorative typefaces were also developed.

The most popular typefaces, among the others illustrated below, are Futura and Bauhaus, developed in the 1920s.

FUTURA
*Futura*
Bauhaus
Kabel
**Kabel**
Gill Sans
**Gill Sans**
Typeface illustrations. Parisian

## POSTERS

Desirable and sometimes very expensive, Art Deco posters are hot collectibles that in recent years have been staging a comeback after a big dip in prices. Overspeculation in 1979 to 1981 led to a downturn in the market, especially in higher-priced work. Art Nouveau posters by Mucha, which skyrocketed in the early 1980s, have not regained those prices on the market. Works by Toulouse-Lautrec have held their market value, and those by Jules Cheret have rebounded and gone higher.

Art Deco posters, too, have shown gains and are being purchased by more individuals, and also by museums as their collections expand to include significant 20th-century art.

"People care about posters," says Jack Banning of Poster America in New York. "It's no longer a question of nationality. Good, well-designed posters from any country are finding a market today. There has been a movement away from the mediocre French stuff to the benefit of fine posters from other countries. Sure, people go through the trends, and the smart dealers admit that they are always learning."

The great charm of posters, Banning adds, is "that they were not meant to be saved. They were purely commercial—here today, gone tomorrow. On top of that, they are the quintessential original source—popular culture documents. Topically wonderful and unusual. Each one tells a story."

New exposure certainly helped the prices on posters of the Viennese Secession, especially after the 1986 Museum of Modern Art exhibition "Vienna 1900." Some of these posters are very high-priced and extremely scarce, doubling or tripling in price in the last few years as wider markets come to appreciate their quality.

After disputes between the older and younger members of the Austrian Künstlerhaus, which was the stronghold of the Jugendstil (German Art Nouveau) Movement, Gustav Klimt and other Austrian artists broke away to form the Union of Creative Artists of Austria, which became known as the Secession.

We've noted the effect of these artists in the area of decorative arts, and their effect on graphic arts was also strong. From the very first poster for the first Secessionist exhibition, by Gustav Klimt (1862–1918), it was clear that the poster's role in Vienna would be to advertise and to make known the Secession's artistic values.

Koloman Moser (1868–1918), Josef Hoffmann (1870–1956), Leopold Stolba (1863–1929), Egon Schiele (1890–1919), Berthold Löffler (1874–1960), Julius Klinger, and Imre Simay introduced bold geometric shapes and patterns and radical use of typography to achieve graphic effects. The use of stylized figures, simplified lines, and bold colors set them in opposition to the Jugendstil Movement. (See the photo in our color section, "An Art Deco Portfolio.")

Color lithography was slower to be developed in Vienna than in France, and photomechanical processes were introduced at an earlier date. In many cases woodcuts were preferred to lithographic processes. Hand-produced posters from the Viennese Secession are therefore rarer.

The best-known French Art Deco posterist is A. M. Cassandre (1901–1968), born Adolphe-Jean-Marie Mouron of French parents in Russia in 1901. He won the Grand Prix for poster design at the 1925 Paris Exposition, had a prolific career, and is today the single most sought after French poster artist of the era.

Cassandre's first poster, "Le Bucheron," for a furniture maker, appeared in 1923. It set the tone for a new style of advertising art in which typefaces played an important role. Posters from previous years now looked old-fashioned with their small, relatively plain lettering.

In 1984 Cassandre's 1928 poster "L.M.S. Bestway" sold in New York for $25,000 and would probably sell for $35,000 to as much as $50,000 . . . if one could be found. (See the photo in our color section, "An Art Deco Portfolio.")

Cassandre began publishing his own work after 1930 when he created the Alliance Graphique advertising agency with two partners. From 1936 until just before World War II he was commissioned to produce a number of illustrations for *Harper's Bazaar*. These can still be found, although his fame today means they are snatched up quickly.

It was not until 1951 that the Musée des Arts Decoratifs in Paris held a retrospective of his work. His famous "Etoile du Nord" (1927), which depicts railroad lines disappearing to a point on the horizon, now sells in the range of $4,500 to $6,000, depending on condition. Several other Cassandre lithographic posters sell easily in the $5,000 range.

Even later, nonlithographic Cassandre posters are gaining higher prices. His 1951 travel poster entitled "Venezia," which depicted an appropriately Deco-slim gondolier leaning in his boat, sells for $400 to $500 today.

Travel and transportation posters are the most highly realized designs of the era, and Cassandre was a master of these; however, posters for entertainers are also prized. Advertising posters were created for everything from cars and soap to cigarettes by a host of talented French artists.

Paul Colin (1892–1985) launched his poster career with the 1925 Theatre des Champs Elysées poster for *La Revue Negre*. In the 1920s in Paris, everything "Negro"—dancing, jazz, and more—came into fashion. Colin would also become known for his posters for Paris's favorite nightclub entertainer, Josephine Baker, and he designed numerous posters for exhibitions, commercial enterprises, and even for the war effort.

Jean Carlu (1900–1983) was the creator of neon tube posters, both in three dimensions and as graphic designs. Carlu also designed posters for everyday items such as toothpaste and created neon-inspired designs for the cover of Condé Nast's *Vanity Fair*.

An artist known as Zig (whose real name was Brummer) also created posters for Josephine Baker and Mistinguett. Another artist who designed for Mistinguett is Charles Gesmar (1900–1928).

Charles Loupot (1892–1971), who often worked with Cassandre, began as a fashion illustrator. Perhaps his most famous poster was for the 1925 Paris Exposition. With its industrial smokestacks, it would probably make today's environmentalists cringe, but at the time it represented the marriage of industry and art which was the overall exposition theme (see frontispiece).

Pierre Fix-Masseau (1869–1937), who had been a sculptor, became a poster artist between the wars. With a design similar at times to Cassandre's, he is best known for his travel and transport posters.

Georges Lepape (1887–1971), best known for his magazine covers for fashion magazines, created posters as well. His posters for the department store Galleries Lafayette and for the Theatre des Champs Elysées are bought up quickly. One of his best-known designs is "Spinelly," created in 1914 and printed by Lucien Vogel's poster company, Affiche du Bon Ton.

In England the Modernist idiom finally took hold in the 1930s, and there the finest posterist was an American, Edward McKnight Kauffer (1890–1954), best known for his posters for the London Underground and the railways.

McKnight Kauffer's work first met with criticism but ended as the standard for other English artists. Later he was commissioned by the prestigious art journal *The Studio*. He was married to Marion Dorn, a talented carpet designer. He also designed posters for the *Daily Herald*, Shell Oil, and other companies. His posters command the highest prices for English posters, and his reputation is firmly established.

It is perhaps through the appreciation of McKnight Kauffer's design genius that other English poster artists of the day have been rediscovered: F. C. Herrick, Frank Bragwyn, Lionel Edwards, Tom Purvis, Norman Wilkinson, John Atherton, Austin Cooper, Frank Newbould, and others.

One of the most successful (and longest-running) poster advertising campaigns was that for Shell Oil in England, using variations of the slogan "Motorists Prefer Shell."

German poster artists have not been as appreciated in the past as they are becoming today, although prices for German posters are still overall less than for French.

Ludwig Hohlwein (1874–1949) is the master Modern designer in German posters. He created literally thousands of designs in a dramatic style using striking color combinations. His depictions of animals, especially for the Munich Zoo, are prized, and he was also skilled at film, travel, and advertising posters.

Lucian Bernhard (1883–1972) is notable because of his typography; he was the creator of the Bernhard and Bernhard Gothic typefaces. Hans Rudi Erdt (1883–1917) produced an enormous number of posters for the theater, cars, cigarettes, and more. His posters often depict a sport like horseriding, race driving, or tennis playing. Walter Schnackenberg (1880–1961) created German posters with a "cabaret" feel and is noted also for his magazine covers.

German poster art of the era was centered in Berlin, and the foremost printers were Hollerbaum & Schmidt, who employed many of the artists mentioned above.

The German design style that evolved before World War I is called Expressionism, a title applied to much Modern German production. Expressionism uses exaggeration, emotion, and intensity to achieve its effects. The rise of Hitler in Germany put an end to the inventiveness of posters of the era, turning them into little more than propaganda.

Switzerland, Belgium, Italy, and other countries also had some fine posterists.

Leonetto Cappiello (1875–1942) was a painter who was born in Italy but worked in Paris. He was one of the earliest poster artists to recognize the need for bold graphics and clear, simple messages. Many posters by Cappiello can still be purchased in the range of $500, but his most popular poster for the entertainer Mistinguett at the Casino de Paris can bring $2,500 or more.

Leo Marfurt (1894–1977) was born in Switzerland but played an important role in Belgian poster art through the agency he established, Les Créations Publicitaires.

Herbert Matter (1907–1984) pioneered the use of photography and photomontage in posters and is well known for his designs for the clothing manufacturer PKZ.

One might assume that the popularity of the Modern style in the United States would yield a wealth of fine posters. However, magazines and other advertising media were more appropriate for the vastness of this country. In addition, advertising art in America used photographic images much earlier; when illustrations were used, it was often European designers who were commissioned to execute them.

Hollywood developed its own style of poster art, which borrowed on some of the graphic effects of Art Deco but was decidedly different in its use of photographic imagery, multiple imagery, and enormous amounts of text—everyone got "billing."

Ironically, two of the most collectible Art Deco American posters are by Viennese immigrant Joseph Binder (1892–1972), who designed the official poster for the New York World's Fair of 1939, and Englishman John Atherton, who also designed a poster for the great fair.

## *Special Focus: Dutch Posters*

Perhaps the fastest-breaking field in poster collecting today is the Dutch lithographic posters of 1920 to 1940. Concord, Massachusetts, dealer and collector Bernice Jackson helped coordinate an exhibition of Dutch posters that will tour nine American museums, finishing at the Cooper-Hewitt Museum in New York from October 1988 to January 1989.

"The poster market is more sophisticated today," she comments. "French posters once predominated and have had much more exposure, but that's just no longer the case. The market has generally broadened to include many other countries."

She believes that Dutch posters have had a lower visibility and popularity on the collecting market than their numbers and quality deserve. It is certain that the new exhibition will raise consciousness as well as prices. "But the word 'poster' has been given a bad name," she cautions. "You should call them vintage posters or lithographic posters. Posters like these just aren't made anymore."

Of course, not all Dutch posters can be classified as Art Deco. Those that come closest were produced for advertising products and the transportation industry in the late 1920s and 1930s.

One notable poster designer was Jacob, or Jac, Jongert (1883–1942), who made a transition from his previous style to commercial Deco-style advertising. Another is Wim ten Broek (b. 1905), whose posters for Holland-America Line ocean liners are reminiscent of A. M. Cassandre. It is no wonder—Cassandre also designed posters for Holland-America and other Dutch companies.

Other artists in the same vein include Jan Wijga (1902–1978), notably his posters for KLM (Royal Dutch Airlines), and Johann von Stein (1896–1965) for Lloyd Lines.

Nicolaas Petrus "N. P." de Koo (1881–1960) and Agnes Canta (1888–1964) have also scored on the collecting market. In addition, some earlier commercial poster artists, such as Piet van der Hem, can be seen as experimenting with a more modern style of advertising art as early as 1912.

Photolithographic, or photomontage posters as they are called, appeared earlier in Holland than in many other countries. Generally speaking, photomontage posters tend to fall outside the range of the Art Deco style. However, one fine Dutch example in the Deco style (and there are more) is Willem Gispen's (1890–1981) poster for Giso Lamps.

Another interesting group of posters for collectors of Modern design are those of the Dutch De Stijl movement. The De Stijl was a design school influenced both by the Vienna Secession and the Deutscher Werkbund. The posters of this movement made incredibly clever use of typography to achieve their geometric and abstract designs, often without any other visual representation.

One of these is in red and black on white by H. Th. Wijdeveld (b. 1885), one of the best-known designers of the movement, for Frank Lloyd Wright's first exhibition in Holland in 1931. Today this poster can bring up to $12,500. Other talented artists influenced by Wijdeveld include J. J. Hellendoorn (1878–1959) and Antoon Kurvers (1889–1940).

Dutch posters are smaller, and earlier ones are harder to read at a glance than French posters. One possible reason for this is that French posters needed to be read quickly and from a distance on wide Parisian boulevards, whereas the Dutch, with their tiny streets and more leisurely pace, could afford to use smaller posters and more complex designs. However, as time went on, the commercial advertising style of the day took hold in Holland as it had in so many other countries: a striking central visual image, the name of the product, and usually little else.

Collectors should note that editions of Dutch posters also tended to be smaller than those of French. Some are already selling at record-breaking prices, and others will inevitably go up as the demand for them increases.

The most distinctive Dutch posters tend to be noncommercial in nature or created for a cultural event. One stunning 1932 example is "Chaliapine" by Joop Sjollema (b. 1900), a Cubist-influenced Boris Godunov poster for the Wagner Society of Amsterdam, richly colored with gold. Today it easily brings over $5,000.

By far the most memorable image, and one of the most expensive on the Dutch poster market today, was created by Jan Toorop (1858–1928) in 1919 to advertise the play *Pandorra* by Arthur van Schendel. While some of its swirled lines may be reminiscent of the 1890s, its clashing diagonals and planes certainly reflect the impact of Cubism and Futurism. (See the photo in our color section "An Art Deco Portfolio.")

Dutch posters are bound to continue to play a role in the Art Deco collecting field in the years ahead as more collectors become aware of their richness and variety.

## A NOTE ON THE POSTER LISTINGS

For the poster price listings given below, please note the following points.

Many of the posters of the day were signed in the lithographic stone or block. When the name of the artist is given in the listings below, it indicates that the poster is signed in this manner. The dates for the posters may also be in the lithographic stone.

Most posters are hard to find in mint condition. We have noted, where known, any tears, repairs, or border damage. To preserve them, lithographic posters are backed on linen and then matted with acid-free paper in museum-quality mounts. The backing on linen helps the restoration, and small tears and other imperfections can be touched up so that they are almost invisible to the eye. Where the work is sold with linen backing, it is noted in the description. A non-linen-backed poster may be less expensive, but remember, you will have to pay for backing and restoring, and this can add $150 or more to the cost.

These measures are necessary for the preservation of posters, as paper degrades fairly easily. Keep your posters in a dry place even after framing, and try to avoid direct sunlight, which can fade the colors.

## POCHOIR ILLUSTRATIONS

Many graphic artists, like Erté, began as fashion illustrators, rendering the fashion designs of Parisian *couturiers* such as Paul Poiret, Doeuillet, Paquin, Lanvin, and Worth, usually in gouache, an opaque paint mixed with water and applied like watercolor.

The growth of fashion magazines allowed designers to reach new audiences, and the development of *pochoir*, or stencil printing, became popular in fashion magazines. These illustrations were published in numerous French magazines such as *Gazette du Bon Ton, Modes et Manières d'Aujourd'hui, Art, Gout et Beauté, Journal des Dames et des Modes, Falbalas et Fanfreluches, La Guirlande des Mois, Les Idées Nouvelles de la Mode,* and *Les Feuillets d'Art*. Some German magazines also used *pochoir* printing. Within a few years, however, most magazines had turned to photomechanical printing.

*Pochoir* fashion plates are great collectibles of the period. Because they were hand-painted, they were more likely to be saved than later magazine illustrations. In some cases color was hand-applied. This may sound laborious, but it produced a high-quality illustration that suited the deluxe marketing of fashion.

*Gazette du Bon Ton* publisher Lucien Vogel brought the *pochoir* method to perfection, and its *pochoir* illustrations from 1912 to 1925 are among the most valuable, bringing up to a high of $200 to $275. However, *pochoirs* from many other magazines can still be found in the general market range of about $75 to about $125, or higher if framed and ready to hang.

Artists who created *pochoir* illustrations include Georges Barbier, Paul Iribe, Georges Lepape, Charles Martin, Léon Bakst, Erté, André Marty, and Pierre Brissaud.

In many ways Paul Iribe (1883–1935) set the standard for such illustration with his 1908 album of designs, *Les Robes de Paul Poiret*. Another album for Poiret, by Georges Lepape, followed in 1911.

Collecting fashion illustrations is often a double treat: a *pochoir* illustration of a Cinderella gown by Doucet executed by the well-known illustrator André Marty, or a Rodier "afternoon dress" illustrated by Georges Lepape, are twice as interesting for the collector.

Many of these same designers were also gifted book and portfolio illustrators. Several portfolios of *pochoirs* were designed during the early Art Deco period to illustrate legends, biographies of artists such as Nijinsky, or as fashion portfolios that designers would show or offer to their clients.

On the auction market in recent years, complete portfolios have been offered for sale, including works by Barbier; Colin; Benedictus, who did portfolios of designs for textiles; André Marty; and Paul Iribe. When purchased by a dealer, these *pochoir* portfolios often are broken up and sold as individual pieces. Finely framed, each can bring several hundred dollars.

The *pochoir* is coming into its own in the collecting market, but it is still a relatively easy acquisition, especially when compared to the prices for posters of the era. We feel that the years to come will see stronger interest in these often stunning limited-edition designs.

## MAGAZINES—COVERS AND GRAPHICS

Offset-printed magazines, magazine covers, and advertising art are also important graphic collecting areas.

In Austria the magazine *Ver Sacrum* was filled with illustrations and works by the leading Viennese Secessionist artists. The magazine was published from 1898 to 1903, at first in editions of six hundred and then in editions of only three hundred. Today complete issues of *Ver Sacrum* are rare and bring high prices.

Another sought-after magazine is the Dutch *Wendigen*, which was published from 1918 to 1931 and served to promote the work of both Dutch artists and Americans like Frank Lloyd Wright. The Constructivist art leader Kazar El Lissitzky also produced a 1921 cover for *Wendigen*, which today can bring as much as $3,000 on the collecting market.

In England *The Studio* had some outstanding Modern covers by E. McKnight Kauffer and others. In Germany in the 1910s and 1920s *Das Plakat* published covers by noted artists Walter Schnackenberg and Ludwig Hohlwein.

By 1900 the magazine business had exploded, and by the 1930s *Art Gout et Beauté* was the only fashion magazine still using *pochoir* hand-colored illustrations. It stopped publication in 1932.

Magazine covers were still rendered first in watercolor, gouache, pen and ink, and other media and then were photographically reproduced. The original works of art from which the covers were made can be much higher priced than the covers themselves.

Notable magazines that featured covers in the Art Deco and Moderne styles include *Harper's Bazaar* (which changed its name from "Bazar" in 1929), *Vanity Fair* (which was published until 1936 and is being republished today), *Vogue,* and *Fortune.*

Some imaginative examples of Deco design come from the covers of a lesser-known magazine, *Asia*, which employed artist Frank McIntosh from 1924 to about 1933.

French magazine cover artists include Léon Baskt, Georges Barbier (1881–1932), and Louis Icart. (See our special section on Icart later in this chapter.)

However, the most notable was Georges Lepape. He designed numerous magazine covers, including those of *Femina, Modes et Manières d'Aujourd'hui, Art et Décoration,* and Lucien Vogel's *Gazette du Bon Ton.* He also designed for *Vanity Fair* starting in 1915 and for *Vogue* starting in 1916, both Condé Nast publications.

Lepape's 114 covers for *Vogue*, created from 1916 to 1939, are highly collectible. He had an eye for lettering and changed the style of the magazine's name with each design. Today it is unthinkable that a magazine could compete on the stands if it changed its logo with every issue.

Erté designed covers for *Harper's Bazaar* from 1915 to 1936. Today it is believed that no one but Erté himself has a complete collection of the 240 covers he designed, and his illustrations for various Hearst publications may number closer to 2,500. (For more on Erté, see the special section in this chapter.)

John Held, Jr. (1889–1959) was known for his humorous covers for *Vanity Fair*, as was Anne H. Sefton, who used the pseudonym "Fish." Miguel Covarrubias was another designer whose magazine covers abounded in the 1930s. Perhaps most famous is his February 1932 *Vanity Fair* cover featuring Greta Garbo, whose pointed shoulders match her pointed eyebrows.

In the 1930s *Vanity Fair* called on the talents of Frederick Chance and Paolo Garetto, and covers started depicting the political and social realities of the day as opposed to mainly fashion. One outstanding Garetto cover, for the November 1932 *Vanity Fair*, is a bold red, white, and black graphic in which the German swastika forms the body of a very Cubist-faced Hitler.

News magazines such as *Fortune*, which started one month after the Stock Market Crash of 1929, also featured Modern idiom graphics and covers. Joseph Binder created several covers for *Fortune*, inspired by skyscrapers, tractors, and other industrial motifs.

*Fortune* is a good source for covers in mint condition because it came with a box for storage. Covarrubias and Garetto also designed for *Fortune*.

One of the few magazines that has not changed its design over the years is *The New Yorker*. Every February the magazine reproduces the first cover of February 21, 1925, a caricature of Eustace Tilley in his top hat and monocle by artist Rea Levin. A first-edition cover of *The New Yorker* now commands as much as $600 to $700 on the collecting market. Ilonka Karasz also designed covers and graphics for *The New Yorker* and *Vanity Fair* in the 1920s.

With relatively low prices, magazine covers are a popular collectible, and one can often still find them in rummage sales for $5 to $7. However, covers in perfect condition are becoming harder and harder to find, especially in urban markets, and dealers are more aware of their value than before. Most Deco magazine covers now command between $25 and $75. They may cost more if already matted and framed for hanging, but they are still a place for the young graphic collector to begin.

Apart from the magazines already mentioned, others that have had Deco covers and/or advertising graphics include *Woman's Home Companion, House Beautiful, Esquire, The American Home, Better Homes and Gardens,* and *Colliers.*

The single most affordable Deco graphics field is advertising art, and some collectors make subject collections of different types of advertising. Fashion advertising and illustrations are popular, but other areas are also notable.

For example, for Deco lovers who are also automobile lovers, advertising art from magazines can be particularly appealing. Not only will you find advertisements for the famous Pierce Arrow Towne Car, Rolls Royce, Packard, and Bugatti but also for less well known models such as the German Brennabor, the English Hupmobile, and the Simson Supra, among many others.

Rockwell Kent (1882–1971), most noted as a book illustrator, also designed advertising, and his Rolls Royce and Steinway and Sons piano advertisements were used in many magazines. Advertising was produced in great quantity, and it is easily acquired, but prices for the best today may appear modest five years from now, especially if the designs are by noted artists.

## PRICE LISTINGS

### Posters

*"Hamburg Sud,"* by Otto Anton, German, 1935. Dramatic ocean liner poster of the liner docked in Brazil on a starry night, with the cruise passengers in evening wear and natives balancing baskets on their heads. 38" tall x 25" wide.

$700–$900

*"Arts Menagers,"* by Francis Bernard, French, 1933. For the 10th Salon of Household Arts. Color photolithographic poster of a geometricized woman with a broom and an inset photo of a French couple. Backed on linen. 63" tall x 42" wide.

$600–$800

*"Nitrolian,"* by Leonetto Cappiello, Italian, 1929. Color lithograph of a man painting steps, with lady descending. Bottom steps are white; they have not yet been painted and neither has the outline of the woman's legs. In red, black, white, and blue. Backed on linen. 63" tall x 47" wide.

$700–$900

"Hamburg Sud" by Otto Anton. *(Photo courtesy of George Theofiles, Miscellaneous Man)*

"*Fêtes de Paris,*" by Jean Carlu, 1935. Color lithograph. Backed on linen. 38¾" tall x 24½" wide.

$2,860 (1986)

"*L.M.S. Bestway,*" by A. M. Cassandre, French, 1928. Lithographic rail travel poster, last sold at auction a few years ago for $25,000. It depicts a close-up graphic of the wheels of a train in red, grays, and black, with outline type for "L.M.S." in black and white and "Bestway" curved in red neonlike lettering. If one could be found today in excellent condition, it would probably sell for (for illustration see color insert):

$35,000–$50,000

"*Nord Express,*" by A. M. Cassandre, 1929, for the Chemin de Fer du Nord. Well-known design by the undisputed master of Deco poster graphics. Train engine speeding into the distance with rail lines and telephone wires leading the viewer's eye into the distance. Backed on linen. 40" tall x 25" wide.

$5,000–$7,000

"*L'Oiseau Bleu,*" by A. M. Cassandre, French, 1929, for the Chemin de Fer. Color lithograph in red, blue, and yellow. Stylized, racing bluebird flies alongside a train car. Printed by "Imprimerie L. Danel,

"Nord Express" by A. M. Cassandre. *(From the collection of Pat Kery)*

Lille." Some repairs to corners; backed on linen. Approx. 35" tall x 24½" wide.

$3,800–$4,000

*"Etoile du Nord,"* by A. M. Cassandre, 1927. Color lithograph for the Chemin de Fer du Nord, depicting rail lines converging at a distant point on the horizon, where the North Star shines. Backed on linen. 41⅜" tall x 29½" wide.

$4,500–$6,000

*"Chemin de Fer du Nord,"* by A. M. Cassandre, 1929, subtitled "Vitesse—Luxe—Confort" ("Speed—Luxury—Comfort"). Color lithograph depicting a huge compass with the needle pointing almost north, superimposed on a view of rail lines disappearing into the distance. Backed on linen. 39" tall x 24½" wide.

$2,700–$3,500

*"Challenge Round de la Coupe Davis,"* by A. M. Cassandre, 1932. Color lithograph for tennis tournament shows the extreme ability of the artist to convey with simple imagery, with tennis ball as central image, closest to viewer, and court line, net, and "challenger" in reverse outline. Backed on linen, framed. 34½" x 25½".

$2,500–$3,000

## ART DECO

"La Coupe Davis" by A. M. Cassandre. *(Photo courtesy of Nancy McClelland, Christie's)*

*"Grandes Fêtes de Paris,"* by A. M. Cassandre, 1934. Color lithograph depicting a rearing horse in stylized design on paper, signed and dated within the stone upper right. Framed, small tear to left side; backed on linen. 37" x 22½".
$770 (1986)

*"Bonal,"* by A. M. Cassandre, c. 1935. Advertising poster for the aperitif, with geometric white figure drinking from bottle, red liquid with stars pours into his stomach while large geometric key "unlocks his appetite." Color lithograph. Backed on linen. 40" tall x 25" wide.
$1,000–$1,400

*"Ste. Anyme. de Gérance & D'Armement, Cie. des Bateaux à Vapeur Du Nord,"* by A. M. Cassandre, 1927. Lithograph in colors on paper, depicting a stylized ship anchored at the dock, slight staining, few small creases at top. Backed on linen, framed. Printed by "Hachard & Cie." 42½" x 27⅜".
$2,000–$2,500

*"Tabarin,"* by Paul Colin, 1928. Color lithographic poster for the nightclub, depicting a triple image of a woman dancing the Charleston. Some stains. 23½" tall x 15⅜" wide.
$528 (1986)

"French Lines," by Paul Colin, French. Color lithograph ocean liner poster with image of the prow of *La France* as seen through a veil-like French flag. Good condition, some border repair. 38" tall x 24" wide.

$450–$600

"Journées D'Esperance," by Paul Colin, 1930s. Color lithograph depicting the stylized head of a man looking up to the sky. Color is banded horizontally in a sunset effect. 62" tall x 48" wide.

$1,500–$1,800

"Leroy, Premier Opticien de Paris," by Paul Colin, 1938. Commercial color lithographic poster in black, reds, grays, and whites showing a gentleman with white gloves trying on glasses. Backed on linen. 63" tall x 46" wide.

$2,500–$3,500

"Haut de Cagnes ou la Joie de Vivre," by Paul Colin, c. 1935. Travel color lithographic poster on paper. Backed on linen. 48" tall x 32¾" wide.

$176 (1987)

"Arts Menagers," by Paul Colin, c. 1939, for the 16th Salon of Household Arts. Geometricized figures show a chef, a repairman, and an artist with palette painting a small house. Color lithograph. 59" tall x 44" wide, framed.

$385 (1986)

"Cie. Gle. Transatlantique, French Line," by Paul Colin, c. 1937. Lithograph in colors on paper of the *Transatlantique* ocean liner, against a backdrop of the French flag. Slight spotting, small abrasion at middle left. Backed on linen, framed. 39" x 24½".

$900–$1,000

"Rayon Des Soirées," by Maurice Dufrène, 1930. Lithograph in colors on paper depicting a loud band of black musicians playing, while one customer yells "I can't hear what I'm drinking." 47" x 31⅜", framed.

$800–$1,000

"Cherry Maurice Chevalier," by Fernel, French, 1930s. Color lithograph for the singer/actor who bridged the Atlantic in the Art Deco period. 63" tall x 47" wide, framed.

$496 (1986)

"Arts Menagers" by Paul Colin. *(Photo courtesy of Christie's East)*

"Exactitude" by Pierre Fix-Masseau. *(Photo courtesy of Nancy McClelland, Christie's)*

*"Exactitude,"* by Pierre Fix-Masseau, French, 1932. Lithograph in color depicting a massive black railroad engine, with the train behind it diminishing to a point on the horizon. Small tear on lower left margin. 39½" x 24½".

$2,860 (1987)

## Posters and Graphics 353

*"Mistinguett,"* subtitled "Casino de Paris," by Charles Gesmar, French, 1922. Color lithograph of the famous nightclub entertainer sitting on a stool with a green bird perched on her finger. Backed on linen. Approx. 6' tall x 4' wide in frame.

$6,500–$7,000

*"International Einfurh-Messe,"* by Ludwig Hohlwein, German, c. 1919. Exports Exhibit poster, color lithograph in green, reds, and yellows depicting a train speeding over an arch. Backed on linen. 35" tall x 25" wide.

$1,500–$2,000

*"Riquetta Schoklade,"* by Ludwig Hohlwein, c. 1921. Poster for chocolate, color lithograph in pink, gray, brown, and green, depicting an elephant and two riders. Backed on linen. 29" tall x 41" wide.

$2,000–$2,500

*"Passau,"* by Ludwig Hohlwein, c. 1930. Travel poster color lithograph in green, yellow, brown, and black, depicting the city and seal of Passau. Backed on linen. 24" tall x 32" wide.

$900–$1,000

*"Cenovis Macht's!"* by Ludwig Hohlwein, c. 1930. Commercial color lithographic poster depicting wide variety of products made by Cenovis, with stylized horses and riders in the background in green, brown, yellow, and black. Backed on linen. 11" tall x 16" wide.

$400–$600

*"400 Tentoonstelling,"* by Roland Holst, German, c. 1935. Lithograph in black and tan on beige paper. Backed on linen. 31¼" x 24½".

$400–$600

*"Spinelly,"* by Georges Lepape, French, 1914. Perhaps the best-known poster for the actress. Close-up of her face in a circle. She wears a gauzy fanlike collar, through which we see her smile, and a beaded necklace. 42½" x 31", framed.

$242 (1986)

*"Exposition Internationale Arts Decoratifs et Industriels Modernes,"* by Charles Loupot, French, 1925. Color lithograph for the great 1925 exposition, depicting billowing smokestacks and a huge flower in the sky. Backed on linen. 36" tall x 22¼" wide. (For illustration see frontispiece.)

$2,000–$2,500

"*PKZ*," by Herbert Matter, Swiss, c. 1928. Lithograph in color on paper for the clothing manufacturer PKZ, valet holding up a man's coat with another over his arm. 49½" x 34¾", framed.

$2,860 (1986)

"*Power, The Nerve Center of London Underground,*" by E. McKnight Kauffer, American who worked in England, 1930. Color lithograph, depicting a factory and a train wheel from which a fist protrudes, emanating zigzag lightning bolts. 39½" tall x 25" wide. Good condition.

$3,500–$5,000

"*Magicians Prefer Shell,*" by E. McKnight Kauffer, 1934. Color lithograph in the Shell advertising series. Backed on linen. 30" tall x 45" wide.

$5,000–$7,500

"*A Postman in Northern Scotland,*" subtitled "Outposts of Britain," by E. McKnight Kauffer, 1930. Photomontage; backed on linen. Excellent condition. 26" high x 21" wide.

$700–$900

"*B P Ethyl Horse-Power,*" by E. McKnight Kauffer. Lithograph in colors, signed in plate, backed on linen. 28½" x 43½".

$385 (1986)

"*Aeroshell Lubricating Oil,*" subtitled "Artistocrat of Lubricants," by E. McKnight Kauffer, 1932. Depicting a race car in yellows and blues. Excellent condition; backed on linen. 31" high x 45" wide.

$3,900–$4,200

"*Turnfest Luzern,*" by E. Mossdorf, Swiss, 1928. Sports poster in color on paper depicting stylized heads of athletes. 46" tall x 38" wide.

$950–$1,000

"*Bonbonniere,*" by Walter Schnackenberg, German, c. 1920. Cabaret poster in yellow, black, and red, depicting a cabaret girl pinching a customer's nose. Backed on linen. 47" tall x 35" wide.

$1,800–$2,400

"*Pavillion Gruss,*" by Walter Schnackenberg, c. 1920. Poster for the German club. Color lithograph in red, yellow, and black depicting a man kissing a woman's hand, dancers in the background. 48" tall x 35" wide.

$2,000–$2,400

"Turnfest Luzern" by Mossdorf. *(Photo by R. Four; courtesy of Bernice Jackson)*

*"Casino de Paris,"* subtitled "Paris Qui Brille" and "La Plus Belle Revue du Monde," by Zig (Brummer), French, c. 1926. Lithograph with vibrant colors; stamped "Central Publicite." Backed on linen. Approx. 7½' tall x 2½' wide in frame.

$3,500–$4,000

*"Success,"* subtitled "Mistinguett," by Zig (Brummer), 1928. Colorful lithograph showing the performer at the height of her fame, with a basket of flowers. Backed on linen. Approx. 6' tall x 4' wide in frame.

$6,000–$6,500

*"Mistinguett—Casino de Paris,"* by Zig (Brummer), 1931. Another in the series of posters for Mistinguett. Lithograph in colors on paper. 33½" x 14¾", framed.

$825 (1986)

## Viennese Posters

*"Darmstadt Spiele 1901 Mai–October Ausstellung,"* by Hans Christiansen, 1901. Lithograph in colors on paper, center folds and creases show. 24¾" x 20", framed.

$1,320 (1986)

## ART DECO

*"1904 Darmstadt Ausstellung der Kunstler Kologne,"* by J. V. Cissarz, 1904. Lithograph in colors on paper, signed and dated in the stone, some tears and worn. 29½" x 19¼".

$770 (1986)

*"Kaiser Huldigungs Festzug, Wien Juni 1908,"* by Berthold Löffler, 1908. Lithograph in colors on paper, signed in the block, lower right, with monogram. 40½" x 15", framed.

$2,420 (1986)

*"Der Toupet Kunstler,"* by Berthold Löffler, circa 1903. Gouache and pencil on paper, a maquette for the book by Nikolai Ljesskow, signed upper left. 7¾" x 6", framed.

$2,200–$2,600

*"Kunstlerhaus Weihnacht Schau,"* by Berthold Löffler, 1930. Lithograph in colors on paper, signed in the stone lower right. 37" x 23¼", framed.

$3,520 (1986)

*"Secession 49. Ausstellung,"* by Egon Schiele, 1918. Lithograph in colors on paper, signed in the stone lower right, with horizontal crease. 25¼" x 18¾", framed. (For illustration see color insert.)

$15,000–$20,000

"Kunstlerhaus Weihnacht Schau" by Berthold Löffler. *(Photo courtesy of Nancy McClelland, Christie's)*

*Posters and Graphics* 357

*"Kunst Ausstellung (Secession),"* by Franz Stuck. Lithograph in colors on paper, signed in the block. 27" x 14" framed.
$1,320 (1986)

## Dutch Posters

*"Moederlegende,"* by Alex Asperslagh, 1925. Theater poster, color lithograph depicting woman in flowing robe with lighted candles in foreground and image of a skull in background. Printed by J. Smulders & Co. Backed on linen. 41" tall x 29" wide.
$850–$900

*"Giso Lampen,"* by Willem Gispen, 1928. Color photolithographic poster for Giso Lamps in red, black, and white. Printed by Kuhn & Son, Rotterdam. Backed on linen. 39¼" tall x 27½" wide.
$8,000–$9,000

*"Jaarbeurs Utrecht,"* by Leo Gestel, 1922. Trade Fair lithographic poster in black and white depicting stylized head of Mercury. Backed on linen. 42" tall x 31" wide.
$2,500–$2,750

*"Spyker-Auto's,"* by P. van der Hem, c. 1912. Automobile poster for Spyker cars. Color lithograph of man lighting a cigarette, standing by a woman and a servant with a suitcase. The Spyker car and chauffeur

"Giso Lampen" by Willem Gispen. *(Photo courtesy of Bernice Jackson)*

are waiting in the background. Printed by Senefelder, Amsterdam. Backed on linen. 28" tall x 21" wide.
$1,100–$1,200

*"Tentoonstelling van Nederlandsche Cemeente Werken,"* by Antoon Kurvers, 1926. Exhibition poster for Dutch Cement Works. Typographic poster lithographed in red and white. Printed by Van Leer, Amsterdam. Backed on linen. 38" tall x 31" wide.
$2,200–$2,400

*"Volksblad,"* by Jan Rot, 1930. Typographic poster in red, black, and white for the newspaper *Volksblad*. Color lithograph. Backed on linen. 27" tall x 22" wide.
$650–$700

*"Chaliapine,"* by J. Sjollema, 1932. Cubist-influenced Boris Godunov poster for the Wagner Society of Amsterdam. Color lithograph with gold. Printed by Van Leer, Amsterdam. Backed on linen. 35" tall x 48" wide.
$5,500–$6,000

*"Pandorra,"* by Jan Toorop, 1919. Color lithographic theater poster for the play by Arthur van Schendel. A distinctive design with Cubist and Futurist influences. Printed by S. Lankhout & Co., The Hague. Backed on linen. 44" tall x 33" wide. (For illustration see color insert.)
$20,000–$22,000

"Volksblad" by Jan Rot. *(Photo by R. Four; courtesy of Bernice Jackson)*

## Posters and Graphics 359

*"Architectur—Frank Lloyd Wright,"* by H. Th. Wijdeveld, 1931. Typographic poster lithographed in red, white, and black for the first Frank Lloyd Wright exhibition in Holland. Printed by Jon Enschede en Zonen, Haarlem. Backed on linen. 30" tall x 20" wide.
$12,500–$13,000

*"Koninklijke Luct Vaart—De Fliengende Hollander,"* by Jan Wijga, c. 1930. Color lithographic poster for KLM that shows a plane flying over a very ghostlike "Flying Dutchman" sailing vessel. Printed by Luii and Co., Amsterdam. Backed on linen. 39" tall x 25½" wide.
$1,400–$1,500

*"Rotterdamsche Lloyd,"* Johann von Stein, c. 1930. Ocean liner color gravure poster advertising Sumatra and Java. White steamship with straight white reflection echoes long straight palms and elongated type style. Some crumplings along the edges. Printed by Nederlandse Rotogravure My N. V., Leiden. Backed on linen. 28½" tall x 18" wide.
$2,200–$2,500

*"Statendam,"* by A. Zut Huff, c. 1930. Color lithographic travel poster for Holland-America Line with Cubist design in yellow, blues, and grays. Backed on linen, framed. 43" tall x 33" wide.
$2,500–$2,750

**"Holland-America Line" by A. Zut Huff.** *(Photo by R. Four; courtesy of Bernice Jackson)*

# ART DECO

## Pochoirs and Gouaches

### Fashion Magazine Pochoirs

*General Market Note: Pochoir* prints from French magazines of the era until about 1932, such as *Gazette du Bon Ton, Modes et Manières d'Aujourd'hui, Art, Gout et Beauté, Journal des Dames et des Modes, Falbalas et Fanfreluches, La Guirlande des Mois, Les Idées Nouvelles de la Mode,* and *Les Feuillets d'Art:*

| | |
|---|---:|
| General price range: | $75–$125 |
| Selected designers or well-known artists: | $150–$275 |

*Pochoirs,* from *Très Parisien* magazine, French, 1927–1928. Women's fashions, with hand-applied color. Approx. 8" tall x 6" wide each. Set of 3 in single frame.
$150–$175

*Pochoir,* from *Gazette du Bon Ton* magazine, French, 1920. "Cinderella" gown by Doeuillet, rendered by André Marty. As Cinderella flees the party, one of her shoes falls to the floor. In black, brown, beige, and pink. 8½" tall x 6½" wide, matted and framed.
$200–$250

*Pochoir,* from *Gazette du Bon Ton* magazine, 1921. Print of an "afternoon dress" by Rodier, rendered by Georges Lepape. Lovers embrace in a manner that shows the elegant, long lines of the dress. In grays, blue, and black. Approx. 8½" x 6½", matted.
$250–$275

*Pochoir,* anon. Print of woman's fashion, rendered and signed by "Benito" with hand painting. Approx. 8½" x 6½".
$80 (1987)

### Pochoir-Illustrated Books and Portfolios

*Les Liasons Dangereuses,* book with *pochoirs* by George Barbier, written by Choderlos de Laclos, volumes 1 and 2, Le Vasseur et Cie, Paris, 1934. Number 120 of 650 copies in a limited edition of 720. Both volumes with illustrations by Barbier and with slipcases.
$900–$1,200

*Nijinsky,* illustrated by George Barbier, written by Francis de Miomandre, A La Belle Edition, Paris, 1913. Number 156 of 340 copies in a limited edition of 390. A rare work with 12 *pochoirs* of the dancer.
$1,000–$1,400

Fashion *pochoir* by Georges Lepape. *(From the collection of Pat Kery)*

*Album Dédié A Tamar Karsavina,* illustrated by George Barbier, written by Jean-Louis Vaudoyer, Collections Pierre Corrard, Paris, 1914. Fashion portfolio with 12 *pochoirs.* Number 155 of 500 copies in a limited edition of 512.

**$1,000–$1,400**

*Le Tumulte Noir,* by Paul Colin, Editions d'Art, Paris, c. 1925. Limited edition of 520 copies. Artist's portfolio consisting of 44 *pochoirs.*

**$4,400 (1986)**

*Bleu Blanc Rouge,* illustrated by Paul Iribe, edited by Nicolas, Paris, 1932; *Blanc et Rouge,* 1930, same illustrator and editor in a limited edition of 520 copies; *Rose et Noir,* 1931, same illustrator and editor, in a limited edition of 520 copies. Each with humorous and provocative illustrations of drinkers.

**$660 (1986)**

"*Révillon Frères—Catalogue de Fourrures,*" Ronaldo Louza, illustrator, Draeger, Paris, 1926–1927. Fashion fur catalog with ornate cover and eight lithographs of fur designs.

**$700–$900**

*Constance Dans Les Cieux,* André Marty, illustrator, written by Comte de Bondy, Editions de la Lampe d'Argile, Paris, 1925. Number 113 of 250 copies in a limited edition of 287, with 12 *pochoirs.*

**$400–$450**

## Original Gouaches for Graphic Designs

"*Spiral Le Tuyan,*" by Paul Colin. Gouache on paper depicting an abstract pattern of pipelike spirals, probably executed for a poster design. Signed lower right. 56¾" tall x 37" wide, framed.

$3,800–$4,400

*Original drawings with gouache,* by Madeline Paenizon, French, c. 1913, for designer Paul Poiret. This portfolio of original designs may have been printed later in the *pochoir* method. 12" tall x 10" wide, framed. Each.

$400–$600

*Costume design,* by Zig (Brummer), French, 1930s for Mistinguett. Very colorful with working drawing annotations. Signed. 14" tall x 11" wide.

$150 (1987)

## Magazines—Covers and Graphics

*Ver Sacrum* (Sacred Spring), Viennese, Sept. 1901 (20 pages). Featuring Koloman Moser typography and design layout, one Moser embossing for poem by Arno Holz plus two woodblocks by F. Konig. (Note: *Ver Sacrum* was 9⅝" x 10¼" and was printed on fine laid paper with cotton fiber.)

$950–$1,000

*Ver Sacrum,* May 1, 1901 (12 pages), from the Tenth Exhibition of the Artists of the Secession. Seven photographs showing paintings and sculpture with their room settings.

$225–$250

*Ver Sacrum,* August 15, 1903 (7 pages). Featuring 12 studies from nude figures by Gustav Klimt.

$1,700–$1,750

*Ver Sacrum,* June 15, 1903 (8 pages). Featuring seven original woodcuts and cover design by Leopold Stolba.

$1,200–$1,300

*Posters and Graphics* 363

*Wendingen Magazine*, Dutch, 1922. Special issue on posters with cover illustration by Russian graphic artist and painter El Lissitsky (full issue). (Note: *Wendingen* was a large square magazine, printed on fine paper, and bound with woven thread.)
**$2,500–$3,000**

*Wendingen Magazine*, artist's proof for 1919 cover by Roland Holst. Double-track image, front and back cover on single sheet, each design 13¾" x 13¼".
**$1,000–$1,200**

*The Studio*, English, cover design by E. McKnight Kauffer for July 1929 issue (Vol. 98, No. 436). Modernistic Venus de Milo superimposed on a classic McKnight Kauffer Cubist-influenced bird in flight.
**$200–$300**

*General Market Note:* Prices for French and American magazine covers usually range from $25 to $50, though some are less. Scarcer covers bring $60 to $75, and historic covers or covers by well-known artists can bring as much as $200 or more. These prices do not necessarily include the cost of matting and framing, which dealers may provide.

**Wendingen** magazine. *(Photo by R. Four; courtesy of Bernice Jackson)*

Magazine covers from fashion magazines including *Vogue, Vanity Fair, Harper's Bazaar,* and others, depending on the designer featured, the illustrator, and condition.

| | |
|---|---:|
| Common covers: | **$15–$20** |
| Common but well-designed covers: | **$25–$40** |
| Scarcer covers: | **$50–$150** |

*Cover,* from *Vanity Fair,* by Paolo Garetto, November 1932. Featuring a bold red, white, and black graphic, German swastika forms the body of a very Cubist-faced Hitler.

**$60–$70**

*Cover,* from *Vanity Fair,* by Miguel Covarrubias, February 1932. Featuring Greta Garbo, whose pointed shoulders match her pointed eyebrows.

**$60–$70**

*Cover,* from *Harper's Bazaar,* by Erté, March 1921. Woman lounging at the bottom of the page, raising a hand toward flocks of swallows that spell out the word "Spring," matted. (For other Erté listings see the "Special Focus" section in this chapter.)

**$65–$75**

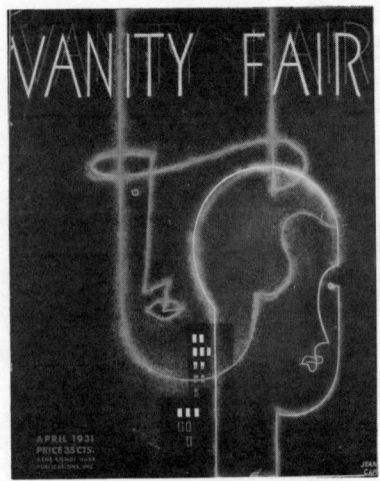

*Vanity Fair* cover by Jean Carlu.
*(From the collection of Pat Kery)*

*Covers*, from *Fortune*, various designers, early 1930s. *Fortune* covers often depict bold designs of machines, industry, and the business world. *Fortune* came in a boxed set, and consequently good covers are easier to find than for many other magazines.
$10–$25

*Covers*, from *Asia*, American, designed by Frank McIntosh, 1924–1930s. McIntosh designs are usually signed "FM" somewhere in the design. The covers of *Asia* are in stunning colors and depict a wide range of Near and Far Eastern cultures in stylized Art Deco designs.
$20–$35

*Advertisements*, from *Vanity Fair*, 1930s. Matted and framed advertisements for:

*Marmon Sixteen automobile*, designed by Walter Dorwin Teague. Ad is elegant Deco styling in silver and black.
$60–$75

*Cadillac's V8, V12, and V16 models*. Good typography and graphics in gold, green, and black.
$60–$75

*Dunlap Hats*. Good design and bold graphics.
$40–$50

*Asia* magazine cover by Frank McIntosh. *(From the collection of Pat Kery)*

*Advertisements,* from *Esquire,* 1930s. Illustrated editorial pages for men's clothing designs, unframed.

$5–$8

*Photographs of Hollywood stars,* from *Vanity Fair,* including such luminaries as Claudette Colbert in full Egyptian-Deco garb on the set of *Cleopatra,* produced by Cecil B. DeMille.

$15–$25

### Special Focus: Louis Icart

Louis Icart (1889–1950) arrived in Paris in 1907, the same year that Picasso's *Demoiselles d'Avignon* set off the Cubist revolution in art. But Picasso and the Cubists had little influence on Icart's romantic style, derived more from the Impressionists than 20th-century Deco or Modern design.

Icart began as an apprentice fashion designer, which allowed him to learn the etching process of the time. Drawn to the female figure, he soon developed his own individual style. Etchings of women became his formula for commercial success.

His chose his women from legends, operas, and the day's entertainers and celebrities. Their elongated figures are exaggerated even further by their lounging positions. Icart's women are also often accompanied by greyhounds or other dogs, and their long furs and high heels show that they were women of some means.

You won't find any harsh zigzags or bold geometric patterns in Icart etchings—or in his book illustrations, other graphics, and paintings, which are also sought after today. Instead, you will find rounded spiral curves and the softer colors of early Art Deco.

Unlike many artists, Icart had a firm grasp on the market, and he produced his works to meet the demand. He first exhibited in the United States in 1922 at John Wanamaker's department store in New York. In 1925 a German, Anton Schutz, who had a decorative arts business called the New York Graphic Art Society, negotiated the exclusive distribution of Icart's work in America. He created the Louis Icart Society, and very soon Icart became the wealthiest artist in France.

At the height of his career, several hundred thousand etchings had been exported to the United States. According to a 1933 catalog, most of these etchings sold for $12 to $15, with some as high as $20.

They were popular during the Depression for their gaiety and color. However, when the war broke out, Icart could not obtain copper for more etchings and turned to oils. After the war, the world and the market had changed, and Icart's etchings had lost their appeal. Though he made a promotional tour of America in 1948, his popularity was over as suddenly as it had begun. When he died in 1950, many of his works could be bought for pennies.

Since the revival of his popularity in the 1960s, prices for his work have risen dramatically, sometimes phenomenally.

His earlier French distributor, L'Estampe Moderne, listed forty-two works in its 1922 catalog. These were printed in editions of three hundred each, and the copper plates were then scratched with an X to prevent further printing. The actual quantity of impressions of later works is harder to establish. The Louis Icart Society reissued many of his most popular designs to meet the demand. Initially, perhaps an edition of three hundred of a work was printed and numbered, but the plates were not destroyed. Also, some copper plates were steel- or nickel-plated to allow for additional printing.

The highest-priced Icart etching, "Leda and the Swan," was created in 1934. His most popular etching called "Vitesse" (Speed) was produced in two different versions. Created originally in 1929, it shows a woman with three greyhounds on leashes, and the gray greyhound leads the pack. Re-etched in 1933, the black dog is in the lead. Thousands of copies of "Vitesse" were sold, and they still command high prices on today's market. "Le Cocktail," also called "Martini," created in 1932, is also popular, with its depiction of animated, expressive dogs sitting at the bar with their mistress.

Many of Icart's works were registered with the U.S. Copyright Office by numerous distributors: F. H. Bresler Company of Milwaukee, L'Estampe Moderne and Gravures Modernes of France, and the Louis Icart Society. The copyright on an Icart etching can usually be found in the top right or left corner. A number of the copyrights were renewed after his death and are still active.

In the listings below a few terms should be explained. Etchings marked "Ep. d'artiste" or "ep. d'Ar" are artist's proofs, and "foxing" means rusting or water marks. Many Icarts were stored disrespectfully in humid cellars after World War II.

## PRICE LISTINGS

### Etchings

*"Basket of Apples,"* by Louis Icart, c. 1926. Etching and drypoint in colors, pencil signed lower right, and annotated "ep'd'Artiste." 16¾" x 12¼", framed.

**$1,000–$2,000**

"Bathers," by Louis Icart, c. 1926. Etching and drypoint in colors, signed in pencil lower right and numbered 131. 24½" x 17".
$1,210 (1987)

"Blue Buddha," by Louis Icart, c. 1926. Etching and drypoint in colors, signed in pencil lower right, numbered 225. 14" x 19½", framed.
$880 (1987)

"Can Can," by Louis Icart, c. 1935. Etching and drypoint in colors of four women doing the can-can. Pencil-signed lower right, with artist's blindstamp. 15½" x 25", framed.
$7,150 (1987)

"Casanova," by Louis Icart, c. 1928. Etching and drypoint in colors, signed in pencil lower right. 21" x 14", framed.
$880 (1987)

"Coursing II," by Louis Icart, c. 1929. Etching and drypoint in colors, of woman in flowing gown playing with three greyhounds, two dark, one light, signed in pencil lower right, numbered 35 21/500 and with artist's blindstamp, framed. 15½" x 26".
$3,300 (1987)
$2,640 (1987)

"The Follies," by Louis Icart, c. 1935. Etching and drypoint in colors, signed lower right, with blindstamp. 25" x 15½", framed.
$3,000–$5,000

"Eve," by Louis Icart, c. 1928. Etching and drypoint in colors, in oval-cut mat, of nude woman outstretched on soft surface, with four apples on the ground. Pencil-signed lower right with artist's blindstamp. 14" x 19½".
$1,540 (1987)
$1,650 (1987)

"Gay Trio," by Louis Icart, c. 1936. Etching and drypoint in colors, of woman sitting at a bar with legs crossed and exposed, with a dark schnauzer sitting on a stool to the right and a lighter-colored one on the bar to the left, sipping from a straw. Signed lower right, with artist's blindstamp. 19½" x 11½", framed.
$3,630 (1987)

"Joy of Life," by Louis Icart, c. 1929. Etching and drypoint in colors. Portrait of a woman with two dogs on windy day, holding her hat on her head to keep it from blowing away. Pencil signed lower right, numbered 417, with artist's blindstamp. 23½" x 15", framed.

$2,310 (1987)
$2,680 (1987)

"*Kittens,*" by Louis Icart, c. 1926. Etching and drypoint in colors, signed in pencil lower right, numbered 69 and with artist's blindstamp. 9½" x 10", framed.

$825 (1987)

"*La Dame aux Camelias,*" by Louis Icart, c. 1927. Etching and drypoint in colors signed in pencil lower right, with artist's blindstamp, framed.

$1,320 (1987)

"*Leda and the Swan,*" by Louis Icart, c. 1934. Etching and drypoint in colors, of nude woman at stream's edge, dangling her feet in the water, with her arms wrapped around a black swan. Signed in pencil lower right, with artist's blindstamp. 21" x 31", framed.

$6,000–$8,000
$3,740 (1986)

"*Love's Blossom,*" by Louis Icart, c. 1937. Etching and drypoint in colors, of reclining woman with wide-brimmed hat and flower in her

"Leda and the Swan" by Louis Icart. *(Photo courtesy of Christie's East)*

hand. Signed in pencil lower right, with artist's blindstamp. 17" x 25", framed.

$2,420 (1987)
$2,860 (1987)

*"Madame Butterfly,"* by Louis Icart, c. 1927. Etching and drypoint in colors, signed in pencil lower right, marked "ep art," with artist's blindstamp, framed. 20" x 13".

$800–$900

*"Martini,"* by Louis Icart, c. 1932. Etching and drypoint in colors, depicting a woman in a bare-back evening gown, sitting on a stool at a bar, legs dangling, sipping on a martini, with a dark schnauzer at her feet and two other dogs sharing a stool next to her. Pencil-signed lower right, with artist's blindstamp. 12½" x 16½", framed.

$3,190 (1987)

*"Modern Eve,"* by Louis Icart, c. 1933. Etching and drypoint in colors, of nude woman sitting with back to viewer, turning her head to one side to put on lipstick. Pencil-signed lower right, with artist's blindstamp. 21" x 16½", framed.

$1,400–$1,800

**"Martini" by Louis Icart.** *(Photo courtesy of Christie's East)*

"Modern Eve" by Louis Icart.
*(Photo courtesy of Christie's East)*

*"Musetta,"* by Louis Icart, c. 1927. Etching and drypoint in colors, signed in pencil lower right, numbered "302," with artist's blindstamp, framed. 20" x 13".

**$700–$900**

*"Orchids,"* by Louis Icart, c. 1937. Etching and drypoint in colors, signed in pencil lower right, inscribed "9 L z," framed. 28" x 19½".

**$2,000–$2,500**

*"Repose,"* by Louis Icart, c. 1933. Etching and drypoint in colors, of nude woman reclining with face partially covered by right arm, pencil-signed lower right, with artist's blindstamp, annotated A/12 (restored). 19" x 45", framed.

**$3,300 (1986)**

*"Shéhérezade,"* by Louis Icart, c. 1927. Etching and drypoint in colors, of woman sitting cross-legged on carpet in Persian desert motif. Pencil-signed lower right, numbered 22, with artist's blindstamp. 13" x 20", framed.

**$2,000–$2,500**

*"Singing Lesson,"* by Louis Icart, c. 1926. Etching and drypoint in colors, pencil-signed lower right, numbered "Ep. d'ar," with artist's blindstamp. 18¼" x 14", framed.

**$880 (1986)**

# ART DECO

*"Sleeping Beauty,"* by Louis Icart, c. 1927. Etching and drypoint in colors, pencil-signed lower right, with artist's blindstamp. 15½" x 19½", framed.
$825 (1986)

*"Smoke,"* by Louis Icart, c. 1926. Etching and drypoint in colors, pencil-signed lower right, numbered "103," with artist's blindstamp, framed. 15" x 20½".
$1,500-$2,000
$1,100 (1986)

*"Sofa,"* by Louis Icart, c. 1937. Etching and drypoint in colors, of woman wearing long gown, lounging in black love seat, signed lower right, with artist's blindstamp. 17" x 25", framed.
$3,960 (1987)

*"Speed,"* by Louis Icart, c. 1929. Etching and drypoint in colors, of three dogs racing off, gray dog in the lead, with woman in flowing gown trying to restrain the last dog. Signed in pencil lower right, numbered "80," with artist's blindstamp (foxing), framed. 15½" x 25".
$1,500-$2,000

*"Speed,"* by Louis Icart, c. 1933. Etching and drypoint in colors of three dogs racing off, black dog in the lead, with woman in flowing gown trying to restrain the last dog. Signed in pencil lower right, numbered "80," with artist's blindstamp (foxing), framed. 15½" x 25".
$2,750 (1987)

*"Thais,"* by Louis Icart, c. 1927. Etching and drypoint in colors, of a reclining woman with two leopards sitting at her feet. Signed in pencil lower right, with blindstamp. 16" x 20", framed.
$1,980 (1986)

*"Under the Apple Tree,"* by Louis Icart. Etching and drypoint in colors, of woman with hat sitting under an apple tree, signed in pencil lower right, numbered 98. 11" x 18½", framed.
$3,190 (1987)

*"Venetian Nights,"* by Louis Icart, c. 1926. Etching and drypoint in colors, of stylized nude woman standing in open doorway with her back to the viewer and a black shawl draped over her arm, looking out over twilight. Pencil-signed lower right, numbered 121. 21" x 13", framed.
$385 (1987)

"Venus," by Louis Icart, c. 1928. Etching and drypoint in colors, pencil-signed lower right, with artist's blindstamp, numbered E76. 14" x 19½", framed.

$935 (1986)

"Youth," by Louis Icart, c. 1930. Etching and drypoint in colors, signed in pencil lower right, numbered "309," with artist's blindstamp (minor foxing), framed. 24" x 15½".

$2,000–$2,500

"Zest," by Louis Icart, c. 1928. Etching and drypoint in colors, of woman and three dogs, appearing to be in motion, signed lower right, with artist's blindstamp. 19" x 14", framed.

$2,860 (1987)

## Oil Paintings, Watercolor, and Bookplates

"Au Péysage" (In the Countryside), by Louis Icart, c. 1940. Oil on canvas, signed lower right, reverse marked "Au Péysage, XII-49, L.I./Paris," framed. 15¼" x 18¼".

$3,000–$5,000

"Lake of Swans," by Louis Icart, c. 1940. Oil on canvas, signed lower right, reverse marked "le lac aux cygnes, XVII-30, L.I.," framed. 12½" x 15½".

$3,000–$5,000

"Golden Girls," by Louis Icart, c. 1920. Oil on canvas, signed lower right. 15¼" x 23", framed.

$4,950 (1987)

"Flowers," by Louis Icart, date unknown. Watercolor and pastel on paper, signed lower right, the reverse with Icart atelier stamp. 37½" x 24", framed.

$2,350 (1987)

Three erotic bookplates, from Gargantua et Pantagruel, by Louis Icart, 1936. Color photogravure illustrations, pencil-signed lower right. Each 7¾" x 5¼". Set of 3.

$500–$600

Two bookplates, from La Vie des Seins, by Louis Icart, 1945. Etching and drypoint in colors, each signed in pencil lower right. Each approx. 10¾" x 8⅜", framed. Pair.

$550–$600
$418 (1987)

## Special Focus: Romain de Tirtoff (Erté)

For many, Erté is the master of the Art Deco style. He was born in Russia, and as of this writing he is still actively designing at 95. Some say "Erté" is a nickname derived from the French pronunication of his real initials, "R.T."

His early gouache fashion designs and renderings in the 1910s and 1920s, when he worked in Paris, were influenced by the Ballets Russes. However, from the very beginning his work was highly individualistic, flamboyant, and whimsical. These early gouaches are valuable today as one-of-a-kind collectibles but often bring no more than a work produced in 1986.

Early in his career he created fanciful costumes for opera stars, millionairesses, and cabaret singers—from Anna Pavolva to Mrs. William Randolph Hearst and Josephine Baker. He designed covers for Condé Nast's *Vogue* until the Hearst publications stole him away in 1915 on a ten-year contract with *Harper's Bazaar*. (See the section on magazines in this chapter.) He designed sets and costumes for the Folies-Bérgères and the Ziegfeld Follies and went to work in Hollywood in 1925, where his style would influence countless productions.

Erté's career hadn't ebbed when the 1960s brought along a resurgence of interest in Art Deco. He was poised and ready to take advantage of it. Barbra Streisand, Liza Minnelli, and other Hollywood stars, many of whom were already collecting Art Deco, began buying his costume and set designs.

The long-lived designer has bridged the gap between the Art Deco of the 1920s and the Art Deco Revival of the 1960s and 1970s.

As many readers know, Erté's costumes, gouaches, lithographs, and serigraphs are popular today in part because the Erté revival was led by Erté himself. He started making serigraphs again in 1974 and is today undoubtedly the most commercially successful artist alive.

As this book was being written, Erté was celebrating his ninety-fifth birthday in New York. He is still creating serigraphs and also objets d'art, luminaires, and sculptures, each published and distributed by a different company. His poster designs for recent shows fetch hundreds of dollars almost the minute they hit the street.

Fine Art Acquisitions, now called Dyansen Corporation, published Erté's first sculpture collection in 1981 and another in 1984. The first piece, called *Victoire,* sold then for $2,400; today it can bring many times that amount. Many of the Erté sculptures on the New York auction market in recent years have fetched prices of $4,000 to $8,000.

Of course, before you buy an Erté sculpture for investment purposes, like any other work of art or antique you must love the piece. However, the company has a "price performance sheet" on the pieces that it has published and buys back pieces from the secondary market to resell in one of their nine gallery locations across the country and in Hawaii.

Can the market for these works continue to broaden enough to support ongoing price increases? Only time will tell. At first each bronze in the collection was published in editions of 250 and more recently in editions of 375. The bronzes themselves are certainly finely executed, appealing to the dramatic imagination many of us share when it comes to fantasy, fashion, and the theater.

Some of them are the three-dimensional representations of designs Erté previously executed as graphics and serigraphs. In addition, his line of art products has broadened and still seems to find its market. (See "Today's Market.")

Erté has worked with fine-art publishers such as Circle Graphics and Chalk & Vermilion to produce many of his serigraphs. Today his serigraphs retail for about $1,200 up to about $10,000. Popular serigraphs include those from special series such as *The Alphabet* (1976–1977), *June Brides* (1979), *The Emotions* (1979), *The Zodiac* (1982), and *Metropolis Suite* (1986).

His objets d'art, including vases, bowls, hand mirrors, and unique table mirror sculptures, are published by Concord Fine Arts and retail for $1,400 up to about $10,000.

In about 1985 Erté started creating a line of luminaires in editions ranging from less than 100 to about 250. These sell today for $900 to $5,000. Erté designs are hand-drawn and hand-etched into clear European lead crystal, in circular, semicircular, and other shapes. They are mounted on electrified bases of lacquered wood, and color filters are used to project an overall light. The hand-etching and sandblasting is executed by Crystal Haze, Inc., a San Francisco company. Many of the luminaire editions have completely sold out, and again some of the designs are previous Erté creations.

As with any successful artist, Erté has his imitators and knock-offs, but the authorized, highly controlled editions produced by his publishers today are issued with certificates of authenticity signed by the publisher. In addition, the bronzes will always carry the stamp of Fine Arts Acquisitions, a copyright number, and the foundry seal for Joe Meisner, or "JM," which uses the expensive lost-wax method of casting and patinates the sculptures in a range of both vivid and subdued colors.

## PRICE LISTINGS

### Serigraphs

*"Angel,"* by Erté (Romain de Tirtoff). Serigraph in colors, pencil signed lower right, numbered. 26¼" x 37½", framed.
**$352 (1986)**

*"The Arctic Sea,"* by Erté, November 1981. Embossed serigraph with foil stamping, of woman standing, arms spread apart with a drape over her arms, the head piece becoming a part of the drape. Pencil-signed lower right, numbered of 300, printed by Mark Rowland Studios, published by Circle Fine Arts, framed.
**$2,310 (1986)**

*"B,"* from *The Alphabet,* by Erté, November 1976. Serigraph in colors, pencil-signed lower right, numbered 213/350. 15¾" x 10½".
**$800–$1,200**

*"Broadway's in Fashion,"* by Erté, June 1978. Embossed serigraph in colors on paper, depicting stylized woman standing, arms spread apart, wearing a cape with the comedy and tragedy masks on either side of cape. Pencil-signed lower right, numbered 183/300 (plus Roman-

"Angel" by Erté. *(Photo courtesy of Christie's East)*

numbered edition of 35), printed by Chicago Serigraph Workshop, published by Circle Fine Arts. 17½" x 13⅛", framed.
$770 (1986)

"*Brown Boot,*" by Erté, September 1974. Serigraph on paper, pencil-signed lower right, inscribed "86/260," printed by Chicago Serigraphs Workshop, published by Circle Fine Arts, 13" x 10".
$352 (1986)

"*C,*" from *The Alphabet,* by Erté, August 1976. Serigraph in colors, signed in pencil lower right, numbered 213/350. 15¾" x 10½"
$605 (1987)

"*Carnations,*" by Erté, 1987. Serigraph in colors with embossing and gold foil hot-stamping, pencil-signed lower right, numbered 100/300, published by Chalk & Vermilion. 19½" x 16½".
$770 (1987)

"*Diva,*" by Erté, 1984. Serigraph on paper, pencil-signed lower right, numbered HC6/300, published by Chalk & Vermilion, 36" x 28", framed.
$2,640 (1986)

"*Enchanted Melody,*" by Erté, 1984. Serigraph in colors with embossing and gold- and silver-foil hot stamping, pencil-signed lower right, numbered LIII/CL, published by Chalk & Vermilion. 42½" x 29¾".
$2,000–$2,250
$1,540 (1986)

"*French Rooster,*" by Erté, April 1980. Serigraph in colors, of stylized woman and rooster. Pencil-signed lower right, numbered 97/300, printed by Chicago Serigraphic Workshop, published by Circle Fine Arts.
$2,310 (1986)

"*Fringe Gown,*" from the *June Brides* suite, Erté, 1986. Serigraph in colors, pencil-signed lower right, numbered HC 16/25, published by Chalk & Vermilion. 33" x 28" framed.
$2,970 (1987)

"*Gemini,*" from *The Zodiac,* by Erté, 1982. Serigraph in colors, signed in pencil lower right, numbered 275/350, published by Tristar Publishing Inc. 19" x 14", framed.
$308 (1987)

"*H*," from *The Alphabet*, Erté, November 1976. Serigraph in colors, pencil-signed lower right, marked "AP." 15¾" x 10½", framed.
$660 (1987)

"*I*," from *The Alphabet*, Erté, December 1976. Serigraph in colors, penciled-signed lower right, numbered 133/350. 15¾" x 10½", framed.
$220 (1987)

"*J*," from *The Alphabet*, Erté, December 1976. Serigraph in colors, pencil-signed lower right, numbered 159/350. 15¾" x 10½".
$495 (1987)

"*Kiss of Fire*," by Erté, from the *Love and Passion Suite*, 1984. Serigraph in colors, of a couple dressed in theatrical plumage, standing face to face with their arms on each other's shoulders, frondlike feathers streaming from their heads and hands. Pencil-signed lower right, numbered LXVII of CLXXV, published by Chalk & Vermilion, 34" x 29", framed.
$2,420 (1986)

"*L*," from *The Alphabet*, by Erté, January 1977. Lithograph and serigraph on paper of woman in leopard-skin outfit with leopard at her feet, forming the letter *L*. Signed in pencil lower right, inscribed 203/350 of 542. (Note: Like several of Erté's designs, this one was recreated as a bronze. See "Bronzes" below.) 10½" x 15¾".
$3,960 (1986)

"*L'Indifference*," by Erté, from *The Emotions*, November 1979. Serigraph in colors, pencil-signed lower right, numbered 51/300, published by Circle Fine Arts. 22¾" x 17⅝", framed.
$1,045 (1987)

"*O*," from *The Alphabet*, by Erté, November 1976. Serigraph in colors, pencil-signed lower right, numbered 159/350. 15¾" x 10½".
$200–$250

"*On the Avenue*," from the *Metropolis Suite*, by Erté, 1986. Serigraph in colors with embossing and gold-foil hot stamping, pencil signed lower right, numbered CXXXX/CL, published by Chalk and Vermilion. 28½" x 22½", framed.
$2,640 (1987)

"L," from *The Alphabet* by Erté. *(Photo courtesy of Christie's East)*

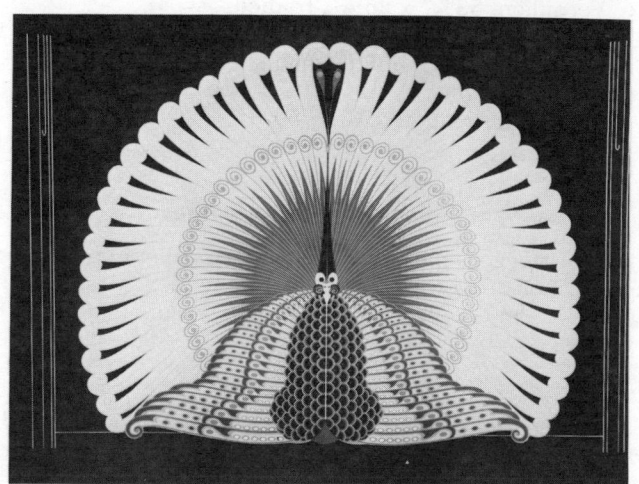

From *Phoenix Suite* by Erté. *(Photo courtesy of Christie's East)*

*Phoenix Suite*, by Erté, 1983. Comprising "Phoenix Reborn" and "Phoenix Triumphant," serigraphs in colors, signed in pencil lower right, numbered 37/300, printed by Chromocorp Inc., published by Chalk & Vermilion. Each 30″ x 40″, framed. Pair.

**$2,090 (1987)**

"R," from *The Alphabet*, by Erté, February 1977. Serigraph in colors, pencil-signed lower right, numbered 159/300, published by Circle Fine Arts. 15¾" x 10½", framed.
$2,420 (1987)

"T," from *The Alphabet*, by Erté, February 1977. Serigraph in colors, pencil-signed lower right, numbered 336/350. 15¾" x 10½".
$880 (1987)

"Top Hats," by Erté, May 1975. Serigraph in colors, of six men standing in line, going backward, with woman in fur in the front of the line and stylized skyscrapers in the background. Pencil-signed lower right, numbered 69/260, printed by Chicago Serigraphic Workshop, published by Circle Fine Arts.
$3,190 (1986)

"Veil Gown," from the *June Brides* suite, by Erté, 1986. Serigraph in colors, pencil-signed lower right, numbered HC 16/25, published by Chalk & Vermilion. 33¾" x 26¼", framed.
$3,300 (1987)

"W," from *The Alphabet*, by Erté, 1976. Serigraph in colors, pencil-signed lower right, numbered 133/350. 15¾" x 10½".
$440 (1987)

## Gouaches and Drawings

"Le Fer," by Erté, gouache and silver paint on paper depicting female warrior in armor dress with sword, pen-signed lower right, stamped "Erte (Romain de Tirtoff), Composition originale," numbered 6714. 14½" x 10¼".
$1,100 (1986)

"L'Or Revue Danseuses," by Erté, 1942. Gouache, pencil and gold paint on paper, of stylized woman in costume with full top skirt and straight lower skirt with slit up right leg. Pen-signed lower right, stamped "by Erte" and "Composition Originale," titled, numbered 6681. 12½" x 9¾", framed.
$1,430 (1986)

"Pipe Dreams," by Erté, c. 1925. Pen and ink on paper, of man smoking a pipe, the smoke of which swirls upward, forming the image of a woman. Signed lower right, stamped on reverse "Erte Romain de Tirtoff, 124 Rue de Bracas, Sevres, no. 1004, II-1925," (3 tears to paper). 11¼" x 9".
$1,650 (1986)

"L'Or Revue Danseuses" by Erté. *(Photo courtesy of Christie's East)*

*"Tabarin, from French Can-Can,"* by Erté, 1939. Costume design for a man, gouache on tan paper, signed lower right, titled on reverse with two stamps, "Erte" and "Composition originale," numbered 470. 13¼" x 9¾".

**$1,200–$1,600**

*Set design,* for *Les Noces du Dauphin,* by Erté. Gouache and gold paint on paper mounted on board, depicting four pages holding standards supporting a canopy against stairway landing, with tall, oval, colored-glass windows, signed lower right, titled and numbered 5512 on verso, stamped "Erte (Romain de Tirtoff), Composition Originale." 7¼" x 10½".

**$3,520 (1986)**

*Set design,* for *Le Jeu de l'Amour et du Hasard,* act 1, scene 5, by Erté. Gouache on paper depicting ornate stage with masked cupid panel flanked by Colombine's vanity and two male characters against curtain of suit designs, pen-signed lower right, titled and numbered 10,987, stamped "Erte (Romain de Tirtoff)" and "Composition Originale." 6¼" x 8".

**$3,520 (1986)**

## Costumes

*"Champagne,"* chorus girl costume, designed by Erté, executed by Vicaire & Madells, Paris, millinery by Covalie. Pink and yellow sequin-embroidered suit trimmed with white ostrich feathers at the bust, the

center having a champagne bottle motif and odd-shaped geometric plastic rhomboids, resembling ice cubes, suspended at the hips; headdress consists of a net cap covered with ostrich feathers and plastic balls representing bubbles of champagne.

$1,000–$1,200

*"Paris by Night: Can-Can Fan,"* designed by Erté. Circular red-ruffles screen with reticulated net-stockinged legs on one side and feathers on the reverse, with mirrored handle. 26″ diameter.

$660 (1986)

## Bronzes

*Figural group, "Amants,"* cast from a model by Erté. In parcel-gilt and patinated bronze, a pair of lovers at play, numbered 26/300 and stamped "Fine Art Acquisitions c, 1980." 19″ high.

$5,280 (1986)

*Figure of an angel, "Angel,"* cast from a model by Erté. In parcel-gilt and patinated bronze, a kneeling angel with hands outstretched in prayer, her wings sweeping out over her streamlined robe, numbered 293/300 and stamped "Fine Arts Acquisitions c, 1984." 13½″ high.

$4,840 (1986)

*Figure of a woman, "Beauty and the Beast,"* cast from a model by Erté. Bronze regal beauty in elaborate headdress, viewed from behind as a black panther emerging from the folds of her dress, patinated in colors, numbered 193/250, and stamped "RKP Int. Corp. c, 1980." 16½″ high.

$7,480 (1986)

*Figure of a woman, "Directoire,"* cast from a model by Erté. Parcel-gilt bronze of a woman posed majestically in a long buttoned-down dress and helmet with large arching plume, numbered 123/350, and stamped "Fine Art Acquisitions c, 1984." 23″ high.

$4,400 (1986)

*Figure of a woman, "Diva,"* cast from a model by Erté. Parcel-gilt and green-patinated figure of woman standing in beaded raiment, the left sleeve designed as a bird with exotic plumage, numbered 198/300, and stamped "Fine Arts Acquisitions c, 1984." 18″ high.

$6,380 (1986)

*Figure, "Firebird,"* cast from a model by Erté. Parcel-gilt bronze of a fantastic birdlike woman, her winged torso supported on the crest of her curved tail plumage, in colored patination, numbered 9/250, and stamped "RKP Int. Corp. c, 1980." 16½" high.

$5,280 (1986)

*Figure of a woman, "In the Evening,"* cast from a model by Erté. Silvered and patinated bronze of a woman posing in a dramatic evening gown with full sleeves, wrapped waist and slim, pleated skirt, numbered 243/300, and stamped "JM-FAA Fine Art Acquisitions c, 1980." 20" high.

$5,720 (1986)

*Figural group, "Kiss of Fire,"* cast from a model by Erté. Parcel-gilt and patinated bronze of a couple dressed in theatrical plumage standing face to face with their arms on each other's shoulders, numbered 79/300, and stamped "Fine Art Acquisitions c, 1984." 21" high.

$5,060 (1986)

*Figural group, "La Femme et la Panthère,"* cast from a model by Erté, based on the serigraph for the letter *L*. Bronze figure of a woman in an exotic animal skin, her pet panther crouched at her feet, numbered 222/250, and stamped "RKP Int. Corp. c, 1980." 15" high.

$9,900 (1986)

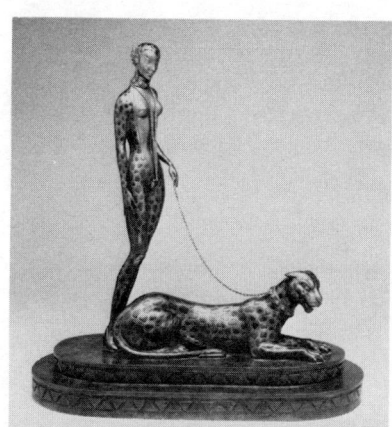

"La Femme et la Panthère" by Erté. *(Photo courtesy of Christie's East)*

*Figure*, *"La Plume,"* cast from a model by by Erté. Parcel-gilt and green-patinated bronze of a kneeling woman with bowed head in a fantastic plumed headdress, stamped "RKP Int. Corp. *c*, 1980," numbered 138/250. 15¼" high.

$5,060 (1986)

*Figure of a woman*, *"Le Soleil,"* cast from a model by Erté. Parcel-gilt bronze, her fantastic curved head piece arching above with strands of beadwork descending behind her, in red and brown patinas, numbered 16/300, and stamped "RKP Int Corp. *c*, 1980." 17½" high.

$8,800 (1986)

# MODERN LIVING

## OCEAN LINER COLLECTIBLES

Today ocean liner memorabilia collectors turn to two different sources for finding items for their collections: attics and specialized dealers in the field. It wasn't so long ago that our parents and grandparents were setting sail on luxurious ocean liners bound for faraway shores. Today, although still popular, ocean liners have to compete with air transport as the favorite mode of vacation travel, especially when people have less time.

The Art Deco era of the 1920s and 1930s was also the heyday of the great luxury *paquebots,* or ocean liners. Many of the French liners were floating museums of the finest in Art Deco design. Perhaps they were inspired by the French or perhaps it was something in the very design of these great vessels, but other nations, too, designed and furnished their liners in the sleek, stylish International Style.

Then again, perhaps it was because the liner companies had to appeal to a sophisticated clientele, a clientele that had already developed a taste for the new design as part of their up-to-date life-style. Later they would have to fulfill tourists' dreams of romance and style as epitomized in Hollywood films.

The opulence and good taste of the *Normandie* decor included French coffee service by Christofle, with circular coffeepots and creamers and semicircular sugar bowls, set on triangular bases. Still considered stylish today, the set was reproduced in a numbered edition by Christofle for Bloomingdale's in silver plate with semicircular ebony handles.

Other French ocean liners that are favorites with Art Deco collectors are the *Ile De France, L'Atlantique,* and *Paris.* Several vessels of the Dutch Holland-America Line, the English Cunard Line, and the German Lloyd Bremen line also have prized Art Deco furnishings and decorative and functional objects.

It would take more than one book to describe the fine antiques and collectibles of the ocean liners. The range of what is collected is phenomenal—the same range as is represented in this book for the entire field of Art Deco: architectural elements, furnishings, silver, glass, ceramics, posters, advertisements, and fashion accessories.

In the chapter "Posters and Graphics," for example, ocean liner memorabilia collectors will find many fine color lithographic posters depicting the liners' sleek forms in even sleeker graphics. In the chapter on "Architecture," you'll find lighting fixtures by Sabino for the *Normandie,* and in "Today's Market," you can read about the sale of wall panels from the same famous liner, sculpted by Jean Fupas and lacquered by Jean Dunand, which were sold for a reported $2 million.

Below is just a sample of treasures from a few of the well-known liners that used Art Deco design extensively.

## Cunard Line

*Tea service,* by Foley Potteries & China Co., English, for the Cunard Line, 1930s. One cube-form teapot, two cube-form hot water pots, one cube-form creamer, one cube-form sugar, three teacups and saucers, two cake plates, three napkin rings, and three cube-form waste dishes, decorated with mustard, gray, and black rings on cream ground, printed firm's and liner's marks. Hot water pot 4" high. Set of 16.
$500–$600

## Europa

*Ashtray,* from *Europa,* Lloyd Bremen Line, German, 1930s. In china, triangular, with ship's full-color portrait in the center.
$65–$75

*Deck plan, Europa,* 1936. Color-coded, in page form.
$45–$50

*Folder,* for *Europa*'s Christmas/New Year's cruise, 1936–1937. Includes photos of interiors/exteriors.
$15–$20

*Menus,* from *Europa.* Each.
$7–$9

*Passenger list,* from *Europa,* first class, 5/28/32.

$15–$20

*Poster, Europa* racing along at sea. Caption on the mat below the ship, "The North German Lloyd Flier 'Europa,' Sister Ship of the 'Bremen,' the two fastest liners afloat." 19" x 13", framed.

$125–$135

## Holland-America Line

*Ashtray,* from Holland-America Line, Dutch, 1930s–1940s. Silver-plated, with house logo raised out in the center.

$35–$40

*Candy dish,* from Holland-America Line. In cream-colored china with house logo and borders in gold.

$25–$35

*Deck of playing cards,* from Holland-America Line, 1930s. In original box, red with full-color house flag.

$45–$50

*Deck plan,* for the *Volendam,* Holland-America Line, June 1936. Photos of interiors/exteriors.

$35–$40

*Passenger list,* from the *Noordam,* Holland-America Line, first and second class.

$15–$20

## Ile de France

*Color postcards,* of the *Ile de France,* French, 1930s. A series of postcards by John Frey that has become well known. Unused. Each.

$15–$20

*Postcards,* of the *Ile de France.* Various interiors and exteriors including photos of the Grand Salon, Dining Salon, Smoking Room, and the deck of the ship. Each.

$8–$10

*Poster,* of the *Ile De France,* by Albert Sebille. In color, showing her leaving New York harbor, over a map of French Line routes. 36" x 25", under glass.

$450–$500

*Silk scarf,* depicting portrait of *Ile de France,* c. 1940. Crest and name surrounded by the company's, and in each corner a French Line sailor and house flag. In tones of greens, reds, and blues on a cream background.

$65–$75

## L'Atlantique

*Booklet,* from *L'Atlantique,* French, 1930s. Color interior/exterior renderings from pre-maiden voyage, 34 pages, foil cover with ship's portrait against tri-color.

$500–$550

*Bronze medallion,* from maiden voyage of *L'Atlantique,* designed by Bazor and executed by the French Mint, 1931. Medallion depicts portrait of the ship on one side and a sea goddess led by four horses on the other.

$350–$400

*News report,* about *L'Atlantique.* Complete copy of *Illustrated London News,* from January 14, 1933, including three-page photo article on destruction of *L'Atlantique,* with 15 photos before and after.

$45–$60

*Magazine feature,* on *L'Atlantique,* from *L'Illustration,* November 1931. Eight pages devoted to *L'Atlantique,* including photos of interiors, exteriors, a deck plan, and full-color interior/exterior renderings.

$50–$60

Bronze medallion from *L'Atlantique. (Photo courtesy of Ken Schultz)*

*Postcard*, of *L'Atlantique*. Depicting lobby of the ship with a car in glass showcase. Printed in the top left corner, "C. De Navigation Sud-Atlantique" and in lower right corner "Paquebot 'L'Atlantique'—Vitrines de la Rue Centrale." Very rare, unused.
$35–$40

*Postcard*, *L'Atlantique* at sea. Printed on top of card "Saint-Nazaire (Loire Inf.)—'L'Atlantique' " and at bottom "Le Novueau grand paquebot de la Compagnie Generale Transatlantique. A.B." Unused.
$35–$40

## La Normandie

*Backgammon/checkers/chess set*, from the *Normandie*, French, 1930s. A large wooden game box with a checker/chessboard on top; closed, 20" x 14" x 5"; opened to form board, 28". Top and bottom of the box board decorated with inlaid woods and a brass plaque with the initials "C.G.T." for Compagnie Generale Transatlantique. Front sides decorated with brass fittings and latches to hold shut. When opened, becomes felt backgammon board. Also included is a set of 2"-diameter checkers, set of chess pieces, plus 2½"-high leather dice cup with "C.G.T." imprinted on it. Three sets of different-size dice inside.
$2,500–$2,750

*Chairs*, designed by Francis Jourdain, for the *Normandie*. Legs clad in metal. 31½" tall. Pair.
$4,000–$6,000

*Champagne cooler*, by Christofle, for the *Normandie*. In silver-plated metal, slightly flaring cylindrical body, the lower portion encircled with horizontal ridged bands, flanked by lug handles with conforming decoration, impressed marks and "Christofle." 8⅛" tall.
$2,420 (1986)

*Champagne goblets*, by Christofle, for the *Normandie*. In silver-plated metal, the shallow bowls raised on cylindrical stems on gently domed and stepped feet, stamped with the "Compagnie Generale Transatlantique" logo. 3⅝" tall. Set of 6.
$330 (1986)

*Deck chair*, from the *Normandie*. Original rust-colored pads, with a 6" house logo on both front and back in cream color, the pad covering entire chair. The chair has been totally restored and recaned. Comes with signed, notarized statement from previous owner stating it was

Backgammon/checkers/chess set from the *Normandie*. (Photo courtesy of Ken Schultz)

purchased at the auction of the ship's contents in 1942. 36" tall x 44" long x 23" wide.

$2,500–$2,750

*Dishes*, by Christofle, for the *Normandie*. In silver-plated metal, concave-center circular dishes, rims stamped with the "Compagnie Generale Transatlantique" logo. 8¾" diameter. Set of 4.

$300–$400

*Games table*, attributed to Jean Dunand, designed for the *Normandie*, c. 1934. Made for the first class lounge, the orange-lacquered wood table with flip top decorated with eggshell-lacquer chessboard. 28" square.

$5,250 (1987)

*Lacquered wall panels*, sculpted by Jean Dupas and lacquered by Jean Dunand, for the *Normandie*. Incredibly beautiful stylized sculpted wall panels, decorated by the master of lacquer. Total of 32 panels, which formed a wall 18' tall x 26' long. (See "Today's Market" for more details.)

$2,000,000 (1984)

*Medallion,* from the maiden voyage of the *Normandie,* designed by Jean Vernon and executed by the French Mint in sterling silver. Very limited edition (possibly only 25). 2½" diameter.

**$1,500–$1,750**

*Book, Normandie,* by Claude Roger-Max. Large illustrations of the *Normandie*'s interior, for Compagnie Generale Transatlantique, Paris, c. 1935.

**$440 (1986)**

*Plates,* by Haviland Limoges, for the *Normandie.* In porcelain, each circular plate with double-gilt ring banding, concave center, the rim with gilt "Compagnie Generale Transatlantique" logo, printed firm's mark. 9" diameter. Set of 5.

**$250–$300**

*Postcard,* of the *Normandie* at the French port of Le Havre, by Hamon. Printed on lower right corner, "Le Paquebot 'Normandie.' Photo Hamon." Unused.

**$15–$20**

*Postcards,* of the *Normandie.* Various interior rooms, including the Grand Saloon, the Grand Hall, the Guignol Theater, and various shops on the ship. On some, back shows where attached to album. Each.

**$15–$20**

*Poster,* of the *Normandie,* by Nascon. Color photographic poster of the *Normandie* leaving New York, in tiered silver-leaf frame with chrome nameplate (name of the ship and company). 33" x 19", framed. Excellent condition.

**$250–$275**

*Salt and pepper shaker and mustard pot,* French, depicting the *Normandie,* c. 1935. In porcelain, in the form of the ocean liner, in red and black on cresting green waves, gilded "Normandie" and stamped "Porcelaine de France." 6¼" long.

**$352 (1986)**

*Sauceboats,* by Christofle, for the *Normandie.* In silver-plated metal, en suite, of oval form with generous pulled lip, on short foot with extended spherical handles, with stamped "Compagnie Generale Transatlantique" logo, impressed firm's marks. 6¼" long. Set of 4.

**$900–$1,100**

*Teapots and hot water pots,* by Christofle, for the *Normandie.* In silver-plated metal, cylindrical form, with strap handles, extending to tubular spouts descending the bodies, each with hinged cover and ball finial, stamped with "Compagnie Generale Transatlantique" logo, impressed worn marks and numerals. Hot water pots 4½" tall. Pair.
$1,000–$1,400

*Tureen and cover,* by Christofle, for the *Normandie.* In silver-plated metal, the circular bowl flanked by rectangular extensions bisecting ball handles, dome cover with half-ring central handle, bowl and cover stamped with "Compagnie Generale Transatlantique" logo. 6⅝" diameter.
$600–$700

*Vegetable servers,* by Christofle, for the *Normandie.* In silver-plated metal, each circular bowl with narrow rim flanked by scalloped lug handles, on stepped foot, stamped with the "Compagnie Generale Transatlantique" logo. 5⅞" diameter Pair.
$400–$500

*Wine bucket,* by Christofle, for the *Normandie.* In silver-plated metal, of slightly flaring cylindrical form, flanked by spherical handles half-bisected by rectangular extensions, the rim encircled by single incised ring, stamped with the "Compagnie Generale Transatlantique" logo, impressed "Christofle 3 0." 8¼" tall.
$2,400–$2,800

## Paris

*Ashtray,* from the *Paris,* French, 1930s. Cut crystal, in the style of Lalique. Frosted in the center, with the ship's three funnels and the French Line name. 5" x 1¼" tall.
$250–$275

*Booklet, Paris,* April 1937. Photos of interiors/exteriors, 16 pages.
$75–$85

*Cigarette case,* from the *Paris.* Portrait of the ship enameled on the entire front. 3½" x 3".
$125–$135

*Deck plan,* from the *Paris.* Color-coded, for West Indies cruises of 1938. Stylized graphic Art Deco cover.
$65–$75

Cigarette case from the *Paris*.
(*Photo courtesy of Ken Schultz*)

*Folder*, from the *Paris*. Depicting first class interiors and exteriors with a dazzling color cover.

**$75–$85**

*Postcards*, of the *Paris*. Showing various rooms, including the dance floor, the grand staircase entrance to the smoking room, the dining salon, the playroom, the promenade deck, and other exteriors. Each.

**$10–$12**

## WORLD'S FAIR SOUVENIRS

Souvenir collecting in general encompasses both quality and kitsch. There are people who collect five-and-dime Art Deco ceramic souvenirs and those who collect finely sculpted bronze medallions from famous expositions and fairs.

World's fair collecting is a field unto itself, with its own publications, clubs, and networks of collectors. Historically unique, each world's fair seems to have something to offer to collectors that none other has. For the Art Deco/Art Moderne buff, the most popular are the 1933 Chicago "Century of Progress" and the 1939 New York World's Fair, "The World of Tomorrow." In addition, the Dallas, Texas, Centenary Exposition of 1936 and the Golden Gate International Exposition, held in San Francisco in 1939, also produced some outstanding Art Deco design.

These souvenirs are double collectibles—both for their history and in many cases for their design quality.

The Chicago "Century of Progress," held in 1933 at the height of the Depression, was intended to be an uplifting fair, one that would set America back on track.

It was a showcase for modern materials, modes of transportation, and glimpses of what the future looked like in 1933. Though the effort had to be scaled down from its original plans due to economic constraints, the fair was popular enough to attract over 35 million visitors! (You can just imagine how many souvenirs that means, even though people did not have a lot of money to spend.)

Many notable architects and designers who have been mentioned in other sections of this book worked on the fair, including Joseph Urban, Lee Lawrie, and Raymond Hood.

The 1939 New York World's Fair, entitled "The World of Tomorrow," was even more optimistic, given that it was presented just before World War II. The vision of a technological future was even more evident at this fair. Much of the design of the fair itself and of its souvenirs is in the Modern style.

Some incredible exhibits captivated the thoughts of Americans, such as the spacious automated freeways of the General Motors "Futurama" exhibit, designed by Norman Bel Geddes. Other stunning examples of modern exhibition architecture were created by Walter Dorwin Teague, who designed Consolidated Edison's "City of Light," Ford's "Road of Tomorrow," and the giant National Cash Register.

It is estimated that there were over 25,000 different souvenirs produced for the 1939 World's Fair, some of them authorized, some not. The vast majority of them, including photographs, postcards, ashtrays, spoons, matchboxes, and so much more, can be collected for $10 to $100.

The proliferation of these souvenirs in the millions is considered by some to signal the end of Art Deco. As the style became popularized to the masses, it lost its appeal with the artists who were creating it. Nevertheless, the souvenirs of this great fair have captured the imagination of many avid collectors.

## PRICE LISTINGS

### 1933 Century of Progress

*Bookends*, from 1933 Century of Progress, Chicago. Chrome greyhounds on marble base, with Century of Progress seal in metal affixed on base, excellent condition. 6" tall. Pair.

$375–$475

**World's Fair souvenirs.** *(Photo courtesy of Ken Schultz)*

*"Child in Outhouse,"* souvenir from 1933 Century of Progress. Wooden outhouse with child inside. Approx. 8" tall.

$65–$75

*Glasses,* from 1933 Century of Progress. Blue and white logo on side. Approx. 5" tall. Set of 6.

$200–$225

*Playing cards,* from 1933 Century of Progress. Two-pack, depicting Art Deco graphic rendering of Walgreen's Drug Store in monochrome green ink. One deck still in plastic wrapper with tax stamp.

$35–$45

*Refrigerator water bottle,* souvenir of 1933 Century of Progress. Depicts the skyline of the fair with horizontal ribbing and screw-on cap. Approx. 6" tall.

$12–$15

*Vases,* from 1933 Century of Progress. In ceramic with brown and orange design. Approx. 4" tall.

$45–$50

## 1939 New York World's Fair

*Alarm clock*, from 1939 New York World's Fair, "The World of Tomorrow." Blue and white face with the Trylon and Perisphere, the fair's logo. Approx. 4" tall.

$250–$225

*Board game*, depicting the site of 1939 World's Fair in color, including Trylon and Perisphere. Box 12" x 8".

$100–$125

*Bowl*, from 1939 World's Fair. In ceramic with Trylon and Perisphere logo in bottom of the dish, maroon and brown pattern along the rim. Approx. 10" diameter.

$50–$60

*Cup and saucer*, from 1939 World's Fair. Orange and blue ceramic set, decorated with the Trylon and Perisphere logo.

$65–$70

*Drink stirrers*, from 1939 World's Fair. In blue, green, and red glass, all with the Trylon and Perisphere logo on the side. Boxed set of 12.

$100–$125

*Fan*, from 1939 World's Fair. Designed with thumb hole, depicting scenes from the fair, multicolored, with the Trylon and Perisphere logo. Approx. 8" x 10".

$65–$75

*Flatware set*, from 1939 World's Fair. Service for eight, 56-piece set, plus one service piece, in silver plate. Each handle marked "1939 World's Fair" vertically and has the Trylon and Perisphere.

$715 (1987)

*Game*, from 1939 World's Fair. Multicolor front. 8" x 6".

$65–$75

*Guide book*, from 1939 World's Fair. Orange cover with gold lettering, the Trylon and Perisphere logo on front. Approx. 10" long x 5" wide.

$35–$45

*Pitcher and set of glasses*, from 1939 World's Fair. In frosted orange glass, with blue Trylon and Perisphere logo. Pitcher approx. 10" tall, three glasses approx. 4" tall. Set of 4.

$500–$525

*Plate*, from 1939 World's Fair. In ceramic, blue and orange, decorated with the Trylon and Perisphere logo. Approx. 6" diameter.

$45–$50

# CHROME AND OTHER METALS

To many collectors, what is most "Deco" about Deco is reflected (pardon the pun) in chrome. World War I weapons research perfected the technique of chromium plating, and as early as the 1920s chrome was being used with brass and other metals for furnishings and decorations, some of them quite elegant. By the 1930s almost any household item you can think of was available in shiny chrome with colorful ivory or black Bakelite plastic handles.

People in the Depression could not afford silver for their dining rooms and homes. Chrome, brass, and copper were solutions for filling the gap. The spring of 1930 saw many manufacturers introducing lines of household items in chrome. The most successful manufacturer was the Chase Brass & Copper Company of Waterbury, Connecticut, which had been founded in 1876.

Primarily an industrial manufacturer of pipes, wires, and tubing, Chase branched out into the domestic field in the 1920s, and in 1930 the company started introducing a voluminous range of household products. Chase produced chromium housewares from the beginning of the 1930s until 1941 when the metal was no longer available for civilian production. Department stores everywhere were suddenly filled with displays of Chase Chrome.

Cocktail shakers, ashtrays, serving utensils, breakfast sets, serving trays, lamps, cigarette boxes, and other accoutrements used mainly to impress dinner guests were widely distributed. Many of these items originally sold for less than a dollar according to the original Chase Chrome catalog for 1936–1937. Today they bring $25, $50, and even $500, especially if the designer is well known. Chase also offered many of the same designs and similar items in brass and copper, as did other companies.

The new chrome brought the shiny status of silver to the average American home at a much lower price. The illusion would not have been complete without the commissioning of the foremost designers of the day to produce the work: Lurelle Guild, Walter von Nessen (1889–1943), Gilbert Rohde (1894–1944), Russel Wright (1904–1976), and Rockwell Kent. Many other designers, anonymous behind the Chase mark, also made contributions.

To maintain the illusion of high style, Chase named its designs accordingly: "Diplomat," "Cosmopolitan," and other evocative names.

Lurelle Guild designed a "smart-looking canape plate" with an inset for a glass and a winglike half-circle handle. According to the 1936–1937 Chase catalog, it allowed one to "hold a cocktail, a canape and a cigarette in one hand and shake hands with the other."

Rockwell Kent, better known for his graphic designs, designed a metal plaque for a wine cooler depicting Bacchus.

Russel Wright designed a seven-inch-diameter ice bowl and tongs, with the handle of the bowl curving crescent-shaped over the bowl to become a holder for the tongs.

Von Nessen's contributions to the Chase line are highly sought after today and include the "Diplomat" tea service. This is the most sought after piece in the chrome collecting field. With its elongated, fluted styling and side pouring handles, it was one of the most popular Chase items and was in production from the 1920s through the mid-1930s. He also designed the "Lazy Boy" and "Stratosphere" smoker stands, service dishes, cheese knives, cake trowels, trays, and more. The handles and trim on these articles were often Bakelite or "ivory composition," a plastic often called ivorene but without any real powdered ivory.

The "Stratosphere," a large ball 5¾ inches in diameter mounted on a fluted, tubular post, stood twenty-six inches high. The top half of the ball swings down in any direction and closes to hide cigarette ashes. The "Lazy Boy" smoker's stand had a compartment for cigars, pipes, or what have you under the pivoting top, which has a fourteen-inch diameter. Standing twenty-two inches high, it was promoted as a "manly" piece for the office and was available in an English bronze finish, a combination of black and satin nickel, or chromium with a red or black top.

Revere Brass and Copper Company entered the chrome housewares market in 1935 with seventeen designs by Norman Bel Geddes (1893–1958). Bel Geddes's design talents had already been apparent in furniture, graphics, and more. He was a household name after he designed the General Motors "Futurama" exhibit at the 1939 World's Fair. Many of Bel Geddes's contributions to the world of chrome were used for the consumption of alcohol—trays, ice buckets, cocktail shakers, and more. By 1935 the cocktail hour had become an American institution.

Revere also had evocative names, such as "Manhattan" for its now-famous skyscraper cocktail shaker. It had a "Normandie" water pitcher and other pieces called "Penthouse," "Empire," "Aristocrat," and "Tuxedo." Revere's line of copper-bottom saucepans with streamlined Bakelite handles was introduced in this era and can still be found in many department stores today.

The Farberware Company had started creating chromium-plated serving pieces as early as 1926. Farberware decorated its candy dishes, snack trays, and other entertaining pieces with Catalin trims. Catalin was yet another machine-age plastic of semitransparent composition. Catalin was more decorative than Bakelite because of its translucency and could be made to look something like tortoiseshell. Collectors today prize their finds of Farber wine and cordial sets, which were made of chromium combined with amber or amethyst Cambridge glass.

Michigan's Howell Chrome Company was another manufacturer who created "Thirties Modern" chrome. Manning Bowman and Company, also known for its Deco-style mantel clocks and other furnishings, produced chrome tea sets that sometimes bring higher prices than those by Chase. In the late 1920s they produced a type of chromium plate that was trademarked as Aranium. Their catalog for 1934 coincided with the end of Prohibition and featuered a liquor service called "The Repealer." Manning Bowman's Craftware was a complete line of streamlined pieces.

Today all chrome items are hot collectibles on the antiques and flea market circuit, and they have also found their way into New York auction houses. Actually, on the East Coast, Chase Chrome began to really take off in about 1980, and there has been some leveling of prices since then.

You can still find pieces of Chase Chrome at flea markets, but you are more likely to find Farberware. However, avid collectors will pay top dollar for a missing piece to complete their collection or to acquire a chrome piece by a noted designer. The resurgence of interest in chrome was due in part to the reprinting in 1978 of the Chase Chrome catalog for 1936–1937.

Aluminum was used for many everyday objects starting in the early 1930s, but unlike chrome, aluminum did not have the appearance of silver. What accounted for the popularity of chrome perhaps more than anything else was the illusion of elegance that it maintained.

Aluminum, though lightweight, durable, and inexpensive, was better suited to industrial production. Toward the end of the 1930s and into the 1940s, when almost all metal was going to the war effort, chromium-plated housewares finally gave way to aluminum, but many of these wares lacked real style or innovative design sense. One of the biggest makers of aluminum home products was West Bend Aluminum.

One popular theme in chrome and aluminum, used by West Bend and others, is the penguin. Why penguins? Your guess is as good as ours. They aren't exactly sleek borzois or gazelles.

Here is Art Deco transformed by the American life-style and sense of humor. Maybe the penguin was poking fun at the image of a tuxedoed gentleman out on the town. In any case, it made its appearance on chrome and aluminum household items and furnishings of the 1930s and 1940s. Ungainly on land, perhaps it was the penguin's streamlined shape and speed in the water that made it so popular for cocktail shakers and as decoration on other items. (See the photo in our color section, "An Art Deco Portfolio.")

The Streamline shape of the zeppelin, a modern flying miracle, was inspiration for some items, including a German cocktail shaker. The listing below gives more details. We think it is the most elaborate piece of chromium we've heard of yet.

Because chrome pieces were so numerous, it is never really necessary to settle for "second best" when collecting them. Make sure that the piece you are buying has its plating intact, especially if you intend to actually use it. Look also for cracks and chips in the Bakelite, Catalin, and glass trims and handles.

While some collectors feel that rechroming the pieces is fine, others feel that an original design should never be touched, no matter what the condition. In addition, we should add that the prices on chrome we have seen vary widely, although certain well-known pieces do have going market rates. This is the kind of collectible you can still find at a flea market or garage sale at real bargain prices or at prices you can bargain down.

It is difficult, if not impossible, to identify the designer of a piece, as more often than not they were unsigned. However, the manufacturer's mark is almost always clearly stamped on the piece, which may also carry a patent number.

You can spend the time researching in a patent library, as some have done. Unfortunately, sometimes the only other resource for identifying chrome pieces are the manufacturers' catalogs and advertisements in publications of the day, and these are difficult and time-consuming to locate. The best rule of thumb is: Don't pay more than you can afford, no matter who the designer is claimed to be.

Caring for chrome is easy. In fact, that was one of its strongest selling points in its heyday. Just use some mild soap and water and a soft drying cloth, and it looks as if you've been polishing silver all day. Displayed on a blue-glass mirror tray, it still has the look of elegant silver service and, as in the 1930s, for a fraction of the cost.

## PRICE LISTINGS

### Chase Brass & Copper Company

*Bagel holder,* by Chase Brass & Copper Co., American, 1920s–1930s. In copper, formed by the silhouette of a laughing waiter lifting a circular platter with central spike, on oval platform, impressed "Chase." 16¾" tall.

$198 (1986)

*Bookends,* by Chase. In brass and Bakelite, each formed as a soldier standing with arms akimbo, next to a brass ball, impressed "Chase." 7¼" tall. Pair.
$242 (1986)
$400–500

*Candlesticks,* by Chase. In chrome, each of U-form on circular base, the two candle nozzles with broad rims at graduated heights, unmarked. 10" tall (pair).
$121 (1986)

*Candy dish,* by Chase. In chrome, with black Bakelite handles and finial and glass liner. Stamped "Chase Chrome." 6" diameter.
$20–$25

*Candy dish,* by Chase, c. 1935. Two chrome dishes joined in center with chrome knob and chrome circular handle. 4" high.
$75–$128

*Cocktail shaker,* by Chase. Cylindrical, with bands of black enamel and chrome and Bakelite knop, stamped with patent numbers and "Chase." 11½" tall.
$45–$65

*Cocktail shaker set,* by Chase. In chrome, comprising a cylindrical shaker, six matching cocktails, each on purple Bakelite foot, on a curved rectangular two-handled tray, unmarked (8).
$110 (1986)

*Coffee service,* "Diplomat" style, by Walter von Nessen for Chase. Coffee server, creamer, and sugar in elongated, fluted styling with black Bakelite side-pouring handles. Stamped "Chase." Coffee server 12" tall.
$500–$550

*Lamp,* by Chase. Spherical copper body with conical copper shade, brass ball finial, impressed "Chase." 8½" tall.
$121 (1986)

*Powder box,* by Chase, c. 1937. In chrome with glass lining, chrome lid with etched flower outline, green Bakelite knob handle.
$50–$85

*Server,* by Chase. In chrome, wood, and glass, circular with wooden handles and turned wooden feet holding three cylindrical Pyrex bowls, each with stepped chrome cover and wood finial, impressed "Chase."

**Cocktail shaker set by Chase.** *(Photo courtesy of Christie's East)*

**"Diplomat" coffee service by Walter von Nessen for Chase.** *(Photo by R. Four; courtesy of Arts & Interiors)*

Patent No. 94568, with electrical cord and original instructions for use. 8″ tall.

$150–$200

*Table lamp*, by Chase. In brass, the swinging spherical body surrounded by fluted arms joining neck to circular foot, impressed "Chase." The body 8½″ tall.

$100–$150

## Other Manufacturers

*Candlestick*, by Farber Brothers, American, 1920s. The chrome holders stepped down from center, holding five and three candles. 12½″ and 10½″ tall. Pair.

$115–$145

*Figural candy dish*, by Farber Brothers, c. 1920. Chrome figure of nude woman holding dish above her head for candy. 7″ tall.

$75–$125

*Cocktail server*, by Farberware (Farber Brothers), American, 1930s. In chrome with brown Bakelite handle, finial, and screw-on/off spout cover. Marked "Farber Bros." 12″ tall.

$20–$25

*Cocktail serving set*, by Farberware. Chrome server has wooden handle, finial, and screw-on/off spout cover. With six wine/cordial cups in chrome. Marked "Farberware, Brooklyn, NY." Server 9″ tall; cups 3″ tall. Set.

$65–$80

*Cocktail serving set*, by Farberware. Chrome server has brown Bakelite handle, finial, and screw-on/off spout cover. With six wine/cordial cups in chrome. Marked "Farber Brothers" and "Krome Kraf." Server 13″ tall; cups 5″ tall. Set.

$80–$100

*Coffee service*, by Manning Bowman, American, 1930s. In chrome with a squared design. Four pieces: coffee server, creamer, sugar, and tray. Brown Bakelite handles, bases, and spout cover. Stamped "Manning Bowman." Server 10″ tall.

$500–$550

*Thermos pitcher/trophy*, "HotaKold," by Manning Bowman, 1930s. Chrome in sleek design with wood-handled cork stopper, streamlined handle, and glass lining. With 1″-diameter bronze medal on front reading "Annisquam Yacht Club" and etched "Squam Day, August, 1935." Stamped "HotaKold" and "Manning Bowman." 12" tall.

$30–$35

*Coffee set*, by Manning Bowman. In chrome with green Bakelite handles and finials, with dramatic angles. Includes tray, 18" long x 7¾" deep; sugar and creamer, 6" tall x 6" wide; and coffeepot, 11" tall x 7¼" wide.

$350–$450

*Penguin cocktail shaker*, by Napier, American, c. 1933. In chrome, shaped like a penguin whose beak opens to rubber stopper and pourer. Marked "Napier." Pat D-101559. 12½" tall. (For illustration see color insert.)

$250–$300

*Cocktail shaker*, "Skyscraper" style, by Norman Bel Geddes for Revere Brass and Copper Co., American, 1930s. Stamped "Revere." Tall, straight design with stepped-back motif on screw-off lid. 14" tall.

$175–$200

**Coffee set by Manning Bowman.** *(Photo courtesy of Peter Boehm, Dualities Gallery)*

*Cocktail shaker*, by Revere Brass and Copper Co., 1930s. Chrome cocktail shaker with long, bright yellow Bakelite finial and spout cover. Semicircular handle, rounded lid, and spout. Stamped "Revere." 14" tall.

$100–$125

*Cigarette lighter*, by Ronson, American, 1930s. In chrome with black-enameled geometric design. Inscribed "H.H." In working condition. 4" long.

$25–$35

*Lighter and cigarette dispenser*, by Ronson, 1930s. Designed in enameled chrome as a Negro bartender shaking cocktails behind a streamlined bar. 6" long. (Missing pieces.)

$440 (1987)

*Hot and cold food server*, "Penguin" style, by West Bend Aluminum, American, late 1930s–1940s. Penguins circle the entire perimeter of this circular server with glass liner and wooden stepped-design handles. Stamped "West Bend Aluminum." 8½" diameter.

$65–$90

*Penguin cocktail shaker*, unsigned, American, 1930s. In chrome, in the shape of a penguin, part of a set with six chrome glasses and tray. (This penguin looks almost identical to Napier's, except that the beak/pourer system is different enough for a new patent.) 11½" high. Set.

$350–$500

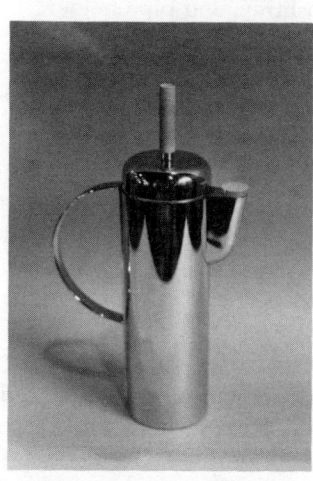

Cocktail shaker by Revere. *(Photo by R. Four; courtesy of Arts & Interiors)*

## ART DECO

*Zeppelin cocktail shaker,* anon., German, c. 1928. Taking its inspiration from the great dirigibles of the era, this cocktail shaker is shaped like the *Graf Zeppelin,* standing on four short rear wings. It contains five spoons in the gondola, corkscrew in the tail, and houses five small cups, funnel, strainer, and storage canister within the body. 12½" tall. Also a miniature version 6" tall.

$700–$900

*Creamer and sugar,* anon., English, 1930s. In chrome with white Bakelite side-pouring handle on creamer and white Bakelite feet. Marked "PBB" and "Made in England." 4½" tall. Set.

$15–$20

*Desk lamp,* anon., probably American. In chrome that has been painted brown. Design of base is stepped-back with insert for holding paper clips or pen nibs. Flexible arm. 14" tall.

$65–$80

*Pie rack,* anon., 1930s. Chrome plated, for commercial diner. 8½" tall.

$50–$75

*Picture frames,* anon. In chrome with silver borders and painted black lines. 8" x 12".

$25–$35

*Smoke stand,* anon., American, mid-1930s. In chrome and pink onyx with built-in interior lights, top and bottom, and cigarette case, lighter, ashtray, and pipe holder.

$225–$275

*Smoke stand,* anon., c. 1930s. Black and chrome, three column legs, circular base, top with sliding doors for storing smoking supplies. 22" high.

$125–$175

*Standing ashtray,* anon., 1930s. Chrome base and table, with black stand. 22" high.

$95–$150

*Teapot,* anon., American, 1930s. In chrome, dome shaped, with incised skyscraper motif on side, red metal handle, and red Bakelite whistling tea plug. 6" high.

$45–$75

## BAKELITE

Celluloid is the oldest of all plastics, first produced about 1870, but Bakelite is the grandfather of modern plastics. According to some sources, it was synthesized as early as 1907 by Belgium's Leo Baeckland. A durable new plastic that was easily molded, Bakelite soon became a popular material for fabricating cheap kitchen clocks, radios, candleholders, and numerous other everyday objects. During the Depression, Bakelite brought inexpensive color into many dull lives.

Celluloid was used into the 1920s for household items. Bakelite, actually a trade name, is used by many to refer to all of the brightly colored, durable plastic of the day. Although many feel that a distinction should be made between Bakelite and other kinds of plastic, it may be a long time before it becomes a practice. Like the vague name "Art Deco," "Bakelite" seems destined to be applied to all objects of the era produced in plastic.

Bakelite radios are collectible both as radios and as plastic design. Bakelite jewelry was and is a highly colorful and popular fashion accessory. (See "Silver, Jewelry, and Fashion" for more information on Bakelite jewelry.) Many other household and novelty items were produced in the new industrial plastics of the day, and many of them are still accessible to beginning collectors.

Today it is radio collectors who are most discriminating when it comes to distinguishing Bakelite and another durable plastic called Catalin. Many so-called Bakelite radios are actually made from Catalin. In high-end markets, Catalin radios bring higher prices than those in Bakelite. Some bring thousands of dollars and have been featured in exhibitions, auctions, and magazines.

Another plastic, with the trade name Plasticon, was also used for radios, which were produced in pastel shades of green, lavender, and yellow, as well as bright red. Earlier than Catalin radios, they are very rare and are commanding unbelievable prices. For example, four Air King Plasticon radios in the Skyscraper motif, designed by Harold L. Van Doren in red, lime green, lavender, and marbled gray, reportedly sold as a set of four for $75,000!

Bakelite and Catalin radios were produced by numerous companies of the day including Bendix, Kadette, RCA Victor, Air King, Fada, De-Wald, and Addison. Catalin cases were made in lead molds that had to set for several days to harden. The molds could be used only once, which added to the cost of production and accounts for their scarcity today. Bakelite radios are much more common than those in Catalin.

Bakelite was generally a plainer plastic, and radios in Bakelite tend to be solid brown, black, or green. Catalin radios were produced in a wide array of crazy colors and color combinations: primary colors of red, yellow, and blue as well as "designer" colors like orange, mustard, purple, and honey. The combinations of these colors would very often be considered less than tasteful today.

Many Catalin radios have a "marbleized" look of swirled colors in the plastic. Two or more different colors of Catalin would be molded together to achieve this effect, and it is one way of distinguishing Catalin from Bakelite. In addition, Catalin tends to be translucent, whereas Bakelite is heavier and usually totally opaque. The differences between Bakelite and Catalin become fairly obvious to the sophisticated collector, but the best way to learn the difference is to go out and look at lots of radios.

Plastic radios were a popular item at the time, as cassette players are today. They sold for as little as $11.95 and were bought for every room in the house: the modern kitchen, den, playroom, and children's rooms.

Radio designs varied widely, even though many look alike. Some have handles, some were designed like mini-skyscrapers, and still others have rounded sides or interesting bases. The treatment of the grillwork that covered cloth speakers on the faces of the radios is reminiscent of car radiators, with vertical or horizontal bands of plastic. Knobs, dials, and numbers were all stylized. The zigzag or bolt of electricity was a common motif.

Before plastic radios stole the scene, most home radio sets were contained in fairly traditional wood furniture. At first there was a real need for the considerable size of the radios, as the technology had not advanced to a point where the radio components could be held in anything resembling a "portable." Yet even after the components had shrunk, the cabinets continued to be manufactured in wood because it looked better in the home. In other areas of design as well, the Modern age was somewhat hidden behind traditional facades. As technological advances became more acceptable, the machine became a national symbol, and technology was beautiful enough to show itself.

Designers for Bakelite and Catalin radios are difficult to identify. It is usually the company name that is on the radio dial or the case, and the radio may carry a patent number. Look for radios in working order and with plastic in good condition. Exposure to sunlight can shrink or crack the plastic and fade the color.

Other Bakelite items have not reached the prices of radios but are still plentiful and can sometimes be found at flea markets and garage sales for only a few dollars. Items such as salt and pepper shakers, napkin rings, and ashtrays are popular collectibles.

One of the most popular and novel Bakelite creations are crib toys. These colorful, clever little people and animals made of separate parts threaded with elastic hung over many a crib in the 1920s and 1930s and are quite valuable today.

## Modern Living

Caring for your Bakelite is not difficult, but some common polishes and household cleaners will eat through the plastic or dull it, so be careful. There are plastic polishes available to give the plastic back some of its sheen as well.

In the listings below, where the source has been identified as Catalin instead of Bakelite, we have included it in the listing. Some of the radios listed may be sold as Bakelite but may in fact be made of the other plastics.

## PRICE LISTINGS

### Bakelite and Catalin Radios

*Catalin radio,* by Addison. Cathedral shape in green marbleized ground enclosing rectangular dial above fabric-covered speaker. Amber Catalin grillwork, marked. 9" tall.

$880 (1986)

*Catalin radio,* by Addison. Purple case, with mustard-colored speaker grill and base treatment. Marked "Addison" in stylized letters below frequency dial. Approx. 10" long.

$700–$800

*Bakelite radio,* by Bendix. In green case, black speaker grill and green knobs. Marked "Bendix Aviation Corporation" on frequency indicator. Rectangular, bulky. Approx. 12" long.

$900–$1,000

**Bakelite radios.** *(Photo courtesy of Christie's East)*

*Bakelite radio,* by DeWald. Brown case with yellow knobs and speaker grill. "DeWald" marked on both case and frequency indicator. Rectangular. Approx. 11″ long.

$1,150–$1,250

*Bakelite radio,* by DeWald. Rectangular with stepped top, horizontal dial above horizontal grill over two knobs, in allover swirled amber color. 6⅝″ tall.

$220 (1987)

*Bakelite radio,* by Emerson. Amber-colored, rectangular case enclosing circular dial at right and opposing cream-and-black grillwork at left, with black Bakelite handle. Marked. 9″ tall.

$495 (1986)

*Bakelite radio,* by Emerson. Rectangular, in swirled brown Bakelite with cream Bakelite latticework grill over the speaker and enclosing circular Lucite dial, over two circular knobs. 8¾″ x 11″ x 6¼″.

$660 (1986)

*Bakelite radio,* by Fada. Rectangular, amber-colored case with square dial on left over two knobs, green grillwork. "Fada" decal. 5¼″ tall.

$550 (1986)

*Bakelite radio,* by Fada. Blue/green, rectangular case with canted corners, centering rectangular inset speaker at left and dial at right. Two ivorene knobs and woven handle. Model 711, marked. 7¾″ tall.

$495 (1986)

*Bakelite radio,* by Fada. Ivorene oval case enclosing black circular dial on right. Model 845, marked. 6″ tall.

$330 (1986)

*Bakelite radio,* by Fada. Amber-colored, in bullet form with dial enclosed on rounded end. Model 1000, marked. 7″ tall.

$770 (1986)

*Catalin radio,* by Fada. Honey-colored case with red knobs. Rectangular. Approx. 10″ long.

$750–$900

*Catalin radio,* by Kadette. Beige and purple case with gray knobs. Rectangular. Approx. 11″ long.

$475–$500

*Bakelite radio,* by Philips. Rounded rectangular form in brown swirled Bakelite, with stepped Lucite dial, two circular knobs. 7¼" x 10¼" x 5½".

$330 (1986)

*Bakelite radio,* by Radiola. Rectangular with fluted body in dark burgundy, with zigzag Lucite grillwork over the speaker, above Lucite dial flanked by two circular knobs. 6" x 9" x 4½".

$880 (1986)

*Bakelite radio,* by RCA Victor. Brown case with black knobs. Marked "Standard" on frequency indicator. With three knobs instead of customary two. Rectangular. Approx. 12" long.

$1,200–$1,300

*Catalin radio,* by Silvertone. Cylinder shape with tuner on side; black. Approx. 6" tall x 11" long.

$1,000–$1,500

*Catalin radio,* by Sparton. Three decorative ridges across the front. Approx. 6" tall x 15" long x 6" deep.
Metallic blue $3,500–$3,800
Metallic brown $5,000–$5,500

*Bakelite radio,* by Ducretet Thomson. Footed rectangular form in brown, with gold grillwork over the speaker, above rounded dial flanked by circular knobs (wear to fabric over speaker). 8½" x 11¼" x 8".

$1,045 (1986)

*Bakelite radio,* by Ducretet Thomson. Footed rectangular form in ivory Bakelite, molded with ribs, the Lucite dial of waisted rectangular form above four circular knobs. 9½" tall x 12¼" long x 6¼" wide.

$935 (1986)

*Bakelite radio,* by Trav-ler. Molded rectangular body with horizontal grillwork and two circular knobs below Lucite angle-set dial. 6¾" x 10" x 6".

$660 (1986)

*Bakelite radio,* by Westinghouse. Rectangular with horizontal dial on top, in brown Bakelite, with central projecting horizontal grillwork, flanked by four circular knobs. 8¼" x 13¼" x 5½".

$660 (1986)

*Bakelite radio*, by Zenith. Rounded rectangular form in dark brown Bakelite with gold mesh speaker cover and circular sundial tuner, over three circular knobs. 7¾" x 12" x 17".

$715 (1986)

## Other Bakelite Items

*Crib toys*, American, 1930s. In Bakelite, created in the shapes of people and animals, such as elephants and cats, to hang above cribs. Approx. 5"–6" long.

$95–$175

*Clocks*, American, 1930s. In Bakelite, shaped like dice, green with yellow dots or yellow with orange dots. 3" square.

$165–$180

*Clock*, by Westclox, American, 1940s. In yellow Bakelite with flashing light and alarm. Face marked "Westclox, Lasalle Ill." 5" tall x 7½" long.

$75–$85

*Desk set*, American, c. 1920. In striped black and green Bakelite with chrome accents, featuring a double inkstand, the inkwells with stacked covers that move outward, a holder for pens, two letter openers, and a rocker blotter, unmarked. Stand 5¾" tall. 5 pieces.

$550 (1987)

**Bakelite crib toys.** *(Photo by R. Four; courtesy of Frank and Barbara Pollack)*

*Desk set.* Blue Bakelite handles in original case, marbled red and green paper inlay. 9½" x 4". 5 pieces.

$135–$150

*Lamp,* by Jumo, French, c. 1930. In Bakelite, streamlined design with overall look of a car hood when closed, opens and raises on hinged extensor arm. (This style was recopyrighted in 1945 and is issued today in white, black, and brown.)

$1,200–$1,500

*Lighters,* American, c. 1930. In Bakelite, one with blue and red stripes, the other with yellow and orange stripes, offered as a pair.

$395–$425

*Strikers,* American, 1930s. Strike-to-light matchboxes in red, yellow, orange, or marbled blue Bakelite. Each.

$95–$100

*Telephone,* Italian, 1930s. In blue and light blue Bakelite, with rounded design, marked "Telcer" and "Made in Italy."

$1,785–$1,850

## INDUSTRIAL DESIGN

One of the hottest, fastest-growing areas of Modern and Streamline-idiom collectibles is called Industrial Design.

Some would say that the major American designers of the day were designing for industry even when they were designing a lady's writing desk because of the materials used: chrome, spun alumnium, plastics, stainless steel, and other modern wonders. They were faced with the task of making furniture and decorative objects that were stylish and comfortable but could also be mass-produced by machines, often on an assembly line.

"Industrial Design," as it is used in the collecting field today, refers to a whole arena of collectibles that just a few years ago almost everyone overlooked: radios, irons, vacuum cleaners, cameras, typewriters, appliances, housewares, tools of all kinds, adding machines, microphones, thermos sets, and much more—just the kind of stuff you've had lying around the basement and garage for years, right? Well, maybe not.

Radios, jukeboxes, and telephones of the 1920s and 1930s are among those Industrial Design objects considered highly collectible, and you've seen some plastic examples on previous pages. Jukeboxes from the 1930s today range from $1,500 and up—some bring in $5,000 or more. Telephones can range from $50 up to several hundred dollars, and early neon, which is often expensive even in reproductions, can bring $3,000 or more.

Jacques Caussin, owner of First Half, a gallery on Thompson Street in New York, hosted an exhibition of Industrial Design to coincide with Sanford Smith's Modernism show in November 1987. Cleverly, the show was entitled "Pat. Pending."

"The response was overwhelming... just incredible," says Caussin. "It was more than I anticipated, considering the risk I was taking with this show."

Apart from Industrial Design–era clocks by Kem Weber (1889–1963) and Paul Frankl (1878–1962), which many collectors have come to accept and even to prize, Caussin also displayed an outboard motor, a shopping cart, a lawn mower, studio microphones, irons, and much more. Of the fifty-two objects in the show, only about ten were unsold.

"A lot of people understood," Caussin comments. "I have to admit that the outboard motor and shopping cart did not sell, but the lawn mower sold very quickly to a German collector."

Who is collecting Industrial Design? "There are people who have collected for many years in a low-key way," states Caussin. "I have a lot of regular customers and others who started coming here after The Brooklyn Museum show, 'The Machine Age.' Other customers came out of the blue. Some were industrial designers themselves. I feel we even reached the upscale, sophisticated buyer, the person who can see the sculptural value of these pieces."

First Half usually shows a good selection of Modernist design from Bel Geddes, Eugene Schoen, and others. However, the Industrial Design show was so successful it is likely to be repeated in November 1988. "It took eight months and tons of research to put this show together," says Caussin, "but it was definitely worth it."

Among the items sold was an air compressor designed by Roland Manning in 1939 for Sears in cast iron and aluminum. The price tag? $250. "You have to remember that prices in New York will be higher than in other parts of the country and that dealers here have high expenses," Caussin cautions. "I don't think that people in other parts of the country can expect to get those prices, but it is a field that will go up in the years ahead."

It was only a matter of time before the rest of the spectrum of Industrial Design would become just as collectible. At first the industrial designer influenced the streamlined look of many of the home furnishings of the era. Automobile, airplane, and other transportation design was applied to couches, chairs, bedroom furniture, and the like.

In the 1920s and 1930s manufacturers of every kind were faced with new economic pressures. Advertising in American magazines increased rapidly, especially advertising aimed at women in the home.

The pressure to manufacture larger and larger quantities of well-designed goods forced most to update their design, materials, and processes. The new Industrial Design could help them increase productivity and reach new markets.

The advent of personal credit and charge accounts enabled the middle classes to "buy now—pay later." Manufacturers needed good new designs to appeal to the readers of *House and Garden, American Home,* and other publications, and at the same time it was to their benefit to change the design frequently. New models, new purchases.

The leading designers were sought by manufacturing firms throughout the country. Today in the American "Machine Age" collecting area you will hear the same names over and over: Russel Wright (1904–1972), Paul Frankl, Henry Dreyfuss (1904–1972), Donald Deskey, Walter Dorwin Teague (1889–1943), Raymond Loewy (1893–1986), Norman Bel Geddes (1893–1958), and others. These American designers, and anything by them, will certainly find their way into American and foreign museums at an increasing rate over the next decade. However, we are confident that other American designers from this period will be discovered—maybe by you.

Streamlining became more popular in Industrial Design. One of the great motifs of many of the Industrial Design objects of the era are three horizontal, parallel lines, which represented speed. The style is often identified by smooth, rounded surfaces and parabolic curves. One collector even reportedly had a teardrop-shaped camper parked behind the garage. Also, the logos of many corporations were also "modernized" at the time and became a part of the overall design of the object.

This area of collecting already has its favorites as well, and we've described several of them in the price listings below. The prices that some of these collectibles are bringing today may be nothing compared to tomorrow. Many of them are rarely found in excellent condition because they were used, banged around, and taken on journeys.

When something nice owned by grandmother went out of fashion—a vase, a Chanel dress, a table, a lamp, a Chase Chrome coffee service—she wasn't likely to throw it away. Instead, it was packed away in the attic or given to a child setting up his or her own apartment. The situation was very different with industrial design. When a pressing iron had outlived its usefulness, it was not enshrined with the family photo albums; it was thrown on the junk heap. Even broken vases can be glued. Broken pencil sharpeners are just replaced.

In fact, Raymond Loewy designed pencil sharpeners, scissors, and other office equipment that is highly collectible today, especially if it is in working order. As the field of Art Deco collecting expands to embrace this area, you may want to know that Loewy also designed the Coldspot Super Six refrigerator, and we haven't seen anyone collecting these yet (you notice we say "yet").

## ART DECO

## PRICE LISTINGS

*Adding machine,* by Victor, 1920. Bakelite with green keys in streamlined, teardrop style. In working order. Stamped "Victor" on case. 13" long.

$625–$675

*Air compressor,* by Roland Manning for Sears, 1939. In cast iron and aluminum with a streamlined design. Approx. 14" tall x 18" wide.

$250–$275

*Barber chair,* 1930s, probably American. Deep leather seat, chrome trim, curved chrome arms, and headrest; chair raises and lowers.

$400 (1987)

*Camera and box,* "No. 1A Gift Kodak," designed by Walter Dorwin Teague for Kodak, 1930. In brown leather case with metal-hinged lid set with chromed-metal geometric design of rectangles and circles, enameled in red, silver, and brown. Fitted black lacquered box, with chromed-metal lid and same enamel design. Impressed metal tag "No. 1A Gift Kodak Made in USA By Eastman Kodak Co. Rochester, NY." 8¾" long x 4⅜" wide.

$1,500–$2,000
$2,860 (1986)

Victor adding machine. *(Photo by R. Four; courtesy of Meisel-Primavera)*

Modern Living 417

**1A Gift Kodak by Walter Dorwin Teague.** *(Photo courtesy of Peter Rakelbusch, 21st Century Antiques)*

*Camera*, "Beau Brownie," by Eastman Kodak, 1929. Geometric design in blue and turquoise blue. With original box. Patent number visible. Camera face 3" x 5".

$450–$485

*Camera*, "6-20 Jiffy," by Eastman Kodak, 1935. Fold-out design with geometric decoration. Patent number visible.

$75–$95

*Camera*, "Banta M Special," designed by Walter Dorwin Teague, executed by Kodak, 1936. Black-enameled body divided by horizontal chromed-metal bands, hinged lens cover. Molded "Kodak Banta M Special Made in USA by Eastman Kodak Co. Rochester, NY." 4¾" long.

$625–$700
$825 (1987)

*Iron*, "American Beauty," by American Electric Heater Company, American. Streamlined design and see-through red plastic handle. Stamped "American Electric Heater Company, Detroit."

$30–$40

*Iron*, "General Mills," by General Mills, American, 1930s. Very streamlined design. From the front, the black industrial plastic handle's V-shape looks like an ocean liner. Stamped "General Mills."

$40–$50

## ART DECO

*Iron*, "Lady Dover," by Knaff-Monarch, American, 1930s–1940s. In streamlined design. Stamped "Knaff-Monarch Co., St. Louis."
$25–$35

*Iron*, "Petipoint," by Clifford Brooks Stevens and Edward P. Schreyer, American, 1941, for the Waverly Tool Co. In metal and black plastic with streamlined oval shape and stepped-back, protruding wings. Stamped "Waverly Tool Co., Sandusky, Ohio." Patent number visible. 4⅞" tall x 5" wide x 10" long.
$725–$785
$660 (1987)

*Iron*, "Silver Streak," by Saunders, c. 1940. Clear and crimson glass handle and body with chrome-plated metal ironing surface, impressed "Silver Streak Saunders Since 1858 Model 1038 1000 Watts 110–120 Volts AC only." 8¾" long.
$1,045 (1987)

*Iron*, "Silver Streak," by Saunders, c. 1940. As above, except in green and clear glass. (Also sold in blue glass.) Impressed with same marks as above.
$300–$450

*Iron*, "Ultramatic," French, 1930s. Streamlined design with maroon Bakelite handles by Novex Stebert. Metal label intact and marked "Ultramatic #44."
$450–$485

"Petipoint" iron. *(Photo by R. Four; courtesy of Meisel-Primavera)*

*"Juiceomatic,"* by Rival Manufacturing Company, American, 1940s. White-painted steel and chrome with streamlined design. Marked "Juiceomatic" with patent and catalog numbers. 10" tall.
$25–$35

*Microphones,* American, mid- to late 1930s. Tabletop microphones used in radio and recording studios. Some have tags, rarely have patent numbers. Created and designed by specialized companies of the era.
$100–$300

*Portable phonograph,* designed by John Vassos, "Victor Special Model M" for RCA, 1946. In red, streamlined polished-aluminum case with velvet turntable cover. Red Bakelite handle. Battery-operated, electrically amplified sound turntable. May be closed to play. 8" tall x 15½" wide x 17½" deep. Working.
$2,600–$2,800

*Radio,* "Spartan," by Walter Dorwin Teague, for Sparks-Wittington Co. of Michigan, 1930s. Table-model radio, round front with blue mirrored glass and chrome. Circular dial is circumferenced by another circle of chrome, and has three horizontal, parallel bands of chrome running across it. In working condition. Mirror approx. 12" diameter
$2,200–$2,700

*Radio,* French, c. 1935. In mirrored peach glass, the rectangular case housing multiband radio and speaker above adjusting knobs, bordered with curved mirrored peach glass panels and foot. 13¾" x 24¼" x 11⅜".
$1,600–$2,000

*"Stormoguide,"* designed by Walter Dorwin Teague for Taylor Instrument Company, 1931. Chrome and black plastic with dial readings for rain, snow, and even tornadoes. Face stamped "Taylor Stormoguide." 5" square.
$225–$265

*Thermos bottle,* designed by Henry Dreyfuss, American, for American Thermos Bottle Co., Norwich, CT, 1935. Aluminum, steel, glass, and rubber. Enameled brown, glass-lined body. Stamped with Henry Dreyfuss's signature, Thermos company mark, and "Pat. Office No. 549." 7¼" tall x 5¼" base diameter. Sometimes found with matching tray. Without tray:
$1,000–$1,150
$605 (1987)

*Thermos set,* designed by Russel Wright for American Thermos Company, 1932. Spun-aluminum thermos with wooden top, 10" tall, six 2"-tall spun-aluminum cups, and a 12"-diameter wooden tray with spun-aluminum rim.

$325–$450

*Thermos,* by American Thermos Company, 1930s. Chrome with ribbed design on base. Lid screws off to be used as cup. Glass-lined, with cork. Stamped "American Thermos Company." 10" tall x 3" wide.

$35–$45

*Toasters,* by Son-Chief Electric, American, 1930s–1940s. Double-slice toasters with stepped-back wooden knob handles painted black. Chrome faces have modernist geometric designs. Stamped "Son-Chief." 6½"–8" tall.

$35–$50

*Toaster,* by Toastalor, American, 1940s. Unique design allows the bread to enter through the side of the toaster, move along a chain drive, and come out toasted on the other side. 9" tall x 12" wide x 3" deep.

$100–$150

*Typewriter,* "Streamliner," by Remington Rand, American, 1930s–1940s. Enameled black metal with carrying case. Marked "Streamliner" and "Remington Rand" on typewriter carriage.

$65–$75

# RESOURCES

# RESOURCE GUIDE

## AUCTION HOUSES

ART DECO AUCTIONS LTD., 19528 Ventura Boulevard #153, Tarzana, CA 91356, (818) 996-3509, David Lawrence, president. Specializing in Art Deco posters, lithographs, etchings, and original paintings, including artists such as Icart and Erté.

CHRISTIE'S (Christie, Manson & Woods International, Inc.), 502 Park Avenue, New York, NY 10022, (212) 546-1000, Nancy McClelland, vice president, specialist, 20th Century Decorative Arts. Christie's has led the market in the area of 20th-century decorative arts at auction. Of the 51 objects selling in excess of $100,000 in the past ten years in New York, 45 of them have sold at Christie's.

CHRISTIE'S EAST (Christie, Manson & Woods International, Inc.), 219 East 67th Street, New York, NY 10021, (212) 606-0400, Kathleen Guzman, specialist, Art Nouveau and Art Deco. Four annual Art Nouveau/Art Deco auctions. Christie's East is very well known in the collecting field for its Art Deco auctions.

WILLIAM DOYLE GALLERIES, 175 East 87th Street, New York, NY 10028, (212) 427-2730, Michael Meek, specialist, 19th Century, Art Nouveau, and Art Deco. Auction gallery dealing in all aspects of American and European art, furniture and decorations, jewelry, and rugs. Specializing in estate property. Four annual "Belle Epoque" auctions featuring Art Deco. Third largest auction house in the United States.

GALLERY 68 AUCTIONS, 3 Southvale Drive, Toronto, ON M461G1, Canada, (416) 421-7614, Fedra Horner. Auction house specializing in 19th- and early 20th-century works of art, estate liquidations, and special Art Deco sales.

# ART DECO

PHILLIPS FINE ART AUCTIONEERS, 406 East 79th Street, New York, NY 10021, (212) 570-4830, Marissa Longo. Fine art auctioneers and appraisers, holding auctions in all areas of fine and decorative arts and collectibles.

SAUGERTIES AUCTION SERVICE, 16 Livingston Street, Saugerties, NY 12477, (914) 246-9928, Harold Swart, owner. Auction house with Art Deco auctions twice yearly.

SAVOIA & FROMM AUCTION SERVICES, Route 23, South Cairo, NY 12482, (518) 622-8000, Rebecca Rotzler. Quality antique auction gallery that concentrates on current market trends in all areas, including Arts and Crafts, Americana, and more.

## DEALERS

ALAN MOSS, 88 Wooster Street, New York, NY 10012, (212) 219-1663, Alan Moss, owner. Specializing in American design and furnishings.

ANTIQUE TRADING CO., 28130 Avenue Crocker #328, Valencia, CA 91355, (805) 257-4461, Arthur Condie. European antique furniture importers, featuring original Deco-style cabinets lacquered and refinished in 1980s colors.

ARTS & INTERIORS 1920–60s, 517 Fifth Street, Philadelphia, PA 19147, (215) 928-9325, Kim Hostler. Specializing in American industrial design, jewelry, and furnishings, 1920s–1960s.

BERNICE JACKSON, P.O. Box 1188, Concord, MA 01742, (617) 369-9088, Bernice Jackson, owner. Fine arts consultant and appraiser with a dealership specialized in vintage posters and graphics. Extensive collection of Art Nouveau, Art Deco, Viennese, and Dutch posters.

CALDERWOOD GALLERY, 221 South 17th Street, Philadelphia, PA 19103, (215) 732-9444, Gary and Janet Calderwood, owners. Emphasizing quality European design 1900–1940, including Art Nouveau and Art Deco, with a special selection of less-known designers.

CAROLLE THIBAUT-POMERANTZ, 50 Sutton Place South, New York, NY 10022, (212) 759-6048, Carolle Thibaut-Pomerantz. Specializing in European antiques and decorative arts with an emphasis on unique French design. By appointment only.

CORAM NOBIS ANTIQUARIANS, 34 East 67th Street, New York, NY 10021, (212) 517-5341; and at 825A Broadway, New York, NY 10003, (212) 254-7269. Specializing in fine European period furniture and decorations, and selected works of art.

DECO DELUXE, 125 East 57th Street, New York, NY 10022, (212) 688-2677, and 93 Main Street, Westhampton Beach, NY 11978, (516) 288-4116, Sandi Berman, president. Specializing in fine furniture, art, and jewelry from the 1920s–1940s. Complete interior design service.

## Resource Guide 425

DETOUR, 92 Main Street, Deep River, CT 06417, (203) 526-9797, Irena Urdang de Tour, owner. Appraiser and consultant, with dealership specializing in vintage clothing, accessories, jewelry, vintage luggage and trunks including Vuitton and Oshkosh, and textiles. By appointment only.

DUALITIES GALLERY, 2056 Boston Post Road, Larchmont, NY 10538, (914) 834-2773, Peter Boehm, owner. Specializing in quality design objects, art, and furniture of the past 200 years.

DYANSEN GALLERY, 132A Newbury Street, Boston, MA 02116, (617) 262-4800, Sondra Eddings. Specializing in Erté and contemporary Impressionists and Chinese artists. (Other Dyansen Gallery locations are in New York, California, Hawaii, and Louisiana.)

FER-DUC INC., Box 1303, Newburgh, NY 12550, (914) 565-5990. Specializing in paintings and American art pottery.

FIRST HALF, 131 Thompson Street, New York, NY 10012, (212) 533-2519, Jacques Caussin, owner. Specializing in American chrome and metal furnishings from Bel Geddes, Schoen, and others, as well as Industrial Design.

FLEUR DE LIS ANTIQUES, 489 Broome Street, New York, NY 10013, (212) 964-0400, Arnold Kaufman. Specializing in used and refinished English Art Deco furniture.

FRANK AND BARBARA POLLACK, 1214 Green Bay Road, Highland Park, IL 60035, (312) 433-2213, Frank and Barbara Pollack. Specializing in American country antiques and arts, Bakelite jewelry. By appointment only.

FRENCH AND COMPANY, INC., 17 East 65th Street, New York, NY, 10021, (212) 535-3330, Emily Bouchard. Specializing in European master paintings and 18th-century furnishings, with a fine collection of Art Deco museum-quality furniture. By appointment only.

FRIEDMAN GALLERY, 135 Post Road East, Westport, CT 06880, (203) 226-5533, Mike Friedman, owner. Art Deco, including chrome, clocks, jewelry, glass, and other objects.

FULL SWING, 474 Thames, Newport, RI 02840, (401) 849-9494, Michelle Mancini, owner. Specializing in furnishings and accessories from the 1920s–1950s, including Art Deco living rooms, bedrooms, dining rooms, wicker, draperies, kitchenwares, lighting, and collectibles.

GALERIE METROPOL INC., 927 Madison Avenue, New York, NY 10021, (212) 772-7401, and Dorotheergasse 12, 1010 Vienna, Austria, Wolfgang Ritschka. Specializing in furnishings of the Viennese Secession.

GALLERY VIENNA, 750 North Orleans, Chicago, IL 60610, (312) 951-0300, Leslie Rutz. Specializing in works by Josef Hoffmann and other artists of the Viennese Secession.

HELBURN & HOYT, 1435 Lexington Avenue, New York, NY 10128, (212) 410-5682, Bill Straus, and 543 Eighth Avenue, New York, NY 10018, (212) 563-6026, Nicholas Brown. Specializing in American design and furnishings 1930s–1950s.

## ART DECO

HISTORICAL DESIGN COLLECTION, 305 East 61st Street, #209, New York, NY 10021, (212) 593-4528, Dennis Gallion, Daniel Morris. Specializing in all periods starting with the Japanese impact on design in the 1860s, including Arts and Crafts, Art Nouveau, Symbolism, Vienna Secession, Cubism, Art Deco, Bauhaus, Art Moderne, and others. By appointment.

HONORE JEWELRY, The Shops at Charles Square, 5 Bennett Street, Cambridge, MA 02138, (617) 497-7187. Estate, antique, and contemporary jewelry. (Stores also in Hartford and Essex, Connecticut, and Hackensack, New Jersey.)

KATY KANE, INC., 34 West Ferry Street, New Hope, PA 18938, (215) 862-5873, Katy Kane, owner. Specializing in antique clothing, textiles, and fine linens.

KEN FORSTER AND INGLETT-WATSON, 884 Park Avenue, Baltimore, MD 21201, (301) 244-8064, Ken Forster, associate. 20th-century decorative arts, with particular emphasis on American Machine Age furnishings, Georg Jensen silver, Viennese Secession, and Wiener Werkstätte decorations.

KEN SCHULTZ, P.O. Box M753, Hoboken, NJ 07030, (201) 656-0966, Ken Schultz, owner. Specializing in World's Fair and ocean liner memorabilia.

KURLAND-ZABAR, 19 East 71st Street, New York, NY 10021, (212) 517-8576, Catherine Kurland and Lori Zabar, Owners. Specializing in British and American furniture, silver, and other decorative arts, 1840–1940.

LOST CITY ARTS, 339 Bleecker Street, New York, NY 10014, (212) 645-8311, Jim Elkind. Specializing in architectural and interior design components, including Art Deco.

MADISON GALLERIES, LTD., 840 Broadway, New York, NY 10003, (212) 529-5020, Florence Rubinstein. Extensive inventory of Art Deco, Art Nouveau, bronzes, chryselephantine statues, marble, statuary, Satzuma, Canton, Rose Medallion, Meissen, ivory, and decorative accessories.

MAISON GERARD, 36 East 10th Street, New York, NY 10003, (212) 674-7611, Gerardus A. Widdershoven, owner. Dealer and collector specializing in fine French Art Deco furniture, sculpture, paintings, carpets, lighting, and objets d'art.

MARNA ANDERSON GALLERY, New York City, New York, NY 10021, (212) 249-8484, Marna Anderson. Specializing in interesting Art Deco objects and American folk art. By appointment only.

MEISEL-PRIMAVERA, 133 Prince Street, New York, NY 10012, (212) 677-1340, Louis and Susan Meisel, owners. Specializing in 20th-century design, 20th-century chairs, and Clarice Cliff.

METROPOLIS, 224 Newbury Street, Boston, MA 02116, (617) 267-4825, Roger Cornwell. Specializing in Art Deco furnishings and contemporary fine arts.

MISCELLANEOUS MAN, P.O. Box 1776, New Freedom, PA 17349, (717) 235-4766, George Theofiles, owner. Specializing in posters and select graphic ephemera. Catalog subscriptions available. Call for more information.

MODERNE, 41 North Second Street, Philadelphia, PA 19106, (215) 923-8536, Bob Aibel, owner. Specializing in French Art Deco furniture, lighting, and accessories.

MORTON ABROMSON DECORATIVE ARTS, Brookline, MA, (617) 277-1925, Morton Abromson, owner. Specializing in Art Deco European ceramics from the 1920s and 1930s. By appointment only.

N. BLOOM & SON ANTIQUES LTD., 40 Conduit Street, London, England, WIR 9FV, (01) 629-5060/FAX 01-437-5026, Ian Harris, president. Specializing in estate jewelry, with selected Art Deco jewelry and silver.

NEWEL ART GALLERIES, 425 East 53rd Street, New York, NY 10022, (212) 758-1970, Bruce Newman, president. Perhaps the largest dealership in the country, with six floors of fine antiques from the 15th to the 20th century.

ORPHAN ANNIE'S, 96 Court Street, Auburn, ME 04210, (207) 782-0638, Dan Poulin, owner. Specializing in Art Deco and Art Nouveau furnishings, jewelry, lighting, pottery, French and American art glass, stained glass, and objets d'art.

PAT KERY FINE ARTS, INC., 141 Prince Street, New York, NY 10012, (212) 505-5144, Pat Kery. Specializing in late 19th- and early 20th-century paintings, drawings, sculpture, and prints, including posters by Toulouse-Lautrec and Cassandre, as well as Russian Constructivist and Viennese Secession posters.

PERRISUE SILVER, Box 2353, Princeton, NJ 08540, (609) 924-2141. Specializing in sterling silver, flatware, serving pieces, and hollowware.

POSTER AMERICA, 138 West 18th Street, New York, NY 10011, (212) 206-0499, Jack Banning. Specializing in vintage advertising posters from 1890 to 1950.

PRIMAVERA GALLERY INC., 808 Madison Avenue, New York, NY, 10021, (212) 288-1569, Audrey Friedman. Specializing in fine furniture, jewelry, and decorative arts.

REMEMBRANCES OF THINGS PAST, 376 Commercial Street, Provincetown, MA 02657, (617) 487-9443, Helene Lyons, owner. Featuring both new and old nostalgia, Art Deco, jewelry, neon, and gifts with special focus on 1920s–1950s.

RETRO MODERN, 104 Washington Street, Norwalk, CT 06854, (203) 866-4246, Joan Wheeler and Michael Albert, owners. "Vintage Furniture for Modern Times"—furniture and accessories from 1850 to 1950.

RETRO-MODERN STUDIO, 214 East 10th Street, New York, NY 10003, (212) 674-0530, Arthur and Bronnie Hindin, owners. Specializing in European and American designer Art Deco, including Paul T. Frankl, Walter von Nessen, Kem Weber, and Donald Deskey. Appointments encouraged.

ROSEBUD GALLERY, 1859 Solano Avenue, Berkeley, CA 94707, (415) 525-6454, Ed Forcum, owner. Shop and gallery specializing in high-style sterling jewelry, including Georg Jensen, Bent K, William Spratling, Antonio, Hector Aguilar, and the sculptural makers of the 1950s. By appointment only.

# ART DECO

A ROSE TREE, Norman Crider Antiques, 725 Fifth Avenue, Trump Tower Level D/5, New York, NY 10022, (212) 421-3879. Specializing in costume jewelry and antique gift items.

SAMBEAU'S LTD, 4724 McPherson, St. Louis, MO 63108, (314) 361-4636, Sam Bass, vice-president. Buyers and sellers specializing in antiques, decorative and fine arts, including furnishings and accessories.

STRUVE GALLERY, 309 West Superior Street, Chicago, IL 60610, (312) 787-0563, Michael Fitzsimmons, curator of Arts and Crafts. Specializing in 20th-century architecture and decorative arts with an emphasis on Frank Lloyd Wright and the Prairie School.

THUNDER ROAD, 347 Commercial Street, P.O. #1023, Provincetown, MA 02657, (617) 487-3339, John Kaschak. Specializing in fine jewelry and Cristal Lalique.

21ST CENTURY ANTIQUES, 11½ Main Street, P.O. Box 70, Hatfield, MA 01038, (413) 247-9396, Peter Rakelbusch, owner. Specializing in books and resources in 20th-century art, design, and collecting. Catalog available. Call for additional information.

THE WAREHOUSE, 120 Gordon Street, Allentown, PA 18102, (215) 770-0702, Paul Fuhrman, owner. Specializing in Art Deco upholstered furniture, with an emphasis on American furnishings of the 1930s and 1940s. Large inventory of American mass-produced furniture of the era, sold in both original condition and restored.

## SHOW MANAGEMENT

SANFORD L. SMITH & ASSOC., LTD., 152 Second Avenue, New York, NY 10003. Write: Sanford Smith, president, with photos of current booth and references from three dealers who currently exhibit at Sanford Smith shows. Annual shows: "Modernism 1860–1960—A Century of Style and Design" the weekend before Thanksgiving (started 1986); "Fall Antiques Show" at the Pier, third week of October (started 1979); "Spring Armory Antiques Show," first week of March (started 1984); "Art at the Armory," January (started 1988).

STELLA SHOW MANAGEMENT COMPANY, P.O. Box 482, Paramus, NJ 07652, (201) 368-1130. Contact: Irene Stella, president. Annual shows: 600-dealer "Manhattan Antiques and Collectibles Expo" on three piers last weekend of November and March, features one pier of Art Deco and Art Moderne to 1960s furniture, art, and artifacts.

*Please note:* The above is by no means a comprehensive list of all the dealers, auction houses, and show management companies in this country and elsewhere that promote Art Deco. Rather, it is a list of the resources that helped us compile the information recorded here.

## SOCIETIES AND ASSOCIATIONS

ART DECO SOCIETIES OF AMERICA, 3447 Sheridan Avenue, Miami Beach, FL 33140, (305) 538-8352, Barbara Baer Capitman, president. A not-for-profit membership organization that works on both a local and a national level to preserve America's Art Deco heritage. Through its nationwide network of contacts, this organization is willing to assist individuals who are interested in starting Art Deco societies on the local level. Membership dues: individual, $15; student, $10.

THE BALTIMORE DECO SOCIETY, 2024 West Rogers Avenue, Baltimore, MD 21209, (301) 466-2616. A preservation group dedicated to the preservation/restoration of Baltimore's Art Deco structures and interiors. Membership dues: Call for information.

ART DECO SOCIETY OF CALIFORNIA, 109 Minna Street, S #399, San Francisco, CA 94105, (415) 552-DECO, Michael Crowe, president. A not-for-profit membership organization, with members throughout the United States, Canada, Puerto Rico, and Western Europe. Membership includes a subscription to the newsletter *The Sophisticate,* reduced admission to events, discounts at local Deco stores, and announcements of Deco-related events. Regular monthly programs vary from slide lectures to demonstrations. Call for time and location. Walking tours during the summer months. Special events: Annual Art Deco Weekend by the Bay; Annual Preservation Ball in the Paramount Theater, Oakland; Gatsby Summer Affair Picnic; and additional special weekend activities throughout the year. Membership dues: Call for information.

CHICAGO ART DECO ASSOCIATION, 823 Lake, Oak Park, IL 60301, (312) 383-4348 (9 A.M.–1 P.M.), Lynn Abbie. A not-for-profit, tax-exempt organization with the purpose of education, preservation, and fellowship. Activities include tours, parties, lectures, classes, movies, a television program in conjunction with Chuck Schaden, and networking with other Deco, preservation, and historical/art agencies. Dues from membership support most programs. Membership dues: individual, $15; dual (single household), $20; friend, $50; patron, $100; benefactor, $250; corporate, $500.

ART DECO SOCIETY OF LOS ANGELES, P.O. Box 972, Hollywood, CA 90078, (213) 659-DECO. Dedicated to the appreciation and preservation of Deco in jewelry, architecture, decorative arts, furniture, and music. Membership benefits include newsletter, free or discounted attendance at special events, participation in Society preservation studies and landmark designation, interaction with others interested in Art Deco elsewhere in the United States and abroad. Membership dues: student, $10; participating member, $25; dual (single household), $45; sponsoring member, $50; corporate member, $100.

ART DECO SOCIETY OF NEW YORK, 145 Hudson Street, 7th Floor, New York, NY 10013, (212) 925-4946. A not-for-profit organization that encourages public awareness of all aspects of Art Deco. Goals include not only the study of modern forms but the application of the ideology expressed in the evolving international style. ADSNY sponsors lectures, walking tours, publications, and educational programs and promotes the cataloging and preserving of worthy

Art Deco buildings. Membership dues: participating individual, $35; participating dual (single household), $50; student, $20; sustaining, $75; friend, $250; patron/dual (single household), $500; corporate, $1,000.

ART DECO SOCIETY OF WASHINGTON, P.O. Box 11090, Washington, DC 20008, (202) 231-3793, Richard Striner, president. Annual events: Expo in the spring, featuring dealers from around the country, and concurrent educational programs; and Annual Ball, with formal Deco dress. The Society is significantly involved in the local preservation scene. Membership includes a subscription to the newsletter *Trans Lux* and monthly membership meetings on subjects of interest to Decophiles. Membership dues: individual, $20; couple/family, $30.

*Please note:* We also tried to contact Art Deco societies that we were informed existed in Texas (Lone Star Art Deco Society), Philadelphia, San Diego, Ohio (Deco Enthusiasts of Ohio), San Joaquin Valley, Kansas City, the Palm Beaches, and Napier, New Zealand. In England the closest organization to these is called The Thirties Society.

## PRESERVATION ORGANIZATIONS

MIAMI DESIGN PRESERVATION LEAGUE, P.O. Bin L., Miami Beach, FL 33119, (305) 672-2014. A nonprofit historic preservation group founded in 1976 that has led the worldwide movement for the preservation of 20th-century design and art. The MDPL is active in the fight to maintain the Art Deco District of Miami Beach and also runs a Welcome Center located at 1201 Washington Avenue. Each January it hosts an Art Deco Weekend festival and regularly offers walking tours and other programs, as well as a quarterly newsletter, *Impressions*. Membership dues: Call for information.

## TOUR SERVICES

"TOURLINK"—A Service of Wallis Gideon Wallis, Inc., 5319 South Lewis #219, Tulsa, OK 74105, (918) 747-2882, Michael Wallis. A for-hire service that permits individuals or groups to see firsthand the Art Deco architectural treasures of Tulsa. Fees: Call for more information.

## ENTERTAINMENT AND PRODUCTION COMPANY

RADIO CITY MUSIC HALL PRODUCTIONS, 1260 Avenue of the Americas, New York, NY 10020, (212) 246-4600. A subsidiary of the Rockefeller Group, this is a diversified entertainment and production company specializing in theatrical production, concert promotion, special events, business productions, television productions, and artist management.

*Resource Guide*

## MUSEUMS AND COLLECTIONS

ART INSTITUTE OF CHICAGO, Michigan Avenue at Adams Street, Chicago, IL 60603, (312) 443-3600. Will be opening the new South Building in fall of 1988, which will house European Decorative Arts and Sculpture department, among others. The collection of some 16,000 objects includes decorative arts in all media—furniture, ceramics, metalwork, glass, enamels, ivory—and sculpture from 1100 to the present. Hours: Mon., Wed., Thurs., Fri., 10:30–4:30; Sat., 10:00–5:00; Tues., 10:30–8:00; Sun. and holidays, 12 noon–5:00. Admission: Tues., free; all other times, suggested fee of $4.50.

BROOKLYN MUSEUM, 200 Eastern Parkway, Brooklyn, NY 11238, (718) 638-5000. Fourth floor galleries of the Department of Decorative Arts include 20th-century furniture, glass, ceramics, metalwork, and lighting. Among those represented are Gorham and Tiffany silver, Frank Lloyd Wright, Marcel Breuer, Emile-Jacques Ruhlmann, Maurice Marinot, Edgar Brandt, Pierre Legrain, and Jean Dunand, as well as a large collection of American Machine Age objects. Also on view is the first 20th-century period room displayed in an American museum, the Worgelt Library (a New York Art Deco room from 1928–1930). Hours: 10:00–5:00 every day except Tuesday, Thanksgiving, Christmas, and New Year's Day. Admission: suggested contribution, $3; students with ID, $1.50; senior citizens, $1; free to museum members and children under 12 accompanied by an adult.

COOPER-HEWITT MUSEUM, 2 East 91st Street, New York, NY 10128, (212) 860-6868. The Smithsonian Institution's National Museum of Design has a collection that includes more than 300,000 objects spanning 3,000 years of design history from cultures around the world. Hours: Tues., 10:00–9:00; Wed.–Sat., 10:00–5:00; Sun., 12 noon–5:00; closed Mondays and major holidays. Admission: general admission, $3; senior citizens and students over 12, $1.50; free admission Tuesday nights 5:00–9:00; Cooper-Hewitt and Smithsonian members, free.

CORNING MUSEUM OF GLASS, One Museum Way, Corning, NY 14830-2253, (607) 937-5371. The most comprehensive museum in the world illustrating the art and history of glass; more than 24,000 objects present a visual and social history of glass over the past 3,500 years. The collection includes Marinot, Lalique, Steuben, and numerous other notable Art Deco designers. Hours: open daily 9:00–5:00; closed Thanksgiving, December 24 and 25, and New Year's Day. Admission: adults, $2.50; senior citizens and students with ID, $2; children ages 6–17, $1.25; families (2 adults and children), $6; children under 6, free.

COWAN POTTERY MUSEUM, at The Rocky River Public Library, 1600 Hampton Road, Rocky River, OH 44116-2699, (216) 333-7610. Rotating exhibition of their collection of more than 800 pieces made by artists at the Cowan Pottery Studio of Lakewood and Rocky River, Ohio, from 1912 to 1932. The museum features the works of Viktor Schreckengost, Waylande Gregory, Russell Aitken, Whitney Atchley, A. Drexel Jacobson, Thelma Frazier Winter, Elizabeth Anderson, R. Guy Cowan, and others. Hours: Mon.–Thurs., 10:00–9:00; Fri. and Sat., 10:00–5:30; Sunday, 1:00–5:00. Admission: free at all times.

CRANBROOK ACADEMY OF ART MUSEUM, 500 Lone Pine Road, Box 801, Bloomfield Hills, MI 48013, (313) 645-3323. The Cranbrook Collection, newly installed in the Museum's main gallery, highlights the achievements of Cranbrook's faculty and students since the school's inception in the 1920s. The Academy attracted artists such as Carl Milles, Harry Bertoia, Eero Saarinen, Maija Grotell, Marianne Strengell, and Marshall Fredericks. The selections from the Collection on display feature sculpture, paintings, furniture, ceramics, textiles, and metalwork by these and other artists. Hours: Tues.–Sun., 1:00–5:00; closed Mondays and holidays. Admission: general admission, $2.50; students and senior citizens, $1.50; children under age 7, the handicapped, and museum members, free.

THE DETROIT INSTITUTE OF ARTS, 5200 Woodward Avenue, Detroit, MI 48202, (313) 833-7900. Included in the Art Deco collection are fine examples of European and American Deco ceramics, silver, and glass. On display are works by Jean Dunand, Edgar Brandt, Eliel Saarinen, Peter Muller-Munk, Georg Jensen, Simon Gate, Lalique, Henry Varnum Poor, and Carl Walters among others. The Institute has recently acquired dinnerware by Russel Wright, Walter Dorwin Teague, Keith Murray, and Susie Cooper Company in order to document mass-produced designs of the Deco period. Hours: Tues.–Sun., 9:30–5:30; closed Mondays and holidays. Admission: free at all times but donations are welcome.

EVERSON MUSEUM OF ART, 401 Harrison Street, Community Plaza, Syracuse, NY 13202, (315) 474-6064. Included in the holdings is a collection of significant 20th-century ceramics, including works from the 1930s by Cowan Pottery, Waylande Gregory, Carl Walters, Viktor Schreckengost, Russell Aitken, Edris Eckhardt, Maija Grotell, Thelma Frazier Winter, Glen Lukens, Vally Wieselthier, Gertrude and Otto Natzler, among many others. Hours: Tues.–Fri., 12 noon–5:00; Sat., 10:00–5:00; Sun., 12 noon–5:00; closed Mondays. Admission: free at all times but donations are welcome.

ISABELLA STEWART GARDNER MUSEUM, 280 The Fenway, Boston, MA 02115, (617) 734-1359. The private home of Isabella Stewart Gardner, which is now a public museum, houses her personal collection. The building is designed after a 15th-century Venetian palazzo. The collection consists of paintings, sculpture, textiles, prints and drawings, furniture, gardens, and decorative objects from the Middle Ages to the 20th century. Hours: Tues., 12 noon–8:00 (except July and August, 12 noon–5:00); Wed.–Fri., 12 noon–5:00; Sat. & Sun., 10:00–5:00; closed Mondays. Admission: donations of $3 for adults; $1 for children and senior citizens.

THE JONES MUSEUM OF GLASS AND CERAMICS, Sebago, Maine. Mailing address: Douglas Hill, ME 04024, (207) 787-3370. Collects, preserves, and interprets the full range of the art of glass, ceramics, and porcelain. The permanent collection contains 6,000 pieces from all time periods and geographic areas, over 50 firms represented from the Art Deco period. Included are designers and artists from America, Great Britain, Germany, Austria, Bohemia, France, and Belgium, as well as Japanese, Russian, and Scandinavian examples. Active year-round workshop and seminar program. Excellent resource library. Open May to November 14. Hours: Mon.–Sat., 9:30–5:00; Sun., 1:00–5:00. Admission: adults, $2.50; students, $1.50; children under 12, $.50; museum members, free.

MUSEUM OF THE CITY OF NEW YORK, Fifth Ave at 103rd Street, New York, NY 10029, (212) 534-1672. Dedicated to documenting the history of New York City. Included in their six curatorial departments is the Costume Collection, a great treasure of clothing and accessories designed or worn by New Yorkers, containing over 25,000 pieces from the mid-18th century to the present. Among the designers represented from the 1900s to 1930s are Coco Chanel, Caillot Soeurs, Madeleine Vionnet, and Louis Vuitton. Also included is the famous Stettheimer Dollhouse, made in the 1920s and furnished entirely in Art Deco with actual sculptures and paintings by famous artists. Hours: Tues.–Sat., 10:00–5:00; Sun. and holidays, 1:00–5:00; closed Thanksgiving, Christmas, and New Year's Day. Admission: free at all times but contributions of $3 for adults and $1 for children are encouraged.

THE NEWARK MUSEUM, 49 Washington Street, Newark, NJ 07101, (201) 596-6550. Examples of ceramics, glass, silver, other metals, and textiles from the United States and Europe from 1920s to 1940s, as part of the general Decorative Arts Collection. The museum is in the midst of a massive rebuilding project, scheduled to be completed in the fall of 1989, but is open on a limited basis to the public, and to scholars by appointment. Hours: Tues.–Sun., 12 noon–5:00; by appointment for scholarly research at other times Mon.–Fri. Admission: free at all times.

VIRGINIA MUSEUM OF FINE ARTS, Boulevard and Grove Avenue, Richmond, VA 23221, (804) 257-0842. The West Wing houses the Sydney and Frances Lewis Collection, consisting of 19th- and 20th-century decorative arts and contemporary paintings and sculpture. Artists and designers included in this significant collection include Emile Gallé, Louis Tiffany, Frank Lloyd Wright, Emile-Jacques Ruhlmann, and many more. Hours: Tues.–Sun., 11:00–5:00; Thurs. eve. until 10:00; Sun., 1:00–5:00; closed Mondays, Thanksgiving Day, Christmas Day, New Years Day, and Independence Day. Admission: free to museum members, senior citizens, and children under 16; all others, $1 requested minimum donation.

WALTER GROPIUS HOUSE, A Property of the Society for the Preservation of New England Antiquities (SPNEA), 68 Baker Bridge Road, Lincoln, MA 01773, (617) 227-3956 (SPNEA). A nonprofit organization dedicated to preserving the New England heritage, owns and operates 23 house museums and 11 study properties in five New England states. The family home of architect Walter Gropius and the first building designed on his arrival in the United States in 1937. Before coming to America, Walter Gropius directed the Bauhaus School in Germany from 1919 to 1928. Hours: June 1–Oct. 15, Fri.–Sun., 12 noon–5:00; November 1–June 30, Sat. and Sun. on the first full weekend of the month. Admission: general admission, $2.50.

*Please note:* The above is by no means a comprehensive list of museums that have collections of Art Deco and other 20th-century decorative design but rather those museums that assisted us in preparing this book. In addition to American museums, the Victoria and Albert Museum in London and the Musée des Arts Décoratifs in Paris should be noted as having large and exceptional collections of the Art Deco style.

# BIBLIOGRAPHY

## EXHIBITION CATALOGS

1925. *Encyclopédie des Arts Industriels et Moderns au XXème Siecle.* Imprimeries Nationale. Twelve volumes covering the 1925 exposition. Reprinted in French. New York: Garland Publishers, 1977.

1966. *Les Années 1925.* Catalog by Yvonne Brunhammer. Two volumes. Paris: Musée des Arts Décoratifs.

1970. *Art Deco.* Catalog by Judith Applegate. New York: Finch College Museum of Art.

1971. *The World of Art Deco.* Catalog by Bevis Hillier. Minneapolis Institute of Arts, Minneapolis. New York: E. P. Dutton, 1971.

1979. *Thirties.* Catalog by the Arts Council of Great Britain. London: Hayward Gallery, Victoria and Albert Museum.

1980. *George Jensen Silversmithy.* Washington, DC: Renwick Gallery, Smithsonian Institution Press, 1980.

1981. *Glas des Art Deco.* Catalog by Helmut Riche. Exhibition at the Kunstmuseum Dusseldorf. Dusseldorf: Kunst & Antiquitäten.

1983. *At Home in Manhattan: Modern Decorative Arts, 1925 to the Depression.* Catalog by Karen Davies. New Haven, CT: Yale University Art Gallery.

1983. *Design in America: The Cranbrook Vision 1925–1950.* New York: Harry N. Abrams, in association with the Detroit Institute of Arts and the Metropolitan Museum of Art.

1985. *High Styles: Twentieth Century Design.* New York: Whitney Museum of American Art, in association with Summit Books.

1986. *Vienna 1900.* Catalog by Kirk Varnedoe. New York: The Museum of Modern Art.

1986. *The Machine Age in America.* Catalog by Richard Guy Wilson, Diane H. Pilgrim, and Dickran Tashjian. New York: The Brooklyn Museum, in association with Harry N. Abrams.

1987. *The Art That Is Life: The Arts and Crafts Movement in America, 1875–1920.* Catalog by Wendy Kaplan. Boston: Little, Brown, for the Museum of Fine Arts.

1987. *American Art Deco.* Catalog by Alastair Duncan. Washington, DC: Renwick Gallery, Smithsonian Institution, in association with Harry N. Abrams.

## BOOKS

Applebaum, Stanley. *The New York World's Fair: 1939/1940.* New York: Dover, 1977.

Arwas, Victor. *Art Deco.* London: Academy Editions, 1975; New York: St. Martin's Press, 1976.

———. *Art Deco.* New York: Harry N. Abrams, 1980.

———. *Art Deco Sculpture.* London: Academy Editions; New York: St. Martin's Press, 1975.

———. *Belle Epoque Posters and Graphics.* New York: Rizzoli International, 1978.

———. *Glass: Art Nouveau to Art Deco.* London: Academy Editions; New York: Rizzoli International, 1977. Republished in expanded edition, by Harry N. Abrams, New York, 1987.

Battersby, Martin. *The Decorative Twenties.* New York: Walker, 1969.

Belves, Pierre. *Cent Ans d'Affiches de Chemin de Fer.* Paris: Editions La Vie du Rail, 1981.

Borsi, Franco, and Ezio Godoli. *Vienna 1900: Architecture and Design.* New York: Rizzoli, 1986.

Brandt, Frederick. *Late 19th and Early 20th Century Decorative Arts.* The Sydney and Frances Lewis Collection. Richmond, VA: Virginia Museum of Fine Arts; Seattle, WA: University of Washington Press, 1985.

Brunhammer, Yvonne. *The Nineteen Twenties Style.* Milan: Fratelli Fabbri, 1966; London: Hamlyn, 1969.

———. *The Art Deco Style.* New York: St. Martin's Press, 1984.

Cartlidge, Barbara. *Twentieth Century Jewelry.* New York: Harry N. Abrams, 1985.

Catley, Brian. *Art Deco and Other Figures.* London: Chancery House, 1978.

Cerwinske, Laura. *Tropical Deco.* With photos by David Kaminski. New York: Rizzoli International, 1981.

Clark, Garth. *U.S. Ceramics 1878–1978.* New York: E. P. Dutton, 1979.

Darling, Sharon S. *Chicago Ceramics and Glass.* Chicago: Chicago Historical Society, 1979.

Defert, Theirry, and Claude Lepape. *From the Ballets Russes to Vogue: The Art of Georges Lepape.* New York: Vendome Press, 1984.

Delhaye, Jean. *Art Deco Posters and Graphics.* London: Academy Editions, 1977; New York: St. Martin's Press, 1984.

DiNoto, Andrea. *Art Plastic: Designed for Life.* New York: Abbeville Press, 1984.

Duke, Harvey. *Hall China, A Guide for Collectors.* New York: Elo Books, 1977.

Duncan, Alastair. *Art Deco Furniture.* New York: Holt, Rinehart and Winston, 1984.

———. *Art Nouveau and Art Deco Lighting.* New York: Simon and Schuster, 1978.
Etherington-Smith, Meredith. *Patou.* New York: St. Martin's/Marek, 1983.
Frankl, Paul. *Form and Re-Form.* New York: Harper and Brothers, 1930.
Gresleri, Giuliano. *Josef Hoffmann.* New York: Rizzoli, 1985.
Griffin, Leonard, Louis Meisel, and Susan Meisel. *Clarice Cliff: The Bizarre Affair.* New York: Harry N. Abrams, 1988.
Hanks, David. *The Decorative Designs of Frank Lloyd Wright.* New York: E. P. Dutton, 1979.
Hanks, David A., with Jennifer Toher. *Donald Deskey: Decorative Designs and Interiors.* New York: E. P. Dutton, 1987.
Hatton, Hap. *Tropical Splendor: An Architectural History of Florida.* New York: Knopf, 1987.
Hillier, Bevis. *Art Deco.* London: Herbert Press, 1968; New York: Schocken Books, 1985.
———. *Posters.* New York: Stein and Day, 1969.
———. *The Decorative Arts of the Forties and Fifties: Austerity Binge.* New York: Clarkson N. Potter, 1975.
Kery, Patricia Frantz. *Art Deco Graphics.* New York: Harry N. Abrams, 1986.
———. *Great Magazine Covers of the World.* New York: Abbeville Press, 1982.
Klein, Dan, Nancy A. McClelland, and Malcolm Haslam. *In The Deco Style.* New York: Rizzoli International, 1986.
Koch, Robert, ed. *Chase Chrome: The Chase Catalogue for 1936–37.* Reprinted by Gladys Koch Antiques, Stamford, CT, 1978.
Koschatsky, Walter, and Horst-Herbert Kossatz. *Ornamental Posters of the Vienna Secession.* London: Academy Editions; New York: St. Martin's Press, 1974.
Lalique, Marc, and Marie-Claude Lalique. *Lalique par Lalique.* Lausanne, Switzerland: Edipop, 1977.
Le Corbusier. *L'Art Décoratif d'Aujourd'hui.* Paris: G. Crès, 1926.
Lesieutre, Alain. *The Spirit and Splendour of Art Deco.* New York: Paddington Press, 1974.
Lyall, Sutherland. *Hille: 75 Years of British Furniture.* London: Elron Press, in association with the Victoria and Albert Museum, 1981.
Madigan, Mary Jean Smith. *Steuben Glass.* New York: Harry N. Abrams, 1982.
Mandelbaum, Howard. *Screen Deco, a Celebration of High Style in Hollywood.* New York: St. Martin's Press, 1985.
McClinton, Katherine Morrison. *Art Deco: A Guide for Collectors.* New York: Clarkson N. Potter, 1986.
———. *Introduction to Lalique Glass.* Des Moines, IA: Wallace-Homestead Book Co., 1978.
———. *Lalique for Collectors.* New York: Charles Scribner's Sons, 1975.
Menten, Theodore. *Advertising Art in the Art Deco Style.* New York: Dover Publications, 1975.
———. *The Art Deco Style.* New York: Dover Publications, 1982.
Mouron, Henri. *A. M. Cassandre.* New York: Rizzoli, 1985.
Neuwirth, Waltraud. *Wiener Werkstätte: Avant Garde, Art Deco, Industrial Design.* Vienna: Author, 1984.

Packer, William. *The Art of Vogue Covers.* New York: Harmony Books, 1980.
Prokopoff, Marcel, and Marcel Franciscono, eds. *The Modern Dutch Poster.* Urbana, IL: Krannert Art Museum; Cambridge, MA: MIT Press, 1987.
Rademacher, Hellmut. *Masters of German Poster Art.* Translated by Anthony Rhodes. New York: Citadel Press, 1966.
Raulet, Sylvie. *Art Deco Jewelry.* New York: Rizzoli International, 1985.
Robinson, Julian. *The Golden Age of Style.* New York: Gallery Books, 1976.
Scarlett, Frank, and Marjorie Townley. *Arts Décoratifs 1925: A Personal Recollection of the Paris Exhibition.* London: Academy Editions; New York: St. Martin's Press, 1975.
Schnessel, S. Michael. *Icart.* New York: Clarkson N. Potter, 1976.
Schweiger, Werner J. *Wiener Werkstätte.* New York: Abbeville Press, 1984.
Spencer, Charles. *Erté.* New York: Clarkson N. Potter, 1970.
Vlack, Don. *Art Deco Architecture in New York 1920–1940.* New York: Harper and Row, 1974.
Waissenberg, Robert. *Vienna Secession.* New York: Rizzoli International, 1977.
———. *Vienna 1890–1920.* New York: Rizzoli, 1984.
Weber, Eva. *Art Deco in America.* New York: Bookthrift (Exeter), 1985.
Whiffen, Marcus, and Carla Breeze. *Pueblo Deco: The Art Deco Architecture of the Southwest.* Albuquerque, NM: University of New Mexico Press, 1984.
Wirz, Hans, and Richard Striner. *Washington Deco: Art Deco in the Nation's Capital.* Washington, DC: Smithsonian Institution Press, 1984.

## PERIODICALS

Allen, Jane Addams. "The Dynamo of American Art Deco." *Insight,* May 25, 1987.
"Decorative Arts of the Late 19th and early 20th Century." *Art & Design,* June 1986.
Flanagan, Barbara. "Happy Birthday, Corbu!" *Metropolitan Home,* October 1987.
Gordon, Alastair. "Long Island Modern." *New England Antiques Journal,* November 1987.
Grabowsky, Robert. "Radios: The Twentieth Century." *Modernism,* November 1987.
Greenberg, Cara. "The 12 Hottest Collectibles." *Metropolitan Home,* April 1987.
Hanks, David. "Nouveau Riches: Collecting 20th Century American Decorative Arts." *Art & Auction,* November 1987.
Hanna, Anetta. "Ear Candy." *Interior Design,* September/October 1984.
"Machine Age in America." *New England Antiques Journal,* November 1986.
McMullin, Bryan. "Donald Deskey: Modern by Design." *New England Antiques Journal,* November 1987.
*News, the Newsletter of the Art Deco Society of New York.* 1 (September–October 1981, November–December 1981); 2 (January 1982, March 1982, Fall 1982, Winter 1982; 3 (Spring 1983, Summer 1983, Fall 1983, Winter 1983); 4 (Spring 1984, Summer 1984, Fall 1984); 5 (Spring 1985, Summer 1985, Winter 1985); 6 (Spring 1986).

Tyndall, Katie. "Art Deco Graphics: New Life as Art." *Insight,* April 6, 1987.
"What Was Modernism?" *New England Antiques Journal,* December 1986.

# INDEX

Aalto, Alvar, 110
Accessories, 323–325
   price listings, 154–159, 326–334
Adnet, Jacques, 109
Albers, Josef and Anni, 55
Ambassade Française, 69
American Art Clay Company
   (AMACO), 253, 255
American Art Deco, 73–79
   American scene and, 74
   decline of, 78
   Depression and, 77
   Erté and, 73
   historical overview, 33–35
   Hollywood Deco, 77
   kitsch, 78
   major designers, 76
   modern influences, 74, 75
   museums/exhibitions, influence of,
      73, 76, 77
   Pueblo Deco, 77
   skyscraper motif in, 76
   Streamline style, 77
   Tropical (Floridian) Deco, 77
American Arts and Crafts
   movement, 49–51
American Designers' Gallery, 75
American Radiator Building, 90
Ancient architecture, influence on
   Deco, 63

Animal motifs, 42, 43
*Animalier* movement, 42, 43, 170
Arbus, André, 109
Archipenko, Alexander, 168
Architecture, 87–99
   American Radiator Building, 90
   ancient architecture, influence on
      Deco, 63
   Carpenter Center, 88
   Chrysler Building, 91, 92
   Empire State Building, 92
   European influences, 87, 88
   interior design components, 98,
      99
   price listings, 99–104
   Wright's pieces, 99
   Long Island Modern, 93
   movie theaters, 93
   preservation movements, 94–98
      Boston, 95, 96
      Miami Design Preservation
         League (MDPL), 94, 95
      San Francisco, 95
      Washington, DC, 95
   Pueblo Deco, 93
   Radio City Music Hall, 90
   Rockefeller Center, 90, 91
   skyscrapers, 89
   Tropical Deco, 93, 94
   Waldorf Astoria Hotel, 92

Argy-Rousseau, Gabriel, 202
Art Deco
　American Art Deco, 73–79
　architecture, 87–99
　artistic influences, 57–61
　Bakelite, 407–413
　ceramics, 241–288
　chrome collectibles, 397–407
　decorative influences, 44–56
　definition of, 3–5
　designers
　　American, 290
　　European, 289, 290
　fashion, 320–334
　furnishings, 105–116
　glass, 201–240
　global influences, 62–66
　graphics, 335–384
　historical overview, 29–36
　　American Art Deco, 33–35
　　Ballets Russes, influence of, 30
　　Deco as total style, 35, 36
　　"Dime Store Deco," 35
　　fashion designers, 30, 32
　　French Art Deco, 30–33
　　kitsch, 34, 35
　Industrial Design, 413–420
　jewelry, 300–320
　manufacturers, 290
　market for, 6–12
　　American design, 10
　　major dealers, 7–10
　　reproductions and, 11, 12
　materials/techniques, 37–40
　motifs, 41–43
　ocean liner collectibles, 385–393
　Paris Exposition of 1925, 67
　Pavillon de l'Esprit Nouveau, 68, 70–72
　price listings, 291–299
　revival of, 80–84
　sculpture, 168–200
　silver, 289–300
　terms related to, 4
　use of term, 3
　*versus* Art Nouveau, 29, 31
　*versus* fifties furniture, 22, 23
　World's Fair souvenirs, 393–397
　*See also* individual topics.
Art Deco (Hillier), 3
Artistic influences, 57–61
　Ballets Russes, 58, 59
　Cubism, 60, 61

Dadaism, 61
De Stijl Group, 61
Fauvism, 58
Futurism, 60
Surrealism, 61
Art Moderne, 3
Art Nouveau, 44–46
　Deco as reaction to, 29, 31
　in France, 44, 45
　in Germany, *Jugendstil,* 45
　in Italy, 45
　major designers, 45, 46
　opposition to, 47, 48
　origins of, 44
　Turin Exposition of 1902, 45, 46
Arts and Crafts movement,
　influence on Deco, 48–51
*Atlantique,* 75
Aucoc, Louis, 301

Bakelite
　crib toys, 408
　miscellaneous items, price listings, 412, 413
　radios, 407, 408
　　Catalin radios, 407, 408
　　price listings, 409–412
Bakelite jewelry, 304, 305
　price listings, 317–320
Baker, Josephine, 64
Bakst, Léon, 58, 59
Ballets Russes, influence on Deco, 3, 30, 58, 59, 107, 320
　influence of, 107, 320
Barbier, Georges, 30
Bauhaus, 70, 88, 110
　influence on Deco, 54–56
Beardsley, Aubrey, 49
Behmer, Marcus, 53
Behrens, Peter, 87, 88
Bel Geddes, Norman, 34, 113, 398
Bernadott, Sigvard, 289, 290
Bernhard, Lucian, 340
Binder, Joseph, 341, 346
Bing, Siegfried, 44
Biomorphism, 61, 78
Black, Starr & Frost, 302
Blazys, Alexander, 252
Block, R., 109
Boch Frères, 244, 245
　price listings, 263–268
Bon Marché, 69, 107, 169
Bonnard, 45

# Index

Boston, Deco buildings, 95, 96
"Boudoir style," 107
Bourraine, Marcel, 170
Brandt, Edgar, 30, 81, 107, 108
Brandt, Marianne, 55
Breton, André, 30
Breuer, Karl, 54
Breuer, Marcel, 32, 55, 56, 88, 110

Canta, Agnes, 342
Cappiello, Leonetto, 340, 341
Cardew, Michael, 246
Carlu, Jean, 339
Carnival glass, 207
Carpenter Center, 88
Carpets
  designers of, 107
  price listings, 156
Cartier, Louis, 300
Cassandre, A. M., 338, 339
Catalin radios, 407, 408
Century of Progress (1933), Deco souvenirs, 394–396
Ceramics, 241–288
  American ceramics, 249–256
    Cowan Pottery, 250–253
    major companies, 253–255
    price listings, 276–285
  English ceramics, 245–249
    Cliff, Clarice, 246–249
  European ceramics, 241–245
    Boch Frères, 244, 245
    Longwy, 244
    price listings, 256–262
    Robj, 245
  reproductions, 25, 26
Chambellan, René, 90
Chance, Frederick, 346
Chanel, Coco, 32, 35, 302, 322
Chanin Building, 92
Chareau, Pierre, 109
Chase Brass & Copper Company, 397–399
  price listings, 400–403
Chase Chrome, 77, 83, 113
Chicago Century of Progress, 77
Chiparus, Demetre H., 81, 171, 173
Christofle, Orfeverie, 81, 289
Chrome collectibles, 397–407
  designers, 397, 398
  manufacturers, 398, 399
  price listings, 400–406

Chryselephantine statues, 170–174
  artists, 171, 173, 174
  materials used, 172
  reproductions, 171, 172
  as series, 172
Chrysler Building, 76, 91, 92
Cliff, Clarice, 12, 81
  biographical information, 246, 248
  designs of, 248, 249
  price listings, 271–276
  rise in popularity, 247, 248
Clocks
  price listings, 159–167
  varieties of, 114, 115
Clothing
  reproductions, 26
  *See also* Fashion.
Coates, Wells, 88
Cocteau, Jean, 58, 59
Colin, Paul, 339
Colinet, Claire Jeanne Roberte, 169, 173
Collections
  starting a collection, 18–21
  tips for collection, 19–21
Compagnie des Artistes Français, 30
Consolidated Lamp and Glass Company, 204, 207
Contempora, 75
Cooper, Susie, 246
Cornwell, Dean, 91
Cowan Pottery
  artists of, 251, 252
  Jazz Bowl, 252
  price listings, 276–285
Cowan, Reginald (Guy), 75, 250, 251
Cranbrook Academy of Art, 74
Csaky, Josef, 168
Cubism, influence on Deco, 60, 61
Cunard Line, Deco collectibles of, 386

Dadaism, influence on Deco, 61
Daily News Building, 92
Da Silva Bruhns, Bruno, 107
Daum, Auguste and Antoine, 46, 81, 107, 108, 203
Daum, Nancy, 107
Decoeur, Emile, 242
Deco-inspired originals, 27, 28
  Postmodernism, 27, 28
Décoration Intérieur Moderne, 31, 110

Decorative influences, 44–56
  Art Nouveau, 44–46
  Arts and Crafts movement, 48–51
  American Arts and Crafts
    movement, 49–51
  Bauhaus, 54–56
  Frank Lloyd Wright/Prairie
    School, 51, 52
  Viennese Secessionist movement,
    53, 54
Decorchement, Francois, 202
de Koo, Nicolaas Petrus, 342
Depression glass, 207
Descomps, Joé, 173
Deskey, Donald, 4, 34, 90, 93, 112
De Stijl Group, influence on Deco,
  61, 87, 342
de Tirtoff, Romain, 30
Deutscher Werkbund, 47
Diederich, William Hunt, 112, 169
"Dime Store Deco," 35
Dixon, L. Murray, 95
Domin, Andre, 106
Dominique, 106
Dorn, Marion, 107
Doucet, Jacques, 30, 107
Dufrène, Maurice, 3, 30, 69, 107,
  243, 244
Dufy, Raoul, 30, 81
Dunand, Jean, 7, 30, 38, 39, 81,
  106
Dupas, Jean, 7, 75
Dutch posters, 341–343
  price listings, 357–360

Egyptian influences, on Deco, 63,
  301
Empire State Building, 76, 92
Enameling, 38, 39
  technique of, 38
*Ensemblier*, role of, 68
Erdt, Hans Rudi, 340
Erté, 8, 9, 30, 33, 34, 81, 343, 346,
  374–384
  biographical information, 374, 375
  price listings, 376–384
Escargot chair, 107
Etling, 169, 243
*Europa*, Deco collectibles of, 386,
  387
Exposition Internationale des Arts
  Décoratifs et Industriels
  Modernes, 3

Farberware Company, 398, 399
Fashion
  accessories, 323–325
    price listings, 326–334
  design elements, 321
  designers, 30, 32, 321–323
  influences of, 320, 321
  materials used, 39, 321
Fashion designers, influence on
  Deco, 30, 32
Fauvism, influence on Deco, 58
Fayral, 170
Finch College Museum of Art, Deco
  revival exhibition, 81, 82, 255
Fishmuth, Harriet W., 170
Fix-Masseau, Pierre, 339
Floating world etchings, ukiyo-e, 62,
  63, 320
Follot, Paul, 30, 69, 106, 107
Fouquet, Georges, 38, 81, 301
Fouquet, Jean, 38
Frankart Company, 83
Frankl Galleries, 111
Frankl, Paul, 4, 32, 76, 81, 93, 111
Frankoma Pottery, 253
French Art Deco, historical
  overview, 30–33
Fulper Pottery, 249
Furnishings, 105–116
  accessories, price listings, 154–159
  carpets
    designers of, 107
    price listings, 156
  clocks
    price listings, 159–167
    varieties of, 114, 115
  designers, 106–114
    American, 110–114
    European, 106–110
  lamps/lighting
    designers of, 107, 108, 113
    price listings, 148–154
  mass-produced furniture, 115, 116
  materials used, 37, 38, 105
  metalwork, designers of, 108
  price listings, 116
  reproductions, 23, 24
  Thonet company, 108
Futura vases, 253
Futurism, influence on Deco, 60

Gallé, Emile, 46
Galleries Lafayette, 69, 107

*Galuchat*, 38, 105
Gambogi, 170
Garçonne style, 323
Garetto, Paolo, 346
Gaudi, Antoni, 46
Genevrière, Marcel, 106
George Jensen Silversmithy, 303
Gerdago, 170
Gill, Irving, 50, 51
Gillot, Gustav, 170
Gispen, William, 342
Glass, 201-240
  historical overview, 202-205
  Art Nouveau glass, 201, 202
  handcrafted glass, 203
  Lalique, 203, 204
  Orrefors, 204, 205
  Pâte-de-verre method, 202, 203
  Steuben, 205
  Lalique, René, price listings, 225-240
  mass-produced glass, 206-208
  perfume bottles, 205, 206
  reproductions, 24, 25
Glass jewelry, price listings, 306
Global influences, 62-66
  ancient architecture, 63
  Egyptian influences, 63
  Jazz, 64, 65
  machines of industrial age, 65, 66
  Orientalism, 62, 63
  science fiction, 65
Goldscheider, 245
Gorham Manufacturing Company, 170, 290
*Gouaches*, price listings, 362
Goulden, Jean, 108
Graphics, 335-384
  Erté, 374-384
    biographical information, 374, 375
    price listings, 376-384
    *gouaches*, price listings, 362
  Icart, Louis, 366-374
    biographical information, 366, 367
    price listings, 367-373
    magazine covers, 345-347
    price listings, 362-366
    *pochoir* illustrations, 343, 344
    price listings, 360-362

  posters, 337-343
    artists, 338-342
    Dutch poster, 341-343
    Dutch posters (price listings), 357-360
    price listings, 347-355
    Viennese posters (price listings), 355-357
  reproductions, 27
  typography, 336
Gray, Eileen, 30, 38, 109
Greco Deco, 95
Gregory, Waylande D., 169, 251, 252
Gropius, Walter, 32, 52, 55, 70, 88, 110
  family home, 96
Groult, Andre, 12
Guardian Building, 89
Guild, Laurelle, 397, 398
Guimard, Hector, 46

Hagenaur, Atelier, 170
Hall China, 254, 255
Held, John, Jr., 346
Herbst, René, 31, 109
Hermes, 35
Hillier, Bevis, 3
Hoffmann, Josef, 47, 53, 70, 87, 108
Hoffmann, Wolfgang, 112, 113
Hohlwein, Ludwig, 340
Holland-America Line, Deco collectibles of, 387
Hollywood Deco, 77
Holme, Charles, 49
Hood, Raymond, 76, 89, 90, 92
Hotel d'un Riche Collectioneur, 69
Howell Chrome Company, 399
Huntington, Anna Hoyt, 169

Icart, Louis, 78, 366-374
  biographical information, 366, 367
  price listings, 367-373
*Ile de France*, 8, 75
  Deco collectibles of, 387, 388
Industrial Design
  designers, 414, 415
  exhibitions, 414
  items related to, 413, 414
  price listings, 416-420

Interior design components, 98, 99
  price listings, 99–104
  Wright's pieces, 99
International Modern, 3
Iribe, Paul, 30, 106, 107, 321, 344

Jacobson, Drexel, 253
Jallot, Léon, 30, 81, 106
Jazz, influence on Deco, 64, 65
Jazz Bowl, 65
Jennewein, Carl Paul, 169
Jensen, Georg, 289
Jewelry, 300–320
  Bakelite jewelry, 304, 305
    price listings, 317–320
  design elements, 300–302
  designers, 301
  fine jewelry, price listings, 306–313
  firms, 302
  glass jewelry, price listings, 306
  marcasite jewelry, 304
  materials/techniques, 302–304
  reproductions, 27
  silver jewelry, 303, 304
    price listings, 313–317
  technique of, 39
  wristwatches, 304
Joubert, René, 3, 110
Jourdain, Francis, 31, 109
Jouve, Paul, 42
Jugendstil, 45

Kahn, Ely Jacques, 89
Kandinsky, Wassily, 55
Karasz, Ilonka, 112
Kauffer, E. McKnight, 81
Kelety, Alexander, 170, 174
Kent, Rockwell, 347, 397, 398
Kitsch, 34, 35
Klee, Paul, 55
Klimt, Gustav, 53
Kroll International, 110

Lachenal, Raoul, 243
Lacquering, 62, 106
  technique of, 38
Lalique, Marc, 206, 209, 210
Lalique, Marie-Claude, 210
Lalique, René, 8, 30, 45, 81, 107, 210
  biographical information, 208, 209
  imitators of, 203, 204
  at Paris Exposition, 69
  price listings
    car mascots, 225, 226
    lighting, 226, 227
    miscellaneous items, 231, 232
    perfume bottles, 228–230
    sculpture, 230
    vessels, 232–240
Lalique, Sabino, 107
Lalique, Suzanne, 242
Lallemand, Robert, 243
La Maîtrise, 107
Lamps/lighting
  designers of, 107, 108, 113
  price listings, 148–154
La Normandie, Deco collectibles of, 389–392
Lanvin, Jeanne, 30, 322
Lanvin, Madame, 322
L'Atlantique, Deco collectibles of, 388, 389
Lawrie, Lee, 91, 169
Leach, Bernard, 246
Le Corbusier, 31, 48, 53, 65, 88, 89
  and Paris Exposition, 70, 71
  views of, 71
le Faguays, Pierre, 170
Legrain, Pierre, 109
Legratin, Pierre, 30
Leleu, Jules, 30, 75, 106
Lendecke, Otto, 54
Lenoble, Emile, 242
Lepape, Georges, 30, 339, 345, 346
Le Vérrier, Max, 170
Levy, Claude, 243, 244
Lightning bolt, 42
Loewy, Raymond, 34, 415
Löffler, Berthold, 53
Long Island Modern, 93
Longwy, 244
  price listings, 268–271
Loos, Adolf, 47, 87
Lorenzl, Joseph, 173
Loupot, Charles, 339
Lovet-Lorski, Boris, 169
Lowey, Raymond, 76
Lurçat, André, 109

McCoy pottery, 255
Macdonald, Margaret, 46
McGraw-Hill Building, 92
Machines of industrial age, influence on Deco, 65, 66

Mackintosh, Charles Rennie, 46, 53, 87
McKnight Kauffer, Edward, 340, 345
McNair, Herbert and Francis, 46
Macy's, Art in Trade exhibit, 73
Magasins du Printemps, 69
Magazine covers, 345–347
 price listings, 363–366
Magnussen, Erik, 77, 290
Maison de l'Art Nouveau, 44
Maison Laparra, 289
Majorelle, Louis, 46, 106
Mallet-Stevens, Robert, 31, 107, 109
"Manhattan" style glass, 207, 208, 222
Manship, Paul, 91, 169
Marcasite jewelry, 304
Mare, André, 30, 106
Marfurt, 341
Marinot, Maurice, 203
Martine, 30, 59, 321
Marty, André, 30
Mass-produced furniture, 115, 116
 major manufacturers, 115
Mass-produced glass, 206–208
 price listings, 222–225
Materials/techniques, 37–40
 clothing, 39
 furniture, 37, 38
 jewelry, 39
 lacquer/enamel, 38
 metal, 39
 new materials, 40, 112
Matter, Herbert, 341
Mère, Clement, 106
Metals, uses of, 39
Metalwork, designers of, 108
Miami
 Deco buildings, 94, 95
 Miami Design Preservation League (MDPL), 94, 95
 Tropical Deco, 94
Miklos, Gustav, 30, 168
Milles, Carl, 169
Modernism, 68
 and Paris Exposition, 70, 71
Moholy-Nagy, Lazlo and Lucia, 55
Mondrian, Piet, 61
Morris, William, 48
Moser, Koloman, 53

Motifs, 41–43
 animal motifs, 42, 43
 lightning bolt, 42
 of Modern phase, 41
 of romantic phase, 41
 skyscraper motif, 76
 speed lines, 42
 ziggurat, 41, 42
Movie theaters, 93
Mucha, Alphonse, 46
Muller-Munk, Peter, 290
Murray, Keith, 246
Murray, William Straite, 246
Muthesius, Hermann, 54

Nadelman, Elie, 169
New York, Deco buildings, 89–93
New York World's Fair (1939), Deco souvenirs, 396, 397
Nielsen, Harald, 290
Noguchi, Isamu, 91
*Normandie*, 7, 75
Northern Life Tower, 89

Ocean liner collectibles, 75, 385–393
 Cunard Line, 386
 *Europa*, 386, 387
 Holland-America Line, 387
 *Ile de France*, 75, 387, 388
 *La Normandie*, 75, 389–392
 *L'Atlantique*, 75, 388, 389
 *Paris*, 392, 393
Olbrich, Joseph Maria, 87
Orientalism, influence on Deco, 62, 63, 320, 322
Orrefors, 204, 205

*Paris*, Deco collectibles of, 392, 393
Paris Exposition of 1925, 67
 and art of *ensemblier*, 68, 69
 Pavillon de L'Esprit Nouveau, 68, 70–71
 scope of, 68
Patou, Jean, 322, 323
Paul, Bruno, 110
Pavillon de l'Esprit Nouveau, 68, 70–72
Peche, Dagopert, 54
Perfume bottles, 205, 206
 Lalique, René, price listings, 228–230
Pflueger, Timothy, 95
Phillipe, Paul, 170

Phoenix Glass, 204
Piccirilli, Attilio, 91
*Pochoir* illustrations, 343, 344
   price listings, 360–362
Poerzl, Otto, 173
Poiret, Paul, 3, 30, 59, 321, 322
Pomone, 107
Posters, 337–343
   Dutch posters, 341–343
      price listings, 357–360
   price listings, 347–355
   Viennese posters, price listings, 355–357
Practical Equipment Limited, 31, 76, 110
Prairie School, 88
   Frank Lloyd Wright, 51, 52
Preiss, Ferdinand (Fritz), 32, 173
Preservation movements, 94–98
   Boston, 95, 96
   Miami Design Preservation League (MDPL), 94, 95
   San Francisco, 95
   Washington, DC, 95
Price, Will, 49
Prices
   auction prices, 14, 15
   dealers on price guidelines, 15, 17
   and geographic variations, 14
   *See also* individual items.
Primavera, 243
   price listings, 268–271
Privat, Gilbert, 170
Proto-Art Deco, 249
Prou, René, 109
Prouvé, Victor, 46
Pueblo Deco, 63, 77, 93
Puiforcat, Jean, 81, 168, 289

Radio City Music Hall, 76, 90, 112
Radios, 407, 408
   Catalin radios, 407, 408
   price listings, 409–412
Rateau, Armand-Albert, 30, 106
Reeves, Ruth, 112
Reproductions
   ceramics, 25, 26
      Hall reproductions, 25, 26
   clothing, 26
   Deco-inspired originals, 27, 28
      Postmodernism, 27, 28
   and Deco market, 11, 12
   furnishings, 23, 24
   glass, 24, 25
   graphics/posters, 27
   jewelry, 27
   silver, 26, 27
   statues, 24
"Retro," 304
Revere Copper and Brass Company, 398
Revival of Art Deco, 80–84
   Finch College Museum of Art, 81, 82, 255
   kitsch, revival of, 83, 84
   major American exhibitions, 82, 83
Rietveld, 61
Ritchfield Building, 89
Robj, 245
Rockefeller Center, 90, 91
Rohde, Gilbert, 34, 112, 115, 397
Roman Bronze Works, 169
Rosenthal, 245
Roseville Pottery Company, 253
Rousseau, Clément, 30
Ruhlmann, Emile-Jacques, 3, 30, 69, 106

Saarinen, Eliel, 32, 74, 110, 290
Sandoz, Edouard Marcel, 81, 168
San Francisco, Deco buildings, 95
San Francisco Telephone Building, 89
Schoen, Eugene, 111
Schreckengost, Viktor, 65, 252
Science fiction, influence on Deco, 65
Sculpture
   artists
      American, 169
      European, 168–170
   bronze and, 169, 170
   chryselephantine statues, 170–174
      artists, 171, 173, 174
      materials used, 172
      reproductions, 171, 172
      as series, 172
   designs
      animals, 170
      female figure, 170
   Frankart, 174, 175
      design elements, 174, 175
      price listings, 197–200
   price listings, 176–197
Senator Hotel, 95

# Index

Sert, Jose Maria, 91
Sharkskin, galuchat, 38, 105
Silver, reproductions, 26, 27
Silver jewelry, 303, 304
   price listings, 313–317
Singer, Susi, 54
Sjollema, Joop, 343
Skyscraper motif, 76, 89, 111
Skyscrapers
   Chrysler Building, 91
   design influences, 89
   Empire State Building, 92
   examples of Deco skyscrapers, 89
Slater, Eric, 246
Smith, Sanford, 7
Sorensen, Carl, 113
Sornay, André, 9, 109
Speed lines, 42
Spratling, William, 303
Statues, reproductions, 24
Steuben Glass Company, 205
Stile Liberty, 45
Stolba, Leopold, 53
Storrs, John, 169
Streamline style, 4, 70, 77, 112, 113, 415
Stubenville Pottery Company, 254
Studium Louvre, 70
"Style Sornay," 9
Süe, Louis, 30, 106
Süe et Mare, 30–32, 106, 109
Sugawara, 38
Sullivan, Louis, 32, 47, 88
Surrealism, influence on Deco, 61

Teague, Walter Dorwin, 34, 113, 205
Teco pottery, 249
Templier, Raymond, 38, 109
Tétard, Jean, 289
Tétard Frères, 289
Thonet Company, 31, 108
Tiffany, 202, 205, 290, 302
Toulouse-Lautrec, 45
Traverse, Pierre, 170
Trenton Art Pottery, 255
Tropical Deco, 93, 94
   Miami Beach, 94

Union des Artistes Modernes, 31, 109
Urban, Joseph, 32, 35, 54, 111, 290

Van Alen, William, 76, 91
Van Cleef & Arpels, 300, 301
van der Rohe, Mies, 55, 70, 88, 110
van de Velde, Henri, 54
Vera, Paul, 30, 106
Versen, Kurt, 113
Viennese posters, price listings, 355–357
Viennese Secessionist movement, 108, 338
   influence on Deco, 53, 54
Vionnet, Madeleine, 30, 322
Von Frankenberg, Arthur, 175
von Nessen, Walter, 4, 34, 77, 93, 113, 290, 397, 398
von Stein, Johann, 342
Voysey, Charles A., 47, 48
Vuitton, Gaston, 324

Wagner, Otto, 47, 53, 87
Waldorf Astoria Hotel, 92
Washington, D.C., Deco buildings, 95
Waugh, Sidney, 169
Weber, Kem, 34, 112, 113, 115, 290
Wiener Werkstätte, 32, 46, 47, 53, 54, 70, 108
Wieselthier, Vally, 54
Wijdeveld, H. Th., 342
Wijga, Jan, 342
Windt, Jan, 244
Winston, Harry, 302
Wolfsonian Foundation, 11
World's Fair souvenirs, 393–397
   Century of Progress (1933), 394–396
   New York World's Fair (1939), 396, 397
Wright, Frank Lloyd, 32, 51, 52, 65, 75, 88
   and Prairie School, 51, 52
Wright, Russel, 34, 76, 113, 254, 397, 398
Wristwatches, 304

Zach, Bruno, 173
Ziegfeld Theater, 89
Ziggurat, 41, 42, 63
Zigzag Moderne, 4
Zorach, William, 169

# ABOUT THE AUTHOR

Tony Fusco has a wide background as an educator, United States Department of State escort-interpreter, journalist, actor, lecturer, press agent, and consultant to the cultural sector.

He is published in many fields, but specializes in arts, leisure, and antiques. In those fields, his by-line has appeared in over thirty publications including *Bostonia, The Boston Phoenix, The Franklin Mint Almanac, New England Entertainment Digest, The Antiques Journal, Hit Parade, Collectibles Illustrated, Palm Beach Illustrated, Yankee* Magazine's *Guide to New England* and *Guide to New York,* and others.

A member of both the Screen Actors Guild (S.A.G.) and the American Federation of Radio and Television Actors (A.F.T.R.A.), he has appeared in feature and industrial films and television commercials, as well as on radio and television as a talk show guest.

Since 1979 he has been director of Fusco & Four, Associates, a Boston-based public relations, marketing, and organizational development agency specializing in the cultural sector. Along with his partner Robert Four, who serves as art director, the agency has worked with over two hundred arts-related businesses and cultural organizations—museums, theater, classical and popular music, dance, art centers, galleries and dealerships, cultural service organizations, and others.

## The HOUSE OF COLLECTIBLES Series

☐ Please send me the following price guides—
☐ I would like the most current edition of the books listed below.

**THE OFFICIAL PRICE GUIDES TO:**

| | | |
|---|---|---|
| ☐ 199-3 | American Silver & Silver Plate 5th Ed. | $11.95 |
| ☐ 513-1 | Antique Clocks 3rd Ed. | 10.95 |
| ☐ 283-3 | Antique & Modern Dolls 3rd Ed. | 10.95 |
| ☐ 287-6 | Antique & Modern Firearms 6th Ed. | 11.95 |
| ☐ 755-X | Antiques & Collectibles 9th Ed. | 11.95 |
| ☐ 289-2 | Antique Jewelry 5th Ed. | 11.95 |
| ☐ 447-X | Arts and Crafts: American Decorative Arts, 1894–1923 (ID) 1st Ed. | 12.95 |
| ☐ 539-5 | Beer Cans & Collectibles 4th Ed. | 7.95 |
| ☐ 521-9 | Bottles Old & New 10th Ed. | 10.95 |
| ☐ 532-8 | Carnival Glass 2nd Ed. | 10.95 |
| ☐ 295-7 | Collectible Cameras 2nd Ed. | 10.95 |
| ☐ 548-4 | Collectibles of the '50s & '60s 1st Ed. | 9.95 |
| ☐ 740-1 | Collectible Toys 4th Ed. | 10.95 |
| ☐ 531-X | Collector Cars 7th Ed. | 12.95 |
| ☐ 538-7 | Collector Handguns 4th Ed. | 14.95 |
| ☐ 748-7 | Collector Knives 9th Ed. | 12.95 |
| ☐ 361-9 | Collector Plates 5th Ed. | 11.95 |
| ☐ 296-5 | Collector Prints 7th Ed. | 12.95 |
| ☐ 001-6 | Depression Glass 2nd Ed. | 9.95 |
| ☐ 589-1 | Fine Art 1st Ed. | 19.95 |
| ☐ 311-2 | Glassware 3rd Ed. | 10.95 |
| ☐ 243-4 | Hummel Figurines & Plates 6th Ed. | 10.95 |
| ☐ 523-9 | Kitchen Collectibles 2nd Ed. | 10.95 |
| ☐ 291-4 | Military Collectibles 5th Ed. | 11.95 |
| ☐ 525-5 | Music Collectibles 6th Ed. | 11.95 |
| ☐ 313-9 | Old Books & Autographs 7th Ed. | 11.95 |
| ☐ 298-1 | Oriental Collectibles 3rd Ed. | 11.95 |
| ☐ 761-4 | Overstreet Comic Book 18th Ed. | 12.95 |
| ☐ 522-0 | Paperbacks & Magazines 1st Ed. | 10.95 |
| ☐ 297-3 | Paper Collectibles 5th Ed. | 10.95 |
| ☐ 744-4 | Political Memorabilia 1st Ed. | 10.95 |
| ☐ 529-8 | Pottery & Porcelain 6th Ed. | 11.95 |
| ☐ 524-7 | Radio, TV & Movie Memorabilia 3rd Ed. | 11.95 |
| ☐ 081-4 | Records 8th Ed. | 16.95 |
| ☐ 247-7 | Royal Doulton 5th Ed. | 11.95 |
| ☐ 280-9 | Science Fiction & Fantasy Collectibles 2nd Ed. | 10.95 |
| ☐ 747-9 | Sewing Collectibles 1st Ed. | 8.95 |
| ☐ 358-9 | Star Trek/Star Wars Collectibles 2nd Ed. | 8.95 |
| ☐ 086-5 | Watches 8th Ed. | 12.95 |
| ☐ 248-5 | Wicker 3rd Ed. | 10.95 |

**THE OFFICIAL:**

| | | |
|---|---|---|
| ☐ 760-6 | Directory to U.S. Flea Markets 2nd Ed. | 5.95 |
| ☐ 365-1 | Encyclopedia of Antiques 1st Ed. | 9.95 |
| ☐ 369-4 | Guide to Buying and Selling Antiques 1st Ed. | 9.95 |
| ☐ 414-3 | Identification Guide to Early American Furniture 1st Ed. | 9.95 |
| ☐ 413-5 | Identification Guide to Glassware 1st Ed. | 9.95 |
| ☐ 448-8 | Identification Guide to Gunmarks 2nd Ed. | 9.95 |
| ☐ 412-7 | Identification Guide to Pottery & Porcelain 1st Ed. | $9.95 |
| ☐ 415-1 | Identification Guide to Victorian Furniture 1st Ed. | 9.95 |

**THE OFFICIAL (SMALL SIZE) PRICE GUIDES TO:**

| | | |
|---|---|---|
| ☐ 309-0 | Antiques & Flea Markets 4th Ed. | 4.95 |
| ☐ 269-8 | Antique Jewelry 3rd Ed. | 4.95 |
| ☐ 085-7 | Baseball Cards 8th Ed. | 4.95 |
| ☐ 647-2 | Bottles 3rd Ed. | 4.95 |
| ☐ 544-1 | Cars & Trucks 3rd Ed. | 5.95 |
| ☐ 519-0 | Collectible Americana 2nd Ed. | 4.95 |
| ☐ 294-9 | Collectible Records 3rd Ed. | 4.95 |
| ☐ 306-6 | Dolls 4th Ed. | 4.95 |
| ☐ 359-7 | Football Cards 7th Ed. | 4.95 |
| ☐ 540-9 | Glassware 3rd Ed. | 4.95 |
| ☐ 526-3 | Hummels 4th Ed. | 4.95 |
| ☐ 279-5 | Military Collectibles 3rd Ed. | 4.95 |
| ☐ 745-2 | Overstreet Comic Book Companion 1st Ed. | 4.95 |
| ☐ 278-7 | Pocket Knives 3rd Ed. | 4.95 |
| ☐ 527-1 | Scouting Collectibles 4th Ed. | 4.95 |
| ☐ 494-1 | Star Trek/Star Wars Collectibles 3rd Ed. | 3.95 |
| ☐ 088-1 | Toys 5th Ed. | 4.95 |

**THE OFFICIAL BLACKBOOK PRICE GUIDES OF:**

| | | |
|---|---|---|
| ☐ 092-X | U.S. Coins 27th Ed. | 4.95 |
| ☐ 095-4 | U.S. Paper Money 21st Ed. | 4.95 |
| ☐ 098-9 | U.S. Postage Stamps 11th Ed. | 4.95 |

**THE OFFICIAL INVESTORS GUIDE TO BUYING & SELLING:**

| | | |
|---|---|---|
| ☐ 534-4 | Gold, Silver & Diamonds 2nd Ed. | 12.95 |
| ☐ 535-2 | Gold Coins 2nd Ed. | 12.95 |
| ☐ 536-0 | Silver Coins 2nd Ed. | 12.95 |
| ☐ 537-9 | Silver Dollars 2nd Ed. | 12.95 |

**THE OFFICIAL NUMISMATIC GUIDE SERIES:**

| | | |
|---|---|---|
| ☐ 254-X | The Official Guide to Detecting Counterfeit Money 2nd Ed. | 7.95 |
| ☐ 257-2 | The Official Guide to Mint Errors 4th Ed. | 7.95 |

**SPECIAL INTEREST SERIES:**

| | | |
|---|---|---|
| ☐ 506-9 | From Hearth to Cookstove 3rd Ed. | 17.95 |
| ☐ 530-1 | Lucky Number Lottery Guide 1st Ed. | 4.95 |
| ☐ 504-2 | On Method Acting 8th Printing | 6.95 |

| TOTAL | |
|---|---|
| | |

SEE REVERSE SIDE FOR ORDERING INSTRUCTIONS

# FOR IMMEDIATE DELIVERY

## *VISA & MASTER CARD CUSTOMERS*
# ORDER TOLL FREE!
# 1-800-638-6460

This number is for orders only; it is not tied into the customer service or business office. Customers not using charge cards must use mail for ordering since payment is required with the order—sorry, no C.O.D.'s.

## OR SEND ORDERS TO

**THE HOUSE OF COLLECTIBLES**
*201 East 50th Street*
*New York, New York 10022*

### POSTAGE & HANDLING RATES
First Book .................................. $1.00
Each Additional Copy or Title ................. $0.50

Total from columns on order form. Quantity_____ $_____
☐ Check or money order enclosed $_____ (include postage and handling)
☐ Please charge $_____ to my: ☐ MASTERCARD ☐ VISA

Charge Card Customers Not Using Our Toll Free Number Please Fill Out The Information Below

Account No. _____ Expiration Date _____
(all digits)
Signature _____

NAME (please print)_____ PHONE_____
ADDRESS_____ APT. #_____
CITY_____ STATE_____ ZIP_____